Neutrality and Collaboration in South China

The South China enclav [illegible] ean colonial settlement in Ea[illegible] s of different empires. In this highly orig[illegible] opes analyses the layers of collaboration that developed [illegible] ty in Macau during the Second World War. Exploring the intersections of local, regional and global dynamics, she unpacks the connections between a plurality of actors with competing and collaborative interests, including Chinese Nationalists, Communists and collaborators with Japan, Portuguese colonial authorities and British and Japanese representatives. Lopes argues that neutrality eased the movement of refugees of different nationalities who sought shelter in Macau during the war and that it helped to guarantee the maintenance of two remnants of European colonialism – Macau and Hong Kong. Drawing on extensive research from multilingual archival material from Asia, Europe, Australasia and America, this book brings to light the multiple global connections framing the experiences of neutrality and collaboration in the Portuguese-administered enclave of Macau.

Helena F. S. Lopes is Lecturer in Modern Asian History at Cardiff University. She held a Leverhulme Early Career Fellowship at the University of Bristol and lectureships at the University of Oxford and the University of Bristol.

In recent years the field of modern history has been enriched by the exploration of two parallel histories. These are the social and cultural history of armed conflict, and the impact of military events on social and cultural history.

Studies in the Social and Cultural History of Modern Warfare presents the fruits of this growing area of research, reflecting both the colonization of military history by cultural historians and the reciprocal interest of military historians in social and cultural history, to the benefit of both. The series offers the latest scholarship in European and non-European events from the 1850s to the present day.

A full list of titles in the series can be found at: www.cambridge.org/modernwarfare

Neutrality and Collaboration in South China

Macau during the Second World War

Helena F. S. Lopes
Cardiff University

CAMBRIDGE
UNIVERSITY PRESS

CAMBRIDGE
UNIVERSITY PRESS

Shaftesbury Road, Cambridge CB2 8EA, United Kingdom

One Liberty Plaza, 20th Floor, New York, NY 10006, USA

477 Williamstown Road, Port Melbourne, VIC 3207, Australia

314–321, 3rd Floor, Plot 3, Splendor Forum, Jasola District Centre, New Delhi – 110025, India

103 Penang Road, #05–06/07, Visioncrest Commercial, Singapore 238467

Cambridge University Press is part of Cambridge University Press & Assessment, a department of the University of Cambridge.

We share the University's mission to contribute to society through the pursuit of education, learning and research at the highest international levels of excellence.

www.cambridge.org
Information on this title: www.cambridge.org/9781009311762

DOI: 10.1017/9781009311786

First published 2023
First paperback edition 2025

A catalogue record for this publication is available from the British Library

Library of Congress Cataloging-in-Publication data
Names: Ferreira Santos Lopes, Helena, author.
Title: Neutrality and collaboration in South China : Macau during the Second World War / Helena F.S. Lopes, Cardiff University.
Description: Cambridge ; New York : Cambridge University Press, 2023. | Series: Studies in the social and cultural history of modern warfare | Includes bibliographical references and index.
Identifiers: LCCN 2023010283 | ISBN 9781009311793 (hardback) | ISBN 9781009311762 (paperback)
Subjects: LCSH: WorldWar, 1939-1945 – China –Macau (Special Administrative Region) | World War, 1939–1945 – China – Macau. | Macau (China : Special Administrative Region) – History. | Macau (China) – History. | Macau (China : Special Administrative Region) – Politics and government. | Macau (China) – Politics and government.
Classification: LCC D767.3 .F47 2023 | DDC 940.53/5126–dc23/eng/20230330
LC record available at https://lccn.loc.gov/2023010283

ISBN 978-1-009-31179-3 Hardback
ISBN 978-1-009-31176-2 Paperback

For my parents

Contents

Figures

Tables

Acknowledgements

This book results from a decade of research on the history of the Second World War in South China and a long-term interest in Sino–Portuguese encounters in the 1930s and 1940s. I have accumulated many debts to colleagues, mentors, friends and family members all over the world over the years, but all the shortcomings of this book are, needless to say, my own responsibility.

A good deal of the research that went into this book was undertaken during a DPhil in History at St Antony's College, University of Oxford. I would like to thank my supervisor Rana Mitter for his unfailing support, excellent advice and generosity during and after my doctorate and for being a model academic whose scholarly work has been a major source of inspiration in my research and teaching.

My research has benefitted from generous funding from different institutions, and I would like to acknowledge their crucial financial support. This manuscript was finished during a Leverhulme Trust Early Career Fellowship (ECF-2020-514) at the University of Bristol. This Fellowship also funded additional archival visits to Portugal, France, the US National Archives at College Park and the UK National Archives at Kew. My doctoral degree was funded by a doctoral fellowship (SFRH/BD/93872/2013) from the Portuguese Foundation for Science and Technology (Fundação para a Ciência e a Tecnologia/FCT) that granted me a monthly stipend for four years, a settling in allowance and a travel grant. A studentship from the UK Arts and Humanities Research Council (AHRC) covered my doctoral tuition and college fees for three years (AH/K503198/1) and an AHRC Research Training Support Grant helped fund my first research trip to the National Library of Australia (NLA). A research trip to the International Committee of the Red Cross Archives in Geneva was funded by a Student Travel and Research Grant from the Carr and Stahl Fund awarded by St Antony's College, while a Taiwan Fellowship allowed me to conduct research at archives and libraries in Taiwan during a five-month period as a visiting fellow at the Institute of Modern History (IMH)-Academia Sinica. I would like to thank the former director Huang Ko-wu, Lien Ling-ling and all the staff at the IMH and the National Central Library in Taipei for all their welcoming support. My research at the University of Hong Kong Libraries Special Collections benefitted from the help of John Carroll, whilst my trip to the Archives of Macau would not have been possible without the boundless generosity of Natacha Fidalgo and her family, who hosted me during my stay. During my lectureship at Oxford, the Faculty of History funded a conference and research trip to Australia, where I had the chance to see hitherto classified files at the NLA and visit the National Archives of Australia. In Canberra, Shuge Wei, Roald Maliangkay and little Lucas were the most wonderful hosts I could have wished for.

Librarians, archivists and other staff of the archives and libraries I visited in the UK, Portugal, Macau, Hong Kong, Taiwan, Switzerland, France, Australia and the USA have been incredibly helpful, inclusively in granting permission to reproduce some of the photographs in this book. Rachel Hurd, Jane Bloore and the late Myke Tymons at the Presbyterian Research Centre (Archives) of the Presbyterian Church of Aotearoa New Zealand granted remote access to written and photographic sources. I would like to add a special mention of the late Isabel Fevereiro, former director of Arquivo Histórico Diplomático (Ministry of Foreign Affairs Archives) in Lisbon for allowing me to start exploring archival records on wartime Sino–Portuguese relations back in 2008–9. Moisés Silva Fernandes also provided useful tips at that time. Lin Ren-Jie, Amy Lin, Hsiao-Yuh Ku and Yvonne Kong gave me crucial help in deciphering more intricate parts of Chinese documents in in-person meetings or remotely, and I am very grateful for their support and, above all, their friendship of many years.

I began to work on the history of refugees in Macau during a second MA degree at the School of Oriental and African Studies (SOAS), University of London, and I would like to thank my supervisor there, Lars Peter Laamann, for all his assistance and guidance then and ever since. I would also like to thank my first MA supervisor at SOAS, Julia Strauss, for her advice and support. I could not have written this book without the excellent teachers and classmates I had at SOAS or without its magnificent library.

While working as a lecturer at Oxford and Bristol I benefitted greatly from the precious advice and feedback of mentors and colleagues, most especially Micah Muscolino and Robert Bickers. At Merton College, Steven Gunn, Matthew Grimley, Miles Pattenden, Yegor Grebnev and Hatice Yıldız were inspiring colleagues. At Bristol, I also received supportive guidance from Ian Wei, Hilary Carey, Simon Potter, Martyn Powell, Will Pooley, Gonzalo Velasco Berenguer and Su Lin Lewis. Michael Sugarman and Josepha Richard were truly wonderful friends in good and bad times. Robert Bickers, Jamie Carstairs and Shannon Smith welcomed me into the Historical Photographs of China Project team with great kindness, helping me see visual sources in new ways. My brilliant students at Oxford and Bristol have been a joy and a privilege to teach, always stimulating me to find novel approaches to telling global stories.

My work has benefitted from the collegiality and mutual support of research groups at Oxford and at Bristol. A very special thanks is owed to my fellow convenors of the Oxford International History of East Asia Seminar, namely Pete Millwood, Nelson So, Frances O'Morchoe, Sheng Peng, Mark Baker, Chinami Oka, Woody Di Wu and Tom Burnham. The Oxford China Centre writing group led by Gordon Barrett and Pamela Hunt provided a safe and joyful writing environment. Bristol's Asian History Seminar and Decolonising History Reading Group also offered regular opportunities for learning and intellectual dialogue with great colleagues including Vivian Kong, Tom Larkin, Jiayi Tao, Gemma O'Neill, Saima Nasar and Rob Skinner, amongst others. My wonderful team members at the interdisciplinary network Colonial Ports and Global History were a constant source of inspiration and I thank Yvonne Liao for the invitation to join them. All the participants of the Summer Institute 'China in a Global World War II' at the University of Cambridge gave precious feedback on my work on wartime Macau in the last year of my doctorate. Mazi Ghiabi and Hande Yalnizoglu broadened my ideas while sharing my love of film when we organised St Antony's Global South Film Society events together.

Colleagues from various institutions provided feedback on my work in different settings, including at conferences and workshops where I presented different parts of what became this book. For their insightful comments and/or useful guidance I would like to thank (in addition to the aforementioned) Wen-hsin Yeh, Hans van de Ven, Lily Chang, Toby Lincoln, Elisabeth Forster, Yuexin Rachel Lin, Brian Martin, Felix Boecking, Jennifer Altehenger, Gary Chi-hung Luk, Hannah Theaker, Joshua Howard, Daqing Yang, Aaron William Moore, Henrietta Harrison, S. A. Smith, Isabella Jackson, Jenny Bond, Lauren Walden, William Clarence-Smith, James McDougall, James Belich, Margret Frenz, Kevin Fogg, Kaori Abe, Laura Madokoro, Neville Wylie, Melanie Oppenheimer, Ying Qian, Alison McEwan, Tan Chee Sheng, Jessica Fernández de Lara Harada, Nick McGee, Loretta Lou, Michael Yeo, Vivien Chan, Pascal Lottaz, Pia Jolliffe, João da Silva, Mariana Pinto Leitão Pereira, João Paulo Oliveira e Costa and Pedro Aires Oliveira.

Family, friends and colleagues (in addition to the aforementioned) scattered across the world have helped me in many ways while I was working on this project, sharing meals, worries and laughs. Many thanks to Odete Santos, Sofia Lobão, Leo Abrantes, Mário B. Soares, Joana Torres, the late Helena Avelar, Aikaterini Chatzikidi, Reema Fadda, Mathew Mills, Gjovalin Macaj, Özlem Akkurt, Negar Elodie Behzadi, Jodie Yuzhou Sun, Jack Pun, Floriane Perrichon, Natalie Ke, Anne Lin, Iris Lai, Yi-chun Chao, Sally Wu, Justina Hwang, Angela Tung and Elisabeth and José Segura. My eighth-grade history teacher Francisco Assis supported my enthusiasm for historical research and early plans to become a historian in a context where the humanities were shockingly undervalued by most and I will be forever grateful for that.

At Cambridge University Press, Michael Watson and Emily Plater offered great editorial support, and Melissa Ward, Ruth Boyes, Subathra Manogaran and Ami Naramor were amazing during the production process. I thank the editors of the Studies in the Social and Cultural History of Modern Warfare series for welcoming this book and the anonymous readers for their excellent comments and suggestions. I would also like to thank Kate McIntosh for the fabulous index, the Tate & Clayburn team for proofreading and Rui Alves for two wonderful maps.

A section of Chapter 3 appeared in the article 'Wartime Education at the Crossroads of Empires: The Relocation of Schools to Macao during the Second World War, 1937–1945' in *Twentieth-Century China*; a section of Chapter 5 was published in 'Inter-imperial Humanitarianism: The Macau Delegation of the Portuguese Red Cross during the Second World War' in *Journal of Imperial and Commonwealth History*; and a version of Chapter 6 was published as the article 'Ghosts of War: China's Relations with Portugal in the Post-war Period, 1945–49' in *Historical Research*. I thank Johns Hopkins University Press, Taylor & Francis and Oxford University Press, respectively, for authorising the inclusion of previously published material in this book.

Words cannot do justice to how amazing my partner, Carlos, has been over the process of researching and writing this book, including reading through a thousand and one versions of these chapters. Thank you for everything.

Finally, the biggest acknowledgement goes to my parents, Margarida and José Lopes, for all their constant support that I will never be able to repay. I hope they will be happy to see this published!

Oxford, September 2022

Note on Chinese Names

Chinese names are indicated with the surname first (as are Japanese names) and spelled according to the *Hanyu Pinyin* romanisation system with a few exceptions. These include the names of figures who are commonly known in Europe with other spellings (e.g. Sun Yat-sen, Chiang Kai-shek, T. V. Soong), in their English versions (e.g. Robert Ho Tung), or whose *Pinyin* equivalent could not be traced due to the lack of Chinese characters in the sources (e.g. a few Cantonese names mentioned in sources in European languages). Exceptions also include Chinese institutions that still exist today and whose official name romanisation does not follow *Hanyu Pinyin* (e.g. Kuomintang, Kiang Wu Hospital, Tung Sin Tong).

The spelling of Chinese place names will, with few exceptions, follow *Hanyu Pinyin* (e.g. Chongqing, Guangzhou). Other spellings might be used when quoting from primary sources (e.g. Chungking, Canton). 'Macau' is used to refer to the territory known in Mandarin as Aomen and in Cantonese as Ou Mun. 'Macao' will only be used when citing from primary sources.

Unless otherwise stated, all translations are by the author.

Abbreviations

BAAG	British Army Aid Group
BNU	Banco Nacional Ultramarino (National Overseas Bank)
CCP	Chinese Communist Party
CMC	Chinese Maritime Customs
CO	Colonial Office
CRB	Central Reserve Bank, RNG
DAB	Deutsch-Asiatische Bank
FO	Foreign Office, United Kingdom
HKU	University of Hong Kong
HSBC	Hongkong and Shanghai Banking Corporation
KMT	Kuomintang
MC	Ministério das Colónias (Ministry of Colonies, Portugal)
MELCO	Macao Electric Lighting Company
MNE	Ministério dos Negócios Estrangeiros (Ministry of Foreign Affairs, Portugal)
MOFA	Ministry of Foreign Affairs, ROC
NHW	Netherlands Harbour Works Company
OSS	Office of Strategic Studies
PPC	People's Political Council
PRC	People's Republic of China
RNG	Reorganised National Government
ROC	Republic of China
SOE	Special Operations Executive
UK	United Kingdom
UN	United Nations
USA	United States of America
USSR	Union of the Soviet Socialist Republics
WATCO	Macau Waterworks Company
YWCA	Young Women's Christian Association

Introduction: An 'East Asian Casablanca'

In 1938, the British poet W. H. Auden wrote a poem about Macau after visiting the Portuguese-administered enclave during his journey, alongside Christopher Isherwood, through wartime China. Auden described the South China territory as a city of contradictions where 'churches alongside brothels testify / That faith can pardon natural behaviour'. Despite being surrounded by conflict, Macau's seemingly sheltered isolation led Auden to conclude that 'nothing serious can happen here'.[1] Yet very serious things did take place in neutral Macau, as this book will show. Taking the territory as a case study, it explores neutrality and collaboration in South China and how they were framed by multiple connections not only to Europe and to Japan, but also to other parts of the world.

Like some of his contemporaries, Auden was quick to notice that the war unfolding in East Asia was profoundly connected to the 1930s conflicts in Europe. Although no one referred to the war as such at the time, it was the opening salvo of the global Second World War. The global connections of the small enclave that Auden deemed of little consequence remain one of the great untold stories of World War II. The only foreign-ruled territory in China to escape formal occupation by Japan, between 1937 and 1945, Macau saw its population rise almost threefold, reaching around half a million people. The territory, at the time comprising a peninsula and two islands with a combined land area of only 15 km^2, became a refugee city, where the number of newcomers dwarfed that of pre-existing residents. Refugees in Macau shaped the social, economic, cultural, political and diplomatic experience of a globally connected South China. Chinese, Portuguese, British and other refugees filled Macau's streets, intelligence agents for several powers operated in the territory, and activities of resistance, humanitarian relief and smuggling were conducted under the protective shadows of Portuguese neutrality (see Figure I.1). The history of this small enclave shows how, even in the unlikeliest of places, the war was global and those who lived through it were profoundly interconnected.

[1] W. H. Auden and C. Isherwood, *Journey to a War* (London, 1939, repr. 1973), pp. 13–14.

Figure I.1 Aerial view of Macau city centre, late 1930s. Source: Bodleian Libraries, University of Oxford, *Anuário de Macau*, 1939. Per. 20659 e.92.

This book explores the lived experience of neutrality during the Second World War in East Asia, detailing the ambiguities of its practice in Macau and surrounding areas. Concomitantly, it explores how neutrality was marked by many layers of collaboration involving Chinese, Portuguese, Japanese, British and other actors. These layers were often overlapping and even contradictory, but, intended or not, they contributed to keep Macau under Portuguese administration during and after the war.

Despite the frequent assurances Portuguese officials gave of their 'strict neutrality', the uses and abuses of neutrality in China make evident that it was far more flexible than strict. Portuguese neutrality in Macau created a space of freedom for actors with antagonistic interests that coexisted and intersected in the territory. The opportunities Portuguese neutrality offered extended beyond the enclave. In mainland China, neutrality allowed for a range of ambiguous practices, from Portuguese diplomats operating in occupied cities whilst not recognising the collaborationist authorities, to the registration of Chinese ships as Portuguese to straddle wartime restrictions on transportation.

Collaboration was at the heart of Macau's wartime experience. There were various and sometimes competing layers of collaboration. Several of these did not involve Japan. On the part of the Portuguese authorities, imperial collaboration with the British prevailed in a clear example of how the centuries-old Anglo–Portuguese alliance worked on the ground.[2] On some level, the nature of Anglo–Portuguese interactions in South China is better captured by the term *cooperation* than by the notion of *collaboration* with an invading and occupying power. However, as will be addressed later, the term *collaboration* is not entirely unhelpful when considering the imperial dimension that underpinned Portugal's ties to the United Kingdom, and the fact that, despite the two European countries' different positioning vis-à-vis China during the war, they were both implicated in forms of colonial occupation in the region that predated Japan's invasion.

Although diplomacy is paramount to understanding neutrality and collaboration in Macau, practical everyday constraints and opportunities went beyond decisions made in distant capital city bureaux. The territory's global connections vividly come to light when considering the ramifications of the social impact of the war in Macau. Its society suffered the effects of the conflict in ways similar to other areas in China. The case of this peripheral enclave sheds new light on the connected histories of neutral territories in the country, such as the Shanghai International Settlement and French Concession and Hong Kong before Japan occupied them from late 1941 onwards. Indeed, these foreign-ruled territories were not sealed off; in their nominal 'peace', they were very much part of the war.

Due to its strategic geographical position in the Pearl River Delta and the relative weakness of the colonial power administering it (which was not perceived as a threat by any of the major belligerents), Macau was at the crossroads of different forces. Its wartime years illustrate the regime competition between the Chinese central government of Chiang Kai-shek resisting Japan – with which Portugal maintained diplomatic relations – and Wang Jingwei's Reorganised National Government (RNG), the main collaborationist regime in China. After 1941, with the swift Japanese occupation of British colonial territories in East and Southeast Asia, Macau also regained a crucial importance for the United Kingdom that had been unprecedented since the founding of Hong Kong a century earlier. Neutral Macau also appealed to Japanese forces, which exerted a significant degree of economic control over the enclave although a formal occupation never occurred, unlike in the Portuguese colony of Timor (today East Timor), which was under Japanese occupation from 1942 until the end of the war.[3]

[2] The Anglo–Portuguese Alliance, established in 1373 and ratified by the Treaty of Windsor in 1386, is considered the oldest alliance in the world still in place.

[3] G. C. Gunn, *Wartime Portuguese Timor: The Azores Connection* (Clayton, 1988); L. Cunha, 'Timor: A Guerra Esquecida' ('Timor: The Forgotten War'), *Macau*, 45 (1996), pp. 32–46; J. D. Santa, *Australianos e Japoneses em Timor na II Guerra Mundial, 1941–1945*

Several locales in China were sites of intense interaction between occupied and unoccupied areas, experiencing periods of prosperity fuelled by wartime human and material circulations. For example, Keith Schoppa has noted the impact of the trade and smuggling boom in Ningbo and Wenzhou between 1938 and 1941, and the pragmatic choices of local entrepreneurs able to capitalise on wartime opportunities.[4] Mark Baker has observed similar dynamics of temporary wartime vibrancy and a smuggling boom in the inland city of Zhengzhou in specific periods of the war.[5] Parallels with Macau are even more striking when considering territories under foreign rule. Shanghai's foreign concessions and Hong Kong eclipsed Macau, not only in terms of scale – from the number of residents to their economic clout – but also in terms of their importance to Chinese actors. Their exceptionalism has merited much scholarly attention. Histories of Shanghai in particular have highlighted the ambiguities of relief practices, political mobilisation, cultural production and economic prosperity. Almost invariably, they portray the experience of the International Settlement and the French Concession before the Japanese occupation as distinctive, something well captured by the term 孤島 *gudao*, often translated as 'lone island', 'solitary island' or 'orphan island'.[6] Despite the isolationist connotations of this term, scholars of the period in Shanghai – for *gudao* is a temporal descriptor as much as a geographic one – stress the wide array of connections to wartime dynamics. Instead of keeping war completely at bay, neutrality generated different forms of engagements with the conflict, both overt and covert, including different forms of violence.[7] As will be seen in the case of Macau, significant human and material circulations also connected *gudao* Shanghai to the hinterland.[8]

(*Australians and Japanese in Timor in World War II, 1941–1945*) (Lisbon, 1997); K. Goto, *Tensions of Empire: Japan and Southeast Asia in the Colonial and Postcolonial World* (Athens, OH, 2003), pp. 24–38; B. d'Água, *Le Timor Oriental face à la Seconde Guerra Mondiale (1941–1945)* (*East Timor in the Second World War (1941–1945)*) (Lisbon, 2007); P. Cleary, *The Men Who Came Out of the Ground* (Sydney, 2010).

4 R. K. Schoppa, *In a Sea of Bitterness: Refugees during the Sino–Japanese War* (Cambridge, MA, 2011), pp. 261–84.

5 M. Baker, 'City Limits on China's Central Plains: Zhengzhou, Kaifeng, and the Making of Spatial Inequality, 1900–1960' (PhD thesis, Yale University, 2017), pp. 170–1, 200–8.

6 P. Fu, *Passivity, Resistance, and Collaboration: Intellectual Choices in Occupied Shanghai, 1937–1945* (Stanford, CA, 1993), p. xiii; W. H. Yeh, 'Prologue: Shanghai Besieged, 1937–45', in W. H. Yeh (ed.), *Wartime Shanghai* (London, 1998), pp. 1–15; C. Henriot and W. H. Yeh, 'Introduction', in C. Henriot and W. H. Yeh (eds.), *In the Shadow of the Rising Sun: Shanghai under Japanese Occupation* (Cambridge, 2004), pp. 1–14; M. Blair, *Gudao, Lone Islet: The War Years in Shanghai* (Victoria, 2007).

7 For example, F. Wakeman Jr, *The Shanghai Badlands: Wartime Terrorism and Urban Crime, 1937–1941* (Cambridge, 1996); Yeh, *Wartime Shanghai*.

8 P. M. Coble, *Chinese Capitalists in Japan's New Order: The Occupied Lower Yangzi, 1937–1945* (Berkeley, CA, 2003); T. Lincoln, *Urbanizing China in War and Peace: The Case of Wuxi County* (Honolulu, HI, 2015), especially chapters 6–8.

A few scholars have probed the experience of other foreign concessions in China, notably those under French administration such as the French Concession of Hankou.[9] Their findings show striking similarities to Shanghai – and to Macau. French territories in China remained grey areas of neutrality until they were taken over by Japanese forces, mostly in 1943. One of these was the French-leased territory of Guangzhouwan, which was only formally occupied in March 1945. Chuning Xie called it 'China's Casablanca'.[10] The analogy is similar to the one Philip Snow used to refer to Macau in his study of occupied Hong Kong: 'East Asian Casablanca'.[11] The 1942 Hollywood film *Casablanca* is indeed a compelling reference. It fictionalises the dangers and opportunities that a strategic neutral territory – in that case, French-controlled Casablanca – offered different belligerents, refugees and very unneutral neutrals, showing the North African city as a place of transit, of waiting, of opportunity and of unlikely friendships. That was very much applicable to Macau during the war years. Considering the enclave as one amongst several 'East Asian Casablancas', one amongst several 'lone islands', opens new possibilities for assessing the connections that framed these territories' complex experiences of neutrality and collaboration, experiences whose ambivalence was linked to their colonial status during China's War of Resistance against Japanese imperialism. Whilst the epithet *gudao* does transmit the peculiarities of these neutral territories' experience, this book argues against a characterisation of them as completely isolated, putting their connections – through the movement of people, things and information – at the centre.

Neutrality and Collaboration

Neutrality is a legal status that exists only if there is a war. The idea of neutrality can be traced back to antiquity and it began to be theorised and codified in international law in Europe in the early modern period, especially from the eighteenth century onwards.[12] Specific definitions of neutrality abound, but a generally accepted notion is that a neutral state

[9] D. Rihal, 'The French Concession in Hankou 1938–43: The Life and Death of a Solitary Enclave in an Occupied City', in R. Bickers and I. Jackson (eds.), *Treaty Ports in Modern China* (Milton Park, 2016), pp. 220–42. On the end of the French Concession in Shanghai, see C. Cornet, 'The Bumpy End of the French Concession and French Influence in Shanghai, 1937–1946', in *In the Shadow of the Rising Sun*, pp. 257–76.

[10] C. Xie, 'China's Casablanca: Refugees, Outlaws, and Smugglers in France's Guangzhouwan Enclave', in J. S. Esherick and M. T. Combs (eds.), *1943: China at the Crossroads* (Ithaca, NY, 2015), pp. 391–425.

[11] P. Snow, *The Fall of Hong Kong: Britain, China and the Japanese Occupation* (New Haven, CT, 2003), p. 180.

[12] E. Karsh, *Neutrality and Small States* (London, 1988), pp. 13–19.

'is required not only to abstain from all warlike action, but also to treat the belligerents impartially'.[13] If refraining from military intervention is relatively straightforward, an impartial treatment of the belligerents is more difficult to respect in practice than in theory. Indeed, questionable practices of neutrality during World War II are often alluded to in works about neutral countries.[14] Their reasons for neutrality varied, but its maintenance required concessions that might not have been compatible with a neutral status. Scholarship on neutrality tends to be dominated by a Eurocentric perspective, either downplaying or ignoring relevant connections with belligerents in Asia.[15] Amongst the few exceptions are the works by Pascal Lottaz and Florentino Rodao, who have analysed in depth Japan's relations with some European neutrals, namely Sweden, Switzerland and Spain.[16]

Roderick Ogley distinguished four kinds of neutral states: neutralised, traditional neutrals, ad hoc neutrals and non-aligned. Portugal fits into the third category, a small power which sought to 'keep out of a particular war'.[17] In her study of European powers in the nineteenth century, Maartje Abbenhuis proposes instead the term 'occasional neutrals' to emphasise certain governments' tactical choice to opt for neutrality as they were 'well aware of the value of staying out' of a particular conflict.[18] Her observations regarding the use of neutrality as a way of safeguarding imperial interests can easily be applicable to Portugal's situation in the Second World War.[19]

[13] W. Hofer, *Neutrality As the Principle of Swiss Foreign Policy* (Zurich, 1957), p. 5.

[14] R. Ogley, *The Theory and Practice of Neutrality in the Twentieth Century* (London, 1970); D. J. Fodor, *The Neutrals* (Alexandria, VA, 1983); H. R. Reginbogin, *Faces of Neutrality: A Comparative Analysis of the Neutrality of Switzerland and Other Neutral Nations during WWII* (Bern, 2006).

[15] For example, C. Leitz, *Nazi Germany and Neutral Europe during the Second World War* (Manchester, 2000); N. Wylie (ed.), *European Neutrals and Non-belligerents during the Second World War* (Cambridge, 2001); M. af Malmborg, *Neutrality and State-Building in Sweden* (Hampshire, 2001); N. Wylie, *Britain, Switzerland, and the Second World War* (Oxford, 2003); R. Cole, *Propaganda, Censorship and Irish Neutrality in the Second World War* (Oxford, 2006); E. O'Halpin, *Spying on Ireland: British Intelligence and Irish Neutrality during the Second World War* (Oxford, 2008); B. Evans, *Ireland during the Second World War: Farewell to Plato's Cave* (Manchester, 2014).

[16] F. Rodao, *Franco y el Emperio Japonés: Imágenes y Propaganda en Tiempos de Guerra* (*Franco and the Japanese Empire: Images and Propaganda in Wartime*) (Barcelona, 2002); P. Lottaz, 'Neutral States and Wartime Japan: The Diplomacy of Sweden, Spain and Switzerland toward the Empire' (PhD thesis, National Graduate Institute for Policy Studies, 2018); P. Lottaz and I. Ottosson, *Sweden, Japan, and the Long Second World War 1931–1945* (London, 2021).

[17] Ogley, *Theory and Practice of Neutrality*, p. 3.

[18] M. Abbenhuis, *An Age of Neutrals: Great Power Politics, 1815–1915* (Cambridge, 2014), p. 16.

[19] Ibid., p. 19.

Portugal's neutrality during the Second World War was not formally declared, but it was often presented as framed and conditioned by the Anglo–Portuguese alliance.[20] Portugal neither had a tradition of neutrality in European conflicts nor was strong enough militarily to deter a foreign invasion, although there were precedents for neutrality in Macau, as we shall see. In continental Europe, Portugal largely escaped occupation during the Second World War because Germany was unable to mount a naval strategy against the United Kingdom and eventually abandoned plans for entering the Iberian Peninsula, which would have led to a Nazi-backed Spanish invasion of Portugal. In 1943 and 1944, Portugal agreed to British and American requests for basing rights in the Azores and even proposed entering the war in the Pacific to participate in the liberation of Timor from the occupying Japanese forces. The Joint Planning Staff studied the potential consequences of a Portuguese declaration of war on Japan, but these were not believed to be favourable.[21] It would be a burden to train and equip the Portuguese forces and the likely occupation of Macau was something Prime Minister Winston Churchill deemed particularly undesirable. However, the offer alone ended up being enough to guarantee British and American support for the re-establishment of Portuguese administration over Timor and to spare it a military occupation by Australia.[22] A leading Portuguese historian of the war thus concluded that the country remained neutral because both Germany and the Allies got what they wanted from Portugal without it becoming a belligerent.[23] Japan should also be added as a prominent actor in this consideration, for it too attained what it wanted from Portuguese colonial territories in Asia without Portugal entering the war. In the particular case of Macau, the territory served – like Lisbon – as an intelligence collection post, as a smuggling and currency exchange hub, as well as a de facto 'R & R' station for Japanese officers and agents.[24]

In Macau, however, there were precedents for neutrality that had started in the nineteenth century and that made Macau's stance in World War II not totally surprising. The territory remained neutral during the Opium

[20] A. J. Telo, *A Neutralidade Portuguesa e o Ouro Nazi* (*Portuguese Neutrality and Nazi Gold*) (Lisbon, 2000), pp. 19, 38.

[21] See files in the UK National Archives (hereafter TNA), CAB 121/508.

[22] A. J. Telo, *Portugal na Segunda Guerra: 1941–1945* (*Portugal in the Second World War: 1941–1945*), 2 vols. (Lisbon, 1991), vol. 2, pp. 209–18; Telo, *A Neutralidade Portuguesa*, pp. 74–5.

[23] Telo, *A Neutralidade Portuguesa*, p. 360.

[24] On the importance of Macau and Lisbon for Japanese intelligence, see G. C. Gunn, 'Wartime Macau in the Wider Diplomatic Sphere', in G. C. Gunn (ed.), *Wartime Macau: Under the Japanese Shadow* (Hong Kong, 2016), pp. 25–54; F. Rodao, 'Japanese Relations with Neutrals, 1944–1945: The Shift to Pragmatism', in W. P. Brecher and M. W. Myers (eds.), *Defamiliarizing Japan's Asia-Pacific War* (Honolulu, HI, 2019), pp. 104–36.

Wars (1839–42, 1856–60) and the Taiping Civil War (1850–64).[25] Portugal was also neutral during the Russo–Japanese War (1904–5), with fear of Japanese reprisals on Macau listed as one of the reasons for neutrality in that conflict.[26]

Portuguese neutrality in World War II was neither static nor strict. It was 'a pragmatic process of adaptation to the different phases of the war' that 'leaned more to one side or the other depending on the circumstances'.[27] Portugal's neutrality has been analysed by different historians as overall pro-Allies, or, arguably more correctly, as pro-British, especially after 1943, despite the ideological affinities of Portugal's Estado Novo (New State) regime with other fascist dictatorships. Closer ties with Britain had a clear imperial dimension. Regarding the future Cold War superpowers, the Portuguese dictator António de Oliveira Salazar had a deep suspicion of the liberal, democratic and anti-colonial United States, whilst the regime he led, ferociously anti-communist, did not have diplomatic relations with the Soviet Union.[28] This is certainly a key difference between Salazar's Portugal and Chiang Kai-shek's China during the Second World War. Despite Chiang's opposition to the Chinese Communist Party (CCP), both the Soviets and the Americans were crucial allies of Nationalist China, even before 1941.[29] Anti-imperialism informed both the Chinese Nationalists and Communists' stance in the war. They fought to overcome their nation's encroachment by imperialist powers that had begun in the nineteenth century and reached the apex in the war with Japan, a conflict global historian Jürgen Osterhammel has labelled 'the most atrocious war for colonial subjugation fought in modern history'.[30]

The study of Portuguese neutrality in Asia is of particular importance because Portugal was the only colonial power with territorial interests in China to remain neutral for the duration of the war with Japan. Furthermore, it was precisely in Asia that the most serious violation of Portugal's neutrality occurred: the Japanese occupation of Timor, which followed an unauthorised Allied landing in the territory and

[25] R. Ptak, *China, the Portuguese, and the Nanyang: Oceans and Routes, Regions and Trade (c. 1000–1600)* (Aldershot, 2004), p. 69.

[26] J. Milhazes, *Rússia e Europa: Uma Parte do Todo* (*Russia and Europe: Part of the Whole*) (Lisbon, 2016), p. 96.

[27] Telo, *A Neutralidade Portuguesa*, pp. 78, 359.

[28] António de Oliveira Salazar was president of the council of ministers (prime minister) from 1932 to 1968, minister of finance from 1928 to 1940 and minister of foreign affairs from 1936 to 1947.

[29] J. W. Garver, 'China's Wartime Diplomacy', in J. C. Hsiung and S. I. Levine (eds.), *China's Bitter Victory: The War with Japan 1937–1945* (Armonk, NY 1992), pp. 3–32.

[30] J. Osterhammel, 'Semi-colonialism and Informal Empire in Twentieth-Century China: Towards a Framework of Analysis', in W. J. Mommsen (ed.), *Imperialism and After: Continuities and Discontinuities* (London, 1986), pp. 290–314, at p. 291.

lasted from early 1942 until the end of the war in 1945. Therefore, Portugal remained neutral even after flagrant disrespects of its neutrality in Asia, including invasion and occupation – acts that usually dictate a change from neutrality to belligerence. The reasons for that are inextricably linked with the Portuguese regime's conception of its colonial empire, as well as with the usefulness of Macau's neutrality to all the belligerents in the region.

The uses of Portuguese neutrality in Macau reveal a multitude of connections, not only to Timor and to Japan, but also, and most particularly, to China as well as to the country's oldest ally, Britain, notably to its colony of Hong Kong. Ultimately, the history of neutral Macau reveals a multilayered web of collaboration whose reach and relevance went far beyond the small country that lent its neutral status to the South China enclave.

Collaboration(s)

Collaboration is another key idea framing this book. Although the term has largely kept the negative connotation associated with occupied France during the Second World War, it has also been the object of pathbreaking enquiries applied to China's War with Japan and Japanese imperialism in Asia more generally. The historiography of collaboration in China has explored, amongst other topics, cases of 'collaborationist nationalism', local adaptation to occupation in Manchuria, attitudes of Shanghai capitalists and intellectuals, revisionist accounts of the Wang Jingwei regime, contacts between pro-Chiang and pro-Wang factions and the visual culture of the RNG.[31] Margherita Zanasi has alerted scholars to the need to problematise the '"resistentialist" postwar narrative' in China with attention to the global context in which it emerged, drawing attention to the parallels, differences and interactions with the Vichy case in France.[32]

[31] J. H. Boyle, *China and Japan at War, 1937–1945: The Politics of Collaboration* (Stanford, CA, 1972); G. E. Bunker, *The Peace Conspiracy: Wang Ching-wei and the China War, 1937–1941* (Cambridge, MA, 1972); Fu, *Passivity, Resistance, and Collaboration*; T. Brook, 'Collaborationist Nationalism in Occupied Wartime China', in T. Brook and A. Schmid (eds.), *Nation Work: Asian Elites and National Identities* (Ann Arbor, MI, 2000), pp. 159–90; R. Mitter, *The Manchurian Myth: Nationalism, Resistance, and Collaboration in Modern China* (Berkeley, CA, 2000); D. P. Barrett and L. N. Shyu (eds.), *Chinese Collaboration with Japan, 1932–1945: The Limits of Accommodation* (Stanford, CA, 2001); Coble, *Chinese Capitalists in Japan's New Order*; B. G. Martin, 'Collaboration within Collaboration: Zhou Fohai's Relations with the Chongqing Government, 1942–1945', *Twentieth-Century China*, 34/2 (2008), pp. 55–88; J. E. Taylor, *Iconographies of Occupation: Visual Cultures in Wang Jingwei's China, 1939–1945* (Honolulu, HI, 2020).

[32] M. Zanasi, 'New Perspectives on Chinese Collaboration', *Asia-Pacific Journal*, 6/7 (2008): apjjf.org/-Margherita-Zanasi/2828/article.html; M. Zanasi, 'Globalizing *Hanjian*: The Suzhou Trials and the Post-War II Discourse on Collaboration', *American Historical Review*, 113/3 (2008), pp. 731–51.

The need to historicise the experience of collaboration as a process of 'state making' has also been addressed by David Serfass, who noted the relative fragmentation of both Japanese and Chinese actors and synthesised the dynamics of collaboration in the case of the RNG as 'a dialectical tension between autonomy and control'.[33] If we look beyond the Sino–Japanese relationship and consider how foreign authorities engaged with Japanese forces in Shanghai, for example, we see iterations of that tension, but with an element of European colonialism added to the mix of overlapping nationalist and imperialist interests.[34] The different experiences of collaboration in China detailed in Timothy Brook's book, including how local elites and intermediaries were forced to deal with the exceptional circumstances of war and occupation that 'Japan imposed from above' – notably how 'collaboration dealt with more mundane problems' such as food provision – provide useful parallels to understanding wartime Macau, even without a formal occupation.[35]

Keeping in mind the concept of 'collaboration' even when discussing a formally neutral territory such as Macau is feasible. Contemporary observers remarked upon and resented the increasing Japanese interference in Macau and, indeed, perceptions of Portuguese and Chinese collaboration with Japan in Macau existed during and after the conflict, much as they did in other 'lone islands'. Similarly, comparing events and actions in neutral Macau with areas in occupied China lends itself to recognising the similarities and differences of this case study. A narrow dictionary definition of collaboration links it to 'traitorous cooperation with the enemy'.[36] However, for a territory that, considering the literal translation of the Chinese term for 'neutral' (中立 *zhongli*), was 'standing in the middle', who the 'enemy' was depended on the beholder. Frequent Japanese complaints that pro-Chongqing and pro-British activities were taking place in wartime Macau are a case in point. I do not wish to underplay the strength of wartime resistance to Japan – evidence suggests that the vast majority of Macau's wartime residents supported the Allies – but merely to point out that, in a neutral territory, resistance itself was marked by collaboration, a point that other historians have made regarding occupied territories in China.[37] I argue that instances of collaboration

[33] D. Serfass, 'Collaboration and State Making in China: Defining the Occupation State, 1937–1945', *Twentieth-Century China*, 47/1 (2022), pp. 71–80, at p. 77.

[34] Henriot and Yeh, 'Introduction', p. 8; I. Jackson, *Shaping Modern Shanghai: Colonialism in China's Global City* (Cambridge, 2018), pp. 159–62.

[35] T. Brook, *Collaboration: Japanese Agents and Local Elites in Wartime China* (Cambridge, MA, 2005), pp. 26, 7.

[36] B. Wasserstein, 'Ambiguities of Occupation: Foreign Resisters and Collaborators in Wartime Shanghai', in *Wartime Shanghai*, p. 24.

[37] For example, ibid., p. 38; Brook, *Collaboration*, p. 29.

with Japan in Macau need to be considered alongside other, often stronger cases of cooperation with Chinese forces or with the British that can be seen as forms of collaboration that do not involve an occupying power. In the case of Chinese resistance, these forms of collaboration challenge the myth of a Portuguese 'strict neutrality', although Sino–Portuguese local understandings in Macau did not represent a state policy of support for China's anti-imperialist resistance.

At a different level, the British connection points to forms of inter-imperial collaboration, at the top and on the ground, that have been overlooked regarding Macau. As Robert Bickers noted, 'empire was also rooted in collaboration' and ideas of collaboration in colonial contexts are easily applied to this case.[38] If 'collaboration remained a necessity for imperialism throughout the history of China', in Macau, that was the very condition for its survival as a foreign-ruled enclave throughout four centuries.[39] Robinson's theory emphasising the role of mediating elites is also applicable to Macau during the war period, for 'they had to recognise mutual interests and interdependence', not just with the Portuguese colonial authorities, but also with the Japanese military and Chinese collaborationist authorities' pressuring the enclave.[40] Wartime Macau hosted a plurality of often overlapping intermediaries: Chinese intermediaries who linked the majority of the enclave's population with the Portuguese colonial authorities; local elites who served as intermediaries between the Portuguese rulers and the Japanese and collaborationist authorities in the region; Chinese, Portuguese and British intermediaries who linked those in Hong Kong and other occupied territories with Allied authorities in unoccupied areas in China and beyond; and, naturally, the charitable institutions and philanthropists who were key intermediaries between the colonial authorities and the many refugees and urban poor, whom Portuguese officials would have been incapable of managing on their own. Ultimately, Macau itself may be regarded as an intermediary between the Allies and the Axis, those engaged in resistance and collaboration, and occupied and unoccupied areas. Although under exceptional circumstances, it is important to note that wartime Macau was not incomparable. Its position as a node for different agents and interests was akin to other foreign-ruled territories in China – for example, Shanghai's foreign concessions, Hong Kong and Guangzhouwan, until they were taken over by Japanese forces – and in Europe, notably Portugal's capital, Lisbon.

[38] R. Bickers, *Empire Made Me: An Englishman Adrift in Shanghai* (London, 2004), p. 59.

[39] Osterhammel, 'Semi-colonialism and Informal Empire', p. 306.

[40] R. Robinson, 'Non-European Foundations of European Imperialism: Sketch for a Theory of Collaboration', in R. Owen and B. Sutcliffe (eds.), *Studies in the Theory of Imperialism* (London, 1972), pp. 117–42, at pp. 120–4.

China and Portuguese Imperialism

Macau is a relevant example if we are to recognise the plurality of foreign imperialism in China. The enclave may be regarded as a 'semi-colony' in practice, given the issue of disputed sovereignties. The Chinese state – be it the Ming, the Qing, the Republican government or that of the People's Republic of China (PRC) – never unequivocally recognised that what the Portuguese considered as the 'colony of Macau' was not supposed to be a Chinese territory. From the beginning of the twentieth century, if not before, the Portuguese were not the key economic players in the territory. As will become clear in the following chapters, colonial authorities were often dependent on the role of Chinese intermediaries. Socially, economically and even politically, the life of the enclave was connected not only to the British imperial presence in China, but also to mainland China, with whose history the territory had always been intertwined.

Various scholars have noted the ambiguities and contradictions of Portuguese colonialism in Macau in different historical periods. Cathryn Clayton called Portugal the 'hapless imperialist', whilst Christina Mui Bin Cheng portrayed Macau as 'an anomaly in colonization and decolonization'.[41] Historians of empire have increasingly questioned the view of the Portuguese as 'weak' imperialists.[42] However, when considering post–Opium Wars Macau and the Portuguese position in Asia vis-à-vis the United Kingdom, the issue of relative weakness is inescapable, as was also noted for the case of Goa.[43] Some authors have regarded Portugal itself as a British semi-colony, or at least part of an informal British empire. The notion of 'subaltern colonialism' explored by sociologist Boaventura de Sousa Santos – allied to the concept of 'semi-colonialism' as it has been applied to foreign imperialism in China since the late Qing – is illuminating when exploring the

[41] C. Clayton, 'The Hapless Imperialist? Portuguese Rule in 1960s Macau', in B. Goodman and D. S. G. Goodman (eds.), *Twentieth-Century Colonialism and China: Localities, the Everyday and the World* (Abingdon, 2012), p. 212; C. M. B. Cheng, *Macau: A Cultural Janus* (Hong Kong, 1999), p. 9.

[42] F. Bethencourt and D. R. Curto, 'Introduction', in F. Bethencourt and D. R. Curto (eds.), *Portuguese Oceanic Expansion, 1400–1800* (Cambridge, 2007), pp. 1–18, at p. 12; E. Morier-Genoud and M. Cahen, 'Introduction: Portugal, Empire, and Migrations – Was There Ever an Autonomous Social Imperial Space?', in E. Morier-Genoud and M. Cahen (eds.), *Imperial Migrations: Colonial Communities and Diaspora in the Portuguese World* (Basingstoke, 2012), pp. 1–27, at pp. 3–7.

[43] Tristão Bragança Cunha, considered the 'father of Goan [Indian] Nationalism', criticised Portugal for being a 'weak' and 'primitive coloniser' responsible for a form of double (Anglo–Portuguese) colonialism. See P. D. Parobo, 'Tristão Bragança Cunha and Nationalism in Colonial Goa: Mediating Difference and Essentialising Nationhood', *Economic & Political Weekly*, I/31 (2015), pp. 61–8, at pp. 64–5.

case of Macau, whose status as a formal colony was problematic throughout its history and where Chinese people, capital and networks have always played a decisive role.[44] Portuguese authorities were well aware of their weakness in relation to China. In the context of the Second World War, they were also conscious of their lack of military capacity to resist a potential occupation by any of the major belligerents. Neutrality was a way of turning that weakness into a strategy for colonial survival. It worked.

As the existence of colonies was seen by Estado Novo officials as a precondition to the regime's survival, maintaining the empire was a key motivation for Portuguese neutrality. In contrast, anti-imperialism was central to Chinese authorities' decision to resist the Japanese invasion through an all-out war from 1937, and revoking long-resented clauses in the 'unequal treaties' was a core goal of China's wartime diplomacy.[45] Sino–Portuguese relations in this period were complicated also because the countries' leaders had opposing attitudes towards imperialism as key motivations for their stances in the war: Portuguese neutrality was a way of guaranteeing the maintenance of its colonial possessions; Chinese belligerence was a struggle to keep the country independent from an imperial aggressor. Macau was at the crossroads of these two conflicting attitudes towards war, imperialism and change.

Neutral Macau in Wartime China

Those who have written on the war years in Macau have often opted to reinforce the territory's exceptionalism, centring on local actors and dynamics and eschewing an approach that emphasises wider global connections.

The war period in Macau was first examined by scholars in mainland China and Taiwan in the 1990s and early 2000s, drawing on archival materials from Nanjing, Guangzhou and Taipei, as well as on Chinese-language newspapers published in Macau.[46] This scholarship has

[44] B. S. Santos, 'Between Prospero and Caliban: Colonialism, Postcolonialism, and Inter-identity', *Luso-Brazilian Review*, 39/2 (2002), pp. 9–43.

[45] On the history of the term 'unequal treaties', see D. Wang, *China's Unequal Treaties: Narrating National History* (Lanham, MD, 2005).

[46] C. Fei, *Aomen sibai nian (Macau 400 Years)* (Shanghai, 1988), pp. 414–29; W. Huang and L. Chen (eds.), *Haojiang fengyun er'nü: Aomen sijie jiuzaihui kangRi jiuguo shiji* (*Children of Haojiang: Macau's Four Circles Disaster Relief Association Activities of Resistance against the Japanese and for National Salvation*) (Macau, 1990); Z. Tan, *Aomen zhuquan wenti shimo: 1553~1993* (*Disputes concerning Macau's Sovereignty between China and Portugal (1553–1993)*) (Taipei, 1994), pp. 221–36; K. S. Deng, *Aomen lishi (1840–1949 nian)* (*History of Macau (1840–1949)*) (Macau, 1995), pp. 85–110; L. Guo, 'Shilun Aomen zai Guangdong

emphasised the contribution of the 'Macau compatriots' to China's resistance efforts, similarly to some scholarship on Chinese communities in Southeast Asia. Some of the Chinese scholarship on Macau covers the role of the Portuguese authorities in Macau, usually in critical terms for ceding to Japanese pressure. Scholars in Taiwan have also researched Kuomintang (KMT) activities in Macau and the post-war negotiations for extraditing alleged traitors.[47] Over the past years, paralleling a renewed interest in the war in both China and the English-speaking world, there has been a revival of studies of Macau in the War of Resistance, manifested in new journal articles, theses and published sources, notably oral histories and collections of visual materials.[48]

kangzhan zhong de diwei he zuoyong' ('On Macau's Position and Function in the War of Resistance in Guangdong'), *Zhanjiang shifan xueyuan xuebao* (*Journal of Zhanjiang Teachers College*), 20/4 (1999), pp. 99–104; L. Zhang, 'Aomen tongbao zhiyuan zuguo kangzhan chutan' ('The Support of Compatriots in Macau to the Homeland's War of Resistance'), *KangRi zhanzheng yanjiu* (*Journal of Studies of China's Resistance War against Japan*), 1 (2003), pp. 101–14; X. Zhang, 'Kangzhan qianqi Aomen de jingji shehui' ('Macau's Economy and Society during the Early Phase of the War of Resistance'), *Minguo dang'an* (*Republican Archives*), 3 (2005), pp. 82–9; Q. Huang, *ZhongPu guanxi shi (1513–1999)* (*History of Sino–Portuguese Relations (1513–1999)*), vol. 3 (Hefei, 2006), pp. 1029–54.

47 Y. H. Li, 'Lunxian qian guomin zhengfu zai Xianggang de wenjiao huodong' ('Culture and Education Activities by the National Government in Hong Kong before the Occupation'), in *Gang'Ao yu jindai Zhongguo xueshu yanjiuhui lunwen ji* (*A Summary of the Symposium on Hong Kong, Macao and Modern China*) (Taipei, 2000), pp. 440–76; Y. H. Li, 'Wu Tiecheng yu zhanshi Guomindang zai Gang'Ao de dangwu huodong' ('Wu Tiecheng and Kuomintang Party Activities in Hong Kong and Macau during the War'), in H. Y. Chen (ed.), *Wu Tiecheng yu jindai Zhongguo* (*Wu Tiecheng and Modern Chinese History*) (Taipei, 2012), pp. 64–88; S. F. Wu, 'Shenzhang zhengyi? Zhanhou yindu taoni Aomen hanjian (1945–1948)' ('Justice Served? Postwar Extradition of Traitors from Macao by the Nationalist Government, 1945–1948'), *Guoshiguan xueshu jikan* (*Bulletin of Academia Historica*), 1 (2001), pp. 128–60.

48 J. Zou, 'Qianxi kangzhan zhong de Aomen sijie jiuzaihui' ('On Macau's Four Circles Relief Association'), *Xiandai qiye jiaoyu* (*Modern Enterprise Education*), 16 (2012), p. 146; X. Liu and H. Huang, 'Aomen Zhongwen baozhi zai kangzhan moqi de xinwen bianji kuangjia yanjiu' ('The Frame of Macau Chinese Newspaper at the End of the Anti-Japanese War'), *Guoji xinwen jie* (*International Press*), 1 (2013), pp. 134–42; C. Feng and Q. Xia, 'Bentu zhi wai: Aomen kangRi zhanzheng yanjiu shuping' ('Outside the Territory: Studies on the War of Resistance against Japan in Macau'), *Minguo dang'an* (*Republican Archives*), 3 (2013), pp. 125–33; S. Mo, 'Kangzhan qijian PuRi heliu kuitan' ('A Probe into Portugal–Japan Collusion during the War of Resistance against Japan'), *Aomen ligong xuebao / Revista do Instituto Politécnico de Macau* (*Macau Polytechnic Institute Journal*), 16/2 (2013), pp. 42–52; Z. Zheng, *1940 niandai de Aomen jiaoyu* (*Macau Education in the 1940s*) (Beijing, 2016); Z. Chen, 'The Rise of Macao Chinese Cultural Nationalism during the Anti-Japanese War' (MA thesis, University of Macau, 2013); Z. Li, 'Approaches of Chinese Newspapers in Macau and Their Roles in Four Fields under the Influence of Nationalism during the Sino–Japanese War (1937–1945)' (MA thesis, University of Macau, 2013); P. Cai (ed.), *Koushu lishi: KangRi zhanzheng shiqi de Aomen* (*Oral History: Macau during the War of Resistance*) (Macau, 2005); F. Lin and C. Jiang (eds.), *Pingmin shengyin: Aomen yu kangRi zhanzheng koushu lishi* (*Civilian Voices: Oral History of Macau in the War of Resistance*) (Guangzhou, 2015); I. L. F. Barreto (ed.), *Macau during the Sino–Japanese War / Kangzhan shiqi de Aomen /*

This recent scholarship maintains the former matrix of emphasising the role of the Chinese community in Macau in supporting Chinese resistance, and in local mobilisation for humanitarian relief.

Portuguese-language works on the war in Macau have mainly been published in the territory, most authored by journalists with connections to the enclave.[49] These works provide a Portuguese-centred narrative of events and focus on figures such as the governor or the head of the Macau Economic Services, Pedro José Lobo. Scholarly monographs have mostly concentrated on the immediate post-war period as a starting point for works centred on Portugal's relations with the PRC.[50] The publication of primary sources on Macau during the war has also been modest when compared with the plethora of published memoirs on wartime Shanghai or Hong Kong.[51]

Despite the relative dearth of interest in Macau, Portuguese neutrality in the Second World War has attracted considerable scholarly attention. Monographs and articles in Portuguese and English have covered multiple aspects of the country's local and international experience. These overwhelmingly concentrate on the European theatre of war and on Portugal's links to major European powers and the United States.[52]

Macau Durante a Guerra Sino-Japonesa (Macau, 2002); F. Lin and X. Wang (eds.), *Gudao yingxiang: Aomen yu kangRi zhanzheng tuzhi* (*Lone Island Images: Pictorial History of Macau and the War of Resistance against Japan*) (Guangzhou, 2015).

49 L. A. Sá, *A História na Bagagem. Crónicas dos Velhos Hotéis de Macau* (*History in the Luggage: Chronicles of Macau's Old Hotels*) (Macau, 1989), pp. 84–129; R. Pinto, 'Guerra em Paz' ('War in Peace'), *Macau*, 43 (1995), pp. 54–89; J. F. O. Botas, *Macau 1937–1945: Os Anos da Guerra* (*Macau 1937–1945: The War Years*) (Macau, 2012). One rare academic work is the published master's thesis I. M. P. Braga, *Macau Durante a II Guerra Mundial: Sociedade, Educação Física e Desporto* (*Macau during the II World War: Society, Physical Education and Sport*) (Macau, 2003).

50 M. S. Fernandes, *Sinopse de Macau nas Relações Luso-Chinesas – 1945–1995: Cronologia e Documentos* (*Synopsis of Portuguese–Chinese Relations – 1945–1995: Chronology and Documents*) (Lisbon, 2000), pp. 27–70; M. S. Fernandes, *Confluência de Interesses: Macau nas Relações Luso-Chinesas Contemporâneas 1945–2005* (*Confluence of Interests: Macau in Contemporary Portuguese–Chinese Relations 1945–2005*) (Lisbon, 2008), pp. 23–111; F. G. Pereira, *Accommodating Diversity: The People's Republic of China and the 'Question of Macau' [1949–1999]* (Lisbon, 2013), pp. 31–49.

51 M. Teixeira, 'Macau durante a Guerra: Doce Visão de Paz!' (Macau during the War: Sweet Vision of Peace!), *Boletim Eclesiástico da Diocese de Macau* (*Macau Diocese Ecclesiastic Bulletin*), 885 (1978), pp. 497–518; A. A. Silva, *Eu estive em Macau durante a Guerra* (*I Was in Macau during the War*) (Macau, 1991); *A Guerra vista de Cantão: Os relatórios de Vasco Martins Morgado, Cônsul-Geral de Portugal em Cantão, sobre a Guerra Sino-Japonesa* (*The War Seen from Canton: The Reports of Vasco Martins Morgado, Portugal's Consul-General in Canton, about the Sino–Japanese War*), ed. A. V. Saldanha (Macau, 1998).

52 A. J. Telo, *Portugal na Segunda Guerra* (*Portugal in the Second World War*) (Lisbon, 1987); Telo, *Portugal na Segunda Guerra*; F. Rosas, *Portugal entre a Paz e a Guerra 1939–1945* (*Portugal between Peace and War 1939–1945*) (Lisbon, 1995); H. P. Janeiro, *Salazar e Pétain: Relações Luso-Francesas durante a Segunda Guerra Mundial (1940–44)* (*Salazar and Pétain: Portuguese–French Relations during the Second World War (1940–44)*) (Lisbon,

Studies on Portuguese neutrality in Asia have mostly privileged the Timor case, about which a number of primary sources have also been published.[53]

References to wartime Macau in English-language works were for years circumscribed to short mentions in works on wartime Hong Kong that, understandably, placed the enclave in a secondary position to the drama unfolding elsewhere.[54] Some of these publications zoomed in on the experience of the Portuguese community in Hong Kong.[55] Since the mid-2010s, some interest in wartime Macau has resurfaced following the publication of the 1946 memoir of the British consul in the enclave, John Pownall Reeves.[56] The focus on the British, as well as on the Portuguese authorities and their relations with Japanese agents and the

1998); Telo, *A Neutralidade*; F. Rosas, 'Portuguese Neutrality in the Second World War', in *European Neutrals and Non-belligerents during the Second World War*, pp. 268–83; N. Lochery, *Lisbon: War in the Shadows of the City of Light, 1939–1945* (New York, 2011); B. F. Pereira, *A Diplomacia de Salazar (1932–1949)* (*Salazar's Diplomacy (1932–1949)*) (Lisbon, 2012); I. F. Pimentel and C. Ninhos, *Salazar, Portugal e o Holocausto* (*Salazar, Portugal and the Holocaust*) (Lisbon, 2013); I. F. Pimentel, *Espiões em Portugal durante a II Guerra Mundial* (*Spies in Portugal during World War II*) (Lisbon, 2013); C. Ninhos, *Portugal e os Nazis: Histórias e Segredos de uma Aliança* (*Portugal and the Nazis: Histories and Secrets of an Alliance*) (Lisbon, 2017); A. Moreli, 'The War of Seduction: The Anglo-American Struggle to Engage with the Portuguese Ruling Elite (1943–1948)', *International History Review*, 40/3 (2018), pp. 654–82.

[53] C. C. Brandão, *Funo: Guerra em Timor* (*Funo: War in Timor*) (Oporto, 1953); B. J. Callinan, *Independent Company: The 2/2 and 2/4 Australian Independent Companies in Portuguese Timor, 1941–1943* (London, 1953); A. Campbell, *The Double Reds of Timor* (Swanbourne, 1995); C. T. Motta, *O Caso de Timor na II Guerra Mundial: Documentos Britânicos* (*The Case of Timor in the Second World War: British Documents*) (Lisbon, 1997); A. M. Cardoso, *Timor na 2ª Guerra Mundial: O Diário do Tenente Pires* (*Timor in the Second World War: Lieutenant Pires' Diary*) (Lisbon, 2007). For more scholarship on the Japanese occupation of Timor, see note 3.

[54] For example, E. Ride, *BAAG Hong Kong Resistance 1942–1945* (Hong Kong, 1981); Snow, *Fall of Hong Kong*; F. D. Macri, *Clash of Empires in South China: The Allied Nations' Proxy War with Japan, 1935–1941* (Lawrence, 2012).

[55] J. Wordie, 'The Hong Kong Portuguese Community and Its Connections with Hong Kong University 1914–1941', in K. C. Chan Lau and P. Cunich (eds.), *An Impossible Dream: Hong Kong University from Foundation to Re-establishment, 1910–1950* (Hong Kong, 2002), pp. 163–73; F. Yap, 'Portuguese Communities in East and Southeast Asia during the Japanese Occupation', in L. Jarnagin (ed.), *The Making of the Luso-Asian World: Intricacies of Engagement* (Singapore, 2011), pp. 205–28. An important work based on oral testimonies is the unpublished thesis: M. D. Cannon, 'Experience, Memory and the Construction of the Past: Remembering Macau 1941–1945' (MA thesis, University of British Columbia, 2001).

[56] J. P. Reeves, *The Lone Flag: Memoir of the British Consul in Macao during World War II*, ed. C. Day and R. Garrett (Hong Kong, 2014); G. C. Gunn (ed.), *Wartime Macau*; C. Day, 'Not Just Refugee Relief: John Reeves' Work As British Consul in Macao in WWII', *Journal of the Royal Asiatic Society Hong Kong Branch*, 60 (2020), pp. 115–37; R. Smith, 'Keeping the Flag Flying: John Reeves and the British Consulate in Macao, 1941–45', in R. Pastor-Castro and M. Thomas (eds.), *Embassies in Crisis: Studies of Diplomatic Missions in Testing Situations* (London, 2020), pp. 55–70.

Macanese community shared the main concerns of previous works in Portuguese and English but Chinese actors and sources have remained largely overlooked.

Over the many years of research that inform this book I have been intrigued by the absence of Macau in works on modern Chinese history. With a mix of expectation, amusement and frustration, I searched in vain for entries on Macau in indexes of scholarly monographs on imperialism, war and international relations, amongst works on various other topics, including Hong Kong history. Exceptions were few and very often not authored by historians. Macau's invisibility is surely not monocausal, though one possible reason may pertain to the relative English-language bias that remains a feature of how global history is researched and written today.[57] Another explanation is the disperse and fragmentary nature of the available records for the Second World War years in Macau, scattered between continents and archives and split between different languages. Telegrams from the governor of Macau to his superior in Lisbon tell one side of the story, information gathered by Chinese Nationalist agents often tells a very different one, and the perspective of, for example, a Eurasian refugee from Hong Kong provides another piece of the puzzle.

This is a book about the layers of collaboration that sprang from wartime neutrality and the global connections that framed these in a small enclave at the crossroads of different empires. Drawing on multilingual and multisite research, it brings to light, with unprecedented range and depth, the multiple connections framing the intersecting experiences of neutrality and collaboration in Macau. Expanding on the pioneering work of many authors and on a decade of archival research in Europe, Asia, Australia and the United States, this work is the result of many hours reading through Portuguese, Chinese, British, French and American government archives, documents by organisations such as the Red Cross, private papers (notably those in the Braga Collection) as well as newspapers, oral histories and memoirs. No single archival collection contains a complete record of Macau's wartime experience. Information is often piecemeal and some records' stated certainties are often proven to be partial when read alongside sources from a different provenance. This work triangulates data from thousands of pages, mostly read on site, on paper or microfilm. I aim to provide a holistic take on the complexities of neutrality and collaboration in Macau and surrounding areas, though I am well aware that the enclave's

[57] J. Adelman, 'What Is Global History Now?', *Aeon*, 2 Mar. 2017. aeon.co/essays/is-global-history-still-possible-or-has-it-had-its-moment; R. Drayton and D. Motadel, 'Discussion: The Futures of Global History', *Journal of Global History*, 13 (2018), pp. 13, 15.

many wartime stories are not exhausted by this work. Still, as Hans van de Ven has noted, 'moving beyond the battlefield and away from the principal wartime political and military players and places opens up new ways of seeing China's Second World War'.[58] Placing a peripheral territory such as Macau at the centre of analysis will unveil long-overlooked global connections between China and Europe and beyond.

A Centuries-Old History of Autonomy, Diversity and Accommodation

Portugal was the first European country to have a permanent settlement in Chinese territory. It was also the last European colonial power to leave China, with the handover of Macau occurring in 1999, two years after the British colony of Hong Kong reverted to Chinese rule. Despite the impressively long history of Sino–Portuguese contact, Portugal is quite often ignored in accounts of Western relations with China. Unlike Hong Kong and the treaty ports, the European presence in Macau dates back to the age of Iberian maritime expansion in the early modern period. Portuguese imperial borders were then fluid and in constant flux. East Asia, at the other side of the world from the imperial capital, Lisbon, is an illustrative case. Macau was marked by a considerable degree of local autonomy, managing to be outside of effective control by the Portuguese state for decades and remaining outside of Castilian control after the union of the Iberian crowns from 1580 to 1640. Although certain aspects of the Macau administration pointed to a strong level of Portuguese control, such as military defences or the fact that the senate (municipal council) was dominated by Portuguese Eurasian merchants, the exercise of Portuguese power 'was only possible through constant negotiation with the Chinese authorities in Canton [Guangzhou]' and the existence of Macau 'was the result not of central political action but of local negotiation and convergent interests'.[59]

Another important factor in Macau's history is the determinant role played by regional networks of merchants and missionaries that connected Macau with different parts of East and Southeast Asia as well as to territories further afield. Macau was not the first settlement of the Portuguese in China, but it became their first (and last) permanent base, occupied from 1555 or 1557 with the permission of local Chinese authorities, to whom they made an annual land rent payment. No written record has been found of such an agreement. As Cathryn Clayton observed: 'To many historians, the

[58] H. van de Ven, 'Wartime Everydayness: Beyond the Battlefield in China's Second World War', *Journal of Modern Chinese History*, 13/1 (2019), p. 18.

[59] F. Bethencourt, 'Political Configurations and Local Powers', in *Portuguese Oceanic Expansion*, pp. 209, 210.

haziness of this origin story is the origin of Macau's sovereignty problem. To others, this haziness was the condition of possibility for the very existence of Macau.'[60] Fok Kai Cheong identified a much-cited 'Macau formula', an informal Ming strategy that allowed for Portuguese trade activities in order to reconcile the need for coastal defences without giving up on the profits of international trade.[61] Roderich Ptak went further, seeing the Cantonese authorities' stance towards the Portuguese as an expression of 'de facto independence of the southern periphery'.[62] Mutual understandings on a regional scale and the fostering of private connections played a vital role throughout the history of Macau. That was also true during World War II.

As would later be the case with other Western powers with interests in China, private enterprise was central to the development of Macau as a globally connected metropolis. Managing to escape the regional authority of the Portuguese state until the seventeenth century, when the governor of Goa started appointing a permanent captain there, Macau was largely a self-governed merchant community – a 'merchants' republic' in the words of Malyn Newitt – structured around the senate.[63] Established in 1583, it preceded by almost three centuries a somewhat similar but much more studied institution: the Shanghai Municipal Council.[64] Chinese authorities tried to intervene in the affairs of Macau on various occasions and their influence over the population grew as the Chinese residents became more numerous. The enclave's population was very diverse, comprising not only Portuguese and Chinese but also other Europeans (particularly missionaries), Eurasians, Japanese, Indians, Malays, a significant number of Africans (mostly enslaved people, who at one point outnumbered the Europeans) and many others. It was a floating and mixed population. Iona Man-Cheong has argued that its cosmopolitanism was 'due in large part to its position as a city of liminality, of transience and of drift', being 'neither fully Portuguese nor fully Chinese'.[65] This cosmopolitanism was revived centuries later during the war with Japan.

The rise of Macau as a major Asian commercial city was linked to the highly lucrative trade between China and Japan that Portuguese intermediaries had assured at the turn of the sixteenth century. Because the Ming officially forbade Chinese ships to trade with Japan, and Japanese ships

[60] C. Clayton, *Sovereignty at the Edge: Macau & the Question of Chineseness* (Harvard, MA, 2009), pp. 40–1.
[61] F. C. Fok, *Estudos sobre a Instalação dos Portugueses em Macau* (*Studies on the Portuguese Settlement in Macau*) (Lisbon, 1996).
[62] Ptak, *China, the Portuguese, and the Nanyang*, p. 33.
[63] M. Newitt, *A History of Portuguese Overseas Expansion, 1400–1668* (London, 2005), p. 145.
[64] On Shanghai, see Jackson, *Shaping Modern Shanghai.*
[65] I. Man-Cheong, 'Macao: An Early Modern Cosmopolis', in C. X. G. Wei (ed.), *Macao: The Formation of a Global City* (Abingdon, 2014), p. 144.

with China, the Portuguese 'were able to secure a more or less official monopoly of the trade between the two countries' that mostly revolved around the exchange of Chinese silk for Japanese silver.[66] One author considers that Macau was 'the frontier between China and Japan *par excellence* [my italic]' during the late Ming.[67] From 1639 onwards, the Portuguese found themselves barred from Japan, following the country's unification by Toyotomi Hideyoshi and, particularly, after the expulsion of Christian missionaries by Tokugawa Ieyasu. Macau's merchants found alternatives to their businesses, notably in trade with Southeast Asian ports.[68] The Qing authorities also consolidated their presence in Macau by establishing two custom houses and having one representative operating from inside the city's borders. Chinese criminals were sent to be judged by Chinese authorities. At the end of the eighteenth century, 'political power in and over Macau was largely in Chinese hands'.[69] Macau's position as an entrepôt between China and Japan would only re-emerge during the Second World War. The engagement of Macau officials in informal diplomacy, which was of major importance during the 1930s and 1940s, had centuries-old precedents dating back to the Ming–Qing transition.[70]

Before the First Opium War, Macau played a key role in Anglo–Chinese relations, a role it would only reassume during the Second World War. With trade only being allowed in Guangzhou for part of the year, and East India Company men, theoretically, not being permitted to keep families in the city, Macau functioned as a rear base to their activities. Macau was a major nexus of the 'Canton system of trade' and some of its key Chinese merchants were based there. These men 'were central to the rise and advancement of international trade and commerce in the eighteenth century'.[71] Macau was also an important link in contraband trade and played a key role in Sino–American relations, with the first treaty between the United States and China having been signed in Macau.[72]

In the context of foreign assault on China during the late Qing period, the Portuguese crown sought to consolidate its rule over Macau,

[66] C. R. Boxer, *The Portuguese Seaborne Empire, 1415–1825* (London, 1969, repr. 1977), p. 63.
[67] L. F. Barreto, *Macau: Poder e Saber – Séculos XVI e XVII* (*Macau: Power and Knowledge – 16th and 17th centuries*) (Lisbon, 2006), p. 99.
[68] G. B. Souza, *The Survival of Empire: Portuguese Trade and Society in China and the South China Sea, 1630–1754* (Cambridge, 1986).
[69] B. V. Pires, 'Origins and Early History of Macau', in R. D. Cremer (ed.), *Macau: City of Commerce and Culture* (Hong Kong, 1987), p. 13.
[70] J. M. S. Alves, *Macau: O Primeiro Século de um Porto Internacional* (*Macau: The First Century of an International Port*) (Lisbon, 2007), p. 73.
[71] P. A. van Dyke, *Merchants of Canton and Macao: Politics and Strategies in Eighteenth-Century Chinese Trade* (Hong Kong, 2012), p. 213.
[72] K. Maxwell, 'Macao: The Shadow Land', *World Policy Journal*, 16/4 (1999–2000), p. 73. See also Y. Hao and J. Wang (eds.), *Macao and Sino–US Relations* (Lanham, MD, 2011).

Figure I.2 The Barrier Gate (Portas do Cerco) in 1933. Built in 1871, it marked the land border between Macau and mainland China. Author's collection

extending the powers of the governor, establishing a Portuguese customs house and expanding the military presence and defensive infrastructures (see Figure I.2). The bold moves by Governor João Maria Ferreira do Amaral (1844–9) – who, amongst other actions to curb Chinese power in Macau, refused to pay the land lease, demolished the Chinese customs houses, expelled the customs superintendents and destroyed Chinese tombs when clearing land for building roads – were met with ferocious resistance from the Cantonese authorities with Amaral being eventually murdered. Amaral was also responsible for introducing the gambling concession model that became of paramount importance to the territory's economy during the twentieth century, and until today.[73]

In the nineteenth century, Macau's economy was anchored in two controversial activities: narcotics and human trafficking. One author has observed that between 1845 and 1925, Macau was both 'an opium trafficking centre' and 'an international opium refinery', and trade in opium was the first source of revenue for the Macau administration.[74]

[73] J. Godinho, 'A History of Games of Chance in Macau: Part 2 – The Foundation of the Macau Gaming Industry', *Gaming Law Review and Economics*, 17/2 (2013), p. 109.

[74] V. F. S. Sit, *Macau through 500 Years: Emergence and Development of an Untypical Chinese City* (Singapore, 2013), p. 119. A. G. Dias, *Portugal, Macau e a Internacionalização da Questão do Ópio (1909–1925)* (*Portugal, Macau and the Internationalization of the Opium Question (1909–1925)*) (Macau, 2004), p. 41.

Chinese authorities vigorously opposed opium and were active in contesting the appalling conditions of the so-called coolie trade, just as they had opposed previous cases of human trafficking that had taken place via Macau.[75] According to Christina Mui Bin Cheng, in 1873, 300 'coolie-slave recruiting offices' operated in Macau.[76] Most of the Chinese indentured labourers sent to Cuba and Peru from the 1840s to the 1870s were shipped from Macau until the transport of forced labourers was banned in 1874. During the twentieth century, the descendants of some of these Chinese migrants to Latin America returned to Asia, including to Macau.

After the cession of Hong Kong Island to the British in 1841, and the opening of a number of treaty ports in China, Macau's relevance greatly diminished. Foreign traders, their Chinese partners and a significant number of Portuguese from Macau left the enclave for better opportunities in the new British colony or the largely British-dominated colonial world of the treaty ports.

In the mid-nineteenth century, as several countries regulated their relations with China through bilateral treaties – known to this day as the 'unequal treaties' – Portugal attempted to follow suit. A lengthy negotiation of a treaty with the Qing authorities, which would recognise Portuguese sovereignty over Macau in perpetuity, was marred by a number of problems.[77] A Sino–Portuguese Treaty of Amity and Commerce, signed in Beijing in 1887, was considered by the Portuguese as the document that confirmed Macau as a Portuguese colony.

That did not mean, of course, that the territory stopped being deeply enmeshed in Chinese affairs. Similar to what happened during the war with Japan, in the last years of Qing rule, several reformers and revolutionaries sought refuge in Macau, where they established newspapers and gathered supporters. Amongst them were the reformers Kang Youwei and Zheng Guanying, and the future 'father of the Republic' Sun Yat-sen (Sun Zhongshan). Sun lived in Macau for a brief period, working for the Kiang Wu Hospital (Jinghu yiyuan) and contributing to the first bilingual newspaper in Macau, the *Echo Macaense* (*Jinghai congbao*).[78]

Portuguese jurisdiction may have been convenient for Chinese actors at certain times, but it was also contested, and anti-Portuguese protests

[75] C. R. Boxer, *Fidalgos in the Far East 1550–1770* (Oxford, 1948, repr. 1968), pp. 223–40.
[76] Cheng, *Macau*, p. 32.
[77] A. V. Saldanha, *O Tratado Impossível: Um Exercício de Diplomacia Luso-Chinesa num Contexto Internacional em Mudança, 1842–1887* (*The Impossible Treaty: An Exercise in Portuguese–Chinese Diplomacy in a Changing International Context, 1842–1887*) (Lisbon, 2007).
[78] M. K. Chan, *The Luso-Macau Connections in Sun Yatsen's Modern Chinese Revolution* (Macau, 2011); K. C. Fok, *O Dr. Sun Yat-sen e a sua Profissão Médica em Macau* (*Dr Sun Yat-sen and His Medical Profession in Macau*) (Macau, 2014).

preceded the implementation of the Chinese Republic in 1911.[79] Despite the coincidence in dates in implementing a republican regime – October 1910 in Portugal and October 1911 in China – Sino–Portuguese relations in the republican period were not always smooth. Chinese anti-imperialism and China's attempts to end the opium trade in Macau clashed with Portuguese colonial interests. The auctioning of opium and gambling monopolies became the main source of revenue for Macau in the late nineteenth and early twentieth centuries, and these would be the pillars of Macau's economy during the war years. Opium trade and smuggling were denounced, and China was successful in harnessing international support from both the United States and Great Britain, leaving the Portuguese largely isolated.[80] These alignments would become more pronounced after Japan invaded Northeast China in the early 1930s. As will be seen in Chapter 1, this generated immediate reactions in Macau.

Centuries of Sino–Portuguese contacts centred in Macau were marked by a degree of autonomy, a relative openness to a changing and diverse population, precedents of engaging in economic activities of questionable legality and moral standing, as well as flexibility in dealing with different authorities and regional powers and, importantly, neutrality precedents. All of these came to be of crucial importance during the Second World War, as the following chapters will detail.

Structure of the Book

Chapter 1 addresses Macau's place in China's War with Japan from the early 1930s to 1941. Macau was part of the geography of Chinese resistance efforts from the start, but its relevance became more pronounced after 1937, especially after Guangdong province was engulfed in the conflict in 1938. The chapter argues that, due to its neutrality, Macau became an important place of activity for competing Chinese actors. Both those engaged in Chinese resistance – Nationalists, Communists and others – and collaborators with Japan (before and after the consolidation of the RNG) used the enclave to circulate materials and propaganda, to mobilise others for their cause and to reach out to opponents. However, the abuses of Portuguese neutrality were carefully monitored and sometimes questioned.

Neutral Macau was not merely of local importance but was a matter of international diplomacy. Chinese diplomats in Lisbon were paradigmatic

79 E. J. M. Rhoads, *China's Republican Revolution: The Case of Kwangtung, 1895–1913* (Cambridge, MA, 1975), pp. 142–8.

80 Dias, *Portugal, Macau e a Internacionalização da Questão do Ópio*, p. 153.

examples of the internationalisation of republican China's elites, whose educational background was much more global than their Portuguese counterparts. Li Jinlun, who served as minister to Portugal until 1943, was born in New York and educated at New York University and the University of Chicago.[81] His successor, Zhang Qian, had studied at the University of Pennsylvania and the University of Southern California. The Chinese legation in Lisbon remained the most stable channel of bilateral communication during the war. In contrast, Portugal's highest-ranking representative in China, Minister João de Lebre e Lima, remained in occupied Shanghai. Macau's authorities often engineered shadow diplomacy initiatives on their own, dealing directly with both Chiang's representatives and collaborationist authorities in Guangdong province. What happened in diplomatic circles in Lisbon, Shanghai and Guangzhou was connected to developments in Macau in complex ways. Even before the more conventional dating for the globalisation of China's War with Japan in late 1941, events and actors in China and Europe were closely connected. Occurrences in a neutral enclave provide new insight into the everyday tightening of Japanese control in South China in the 1930s and early 1940s, European weakness and Chinese determination to resist Japan, both through underground channels and through official diplomacy.

Chapter 2 analyses Portuguese neutrality in wartime China before the fall of Hong Kong with reference to the British and Japanese presence in the region. It argues that the war in South China saw Macau and its Portuguese administration engage constantly and deeply with these two major imperial powers in a precarious balance marked by continuities in Portugal's relations with Britain and a novel proximity in relations with Japan that generated contradictory practices on the ground.

The Japanese wooing of Portuguese colonial authorities was a transnational affair, articulated in Macau, in Guangzhou, in Tokyo and in diplomatic circles in European capitals. The first wartime governor of Macau, Artur Tamagnini de Sousa Barbosa (who died whilst in post in 1940), was relatively receptive to these overtures.[82] Nevertheless, he still prioritised good relations with Hong Kong. Pro-British actions would become prevalent after a new governor of Macau, Gabriel Maurício Teixeira, took office in 1940. This triangular relationship – Portugal, Britain, Japan – vividly conveys the dynamic interaction of imperial interests in South China.

[81] Li Jinlun belonged to a generation of Chinese Americans who went to China in large numbers during the Republican period, many of whom found employment at different levels of government. For more on this, see C. Brooks, *American Exodus: Second-Generation Chinese Americans in China, 1901–1949* (Oakland, CA, 2019).

[82] Barbosa was governor of Macau three times, in 1918–19, in 1926–31 and in 1937–40.

Although politics and diplomacy were essential to neutral Macau's global connections, those are better understood if analysed in tandem with the social transformations brought about by the conflict. Chapter 3 centres on the social history of the war in Macau, demonstrating that neutrality did not shield the territory from the effects that the conflict generated elsewhere in China, such as a massive refugee influx. The chapter argues that neutrality shaped the experience of displacement in Macau in concrete ways: it turned it into a haven for refugees of different social strata, many of whom had regional and global personal connections.

The arrival of hundreds of thousands of refugees – around 300,000 newcomers between 1937 and 1945 – had a momentous impact on Macau's economic, cultural and educational practices. The chapter centres on Chinese refugees from Shanghai and Guangdong province, and on Portuguese Eurasian refugees from Shanghai and Guangzhou, and it details how the arrival of a great number of displaced persons was both a crisis and an opportunity for the territory's administration, local population and for the refugees themselves. The refugee influx into Macau led to the emergence of a peculiar wartime cosmopolitanism, which sprang from new flows of people, capital and ideas from major treaty-port metropolises, namely Shanghai and Guangzhou. Relief activities depended on the pragmatic interplay and cooperation of multinational state and non-state actors (see Figure I.3). Allowing a relatively unrestrained entrance of refugees was determinant to the wartime experience of Macau and to shelter its administration against allegations of collaboration whilst, at the same time, shaping how the enclave's colonial officials responded to Japanese and RNG pressures.

Chapter 4 centres on Macau's 'lone island' years, from the occupation of Hong Kong until the end of the war (December 1941 to September 1945). Although the isolation associated with the term *gudao* ought not to be overstated, the fact that Macau became the only foreign-ruled territory in China to remain unoccupied by Japan was distinctive, generating heightened pressures and restrictions. In this period, the practice of neutrality in Macau reached a peak of ambiguity, which was marked by the interplay of different forces and new players competing for political legitimacy, economic control and social influence. These included Chiang Kai-shek's government, Wang Jingwei's RNG, Portuguese colonial authorities, Japanese military forces and local elites. Arguing that collaboration through compliance was a way of avoiding occupation, this chapter highlights the significance of the ambiguous connections forged between Macau elites and Japanese and RNG figures,

Figure I.3 Harbour view, Macau, *c.*1938. P-A1.41-111. Courtesy of Archives Research Centre of the Presbyterian Church of Aotearoa New Zealand

illustrating how the strict neutrality the Portuguese authorities claimed to be practising was, in fact, quite ambivalent.

Chiang Kai-shek's government remained interested in Macau's situation and kept contacts with Portuguese authorities there through its agents in the territory, and in the Portuguese capital via its legation. Its concern for the impact of the war on the Chinese population was directed towards Macau, Lisbon and Portuguese-ruled Timor, which hosted the largest Chinese community in the Portuguese empire outside of Macau.

Emboldened by the occupation of British Hong Kong, whose effects left Macau in complete economic dependency, Japanese forces and the RNG authorities in Guangdong tightened their control over the enclave. Constraints on food supplies led to hunger and disease affecting a growing number of refugees as thousands fleeing Hong Kong joined those who had arrived in Macau in the late 1930s. Building on the links between diplomatic and social dimensions addressed in the previous chapters, Chapter 4 demonstrates how the dramatic reality of food scarcity had devastating effects on the enclave's swollen population and was used to justify concessions to Japanese and collaborators. Local businessmen and moneychangers expanded their power and influence, being coopted by the government as key supply providers. Amongst them were gambling tycoons Gao Kening (Kou Ho Neng) and Fu Deyin (Fu Tak Iam), Stanley Ho (then a young newcomer from Hong Kong who joined his uncle Robert Ho Tung in a wartime exile in Macau) and the aforementioned head of the colony's Economic Services, Pedro Lobo. Some of these wartime economic elites would go on to assume an even greater importance in post-war Macau.

Chapter 5 focuses on a second major wave of refugees to Macau: those from Hong Kong. It highlights the significant experience of colonial transplantation that allowed the British to keep a foothold in South China from where the reoccupation of Hong Kong was prepared. It pays particular attention to the role played by the British consulate in Macau in refugee management and intelligence networks, revealing little-known dimensions of pro-British wartime resistance in South China and how Macau was an important base and a connecting node for British operations. This chapter argues that Macau played an important supportive role to many in and from Hong Kong from late 1941 to the end of the war. Although this crucial link remains unacknowledged in the scholarship on Hong Kong, this book posits that the British reoccupation of Hong Kong would have been far more complicated without a neutral Macau nearby.

Macau was a peculiar centre of inter-Allied collaboration. Amongst those drawing relief from the British consulate, assisting escapees from Hong Kong and gathering intelligence for Consul John Pownall Reeves were many Chinese and Portuguese. Some of those involved in these efforts were also closely linked to the Chinese Nationalists and to US intelligence. Spearheading this were individuals whose transnational connections straddled different camps, such as José Maria (Jack) Braga, journalist, businessman, teacher and spy, whose pool of contacts illustrates the plurality of overlapping players in the region. These included the British naval intelligence officer and future historian Charles Ralph Boxer, the former magistrate of Zhongshan and Chinese aviation celebrity Zhang Huichang, the Russian exiled painter George Smirnoff, the tycoon Robert Ho Tung and Hong Kong barrister of Portuguese descent Leonardo (Leo) d'Almada e Castro who would be smuggled out of Macau to integrate the Hong Kong Planning Unit in London in the final stages of the war. This book makes significant use of the Braga Papers, held at the National Library of Australia, which are an invaluable and underused archival source on wartime resistance and relief in South China.

The ambiguities of wartime neutrality in Macau were not settled when the conflict came to a close. Instead, they continued to haunt China's relations with Portugal in the post-war years, as Chapter 6 argues. Five interconnected issues relating to Portuguese neutrality evidence China's post-war quest for justice and recognition: re-establishing formal diplomatic contacts in China, handling Japanese property, extraditing suspects of war crimes and collaboration, abolishing extraterritoriality, and discourses critiquing Portugal's problematic neutrality in calls to retake Macau. These issues raised questions about the meaning of justice and the legitimacy of who got to yield it. In its relations with a small and relatively weak European colonial power, China sought to affirm its new post-war international status, but this process was hampered by resistance to the Nationalists' anti-imperialist goals in South China and constrained by the changing fortunes of Nationalist power as the Chinese Civil War unfolded.

As one of the main Allied powers, China emerged from the Second World War as a victorious power, one of the first in Asia to triumph in what had been a war of liberation against Japanese imperialism. Post-war relations with Portugal reveal not only the Nationalists' determination in assuming their new post-war and postcolonial position but also the challenges they faced in doing so. The layers of collaboration that had marked Macau's wartime neutrality created considerable room for manoeuvre for both Portuguese authorities and Nationalists officials. The first, seeking to salvage their reputation in order to maintain colonial rule in Macau, drew attention to the benefits that neutrality had brought many Chinese people, particularly refugees. However, for the Nationalists, neutrality had other meanings, too: cosying up to their wartime enemies and sheltering people wanted for war crimes and collaboration. Macau's flexible neutrality meant that collaboration had multiple beneficiaries, including on the side of the future winners, which complicated clear-cut post-war assessments and attempts to exercise justice.

The usefulness of Macau's neutrality and global connections gained a renewed importance for the KMT, the CCP and other actors without allegiance to either party. As the Civil War approached the south, Sino–Portuguese relations gradually began to improve, ending attempts to decolonise Macau by force. Yet that improvement, forged by elite personal connections, came too late to translate into a meaningful compromise with the Nationalists. Still, ad hoc practices of accommodation with opposing Chinese sides were enacted during the Civil War just as they had been during the Second World War. Neutrality in the Civil War, building on practices that preceded it, ensured that Portuguese colonial rule remained in Macau despite the post-war wave of decolonisation that swept Asia.

1 Caught in the Middle

Macau between Chinese Resistance and Collaboration

When Japanese and Chinese forces clashed in Shanghai in the early months of 1932, twenty-one-year-old Macau-born Guo Jingqiu (Helena Kuo) was starting a journalism career that would later take her to Britain, France and the United States. The violence of the combat led her to return temporarily to her place of birth, where her family still lived, in search of safety. There, she encountered a completely different reality: 'I went out into the town that first night. The dancing and gambling and vice continued as usual. The hotels were crowded with rich refugees from Shanghai. Macao seemed more like Babylon than ever. No one worried about China's war problem.'[1]

Guo was not the only person in Macau concerned about China's situation, but, in 1932, the Japanese invasion of China was still regarded in the enclave as a distant affair. In 1937, when a continuous state of warfare began, things were very different.

After addressing the limited impact of the Sino–Japanese conflict in Macau in the early 1930s, this chapter explores how the territory came to be an important intersection for competing Chinese forces from 1937 to 1941. It was relevant not only for Chinese resistance activities in Guangdong province – both Nationalist and Communist – but also for the collaborationist movement led by Wang Jingwei. Similarly, Macau was used as a meeting place for Japanese peace feelers towards Cantonese elites and Chiang Kai-shek's envoys. It was a place that did not simply stand in the middle but was caught in the middle of different and intersecting nationalist and imperialist designs.

The great majority of the Macau population – both pre-war and refugee – was Chinese, so understanding how different Chinese actors perceived and engaged with neutrality and collaboration in the enclave is paramount. Macau was used by both Chinese resistance and collaborators in their activities to maintain China's war effort against Japan or convince others to file for peace with the occupiers. The commercial and transportation opportunities neutrality offered were amply explored by both those resisting and those collaborating with Japan.

[1] H. Kuo, *I've Come a Long Way* (New York, 1943), p. 156.

The enclave had a strategic position. Located in the Pearl River Delta, connected by land and water routes to the most important city in South China, Guangzhou (occupied in 1938), it bordered a county, Zhongshan, that was not firmly occupied until 1940, and was well connected to Hong Kong, which until 1941 was a crucial lifeline for Chinese resistance. Whilst the British colony's importance for the Chinese war effort has been acknowledged by several historians, Macau has remained largely in the shadows.[2] This chapter demonstrates that the small enclave mattered locally and regionally and was also discussed in international diplomacy.

Watching from Afar: Macau and the Japanese Invasion of China before 1937

On 18 September 1931, an incident at a railway masterminded by Japanese military figures stationed in north-eastern China escalated into a full-on invasion of three provinces that became known as the Manchurian Crisis. In China today, this marks the official start of China's War of Resistance against Japan and of the Second World War.

In response to Japanese actions, the Chinese government called on the League of Nations, of which China was a founding member, for assistance. Chinese diplomats in Geneva and all over the world conveyed the arguments against the Japanese aggression. Portugal was no exception. Minister Wang Tingzhang wrote to the Ministry of Foreign Affairs in Lisbon and transmitted the appeal being made 'of the Chinese government and people' calling on all the League's signatory powers to examine the 'invasion of Chinese waters by numerous Japanese ships' along the coasts, including in Shanghai, escalating the conflict in Manchuria.[3] The immobility of the League was evident, however.

Meanwhile, in Macau, there were some open manifestations of support for the Chinese resistance, including speeches condemning Japan and fundraising for Chinese victims to be sent to General Ma Zhanshan, a major figure of the resistance in the north-east.[4] There is some evidence to suggest that Portuguese authorities took steps to curb openly

[2] For example, S. Tsang, *A Modern History of Hong Kong* (London, 2004), pp. 114–15; J. M. Carroll, *The Hong Kong–China Nexus* (Cambridge, 2022), pp. 34–7.

[3] Wang Tingzhang, Chinese Minister to Portugal, to Fernando Augusto Branco, Minister of Foreign Affairs, 12 Oct. 1931, Arquivo Histórico Diplomático (Historical Diplomatic Archives of Portugal's Ministry of Foreign Affairs, hereafter AHD), 3P, A9, M125.

[4] 'Macao Chinese Meet: Sum Collected for General Ma Chan-shan', *South China Morning Post* (hereafter *SCMP*) (30 Nov. 1931), p. 14. In the first half of the 1930s, Ma would go from resistance hero to collaborator with the Japanese before returning to a prominent

anti-Japanese activities. For example, in 1931, the Macau authorities sought to prevent the Chinese Commercial Association (the local chamber of commerce) from requesting local merchants to participate in a boycott of Japanese products, as this could be damaging to the territory's commerce.[5]

The spread of hostilities to Shanghai, where Chinese and Japanese armies clashed from late January to March 1932, had more direct effects in the enclave, as well as on Portuguese residing in mainland China that, to an extent, and like other cities in China, anticipated some of the actions that took place from 1937 onwards.[6] The 1932 hostilities, which have been called 'the Shanghai War of 1932' and whose significance has been demonstrated by Donald Jordan, did not leave the Portuguese unscathed.[7] The Portuguese diplomats in the city prepared an evacuation of the community, even dispatching the auxiliary cruiser *Gil Eanes* from Macau. Portugal's Ministry of Foreign Affairs archives hold detailed lists of their material losses and complaint letters on the damage caused to Portuguese properties.[8] A public subscription was started by Macau's municipal council, the Loyal Senate (Leal Senado) to gather donations for relief of Portuguese in Shanghai, an early example of the public–private partnerships that were a dominant practice during the Second World War.[9]

Although Portuguese officials were concerned only with their fellow nationals, Chinese who left Shanghai also sought shelter in Macau, as Guo Jingqiu's case illustrates. Chinese refugees also generated a civil society response. In Macau, the Chinese population likewise organised subscriptions to collect relief funds to be remitted to the victims on the mainland, and refugees who had come to Macau were assisted by local charities.[10] One of those who reportedly sought refuge in Macau in 1932 was the film superstar Ruan Lingyu.[11] Unlike in 1937, however, when the 1932 hostilities in Shanghai came to an end, refugees largely left Macau soon after.

position in the resistance movement. On Ma and the complex situation in the north-east in the first years of the Japanese invasion, see Mitter, *Manchurian Myth*.

5 Council Administrator and Police Commissioner to Director of the Civil Administration Services, 17 Oct. 1931, Arquivo de Macau/Aomen dang'an guan (Archives of Macau, hereafter AM), MO/AH/AC/SA/01/13673.

6 On the 1932 precedents for refugee management in 1937, see, for example, the case of Wuxi discussed in Lincoln, *Urbanizing China in War and Peace*, pp. 120–6.

7 D. A. Jordan, *China's Trial by Fire: The Shanghai War of 1932* (Ann Arbor, MI, 2001).

8 See files in AHD, 3P, A9, M125.

9 Appeal from the President of the Loyal Senate, 16 Mar. 1932, AM, MO/AH/AC/SA/01/13827.

10 'Macao Chinese – Take Part in the Cracker Celebration: Funds for Sufferers', *SCMP* (25 Feb. 1932), p. 14.

11 Cheong K. M., '"Afilhada" de Ho Tung Refugiou-se em Macau durante a Guerra ('Ho Tung's "Goddaughter" Sought Refuge in Macau during the War'), *Jornal Tribuna de Macau* (31 Mar. 2022), p. 9.

A refugee exodus would only unfold again – and with much greater intensity – from 1937 onwards, but, from 1932 to 1937, there were periodic echoes of the Sino–Japanese conflict implicating Macau. These usually took the form of alarmist rumours of Japanese demands. In March 1932, rumours that Japan was using Macau for military activities with Portuguese agreement arose in Chinese newspapers yet the Portuguese authorities denied them.[12] In 1935, a string of news articles reported on hearsay that a Japanese group wanted to build an aerodrome in Macau or, more spectacularly, that Japan had proposed to buy Macau itself. Portuguese authorities always rebuffed such hearsay, but the gossip did generate some international attention.[13]

Even though there was a perception of relative appeasement of Japan by Chiang's government in the mid-1930s, diplomatically, resistance never ceased.[14] Japanese actions in China continued to be brought to the attention of the international community, including small powers such as Portugal. When Manchukuo, a Japanese-sponsored colonial creation under the guise of a supposedly 'independent' state was established out of the three invaded provinces in the north-east, the Chinese Ministry of Foreign Affairs (MOFA) wrote to the Portuguese minister Armando Navarro, urging Portugal 'not to give recognition to the unlawful organization born out of Japanese military action'.[15] Although Portugal did not show signs of recognising Manchukuo, neither was it openly supportive of China in the League of Nations where the Manchurian Crisis would eventually lead to Japan's withdrawal from the international body.

In December 1932, after the findings of the League's Lytton Report that confirmed Japan's aggressive actions in the north-east and Chinese sovereignty over Manchuria, the Portuguese minister of foreign affairs instructed the country's delegate 'not to intervene in the discussion of any resolution project'. When a vote became inevitable, Portugal was to follow the British attitude, 'softening as much as possible what in our

[12] AM, MO/AH/AC/SA/01/25240, Documentos enviados e recebidos de vários consulados portugueses e estrangeiros (Documents Sent to and Received from Various Portuguese and Foreign Consulates), 1931–3.

[13] 'Japan in Macau', *SCMP* (18 Mar. 1935), p. 16; 'Sale of Macao', *SCMP* (14 May 1935), p. 15; 'No Sale of Macao', *SCMP* (20 May 1935), p. 16; 'Japan's Eyes Not on Macao', *North China Herald* (hereafter *NCH*) (2 Oct. 1935), p. 11; Paul d'Hybouville, French Chargé d'Affaires in Lisbon, to Pierre Laval, Minister of Foreign Affairs, 20 May 1935, Centre des Archives diplomatiques de La Courneuve (Diplomatic Archives at La Courneuve), Paris – Ministère des Affaires Étrangères (hereafter MAE), 32CPCOM/784.

[14] S. G. Craft, 'Opponents of Appeasement: Western-Educated Chinese Diplomats and Intellectuals and Sino–Japanese Relations, 1932–37', *Modern Asian Studies*, 35/1 (2001), pp. 195–216.

[15] MOFA to Armando Navarro, Minister to China, 23 June 1932, AHD, 3P, A9, M125.

vote may be disagreeable to China or to Japan'.[16] In other words, Portugal opted for a detached neutrality.

Portuguese diplomats regarded the situation in East Asia differently, but none advocated open support for China. The chargé d'affaires in Tokyo noted the worrying imperial confidence of Japanese authorities whose attitude 'is becoming singularly similar to that of Germany in 1914'.[17] For his part, the Portuguese ambassador in London, Rui Enes Ulrich, considered 'a grave error' the League's decision that Manchukuo should not be recognised. He praised Japanese imperialist plans, offering his 'sincere sympathy for the notable work of Japanese colonisation' and his 'disgust for the liberal Chinese anarchy'.[18] Yet he too thought Portugal should not take any initiative to recognise Manchukuo because Macau's existence made it imperative to 'avoid any friction with China'. Thus, the country should simply follow whatever other states did on the matter. Chinese diplomats continued to monitor Portugal's position vis-à-vis Manchukuo in subsequent years, but Portugal never advanced towards a formal recognition, the main reason for that arguably being because Britain never did.

An all-out war between China and Japan erupted in July 1937 when an incident near Beijing (the so-called Marco Polo Bridge Incident) was met with fierce military resistance. When a new front opened in Shanghai in August, that resistance became clear to the entire world. One of the most important attempts to bring the conflict to the attention of the international community occurred a few months later when the Conference of Brussels was convened in November, bringing together the signatory powers of the 1922 Nine-Power Treaty of Washington – Portugal amongst them.[19] A key power, however, Japan, declined the invitation. Ambassador Wellington Koo (Gu Weijun) made a powerful case for Chinese resistance:

> China had never given any challenge to Japan before the deliberate opening of hostilities on China by Japan. The Chinese armed forces had never invaded a single foot of Japanese territory, nor had the Chinese air forced bombed a single Japanese town. China had not wished to make war on Japan and is fighting today determinedly and bravely only to resist the unceasing onslaught of the invading Japanese forces.[20]

[16] César de Sousa Mendes, Minister of Foreign Affairs, to Augusto de Vasconcelos, Portugal's Delegate at the League of Nations, copy dated 9 Dec. 1932, AHD, 3P, A9, M125.

[17] Justino Montalvão Machado, Minister in Tokyo, to Mendes, 13 Feb. 1933, AHD, 3P, A9, M125.

[18] Rui Enes Ulrich, Ambassador in London, to Minister of Foreign Affairs, 3 Mar. 1934, AHD, 2P, A48, M212.

[19] The Conference list of participants was much wider than those Nine Powers and comprised delegations from eighteen states, including the Soviet Union.

[20] 'Address by His Excellency Dr. V. K. Wellington Koo, of China', in *The Conference of Brussels November 3–24, 1937* (Washington, DC, 1938), p. 41.

Koo's appeal to foreign powers did not bring about the support the Chinese government desired, but Japan's refusal to attend the conference confirmed its refusal to work towards a diplomatic solution that had already been apparent with its retreat from the League.

Portugal's participation in the Conference of Brussels had more to do with projecting an image of colonial prestige than with solving the crisis in Asia. In one of his interventions, the Portuguese envoy, Augusto de Castro, who was the minister in Belgium, used a colonialist discourse that emphasised 'the part played by Portugal in the civilization of Asia', justifying its presence there with the country's 'political and territorial interests' and 'its position in the Far East'. Castro reaffirmed the country's neutrality and merely committed to 'lend its support to all useful work for conciliation' to which the conference may lead 'within the limits and spirit of its neutrality'.[21] The Portuguese chargé d'affaires in Tokyo noted that the local press was conveying the impression that Portugal was sympathetic to Japanese actions in China and its position in the Brussels conference reflected that.[22] However, in Castro's correspondence to Salazar – who combined his post of president of the council of ministers (prime minister) with that of minister of foreign affairs – it was clear that the main preoccupation of the Portuguese diplomat was to act in accordance with the British position and maintain close relations with the United Kingdom despite existing tensions relating to the Spanish Civil War.[23] As will be demonstrated in Chapter 2, the Portuguese authorities' policy to follow the UK position on the Sino–Japanese conflict was shaken in the following years, when Macau came into direct contact with the realities of a continuous state of war in South China. As Britain moved closer to an alliance with China, Portugal's position became more ambiguous, even though Macau gained a new importance for the Chinese resistance.

Macau and Chinese Resistance

Communication between the Chinese Nationalist government resisting the Japanese invasion and the Portuguese authorities in Lisbon and Macau was made through diplomatic channels, personal intermediaries and contacts between provincial and county authorities and the Macau administration. These links had varying degrees of efficiency, but they were constant during the war.

21 'Address by His Excellency Mr. Augusto de Castro, of Portugal', in ibid., p. 45.
22 Antero Carreiro de Freitas, Chargé d'Affaires in Tokyo, to Portugal's Ministry of Foreign Affairs (hereafter MNE), 11 Nov. 1933, AHD, 3P, A49, M134.
23 Castro to Salazar, 30 Nov. 1937, AHD, 3P, A49, M134.

Figure 1.1 Li Jinlun (centre left), Chinese minister to Portugal between 1934 and 1943, after presenting his credentials at the presidential palace in Lisbon, 1934. Empresa Pública Jornal O Século, Álbuns Gerais n.º 31, doc. PT/TT/EPJS/SF/001-001/0031/2226I. Courtesy of Arquivo Nacional Torre do Tombo

Sino–Portuguese diplomatic relations suffered a period of crisis after 1938. Although China's diplomatic representation in Portugal was marked by stability, such was not the case with the Portuguese diplomatic presence in China. The Chinese minister to Portugal throughout the period covered in this chapter was Li Jinlun, who served in Lisbon for a record period, from 1934 to 1943 (see Figure 1.1).[24] When the war erupted, Portugal's highest-ranking diplomat to China was Minister Plenipotentiary Armando Navarro, based at the Portuguese legation in Beijing since 1930. As the Portuguese minister to Tokyo who had worked in Beijing in the 1920s noted, 'Macau justified the existence of the legation', since Portuguese trade and other relations with China were practically nil.[25] An extensive Portuguese community, mostly comprising Eurasian families with ancestral links to Macau,

[24] *Zhonghua minguo shi waijiao zhi (chugao)* (*Diplomatic History of the Republic of China*) (Taipei, 2002), p. 832.

[25] L. E. Fernandes, *De Pequim a Washington: Memórias de um Diplomata Português* (*From Beijing to Washington: Memoirs of a Portuguese Diplomat*) (Lisbon, 2007), p. 47.

lived in some treaty ports where Portuguese consuls and/or vice consuls were either posted from Portugal (namely to Shanghai and Guangzhou) or requested to look after Portuguese interests locally. At the suggestion of Li Jinlun, the Portuguese Ministry of Foreign Affairs ordered Navarro to move from Beijing to Shanghai in October 1937 to better communicate with the government in Nanjing.[26] He died in February the following year, however, depriving Portugal of an experienced diplomat in China.[27] His successor, chosen in April, was João Maria da Silva de Lebre e Lima, who had served in London and at the Ministry of Foreign Affairs in Lisbon.

All was set in August 1938 for Lima to travel from the Portuguese legation in Shanghai to the Chinese wartime capital of Chongqing to present his credentials. Then suddenly his departure was suspended as the war progressed and military operations, including aerial bombing between Hong Kong and Chongqing, made travelling dangerous.[28] Lima ended up staying in Shanghai until his return to Lisbon in 1945, a permanent point of contention mentioned by the Chinese side throughout the war.[29] Although technically accredited to Chiang's government, Portugal's minister lived in an occupied city, mingling in the same diplomatic circles as the pro–Wang Jingwei German and Italian ambassadors. This fact is particularly illustrative of the complexities of Portuguese neutrality in China. Furthermore, all Portuguese consuls in mainland China were, from 1937–8 onwards, living in occupied cities (Shanghai, Guangzhou, Xiamen, Hankou, Harbin), and the Portuguese consul in Hong Kong was transferred elsewhere in 1939 and was not replaced by a 'career diplomat'.[30]

26 Salazar to Portuguese Embassy in London, 3 Oct. 1937, AHD, 2P, A48, M176.

27 'Ministro de Portugal na China' ('Portugal's Minister to China'), *A Voz de Macau* (hereafter VM) (7 Feb. 1938), p. 4.

28 For example, Salazar to Portuguese Legation in Shanghai, 23 Aug. and 1 and 5 Sept. 1938; Portuguese Legation in Shanghai to MNE, 23 Aug. and 5 Sept. 1938, Arquivo Nacional Torre do Tombo (Portuguese National Archives, hereafter ANTT), Arquivo Oliveira Salazar (hereafter AOS), NE-2A2, cx. 422.

29 For example, Academia Historica/Guoshiguan (hereafter AH), Waijiaobu (Ministry of Foreign Affairs), 020000023906A, Putaoya za juan (Portugal–Miscellaneous); Conversation notes by Franco Nogueira, 13 Aug. 1945, ANTT, AOS, NE-2A2, cx. 422, Pt. 8.

30 In some cities, consular representation seems to have been an honorific post with little to do with formal diplomacy. Illustrative of this was the employment of several 'White Russians' as Portuguese consuls, perhaps a remnant of nineteenth-century practices when tsarist diplomats had played a role as intermediaries between Portugal and the Qing. Solomon L. Skidelsky, a Jewish businessman, consul in Harbin since the early 1920s, disappeared from official listings in 1941; he was reportedly imprisoned by the Soviets after the war, dying in captivity (F. Patrikeeff, *Russian Politics in Exile: The Northeast Asian Balance for Power, 1924–1931* (Oxford, 2012), pp. 118, 199; *The Chinese Year Book 1940–1941* (Chongqing, 1941), pp. 800–2). From 1923 to 1947, the Portuguese consul in Hankou was Andrei Terentevich Belchenko, a former Russian diplomat. The Portuguese vice consul in Xiamen was the French consul in the city. The consulate in Fuzhou closed in 1938. The

Diplomatic channels were thus highly uneven. With Portuguese diplomacy in China in such dire straits, Macau assumed a privileged position as a base for communication with both Japanese and Chinese of different factions, sometimes at odds with the Portuguese diplomats.[31] Chinese contacts with Macau requesting assistance from the Portuguese authorities began in the first year of the war.[32] They gained momentum as the Chinese Nationalists began to suffer serious attacks in South China from 1938.

Having attempted and failed to instigate a local coup, the Japanese started to bomb Guangzhou in February 1938. The Portuguese consul in the city witnessed the attacks and manifested sympathy for the Chinese victims in his reports to Salazar: 'The Japanese say the targets are military but until today almost no soldier has been killed in these raids over the city. Students, women, children are the ones that have suffered in these violent and continuous daily attacks on the city. I personally went to see the result of the bombings ... The spectacle is profoundly horrible and desolating.'[33]

As the first city to be under a KMT government in the 1920s, Guangzhou was of great symbolic importance for the Nationalists. In a speech to Nationalist party delegates in April, Chiang Kai-shek declared that 'Guangdong province is our revolutionary base area' and stressed the importance of China holding Guangzhou with its key 'sea links to the outside world'.[34] The Nationalist forces would eventually retreat from Guangzhou, but the city was defended for several months and Guangdong province was never completely occupied.

The Portuguese authorities in Macau assisted the Chinese in neighbouring areas during the Japanese bombings, providing refuge and

well-connected consul in Hong Kong, Álvaro Brilhante Laborinho, was moved to South Africa in June 1939 (Acting Governor (Encarregado do Governo) to Minister of Colonies, 5 June 1939, AHD, 3P, A9, M128–129). Francisco Paulo de Vasconcelos Soares, an aged member of the Hong Kong Portuguese community, stayed as acting consul (B. H. M. Koo, *The Portuguese in Hongkong and China: Their Beginning, Settlement and Progress to 1949*, vol. 2 (Macau, 2013), p. 124).

31 Mutual complaints between the governor of Macau and the Portuguese consul in Guangzhou can be found in some of the existing correspondence to Lisbon. For example, José Carlos Rodrigues Coelho Jr, Acting Governor of Macau, to MC, 23 June 1939, ANTT, AOS, UL-10A1, cx. 767; Monteiro to Lima, 26 Mar. 1940, AHD, 2P, A48, M217; J. da Costa Carneiro, MNE to Lima, 21 May 1940, ibid.

32 For example, in October 1937, a delegate of the Guangdong government visited the Macau governor to request his assistance in trade and supply flows (Barbosa to Ministry of Colonies (hereafter MC), 12 Oct. 1937, transcribed in note from MC to Salazar, 16 Oct. 1937, ANTT, AOS, UL-10A1, cx. 767).

33 Morgado to MNE, 9 June 1938, AHD, 3P, A9, M128–129.

34 R. Mitter, *China's War with Japan, 1937–1945: The Struggle for Survival* (London, 2013), p. 147.

medical care. Borders were relatively porous, which suited the needs of humanitarian assistance. In April, the Japanese bombed the Chinese Maritime Customs (CMC) post at Qianshan, near Macau, leading hundreds of people to head to the enclave.[35] The crews of the nearby boats fled in panic to Wanzai, in the eastern part of Lappa Island, with a few treated for their wounds in Macau.[36] Following a request for help from Chinese authorities, an ambulance went from Macau into Chinese-controlled territory to collect two people seriously injured after a Japanese attack.[37] After a similar request, several wounded in a bombing over Zhongshan's capital, Shiqi, were also assisted in Macau (see Figure 1.2).[38] Chinese Minister of Foreign Affairs Wang Chonghui thanked the Portuguese minister to China in writing in December, and asked him to convey his regards to Governor Artur Tamagnini de Barbosa, the police commander and the staff who had assisted the victims in another attack on Shiqi.[39]

Macau had for centuries been a source of arms supplies for China, and the war with Japan revived the practice.[40] Whilst the role of Hong Kong as a base for military supplies into unoccupied China is well known, Macau's is less so, despite the connections between the two foreign-ruled territories.[41] For example, in May 1939, agents of the Chinese military informally approached the Hong Kong government requesting it to allow the export of war material to Macau for re-export to inland China to be used by Chinese forces in south Guangdong. This was to be done without insisting on a formal authorisation by the Macau government.[42] The Macau chief of police, Lieutenant Colonel Alberto Arez, wrote a personal letter to his Hong Kong counterpart stating that 'we are prepared to help these people'.[43] This source, hinting that at least some amongst the Macau

[35] 'Nippon Night Raiders Visit River Capital', *China Press* (hereafter *CP*) (18 Apr. 1938), p. 2.

[36] 'O bombardeamento de ontem ao Posto Maritimo da Alfandega Chineza de Chinsan' ('Yesterday's Bombing of the Chinese Maritime Customs Post at Qianshan'), *VM* (18 Apr. 1938), p. 3.

[37] Barbosa to MC, 18 Apr. 1938, ANTT, AOS, UL-10A1, cx. 767.

[38] 'Os efeitos do último bombardeamento japones sobre Seaki' ('The Effects of the Latest Japanese Bombing of Shiqi'), *VM* (5 Nov. 1938), p. 4.

[39] João Maria da Silva de Lebre e Lima, Minister to China, to Barbosa, 7 Jan. 1939, AM, MO/AH/AC/SA/01/16831.

[40] D. Faure, *Emperor and Ancestor: State and Lineage in South China* (Stanford, CA, 2007), p. 314.

[41] For example, K. C. Chan Lau, *China, Britain and Hong Kong, 1895–1945* (Hong Kong, 1990), pp. 265–92.

[42] Geoffry Northcote, Governor of Hong Kong to Malcolm MacDonald, Secretary of State for the Colonies, 5 May 1939, TNA, FO 371/23427.

[43] Macau Chief of Police to Hong Kong Deputy High Commissioner of Police, 12 Apr. 1939, ibid.

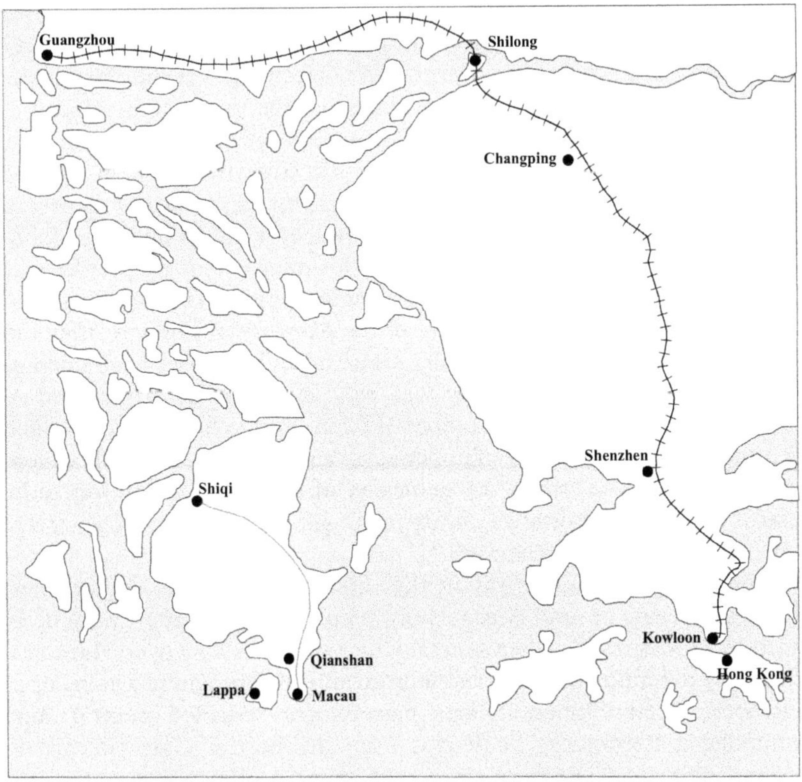

Figure 1.2 Map of South China showing the Macau–Shiqi road and the Kowloon–Guangzhou railway. Map by Rui Teixeira Alves (based on a map by P. C. Chen published in *China Weekly Review*, 13 April 1940, in the public domain via Internet Archive) (https://archive.org/details/millards-1940.04.13/page/228/mode/2up)

authorities were favourable to cooperating with the Chinese, contradicts the governor's assurances to Lisbon that no military assistance was dispensed. However, the plan did not secure British approval.[44] The reason for the denial was that such a proposition posed 'a grave risk of a clash with the local Japanese naval authorities'.[45] Whilst some were willing to take risks, others feared international consequences.

[44] The Hong Kong governor, following the suggestion of the commander-in-chief of the China Station, forbade it and the Colonial Office (hereafter CO) and Foreign Office (hereafter FO) later concurred.

[45] Northcote to MacDonald, 5 May 1939, ibid.

Sino–Portuguese contacts were also established for matters concerning Portuguese interests in the enclave. In May 1938, the governor sent Arez to speak to the provincial governor, Wu Tiecheng, via the Portuguese consulate at Guangzhou. He was to discuss the presence in Macau of Japanese elements spreading anti-Portuguese propaganda and causing problems between Portugal and China. He suggested that, should the Guangzhou authorities know who the troublemakers were and request it, the governor would be willing to hand them over unless they were long-term residents. The consul considered this offer extremely problematic but helped Arez to write a more general note that ended up being received by Diao Zuoqian, special delegate of the Ministry of Foreign Affairs in Guangdong and Guangxi. Equally vague in his response, Diao guaranteed that 'Macau's tranquillity was very important to China and to Guangzhou, given the high number of Chinese who lived there.'[46] Such was the strange coexistence of imperialism and anti-imperialism in exceptional times of war, when the neutrality of a foreign colony was quite useful to Chinese resistance. Attempts to get supplies into Macau were also made via personal channels.[47]

However, cooperation was neither linear nor constant. Sometimes, Chinese actions around Macau prompted protests by the Portuguese, such as in May 1938, when several Chinese planes flew over Macau on their way to bomb Japanese positions outside of Portuguese waters, or in October, when Chinese troops patrolling a so-called neutral zone wounded a Portuguese lieutenant from the Barrier Gate (Portas do Cerco) garrison.[48] Protests were sent from the Portuguese consul in Guangzhou to the provincial authorities and assurances were given in writing or in person, by Diao Zuoqian or the secretary, Ling Shifen.

Diplomatic correspondence between Portugal and China during the war can be described as a litany of complaints and rebuttals, with the Chinese government insisting on official clarifications to any information it received on possible breaches of Portuguese neutrality in Macau. These are indicative that Chinese wartime diplomacy was attuned to a myriad of affairs and did not overlook relations with a small European power. The

46 Morgado to Alberto Carlos de Liz Teixeira Branquinho, Portuguese Chargé d'Affaires in China, 21 May 1938, AHD, 2P, A48, M176.

47 For example, Jack Braga wrote to General Zhang Huichang asking him to intervene in order to allow ships to travel between Shiqi and Macau (Braga to Boxer, 21 Oct. 1938, National Library of Australia (hereafter NLA), MS 4300, Box 9, 3.2/2).

48 Barbosa to Morgado, 12 May 1938, AHD, 2P, A48, M176; Diao Zuoqian, Ministry of Foreign Affairs (hereafter MOFA) Special Delegate for Guangdong and Guangxi, to Morgado, 21 May 1938, AHD, 2P, A48, M176; Morgado to Wu Tiecheng, Governor of Guangdong Province, 14 Oct. 1938, AHD, 3P, A9, M128–129; Morgado to Lima, 18 Oct. 1938, ibid.

Chinese minister in Lisbon, Li Jinlun, went to the Portuguese Ministry of Foreign Affairs several times to get a reaction to news on events in Macau or rumours about Portugal's stance on Japan. Similarly, the dispatches of the Portuguese minister to China to the Chinese minister of foreign affairs in Chongqing usually contained denials of such rumours. For example, in May 1938, Lima wrote to Wang Chonghui, via the Portuguese consulate in Hong Kong, to deny the news that Portugal would recognise Manchukuo. In his rebuttal, he admitted the de facto existence of parallel diplomacy between Macau and Japanese forces:

It is possible that between the Government of Macao and the Japanese authorities there exists some kind of understanding or local agreement in connection with shipping facilities. However, I have the honour and pleasure to assure Your Excellency that the news regarding the existence, for the above purposes, of any treaty or negotiations between the Portuguese and the Japanese Governments have no foundation whatsoever.[49]

The Japanese occupation of Guangzhou added a layer of distance between the Portuguese diplomats and the Chinese central government. The city fell in October 1938 with little military resistance, almost at the same time as the Nationalists lost the temporary wartime capital of Wuhan. The city's occupation may be regarded as the transition between a first phase of the Second Sino–Japanese War and a 'second, defensive stage' that ensued.[50]

As the Nationalists lost ground in South China, Macau made its riskiest move in shadow diplomacy. In February 1939, the Macau police commander, Captain Carlos de Sousa Gorgulho, went to Tokyo, where he met a number of Japanese officials – an event that will be discussed further in Chapter 2.[51] The visit caused a stir in Sino–Portuguese relations. In Paris, Ambassador Wellington Koo lamented the news he had heard of an agreement between the government of Macau and Japan that included the recognition of Manchukuo and the free use of the Macau port. Koo interpreted the affair as part of Japan's efforts to 'poach the lesser signatories of the Washington Treaty'.[52] The minister in Lisbon, Li Jinlun, came to the Ministry of Foreign Affairs to enquire if the news was true. He

[49] Lima to Wang Chonghui, Minister of Foreign Affairs, 10 May 1938, Academia Sinica, Institute of Modern History Archives (hereafter AS-IMH), Waijiaobu, 312.8/0001. Also in AHD, 2P, A48, M217.

[50] Mitter, *China's War with Japan*, p. 200.

[51] Gorgulho was later appointed governor of the West African archipelago of São Tomé and Príncipe in April 1945, where he was implicated in the infamous Batepá Massacre in 1953.

[52] Note from the Direction of Political and Commercial Affairs – Asia–Oceania Division of the French Ministry of Foreign Affairs, 3 Mar. 1939, MAE, 32CPCOM/761.

was told it was not.[53] Li later delivered a note on the matter, noting that there was information that 'some members of the Macau government favour the pro-Japanese policy' advocated by Gorgulho.[54] A document from the Chinese Military Affairs Commission informing the Ministry of Foreign Affairs on Gorgulho's trip and the proposals he had discussed shows how these caused high-level concern. The Nationalists feared Japan was attempting to use Macau as a base and to influence Portugal to join the Anti-Comintern Pact, which was not far-fetched, given Salazar's anti-communism.[55] Shortly after, Li Jinlun presented the ministry in Lisbon with this new set of allegations of Portuguese collaboration with Japan that he wished to see clarified.[56] Those were denied, but increasing Japanese pressure in the vicinity of Macau was a reality, one that Chinese officials were well aware of.

The 'Portuguese' Ships

An illustrative way in which neutrality shaped Sino–Portuguese relations at a non-state level – but that often spilled out into consular démarches – was the registration of Chinese ships under Portuguese nationality, several of which were used for smuggling materiel to both Chiang's China and Japanese troops. As a Portuguese consul wrote at the time, the 'Portuguese merchant fleet' in China was 'the illegitimate daughter of the Sino–Japanese conflict'.[57] Correspondence about detained ships, many of which were involved in the lucrative, albeit risky, transport of weapons, ammunitions or goods destined to both of the belligerents, is one of the sources that attest to the flexibility of Portuguese neutrality in the war. Japanese representatives accused the Macau authorities of protecting Chinese boats that attacked Japanese warships;[58] sometimes it was the arrest of Chinese and their boats that motivated protests by China.[59]

[53] MNE to Portuguese Legation in Shanghai, 6 Mar. 1939, AHD, 2P, A48, M217.
[54] Note handed by Li Jinlun to MNE, sent with dispatch from MNE to MC, 12 May 1939, ibid.
[55] Military Affairs Commission to MOFA, 12 June 1939, AS-IMH, Waijiaobu, 312.8/0001.
[56] Note delivered by Li Jinlun to MNE, 17 June 1939, AHD, 2P, A48, M217.
[57] Monteiro to Salazar, 9 Aug. 1941, AHD, 3P, A9, M135.
[58] The governor of Macau denied this but admitted that wounded Chinese had come to be treated in Macau, an 'humanitarian act' that ought not be considered as 'help to the Chinese forces' (Salazar to Portuguese Legation in Tokyo, 25 Apr. 1938, AHD, 2P, A48, M176).
[59] For example, a case occurred in 1940 (still unsettled in 1948) that resulted in the seizure of the vessel and in the arrest, trial and deportation to Timor of members of the crew (see files in AH, Waijiaobu, 020000003313A).

Japan had informed foreign powers that the transfer of Chinese ships to foreign ownership since August 1937 would be recognised only with bona fide proof of the transfer. A consequence of this was the registration of Chinese boats under foreign flags, of which Portugal's was an easy choice, most likely because the limited financial capacity of the Portuguese in China made them more prone to agree to such a scheme. Throughout 1937 and 1938, Japanese navy patrols often stopped and searched 'Portuguese' merchant ships such as the *Wing Wah* and the *Anjou*, Chinese junks with permits from the Macau Harbour Authority and Chinese junks travelling between Hong Kong and Macau. Some had their cargo seized whilst others were attacked, the crew left to die.[60] A public accusation that Chinese junks and speedboats were using Portuguese territorial waters in South China to launch raids on Japanese warships was made by a Japanese navy spokesman in Shanghai in April 1938, which was amply reported both in Shanghai and in Hong Kong.[61] Although the Macau government and the Chinese military authorities denied this, these cases illustrate the ease with which the ships could be deployed for pro-resistance purposes.[62] In July 1938, the minister of colonies, Francisco José Vieira Machado, wrote to the governor of Macau that it was 'not convenient to facilitate the matriculation of Chinese junks as Portuguese boats [as] it will be [a] source [of] conflicts without any advantage'.[63] Barbosa replied that such measures would only last during the conflict and blamed the trouble on 'the abuse of Chinese boats' using Portuguese flags, as if Portuguese officials had not permitted such use of the flags.[64] However, sometimes that was not the only flag they used: one of the vessels the Japanese detained in 1940, the *Fu An* (*Fuk On* in Cantonese), 'flew the Portuguese flag' whilst having 'a painted flag of the Chiang Kai Shek regime on her stern', evidence of a rushed transfer of ownership or of its true allegiance.[65] However, not all the ships were stopped by the Japanese side. In 1940, the Chinese authorities in Fujian

60 On the case of the *Kamshan*, sank between Macau and Wuzhou, see 'Canton to Defend At All Costs', *NCH* (1 June 1938), p. 358.

61 For example, 'Claims Junks Attack War Vessel', *Hongkong Telegraph* (19 Apr. 1938); 'Macao Accused of Sheltering Chinese Ships', *Hong Kong Daily Press* (20 Apr. 1938), AHD, 3P, A9, M135; 'Japanese Sink Fleet of Junks', *China Weekly Review* (hereafter *CWR*) (23 Apr. 1938), p. 226.

62 'Colony Has Not Deviated from Strict Neutrality', *SCMP* (22 Apr. 1938); 'Japanese Allegations Refuted', *China Mail* (22 Apr. 1938). The Cantonese authorities stated that 'such allegations are made to cover the Japanese navy's nefarious plans to destroy the Chinese fishing industry and as an excuse to fire on fishing boats at will' ('Real Motive behind Japanese Charge', *SCMP* (23 Apr. 1938)). Clippings in AHD, 3P, A9, M135.

63 Francisco José Vieira Machado, Minister of Colonies, to Barbosa, 8 July 1938, ANTT, AOS, UL-10A1, cx. 767.

64 Barbosa to MC, 9 July 1938, ibid. Also in AHD, 3P, A9, M135.

65 Nagao Kita, Japanese Consul General at Guangzhou to Monteiro, 28 Aug. 1940, AHD, 3P, A9, M135.

detained the boats *Tito* and *Santa Rosa*, including the Portuguese captain and crew, accused of collaborating with the enemy.[66] Such were the dangers and opportunities of neutrality: a Portuguese flag could facilitate shipping but was not a stable guarantee against attacks by one of the belligerents.

The registration of former Chinese ships as Portuguese was an open secret and was employed as a strategy for mutual benefit, given that Macau needed supplies from inland China and the Portuguese needed Chinese capital for the ships and could also profit from their trade.[67] Even Portuguese representatives were involved: one prominent case involved the *Luso*, a ship bought by the vice consul in Shanghai, Antonio Augusto Alves Lico. Attempts to tackle the situation were half-hearted. In the summer of 1939, instructions were given to Portuguese consulates in China and to the Macau Harbour Authority not to nationalise Chinese or Japanese ships as Portuguese. Temporary boat passports were to be replaced for definite ones, and in cases where there were legal impediments, solutions were to be found to guarantee that nothing really changed so as not to cause trouble to the Portuguese involved in the traffic. In any case, by 1941, most of the 'Portuguese' ships had been apprehended by Japanese or Chinese authorities. Portuguese consuls at Shanghai and Guangzhou repeatedly pleaded with them, but release of the boats and sometimes their crews was a lengthy and not always successful process. The Portuguese consul in Guangzhou concluded: 'The "Portuguese fleet" is not respected by any of the two contenders, because both know the way in which it was acquired.'[68] The registration of Chinese ships under foreign flags mirrored the registration of businesses in the neutral International Settlement and French Concession in Shanghai.[69] These were strategies for survival in which nationalism and transnational connections overlapped.

The Portuguese ships were one channel amongst others and the important role Macau played in smuggling weapons and other supplies into Free China is attested by contemporary sources of different

[66] *Tito* had belonged to a shipping company owned by Wang Qingpo, a Chinese 'Portuguese protégé', and was sold to Victor Carvalho, a Portuguese from Xiamen in 1937 (Fernand Roy, Responsible for Portuguese Interests in Xiamen, to Morgado, 4 Apr. 1939, ibid.). A later document mentioned that Carvalho's business partner was a Chinese man from Taiwan who was an 'intimate friend of the Japanese' in Xiamen (Report by Álvaro Baião, captain of the *Tito*, 7 Dec. 1940, ibid.).

[67] C. T. da Costa, Merchant Navy Department, 3 July 1939, sent by the Navy Ministry to MNE, 8 July 1939, ibid.

[68] Monteiro to Salazar, 8 July 1941, ibid.

[69] P. M. Coble, 'Chinese Capitalists and the Japanese: Collaboration and Resistance in the Shanghai Area, 1937–45', in W. H. Yeh (ed.), *Wartime Shanghai* (London, 1998), pp. 57–77.

provenances, including a report by the manager of the Banco Nacional Ultramarino (BNU) and an American document noting that 'a considerable amount of railway material' and small quantities of munitions entered China via Macau.[70] Some of these were likely to have been deployed nearby, as Macau's environs became a frontline of hostilities.

Defending Zhongshan

The Japanese Expeditionary Forces in South China had held positions encircling Zhongshan county since the late 1930s but had not moved into the capital, Shiqi, until the end of the decade. They tried to convince local elites to settle for peace and neighbouring Macau was one of the chosen meeting places. According to a British account, based on a pro-resistance source, at least five meetings took place in Macau between Japanese officers and representatives of the Zhongshan authorities between December 1938 and February 1939 to guarantee a smooth occupation without violence. The Japanese side promised the return of foreign concessions and colonies and the abolition of extraterritoriality, but 'the Chinese representatives retorted that it was impossible to reconcile the Japanese protestations of friendliness, with the indiscriminate attacks on the local civilian populace as exemplified in the burning of junks, raping of women ... or the shooting down of the C.N.A.C. [China National Aviation Corporation] plane "Kweilin"'.[71] Appealing to anti-imperialist solidary meant little when it was accompanied by imperialist aggression.

Armed resistance to the Japanese was made not by regular troops but by militia,[72] which, a newspaper claimed, 'imported arms and ammunitions

[70] C. Vasconcelos, 'Relatório de Exercício de 1938 a 1945 da Filial de Macau' ('Macau Branch Activity Report from 1938 until 1945'), pp. 6–7, Arquivo Histórico da Caixa Geral de Depósitos (Caixa Geral de Depósitos Historical Archives, hereafter CGD), AG-012–22–117; Acting Secretary of War to Cordell Hull, Secretary of State, 15 June, 1938, Franklin D. Roosevelt Presidential Library, Collection FDR-FDRPSF, Diplomatic Correspondence, 1933–45, China, 1938: catalog.archives.gov/id/16618367.

[71] Hong Kong Intelligence Report No. 3/39, sent by War Office to Far Eastern Department, FO, 15 Apr. 1939, p. 14, TNA FO 371/23501. Occurring in August 1938 and known as the 'Kweilin Incident', it is considered the first time in world history a civilian airliner was shot down. At the time, some speculated that the intended target was Sun Fo, then president of the Executive Yuan, who cancelled his journey at the last minute ('Descida forçada dum avião pertencente à "China National Aviation Corporation"' ('Forced descent of a plane belonging to the "China National Aviation Corporation"'), *VM* (25 Aug. 1938), p. 4). In a letter to Charles Boxer, Braga informed him he had gone to photograph the site and sent a long report to the *SCMP*, 'but it was crowded out by news of affairs in Europe' (Letter from Braga to Boxer, 31 Aug. 1938, NLA, MS 4300, Box 9, 3.2/2).

[72] Up to 200,000 guerrillas were reportedly operating in Guangdong in 1939 (Macri, *Clash of Empires*, p. 130).

Figure 1.3 A Chinese woman fighting for the resistance in Zhongshan, 1939. Sueddeutsche Zeitung Photo / Alamy

through third parties at the border' – that is, via Macau (see Figure 1.3).[73] This may explain why military historians have largely overlooked the region.[74] Fighting around Shiqi occurred from the spring of 1939 and intensified during the summer and fall when the county was heavily bombed, disrupting food production and supplies, including of manufactured goods, between Hong Kong and Macau and the interior of China. Concerning reports reached diaspora communities as far away as San

[73] 'Japanese Disclose Why Chungshan [Was] Taken', *Canton Daily Sun* (hereafter *CDS*) (9 Oct. 1939). The clipping was attached to a copy of a dispatch from Monteiro to Lima, where he noted that, 'during my short stay in that colony of ours, a trusted person had told me armament had been passed through Macau' (AHD, 3P, A9, M128–129).

[74] M. Peattie, E. Drea and H. van de Ven (eds.), *The Battle for China: Essays on the Military History of the Sino-Japanese War of 1937–1945* (Stanford, CA, 2011). The key exception is Macri, *Clash of Empires*.

Francisco.[75] As Macri observed: 'The Chinese defended the birthplace of Sun Yat Sen with great determination, and although the fight for Shekki [Shiqi] was small in scale compared with other significant battles, its political impact helped prolong the war.'[76] Three assaults on the city failed in September, but on 8 October, Japanese forces occupied it. However, they had to withdraw after two days and the local magistrate, General Zhang Huichang, returned.[77] Like many other Nationalist officials, Zhang's life story was marked by global connections. He grew up in the United States, graduated from a flight school in New York and became an American citizen. He returned to China in 1917, was Sun Yat-sen's aide-de-camp and the leader of his first squadron of aviation corps, later bureau chief of the Canton Aviation Bureau and director of the Nationalist government Aviation Office in Nanjing. An aviation celebrity, he fell from grace after joining the Fujian People's Government, destroyed by Chiang Kai-shek in 1933. He served as a diplomat in Cuba before returning to serve as the head of Zhongshan county. By 1939, anti-Japanese resistance put him again on Chiang's side.[78]

Worried that combat might spread to what was considered a 'neutral zone' between Macau and Qianshan, or that Chinese troops might seek refuge in the enclave, Governor Barbosa sought to reinforce Portuguese defences near the border. He was also involved in contacting the local authorities via intermediaries to convince them to avoid a bloodbath by giving up what he considered a 'pointless opposition'.[79] Chinese resistance in and around Macau was tolerated, but Barbosa would prefer that it did not pose too many problems for the Portuguese in Macau. Others were more understanding, however. Anti-Japanese activities in Macau were a consequence of the brutal invasion, and the Portuguese consul in Guangzhou knew it would be 'almost impossible to completely prevent them in a land where around 200,000 Chinese live who cordially hate the invader and victorious oppressor'.[80]

In early March 1940, Japanese naval units advanced again into Shiqi following the same route as the previous year. An army of around 25,000 men under Wu Fei, who had been the county leader since 1939, resisted the invasion but was overpowered. Japanese naval and land forces

75 'Hongkong Sees New Menace As Japanese Capture Shekki', *San Francisco Chronicle* (9 Oct. 1939), p. 3.
76 Macri, *Clash of Empires*, p. 137. 77 Ibid., p. 143.
78 A. O'Keefe, 'Stars in the Nation's Skies: The Ascent and Trajectory of the Chinese Aviation Celebrity in the Prewar Decade', in P. Pickowicz (ed.), *Liangyou: Kaleidoscopic Modernity, and the Shanghai Global Metropolis, 1926–1945* (Leiden, 2013), pp. 135–59, at pp. 138–46.
79 Barbosa quoted in dispatch from MC to MNE, 12 Oct. 1939, AHD, 3P, A9, M128–129.
80 Monteiro to Lima, 26 Mar. 1940, AHD, 2P, A48, M217.

blockaded coastal areas while naval air units bombed the retreating Chinese. The city was taken in three days.[81] From Chongqing, a Chinese military spokesman dismissed the operation as of 'no military significance' and probably carried out 'for certain political reasons connected with the Japanese attempt at an early establishment of a new regime in China'.[82] News in pro-Japan Chinese newspapers in Guangzhou claimed the pro-Chiang guerrillas, who had provoked the Japanese advance on Shiqi, had been operating from and were aided by Macau. The governor of Macau believed Wu Fei had collaborated with the Japanese. The Portuguese consul in Guangzhou disagreed, confirming the rumours that he was acting under orders of the Nationalist government, fooling both the Japanese and Barbosa.[83] These contradictory views demonstrate how volatile the South China front was, with those engaged in resistance and collaboration not always unequivocally differentiated.

The Kuomintang in Macau

The presence of neutral foreign colonies and concessions bordering Guangdong province was of great importance to harness support for Chinese resistance.[84] At an early stage, Hong Kong and Macau were regarded as one entity and KMT cadres usually operated in both, often being based in Hong Kong, which was deemed more important.[85] As the Nationalists suffered a series of defeats and Japanese-occupied areas expanded, the importance of neutral territories grew and there was a significant rise in the number of party members in Hong Kong, Kowloon and Macau.[86] Wu Tiecheng, the former mayor of Shanghai and governor of Guangdong province, headed the Hong Kong–Macau branch, which had been reorganised and became independent from the tutelage of the Guangzhou one it had formerly belonged to.[87] In 1939,

[81] 'Japanese Spokesman Reviews Chungshan Operation', *CDS* (9 Mar. 1940), AHD, 2P, A48, M217.
[82] 'Chinese Comment on Chungshan Operation', *CDS*, 9 Mar. 1940, ibid.
[83] Monteiro to Lima, 26 Mar. 1940, ibid.
[84] In addition to Macau and Hong Kong, one must consider the French leased territory of Guangzhouwan. Its wartime experience had many similarities with Macau's (Xie, 'China's Casablanca').
[85] Li, 'Lunxian qian', pp. 445–6. [86] Ibid., p. 449; Li, 'Wu Tiecheng', pp. 75–6.
[87] R. Hei and H. Chen, '1927–1949 nian Guomindang Aomen zhibu de dangwu kaocha' ('The Party Affairs of the KMT Macau Branch in 1927–1949'), *Aomen yanjiu (Journal of Macau Studies)*, 54/10 (2009), pp. 131–5, at pp. 131–2. Wu Tiecheng was regarded favourably by Ashley Clarke, a senior British diplomat who later served as ambassador to Lisbon from 1944 to 1946. He cited information by the Officer Administering Government in the Straits Settlements that there was no suggestion in China that Wu

Wu entrusted responsibility for the Macau section to Zhou Yongneng, who earlier in his career had played an important role in establishing a KMT branch in Cuba. Wu also asked the KMT Central Committee to make Zhou the head of the Guangdong Office of Overseas Chinese Affairs.[88] A mass rally supporting the resistance was held on Lappa island in May 1939, with the participation of Macau patriotic associations.[89]

Chinese resistance activities had to deal with increasing interference from the Portuguese authorities. In September 1939, they sent the police to search offices, houses and schools of Chinese representatives in Macau. Chinese sources state that, after the Japanese consul had protested to the governor against the Chinese government in Chongqing having many people engaged in anti-Japanese activities in the enclave, and requested the Portuguese stop them, Barbosa had agreed to send the Macau police to search for propaganda materials. Zhou's house and the Chong Tak [Zhongde] Middle School were searched, materials were confiscated and some people were arrested.[90] The Portuguese police had also asked for the money collected from donations for refugee relief.[91] These actions seem to indicate that Portugal was breaching its neutral status and favouring Japan. The Chinese legation in Lisbon was instructed to protest to the Portuguese government and urge it to enquire about the matter with the Macau authorities.

Further information that the Macau police had raided offices, schools and residences searching for anti-Japanese materials reached the Chinese Ministry of Foreign Affairs in October. This was based on a Chinese intelligence report (*qingbao*) informing on Portuguese–Japanese collaboration that had included the acceptance of payments from the Japanese in exchange for help to arrest Chinese officials and spies engaged in anti-Japanese activities in Macau.[92] Li Jinlun delivered a note to the Portuguese Ministry of Foreign Affairs stating that the Chinese government had been informed of a decision to crack down on Chinese relief institutions in Macau, including the seizure of more than 10,000 Chinese dollars that the Commercial Association had collected for refugees. They had been ordered to dissolve because if the Japanese captured Zhongshan

was blamed for the loss of Guangzhou and that he still enjoyed Chiang Kai-shek's confidence (Ashley Clarke, FO, to Gerard Gent, CO, 20 Oct. 1940, TNA, FO 371/24704).

88 Li, 'Lunxian qian', p. 450; Li, 'Wu Tiecheng', p. 74.

89 Guo, 'Shilun Aomen', p. 100.

90 Military Affairs Commission to Wang Chonghui, Minister of Foreign Affairs, 20 Sept. 1939, AS-IMH, Waijiaobu, 312.8/0001.

91 Military Affairs Commission to Wang Chonghui, 23 Sept. 1939, ibid.

92 Military Affairs Commission to Wang Chonghui, 14 Oct. 1939, ibid.

and demanded a list of Chinese involved in anti-Japanese activities, the Macau government could not be responsible for their safety.[93]

In a follow-up meeting at the ministry, Li insisted on clarifying the rumours, particularly the threat of handing Chinese refugees in the enclave over to the Japanese military authorities if they advanced close to Macau. He wanted guarantees from the Portuguese that the Macau authorities would not do such a thing.[94] Barbosa reported to Lisbon that all of the rumours were false. Chinese merchants who raised funds for refugees were just asked to present their balance sheets to prove funds were not being sent to the resistance as the Japanese suspected.[95] This was a somewhat impossible request given the entanglement of relief and resistance in South China. Once again, however, the Chinese central government was quick to use diplomatic channels to hold the Portuguese accountable for what was happening in Macau.

Despite the Japanese military forces citing KMT activities in Macau to pressure the Portuguese, these continued to take place. A report from Japan's national news agency, Dōmei, claimed that a KMT meeting had been held in Macau in January 1940, where Chiang 'was praised' and Wang Jingwei 'was criticized'.[96] The governor denied this, but Zhou Yongneng later confirmed that the meeting had taken place on Lappa.[97] This is also attested by a letter from Jack Braga, assuring the report was erroneous but confirming that KMT meetings did occasionally take place in Wanzai on the eastern part of Lappa. Braga hailed from an important Hong Kong Portuguese family and lived in Macau from the late 1920s to 1946. He was a Reuters and Associated Press correspondent and a teacher and, as detailed in Chapter 5, also worked for British, Chinese and possibly American intelligence during the war. He stated that the majority of those attending the meeting were Macau residents and the branch was known as the Macau Kuomintang. Braga believed the branch was not engaged in anti-Japanese propaganda 'but concentrate their attention on getting subscriptions for Chinese war charities, and keep an eye on any of their own nationals who happen to be pro-Japanese'.[98] The line between relief and resistance was often a thin one.

Crackdown on KMT activities grew in the later stages of Barbosa's governorship, and from 1940 onwards they were mostly

[93] Note from Li, delivered on 27 Sept. 1939, AHD, 3P, A9, M128–129.
[94] Record of conversation with Li Jinlun, 14 Oct. 1939, ibid.
[95] Barbosa quoted in dispatch from MC to MNE, 18 Oct. 1939, ibid.
[96] 'Japanese Angered by Macao Action', *NCH* (17 Jan. 1940), p. 86; 'Kuomintang Party Holds Conference in Macao', *CDS* (17 Jan. 1940), AHD, 2P, A48, M217.
[97] Barbosa to Monteiro, 23 Jan. 1940, AHD, 2P, A48, M217.
[98] J. M. Braga to S. S. Moosa, 30 Jan. 1940, NLA, MS 4300, Box 14, 4.1/15.

forced underground.[99] In June 1940, Chiang Kai-shek was informed that the Macau governor had reached a tacit agreement with Japanese forces. He would suppress the activities of Chinese patriotic groups and in exchange Japan would prevent a blockade of Macau. Chiang lamented in his diary that Macau was now completely under Japanese control.[100] Zhou Yongneng recalled in his memoirs how his presence in Macau was cut short when he was arrested. When his identity was revealed in a newspaper, the governor of Macau ceded to Japanese pressure and sent the police to arrest him. Wu Tiecheng, with the help of some influential Chinese personalities from Macau, managed to prevent Zhou's extradition to the Japanese. Instead, he was simply expelled from Macau and forbidden to exercise activities there.[101] He went to Hong Kong where he remained until the death of Governor Barbosa and his replacement by Gabriel Maurício Teixeira, whom Zhou described as anti-German and not sympathetic towards the Japanese. Zhou managed to resume work in Macau through Catholic networks and he cultivated good relations with the new governor and others in the administration.[102] Although he lived in Kowloon, Zhou often stayed in Macau. He was there for a party meeting when the invasion of Hong Kong began and he remained stranded in Macau for the following weeks. He then fled to Chongqing after learning that collaborators were planning to kill him.[103] Zhou's case is illustrative of the multiple local and transnational links that sustained Chinese resistance in South China.

Official and shadow diplomacy were occasionally intertwined. At the end of 1940 and in April 1941, Li Shizhong, a former chargé d'affaires in Portugal, came to visit the new Macau governor. He identified himself as an envoy of Chiang Kai-shek, who wanted him to be his delegate in the enclave.[104] Teixeira replied he could only consider him privately – as an official appointment had to be granted by Lisbon – but he did not dismiss him. Indeed, assistance could be and was requested through these semi-informal channels. When the governor was asked to allow the supplying of gasoline to Free China, he told Li that Portugal's 'honest [and] loyal

[99] Guo, 'Shilun Aomen', p. 100.

[100] S. F. Wu, 'Zhongguo kangzhan xia de Aomen juese' ('Macau's Role in China's War of Resistance'), in *Jiang Jieshi yu kangzhan shiqi de Zhongguo* (*Chiang Kai-shek and China during the War of Resistance*) (Yilan, 2013), pp. 43–8, at p. 45. ccfd.org.tw/ccef001/files ys/files/dl/CKS-manual.pdf.

[101] Y. Zhou, *Zhou Yongneng xiansheng fangwen jilu* (*The Reminiscences of Mr. Chou Yung-neng*) (Taipei, 1984), p. 150.

[102] Ibid., p. 151. [103] Li, 'Wu Tiecheng', p. 83.

[104] Teixeira to MC, 28 Dec. 1940, ANTT, AOS, UL-10A1, cx. 767.

neutrality policy could not allow' an approval. When he suggested that perhaps contraband could be permitted, Teixeira's answer was ambiguous: 'when smugglers were caught, they would suffer the legal penalties'.[105] This implied that they would be free to continue their activities if they kept a low profile.

As these contacts attest, Chiang Kai-shek had not given up on Macau as an entrepôt for Chinese war supplies. In February 1941, the governor informed Lisbon that Chiang had sent a special delegate, Wang Zhengting, to Hong Kong and Macau. Wang was a former minister of foreign affairs and had been China's ambassador to the United States between 1936 and 1938. He had not been able to visit Macau, arguably because Japanese were searching boats travelling between the two colonies. Since Wang had asked to exchange views with the Macau government, the governor sent Pedro José Lobo to Hong Kong to meet him. Lobo was one of the most powerful figures in Macau, remaining a key intermediary figure throughout the war years and afterwards. He was instructed to listen to whatever Wang had to say but only to talk about assistance to refugees: '[W]ithin [its] impartial neutrality, the Macau government will continue to assist Chinese refugees not only because [of] the never-interrupted friendship between our two countries but also by compliance with the Christian spirit [which is the] base of the New State [Estado Novo authoritarian regime] doctrine.'[106]

Mentioning Christianity may have been an attempt to stress a common ground given Chiang's Christian faith and the Christian influence over his New Life Movement implemented, like the New State in Portugal, in the 1930s.[107] The reference to the Chinese refugees in Macau – by then already numbering in the tens of thousands – attests to the links between humanitarian assistance and political expediency in the enclave, an issue that will be analysed in Chapter 3. During his meeting with Lobo, Wang transmitted official thanks from Chiang Kai-shek for Portugal's 'correctness [and] friendship with China and assistance [to] refugees', having sent a jade stone ring to the governor as a 'symbol of friendship'.

Before leaving for Chongqing, Wang said he would return within a few months and would visit Macau unless there was a risk of detention by Japanese forces. Teixeira later notified Lisbon that he had information of 'secret negotiations' taking place in Hong Kong between delegates of Chiang Kai-shek and Wang Jingwei. Wang, he said, had been showing resistance towards the Japanese and refused to nominate a pro-Japanese

105 Teixeira to MC, 10 Apr. 1941, ibid. 106 Teixeira to MC, 10 Feb. 1941, ibid.
107 On the Christian elements of the New Life Movement, see F. Ferlanti, 'The New Life Movement in Jiangxi Province, 1934–1938', *Modern Asian Studies*, 44/5 (2010), pp. 961–1000.

candidate to govern Shiqi.[108] Japanese agents were working in Guangdong distributing donations for propaganda purposes and advocating peace. However, according to the governor, Chiang remained the 'main figure'. He told his superior that 'if Chiang does not make peace [,] even if the Japanese keep Wang Jingwei [,] his authority will be more and more fictitious'. The governor then clearly stated his position in the matter. '[O]ur policy is not altered: honest neutrality but, within it, friendship with Chiang.'[109] This was a more open expression of cooperation with Chinese resistance than the actions of his predecessor.

Nationalist resistance's interactions with Macau were part of a wider picture of making creative uses of neutral foreign-ruled territories in China, to which Shanghai's foreign concessions and Hong Kong were key. Chiang's men were not the only ones operating in these, however.

Communist Mobilisation

Communist guerrillas had been recruited in Macau since the early stages of the war. Both the KMT and the CCP were involved in cultural activities taking place in Macau to mobilise support for the war effort, including sonic and visual propaganda such as the 1938 documentary series *Kangzhan teji* (*War of Resistance Special*) shown at the Apollo Theatre in Macau.[110]

The origins of the CCP in Macau have, so far, lacked scholarly attention, but it is known that the party was present in Macau before 1937. Chen Shaoling, a CCP member from Taishan who had fled the KMT to Malaya in 1927, came to the enclave in 1935, where he opened a 'progressive' bookshop and sought to mobilise teachers, students and workers.[111] The Second United Front with the Nationalists during the war provided a golden opportunity for the CCP to expand their activities in places such as Macau and Chen played an important role in mobilisation efforts within and beyond Macau.

One of the city's newly founded charities, the Four Circles Disaster Relief Association (Sijie jiuzaihui), was linked to Communist resistance. The circles were academic, musical, theatrical and sporting. It included more than fifty smaller associations (schools, sports teams, media, musical and theatre groups, etc.) and more than 100 people. Founded in August 1937, it organised a variety of fundraising activities (such as

[108] Teixeira to MC, received 27 Feb. 1941, ANTT, AOS, UL-10A1, cx. 767.
[109] Teixeira to MC, 12 Mar. 1941, ibid. [110] Lin and Wang, *Gudao yingxiang*, p. 99.
[111] Guo, 'Shilun Aomen', p. 100. Chen was expelled from the party in 1939, wrongly accused of Trotskyism, and died in a Japanese bombing that year ('Chen Shaoling', in *Baidu baike*, baike.baidu.com/item/陈少陵).

entertainment events, sports competitions and collection of donations on the street). These groups' work included propaganda activities to mobilise the rural communities and provision of medical treatment, for example, to victims of Japanese bombings, as well as actual fighting.[112] The association provided training to youth teams dispatched to engage in popular mobilisation and guerrilla fighting in inland China. The Macau Chinese Youth Countryside Service Group (Lü Ao Zhongguo qingnian xiangcun fuwutuan) was the first Chinese service group to send members to the interior.[113] Several of its young members lost their lives in the conflict.[114]

After the fall of Guangzhou, the Four Circles Disaster Relief Association Return to the County Service Group (Sijie jiuzaihui huiguo fuwutuan) was set up, with Liao Jintao as leader.[115] Liao, an underground CCP member, was a clerk in a motor company in Macau and was responsible for the propaganda department of the Four Circles Association, travelling to Guangzhou and other places near Macau and mobilising people to support the resistance. The Nationalists arrested him in 1941, and he ended up dying in jail at just twenty-seven.[116]

That same year, General Ye Ting, commander of the New Fourth Army, is mentioned as having come to reside in the enclave. Ye had been arrested and tried in the New Fourth Army Incident that had fatally damaged the CCP–KMT United Front. He was reportedly imprisoned until the end of the war.[117] However, according to a telegram from the governor of Macau, after being arrested by the Nationalists, Ye returned to Macau, where he had sought refuge in 1935.[118] The governor notified Lisbon that he would summon Ye to tell him that 'he would let him stay in Macau as long as he observed absolute correctness [in his behaviour] but at the minimum communist activity he would be arrested and deported'.[119] It is unclear if Ye's return to Macau did indeed take place and, if so, how long it lasted and what its purpose was.

112 Deng, *Aomen lishi*, pp. 90–9. See also Huang and Chen, *Haojiang fengyun er'nü*, and Zou, 'Qianxi kangzhan', p. 146.
113 Fei, *Macau 400 Years*, p. 343.
114 Barreto, *Macau during the Sino–Japanese War*, pp. 157–9.
115 Deng, *Aomen lishi*, pp. 96–7.
116 'Liao Jintao', in *Gang'Ao dabaike quanshu* (*Encyclopedia of Hong Kong & Macao*) (Guangzhou, 1993), p. 800.
117 G. Benton, *New Fourth Army: Communist Resistance along the Yangtze and the Huai, 1938–1941* (Berkeley, CA, 1999), p. 571.
118 Ye Ting's family home in Macau is now a museum open to the public.
119 Teixeira to MC, 13 Mar. 1941, ANTT, AOS, UL-10A1, cx. 767.

As will be detailed later, the CCP presence in Macau became stronger in the 1940s when some future key figures started to operate in the Portuguese enclave. Chinese historians now credit the party with the bulk of anti-Japanese resistance activities in and around Macau.[120]

Macau and Chinese Collaborators

Neutral territories were prime sites for the coexistence and interaction of opposing forces during the Second World War. Macau was important both for those supporting resistance against Japan and for those attempting to settle for peace, most notably Wang Jingwei and his circle. As will become clear in this section and in Chapter 4, the enclave was a peculiar participant observer in the rise and fall of Wang's RNG.

Unable to convince Chiang Kai-shek to accept surrender, the Japanese turned their attention to Wang Jingwei, an important KMT figure who regarded Chiang as a rival who had usurped his 'rightful place as leader of the National Revolution'.[121] Together with a group of close associates, Wang left Chongqing in December 1938, bound for Hanoi in French Indochina, and Hong Kong. In these then-neutral colonial territories, Wang and his circle began to negotiate with Japan, responding to covert overtures for peace that had been happening for some time and would continue for the rest of the conflict. After leaving Chongqing, Wang began to contact a number of figures in areas where he and his wife, Chen Bijun, were well connected. Chen, who had been born in British-ruled Penang, played a key role in Wang's shift towards Japan and actively lobbied for his 'Peace Movement'. She led one of the two main factions of Wang's supporters, the *furen pai* or 'Madame (Wang) Faction', that came to dominate occupied Guangdong's economy and politics.[122]

One of Chen Bijun's colonial stopovers was Macau. In January, the governor reported to Lisbon that Chen had 'come to reside in Macau', believing it to be a safe location.[123] Guangdong province had long been a key area of support for Wang, a native Cantonese who had been a close

[120] A good example of this is the section dedicated to 'Heroes of the Sino–Japanese War' in Barreto, *Macau during the Sino–Japanese War*, pp. 139–65.

[121] Mitter, *China's War with Japan*, pp. 202, 206.

[122] J. K. S. Yick, '"Pre-collaboration": The Political Activity and Influence of Chen Bijun in Wartime China', *Southeast Review of Asian Studies*, 36 (2014), pp. 58–74, at p. 63; J. K. S. Yick, '"Self-Serving Collaboration": The Political Legacy of "Madame Wang" in Guangdong Province, 1940–1945', *American Journal of Chinese Studies*, 21/217 (2014), pp. 217–34.

[123] Barbosa to MC, 5 Jan. 1939, ANTT, AOS, UL-10A1, cx. 767. Also in AHD, 3P, A9, M128–129.

associate of Sun Yat-sen. It is not surprising that the Wangs' first efforts to develop an alternative government to that of Chiang's involved meetings with other Cantonese elites, facilitated by the official neutrality of the foreign-ruled territories in South China. These territories also offered opportunities to reach out to European authorities.

It was via Macau that Wang Jingwei arrived at Guangzhou in July, on the Japanese ship *Shirogane Maru*.[124] He broadcast a key speech in the provincial capital, calling for peace with Japan and condemning Chiang and guerrilla actions in Guangdong, and the suffering they inflicted on the local population.[125] His pleas were not unanimously well received and his attempts to convince key KMT military figures, such as General Zhang Fakui, to defect failed.

In Hong Kong, Wang's supporters faced fierce opposition from pro-resistance circles and were met with a cold, if not downright hostile, position from the British colonial authorities, well exemplified by the difficulties faced by the *Hua nan ribao* (*South China Daily News*), a Hong Kong–based newspaper that was an important propaganda mouthpiece for Wang.[126] Despite this, his moves to gain prominence in occupied South China had some traction. Although Wang ended up relocating to Shanghai, a pro-Wang Guangdong Political Affairs Committee was established later in 1939. By then, Cantonese collaborators were divided into factions, one of them Chen Bijun's, fighting for power. In a bid against Chen's faction, Peng Dongyuan, one of the collaborators the Japanese had put in charge of Guangzhou, made himself mayor of the new Guangzhou Municipal Administrative Office. Eventually, Chen's faction – with the support of the head of the Japanese army special services in Shanghai, Kagesa Sasaki – succeeded in dominating Guangdong province, where a new provincial government was established in May 1940.[127] Several of the provincial government committee members were part of Chen Bijun's faction, and she was appointed to the position of Guangdong political director that granted her extensive powers of supervision over government affairs in South China.[128]

If Wang Jingwei used Macau as a stopover for his démarches in South China, so did Chiang Kai-shek's envoys, who were determined to make Wang's efforts collapse. Wang's rival government had been officially

[124] Acting British Consul General in Guangzhou to Archibald Clark Kerr, British Ambassador to China, 10 Aug. 1939, TNA, FO 676/410.

[125] Kerr to FO, 15 Aug. 1939. An English translation of the speech was published in *CDS* (11 Aug. 1939), ibid.

[126] L. M. W. Chiu, 'The *South China Daily News* and Wang Jingwei's Peace Movement, 1939–41', *Journal of the Royal Asiatic Society Hong Kong Branch*, 50 (2010), pp. 343–70, at pp. 349–62.

[127] Yick, '"Pre-collaboration"', p. 68.

[128] Ibid., pp. 70–1; Yick, '"Self-Serving Collaboration"', p. 223.

inaugurated on 30 March 1940 without formal recognition by Japan, which 'still hoped for a peace settlement with the real power in China, the National Government'.[129] In June, high-level contacts that had begun in Hong Kong between Nationalist agents and Japanese military figures were resumed in Macau. The talks revolved around 'Chinese recognition of Manchuria and Japanese stationing of troops in North China' and went as far as the signing of a memorandum agreeing that Chiang would meet Itagaki Seishirō, chief of staff of the China Expeditionary Army, in Chongqing in August, but then Chiang abruptly cancelled them.[130]

In early November, a more informal meeting took place in Macau between Du Shishan, one of the Nationalists' 'unofficial representatives', and Toyama Shuzo, son of a friend of Sun Yat-sen, who warned of the imminent recognition of the Wang Jingwei regime. This was one of the Nationalists' last efforts to obstruct that recognition.[131] However, they did not stop trying to discredit the RNG and even unlikely actors were used to ensure this. For example, news from Chongqing that the Chinese apostolic vicar of Nanjing, Yu Bin, called for opposing the Wang government, was published in the main Macau daily.[132] The impact of such reports on a considerable local Chinese Catholic population is unknown but is easily imaginable, particularly given the Japanese bombing of Catholic missions in the province that will be addressed in the following chapter.

Meanwhile, the RNG authorities in Guangdong found Macau useful for other purposes. In May 1940, a new Zhongshan county magistrate contacted the Macau authorities with commercial proposals. He was organising an export regime to neighbouring territories and promised to make Macau's harbour a distribution hub, as well as to replace the Lappa island garrison with one more in line with Portuguese interests. In exchange, he wished to obtain 20,000 patacas to cover the district's organisational expenses.[133] In a top-secret telegram to Lisbon, Governor Barbosa expressed his approval, fearing economic reprisals if he did not comply. Everything would be taken care of confidentially, involving only the governor and two other associates, one of them Lobo. With the bluntly racist language sometimes found in official correspondence, he exonerated

[129] M. Huang and H. Yang, 'Nationalist China's Negotiating Position during the Stalemate, 1938–1945', in D. P. Barrett and L. N. Shyu (eds.), *Chinese Collaboration with Japan, 1932–1945: The Limits of Accommodation* (Stanford, CA, 2001), pp. 56–76, at p. 63.

[130] Ibid., pp. 65–6. Also see Mitter, *China's War with Japan*, pp. 220–1.

[131] Huang and Yang, 'Nationalist China's Negotiating Position', pp. 63–4.

[132] 'Um apelo do bispo católico chinês Yi Pin' ('An Appeal by the Chinese Catholic Bishop Yu Bin'), *VM* (8 Apr. 1940), p. 3.

[133] The pataca has been Macau's currency since 1894. In the 1930s, it was the equivalent of 5.5 Portuguese escudos.

himself of any responsibility, noting that 'all Chinamen are venal', it was not such a high amount, 'and the general has volunteered to issue a receipt which is a valuable document for us and places him, in a way, in our dependency'. Ever mindful of colonial comparisons, he added that 'it is like this that other foreign countries have managed their tranquillity and the maintenance of their interests in the Far East'.[134] In other words, since everybody was collaborating, it was not a problem.

The minister of colonies was not particularly enthusiastic at first. Such things 'are perhaps very common [in the] East but they contradict our principles [and] shock our sensibility', he telegraphed. The whole affair was likely to lead to more demands and would look very much like blackmail. However, if the Lappa settlement meant a Portuguese reoccupation of Lappa, he added, using 'these means would not be so repugnant'. The minister approved the operation, hoping for the 'moral sacrifice' to be justified by 'advantageous results'.[135] For the governor, compromise was imperative because the 'maintenance [of] gambling, opium and commerce profits depend[ed] [on the] sympathy [of the] high authority [of the] Zhongshan district'.

Morality was a strange thing indeed, for its sacrifice was, after all, to buy Macau's financial solvency through activities that elsewhere attracted moral condemnation. The money would be considered a loan and the replacement of the Lappa garrison by one less hostile to Portugal would allow the Macau authorities to scale down maritime security measures. In sum, collaboration with the collaborators would be 'very useful at least economically', especially given the unrelenting Japanese pressure.[136] Such desire for stability soon gave way to more demands.

Authorities in Zhongshan tried to control access to Macau in different ways. These interactions served multiple and intersecting purposes, from personal profit to protection of power or expansion of influence. In November, a tax was imposed on everyone who went to Macau. The new governor, Gabriel Teixeira, informed Lisbon he would try to negotiate a reduction. An opportunity came up when, a few months later, the newly appointed magistrate of Zhongshan remained in Macau, hiding from the supporters of his predecessor, 'who wanted to assassinate him', and waiting for the Japanese to 'clean up Zhongshan'.[137]

The case highlights how different collaborationist factions in the south had differing degrees of closeness with the Japanese military forces. The Macau governor granted him protection, including authorisation for gun

134 Barbosa to MC, 2 May 1940, ANTT, AOS, UL-10A1, cx. 767.
135 Machado to Barbosa, 4 May 1940, ibid. 136 Barbosa to MC, 4 May 1940, ibid.
137 Teixeira to MC, 24 Apr. 1941, ibid.

licences for his two bodyguards.[138] In May, the magistrate came to visit Teixeira with customary 'wishes of collaboration' (*desejos [de] colaboração*). Confirming those to be his wishes as well, the governor suggested that a practical way of doing so would be to lower the taxes over people and goods travelling between Macau and Zhongshan, as well as to facilitate the return of refugees in Macau. The magistrate requested to station a representative to deal with Macau–Zhongshan issues, a refugee from Zhongshan who had been living in Macau for four years. He was a graduate of an American university and a 'friend' of the Portuguese. The governor accepted.[139] Personal links, however, were a volatile insurance in a region ravaged by factions and war. In mid-June, the magistrate was assassinated in Macau, shot dead by three Chinese who escaped.[140] Even though the governor assured Lisbon that he had provided everything for the man's safety, the incident was a pretext for the RNG to protest as a state would.

Complaints and demands were opportunities for the RNG to affirm its claims as the legitimate Chinese government. A protest about the magistrate's assassination came via the commissioner for foreign affairs of the Guangdong provincial government, Zhou Bingsan, accompanied by a Japanese adviser. The demands were harsh: a written apology by the Macau government; immediate handing over of the criminals; punishment of the responsible Macau government staff; financial compensation for the family of the deceased; and guarantees that similar incidents would never again take place. Teixeira refused to accept, claiming he had granted all requests for the deceased's protection and had kept good relations with him. The Japanese sided with the governor, and their agent told Teixeira that their investigations in Shiqi pointed towards the assassination having been requested by the Nanjing government itself.[141] This case highlights the divisions amongst collaborators and how internal decisions influenced informal external relations.

As in Shanghai, where – as Frederick Wakeman demonstrated – political terrorism became an everyday reality between 1937 and 1941, political assassinations continued with frequency in South China, sometimes perpetrated in Macau.[142] One of the victims was the Guangzhou police sub-chief.[143] He was the fifth man working for the RNG provincial government killed in Macau between June 1940 and September 1941.[144] A new protest

[138] Teixeira to MC, 18 June 1941, ibid. [139] Teixeira to MC, 8 May 1941, ibid.
[140] Teixeira to MC, 18 June 1941, ibid. [141] Teixeira to MC, 8 July 1941, ibid.
[142] Wakeman, *Shanghai Badlands*. [143] Teixeira to MC, 11 Sept. 1941, ibid.
[144] MNE note based on information transmitted from Teixeira to MC, Mar. 1942, AHD, 2P, A48, M212. One of the five men assassinated was shot and stabbed to death while in hospital.

ensued. The Guangzhou authorities wanted to send their staff in order to, they claimed, cooperate with the Portuguese authorities in 'exterminating dangerous Chongqing elements in Macau'. Licences for carrying guns would be issued to them and their bodyguards. After some negotiating, the governor granted 20 licences – much fewer than the 150 demanded – and tried to get the Japanese representatives to support him. Then he called a representative of Chiang's government in Hong Kong, urging him of the 'imperative need to impose on his supporters respect [for] Macau's hospitality [and] neutrality'.[145] The agent denied Chongqing's involvement in the assassinations. The fact that the governor believed it had been the Nationalists is not surprising as their underground actions against collaborators were common during the war.[146] This episode reveals that, although pressured by the RNG authorities, the Portuguese authorities in Macau continued to maintain contact with Chiang's men.

The Nationalists were paying close attention to what was happening in Macau and regularly sent representatives to ensure the Portuguese authorities had not changed sides. In early May 1941, Ling Shifen visited the governor. He wanted to ascertain whether the Macau government had recognised Wang's, and if the Japanese had espionage services in the enclave and were pressuring Chinese schools and associations to support Wang.

Teixeira confirmed not only that the Macau government had not recognised the RNG, but also that such a decision rested with the metropolitan government. On the other issues, he had no knowledge of Japanese spying in Macau and did not think it necessary given that Japan occupied all the neighbouring territories. As for co-opting the Macau Chinese, he only knew that Colonel Okubo Hiroshi, a Japanese liaison officer, had invited the president of the Commercial Association to support Wang Jingwei. The governor forbade that association from any political activity.[147]

At least until 1941, the core of the Macau Chinese elite remained with Chiang, and this permitted useful communications with a very wide reach indeed. For example, in early July 1941, the British intercepted a message from Macau to the Chinese embassy at Berlin to evacuate the embassy.[148] The warning came shortly after Chongqing's severed relations with the

145 Teixeira to MC, 1 Oct.1941, ANTT, AOS, UL-10A1, cx. 767.

146 For example, P. F. Lo, *It Is Dark Underground* (New York, 1946).

147 Teixeira to MC, 6 May 1941, ANTT, AOS, UL-10A1, cx. 767; Diao Zuoqian to MOFA, 18 May 1941, AH, Waijiaobu, 020000003319A.

148 Wong Yun Une to Wong Hsioh Li (possibly Lin Qiusheng), FO 371/27635. On Lin Qiusheng, see N. F. Glang, 'Back-Channel Diplomacy and the Sino–German relationship, 1939–1945' (PhD thesis, University of Sheffield, 2014), pp. 103–4.

Axis Powers. That month, two years after his defection, Wang Jingwei saw Japan finally recognise his Nanjing government. Germany, Italy and a number of pro-Axis countries, including Spain, also recognised it.[149] Efforts were made, by Wang and Japan, to persuade Portugal to follow suit. Despite many rumours in that direction, such an official recognition never occurred. In fact, Chiang's government asked Portugal to protect Chinese interests and citizens in Spain and its territories after the breaking of relations with Madrid, and Portugal accepted the request.[150] Despite compromises at the local level, Sino–Portuguese state-to-state relations kept an appearance of smooth continuity.

Conclusion

Although Portugal had been part of China's diplomatic resistance against Japan since 1931, Macau's importance for the Nationalists grew significantly from July 1937, when a continuous state of warfare led to profound and unprecedented effects in the neutral South China enclave.

When hostilities reached Guangdong province, the attitude of Portuguese colonial authorities and the actions of Chinese in Macau became an object of scrutiny and a target for mobilisation. Portuguese neutrality was often questioned by the Chinese government, but it was also pragmatically utilised by its agents. Smuggling, propaganda and meetings were conducted in and via Macau by Chinese in opposing camps. As this chapter has demonstrated, Chinese wartime diplomacy was a dynamic endeavour that did not ignore small powers such as Portugal. From the start of the war, the Nationalists used the opportunities neutrality provided, from Macau's entrepôt features to the protection the Portuguese flag could offer renationalised ships.

Portuguese foreign policy towards China was actually nothing more than colonial policy, where every action was taken with the single objective of securing Portugal's outposts in Asia. Whilst Chinese diplomats in Lisbon had a stable presence and acted with professionalism, Portuguese diplomats remained in occupied cities and did not follow the Nationalists

[149] W. C. So, 'Race, Culture, and the Anglo–American Powers: The Views of Chinese Collaborators', *Modern China*, 37/1 (2011), pp. 69–103, at p. 77. On Spain's close relations with Wang's government, see F. Rodao, 'Franco's Spain and the Japanese Empire, 1937–45', *Bulletin of Portuguese–Japanese Studies*, 10–11 (2005), pp. 243–62; F. Rodao, 'Japan and the Axis, 1937–8: Recognition of the Franco Regime and Manchukuo', *Journal of Contemporary History*, 44/3 (2009), pp. 431–47.

[150] Li Jinlun to Salazar, 19 Sept. 1940, AHD, 2P, A48, M212. The Chinese legation in Spain had been moved to the south of France during the Spanish Civil War and was closed in 1940. Shortly afterwards, there were attempts to re-establish diplomatic relations, which the Spanish government did not accept.

to the wartime capital, Chongqing. This contributed to the disruption in state-to-state communication at a time when it was urgently needed. In such a trying context, Macau's authorities often bypassed official diplomatic channels and launched their own shadow diplomacy initiatives, albeit without lasting success. Decisions were sometimes taken in Macau without the prior knowledge and approval of the Portuguese government in Lisbon, even though it was the latter that had to respond to Chinese enquiries and complaints over malpractices of neutrality.

Macau was part of a network of foreign-ruled territories, also including Shanghai's foreign concessions, Hong Kong and Guangzhouwan, which, due to their ambiguous neutrality and colonial status, were used by both resistance activists and collaborators with Japan. These were liminal places, with water and overland links to mainland China, through which people, goods and information circulated. Increasing Japanese pressure to limit Chinese use of Macau for resistance had some degree of success; however, they never completely ceased as the smuggling opportunities on offer were attractive to all sides.

2 Old Allies and New Friends

The Macau Portuguese Administration, Japan and Britain before the Fall of Hong Kong

Keeping 'good relations' with everyone 'without breaking our strict neutrality' is how the acting governor of Macau in 1940 described the attitude of the Portuguese colonial administration shortly after Artur Tamagnini de Sousa Barbosa, the first of the two wartime governors of Macau, suddenly died.[1] By 'everyone' he meant pro-resistance Chinese, Chinese collaborators and Japanese forces, but to the pool of 'good relations' one should add the British in Hong Kong. This accommodating stance towards all sides was precisely what made Portuguese neutrality in Macau anything but 'strict'. Its flexibility made it prone to be used – and abused – by different actors for their own interests.

This chapter argues that Macau functioned as a nexus for multiple layers of collaboration by different imperial actors from the outbreak of the Second Sino–Japanese War in July 1937 until the fall of Hong Kong in December 1941. Macau was a centre for human, commercial and intelligence exchanges between Portugal, Japan, the United Kingdom and, as seen in the previous chapter, also between the Chinese central government and Chinese collaborators. These exchanges were dictated and conditioned by the weakness of the Portuguese authorities in Macau, Portugal's historical alliance with Great Britain, Japanese threats and connections to Chinese authorities in South China. It was precisely Macau's unassuming position that made it so convenient for these different players.

The Portuguese were torn between loyalty to an old ally, Great Britain, and accommodating a new major power in the region, Japan, with whom some Portuguese officials had ideological affinities. This chapter explores this triangular relationship between Portugal, Britain and Japan. Japanese representatives, in both Asia and Europe, employed a mixed strategy towards the Portuguese in Macau, ranging from courtship to aggression and exploiting their colonial anxiety in relation to the

[1] Acting Governor of Macau to MC, 3 Aug. 1940, ANTT, AOS, UL-10A1, cx. 767.

British. The Portuguese were less enthusiastic Japanese partners than Franco's Spain, and often sought to stall demands and seek a united front with the British in Hong Kong. Eventually, however, the Macau authorities ceded to certain Japanese overtures for collaboration and some came to see the Japanese invasion of the south as advantageous for Portuguese colonial expansion at the expense of Chinese interests. This was particularly evident in one of the most flagrant abuses of Portuguese neutrality in South China. By taking advantage of the volatile situation in the region, the Portuguese temporarily occupied part of some Chinese islands they considered under dispute and sought to legitimise that situation in secret negotiations with Japan.

As the war erupted through South China, the Portuguese authorities in Macau turned to their oldest ally and imagined colonial guarantor. British authorities initially downplayed the threat of a Japanese occupation of Macau. Still, they had been on the alert for Japanese attempts to establish a foothold in the enclave since before 1937. The British were well aware that Japanese advances in China threatened their widespread interests in the country, but their interactions with the Portuguese in Macau were not unlike their uncommitted dealings with Chinese authorities. Knowing that to offer the Portuguese concrete commitments to help defend Macau would be unfeasible, the British nevertheless kept official and unofficial channels of communication open for intelligence sharing. Any temptation that Portuguese officials might have of taking a more pro-Japanese line was received with concern and attempts were made to diffuse threats in that regard, with relative success. The Portuguese could imagine a defeated China but never, in a future that included them administering Macau, a Japanese victory over Britain.

Portuguese–Japanese Relations and Macau before the Occupation of Zhongshan

Japanese military advances in China were fast and brutal. Japanese forces moved southwards from 1937, along railway lines and targeting urban areas along the east coast. Cities like Tianjin, Beijing, Shanghai, Hankou or Guangzhou, which had been the most vibrant industrial, commercial and cultural centres of modern China, were (minus foreign concessions) occupied and their administrations delegated to local collaborators. With its most important diplomats and communities based at Shanghai and Guangzhou and with its colonial enclave situated on the Pearl River Delta, the Portuguese presence in China was very much in the line of fire from the beginning of the conflict. Portuguese actors left a paper trail about the hostilities from the virtually unknown perspective of a small

European colonial power that observed the Japanese takeover from a position of military weakness that was different from other countries with important interests in China.

From the Eurocentric perspective that dominates the historiography of the Second World War, the conflict began in 1939 with the German invasion of Poland. Contemporary observers saw the Second World War as a European war, a conflict distinct from the one in East Asia that had been building up since 1931 and that raged on as an all-out armed conflict from 1937 onwards. Little attention has been paid to how actors in Europe and Asia were involved in both of these theatres of a global war in the making. An exception to this is the work of Franco Macri, who has detailed the role of the British in the Second Sino–Japanese War as a 'proxy war' in South China.[2] This chapter decentres the British. Although Great Britain was an important force, it was but one amongst several in the region. Focusing on the experience of Macau as a territory at the crossroads of different empires, it provides a new perspective on the complex interaction of imperialisms in South China during World War II.

By late 1937, Japanese military activities around Macau were an everyday reality. Aerial bombings over ships and land targets were often reported, the sounds of which were heard in the enclave. For the Portuguese authorities, it was clear from the onset that defending the territory against an eventual Japanese attack was a task impossible to achieve. The governor, Tamagnini de Barbosa, was assured by his superior, the Minister of Colonies Francisco José Vieira Machado, that the territory was capable of ensuring its neutrality, but Barbosa insisted on the need to strengthen the enclave's defence capability.[3] His argument was not that Portugal could win over 'the invincible Japanese', but that making a show of protecting its interests would have an important 'moral' effect.[4] Subsequently, Macau's defences were modestly boosted.[5] Showing off

[2] Macri, *Clash of Empires*.

[3] Machado to Barbosa, 30 Oct. 1937, ANTT, AOS, UL-10A1, cx. 767.

[4] Barbosa to MC, 2 Nov. 1937, ibid.

[5] Despite efforts to build up the Portuguese military presence in Macau, by the late 1930s, the territory's defences were still too weak to resist a potential Japanese attack. A garrison of 497 men in 1936–7 had been increased to 794 in 1940 (one battalion of Mozambican soldiers divided into two infantry companies, one machine-gun company and one artillery company). The police force mostly employed Sikh and Chinese men. Defences amounted to a battery of five field guns, six hydroplanes and a sloop (*aviso*) sent from Lisbon on commission. The first, *Gonçalo Velho*, stayed in Macau for fifteen months from September 1937, the second, *Gonçalves Zarco*, stayed in Macau from September 1938 to April 1939, followed by the *João de Lisboa* between April and November of the same year, a second commission by the *Gonçalo Velho* from June 1940 to March 1941, and then the *João de Lisboa* from May 1941 to May 1942, after which the ships returned to

a heightened military capability, however inadequate to meet a potential Japanese attack, was essentially a projection of 'colonial prestige', something paramount for the Estado Novo, a regime whose authoritarian rule was indissociable from its imperial project. Imperialists tend to understand each other, however, and do not hesitate to collaborate when a mutual benefit is perceived.

Similar to the way in which Germany was attempting to woo Salazar's regime in Portugal away from its traditional ally, Great Britain, Japan kept trying to entice the Portuguese authorities in Asia into believing it could be a reliable alternative partner. Vague suggestions and more concrete proposals began to be offered more vigorously from 1938, the year that Japanese military forces started to occupy parts of Guangdong province. Studies on Japanese wartime diplomacy in East Asia often stress its pan-Asian rhetoric, but, in fact, Japan did not completely abandon the Western circles of colonial power with its decision to leave the League of Nations in 1933. Japan remained a skilled player in dealing bilaterally with European nations for its own advantage, as the case of Portugal vividly illustrates.

For the Portuguese authorities, it was unfathomable to cut ties with Britain, but gaining economic benefits out of the Japanese apparent preference for them in South China was sometimes considered. In October 1938, after the fall of Guangzhou, the Macau government received a Japanese request to station an attaché in the enclave. Governor Barbosa informed Lisbon he believed the 'answer should be compliance in principle' but 'with reciprocity'. Portuguese inferiority complexes in relation to the British in Hong Kong were also smartly played. When the circulation of British ships to Guangzhou was disrupted, Japanese officials suggested to the governor of Macau that they would be favourable to a Guangzhou–Macau shipping route to replace the one with Hong Kong.[6]

Japanese propositions became more daring, leaving Portuguese authorities both enticed and worried. A set of proposals that the Japanese military and naval forces aimed to submit to the Portuguese government reached Barbosa in November. Amongst other things, these planned to make Macau a transit hub for passenger and cargo shipping to Guangzhou. Military transport would come close to Coloane (one of

Lisbon as a sign of neutrality. The Centre of Naval Aviation of Macau, closed in 1933, was reactivated in December 1937. Two Osprey seaplanes sent from Lisbon were joined by another four in 1938 and a School of Naval Aviation was established in 1939. The Centre closed in 1942 after one of the Ospreys crashed in central Macau, killing the two pilots. A hangar built in 1941 was destroyed by American bombings in 1945 (R. J. Garrett, *The Defences of Macao: Forts, Ships and Weapons over 450 Years* (Hong Kong, 2010), pp. 114–15, 134–8; Macri, *Clash of Empires*, p. 128).

[6] Barbosa [to MC], received 27 Oct. 1938, ANTT, AOS, UL-10A1, cx. 767.

the islands under Macau's administration); its cargo would pass through Macau on Portuguese boats and from there on to Guangzhou along the Pearl River or overland. Concession of this traffic would not be given to Japanese people or firms and the Japanese would only nominate an agent to help to establish a Portuguese company. The promises seemed too good to be true and worried the governor, who was already wary of the fact that gambling and opium, Macau's financial lifeblood, had become widely available in Guangzhou 'with acquiescence from the Japanese authorities'.[7] If Portugal refused to collaborate, the Japanese could simply block any trade to and from Macau. He was adamant that, should such plans be presented to the Portuguese government, the proposal on military transport should not be accepted but the others could be carefully discussed.

Japanese advances into Guangdong meant a direct threat to European interests in the province – which had always been tightly connected with Chinese actors. If the prospects seemed manageable to officials in Macau, from the rubble of war bombings in Guangzhou, the Portuguese Consul General Vasco Martins Morgado made a more sceptical assessment. He doubted the Japanese capacity to deliver on these proposals and advised that Macau's development should be planned only according to Portuguese ideas.[8]

Despite more cautious views, the wooing of the Portuguese did not abate. In December, the Japanese presented an updated round of thirteen proposals for a cooperation project between Japan and Portugal focused on Macau. Excluding the point on military transport, it included plans: to build a railway line and a road between Macau and Guangzhou; to establish a commercial air service connecting Taiwan (then a Japanese colony), Macau and Guangzhou; to develop shipping between Japan, Taiwan, the Portuguese colony of Timor in Southeast Asia and Portugal's colonies in Africa; to build sugar, cotton and gas factories; and to establish schools in Macau.

These visions of prosperity touched the nerve of Portuguese colonial aspirations, but they remained too rosy to be credible. The governor considered that 'some [of these] proposals are inadmissible', but feared that a negative response could damage the country's 'good relations' with Japan.[9] Barbosa responded with little more than inaction, but the discussions did not go unnoticed. Rumours of future collaboration provoked outrage amongst many Chinese, who criticised them in the Hong Kong

[7] Barbosa [to MC], received 16 Nov. 1938, ibid.
[8] Vasco Martins Morgado, Consul in Guangzhou, to Barbosa, 17 Nov. 1938, AHD, 2P, A48, M217.
[9] Barbosa [to MC], received 16 Dec. 1938, ANTT, AOS, UL-10A1, cx. 767.

press. American information that the Japanese had promised to 'develop Macau as a commercial port at the expense of Hong Kong' was also received with alarm by British officials, who contemplated the possibility of Macau becoming 'a Japanese Headquarters in South China for the smuggling of goods and other kinds of economic exploitation'.[10] This pattern of enticing offers, alarming news and international concern was to mark Macau's war years.

At the same time as these grandiose suggestions were being made, the violence of Japanese military attacks on South China came to affect many Portuguese directly, not only in Macau, but also in Guangdong. In December 1938, Japanese pilots bombed buildings guarded by the country's neutral flag at the Portuguese Catholic mission in Zhaoqing, killing a watchman.[11] In January 1939, the Zhaoqing mission suffered further damage from another aerial attack. Portuguese flags were hoisted up flagpoles and painted on roofs, but still one bomb fell near the flagpole where one had been flying. In a letter protesting to the Japanese consul general at Guangzhou, Okazaki Katsuo, Morgado highlighted the contradiction between words and deeds: 'It is not understandable for our friendship towards the Japanese Empire that such attacks to Portuguese properties could be made.'[12] Complaints and requests for compensation were lodged in Tokyo, but to no avail.

A string of visits from Japanese army and navy officers to Macau and Portuguese officers representing the governor to Guangzhou or to other occupied areas nearby intensified from late 1938, after the occupation of the provincial capital had been completed. The new masters of the house came to call on the neighbours to give and to get assurances regarding the new state of affairs in the region. The governor of Macau embraced the centuries-old precedents of Macau's autonomy, informing his superiors in Lisbon that what was going on needed compromise with his military interlocutors, not with diplomats. A Japanese military attaché arrived in Macau in December, and that same month a major, representing Lieutenant General Ando Rikichi, the commanding officer of the South China Area Army, came to visit the governor.[13] Barbosa reported to

[10] Home Office, Drugs Branch, to FO, 18 Jan. 1939, TNA, FO 371/23501.

[11] The Zhaoqing Mission, which Michele Ruggieri and Matteo Ricci opened in 1583, was the first Jesuit residence in Chinese territory. It was abandoned in the eighteenth century due to persecution from Qing authorities and reopened in the beginning of the twentieth century under the jurisdiction of the Macau Diocese (A. F. Netto, *Breve Notícia Histórica da Missão de Shiu-Hing na Província de Cantão* (*Brief Historical Account of the Shiu-Hing Mission in Canton Province*) (Macau, 1924), pp. 12, 16).

[12] Morgado to Okazaki Katsuo, Japanese Consul in Guangzhou, 4 Feb. 1939, AHD, 2P, A48, M176.

[13] Barbosa to MC, 16 and 23 Dec. 1938, ANTT, AOS, UL-10A1, cx. 767.

Lisbon on the usefulness of these contacts: '[W]e will get nothing without a prior understanding [with the] military and naval authorities [and] only later take the subject [to the] diplomatic field.'[14] Without hesitation, he did just that.

At a Japanese invitation, the governor sent the police commander Carlos Gorgulho to Guangzhou to meet with Japanese military authorities. Gorgulho was accompanied by Wada Shinzo, a Japanese secret services agent who posed as a businessman and dentist, much to the displeasure of the Portuguese and the Japanese consuls in the city, who disapproved of serious issues regarding Macau being discussed by someone without an official position.[15] This left little doubt where power in South China lay, and it was not in the hands of civil servants. This unofficial parallel diplomacy with the Japanese armed forces centred on Macau continued, however. Several officers (at least one rear admiral, four colonels and two majors) visited Macau between January and May 1939.[16] Local moves towards accommodation trumped a national policy of 'strict neutrality' and bypassed regular diplomatic channels, but they were defended with a rhetoric of patriotism. It was not so dissimilar to what was happening in occupied China, where collaboration was often justified with the higher interests of the nation.[17]

The most significant initiative of parallel diplomacy was the visit of the chief of police in Macau to Japan. Gorgulho left for Tokyo in the beginning of February 1939, accompanied by Wada, who, according to British sources, was being paid a monthly fee of 1,000 [patacas or Chinese dollars] to assist the easy passage of a scheme for Lappa island.[18] The pretext for Gorgulho's visit was to hand over a cypher book to the Portuguese legation in Tokyo. The Macau authorities had instructed him to approach the Japanese authorities about the release of some Portuguese boats detained at Guangzhou, compensation for the bombing

14 Barbosa to MC, 23 Dec. 1938, ibid.

15 Morgado to Salazar, Minister of Foreign Affairs, 26 and 31 Dec. 1938, AHD, 2P, A48, M217. A long-term resident of Macau, Wada was believed to be a retired or reserve naval officer and working for navy secret services. Japanese spies in China apparently used the dentist cover often (Antero Carreiro de Freitas, Portuguese Chargé d'Affaires in Tokyo to Salazar, 4 Mar. 1939, ibid.; on Wada's business activities, see L. Cunha, *A Publicidade em Macau (1822–1965) (Advertising in Macau (1822–1965))* (Macau, 2000), p. 42.

16 Barbosa to MC, 5, 11 and 19 Jan. 1939, and Coelho Jr to MC, 6 and 18 May 1939, ANTT, AOS, UL-10A1, cx. 767.

17 For example, Brook, 'Collaborationist Nationalism in Occupied Wartime China', pp. 159–90.

18 Barbosa to MC, 7 Feb. 1939, ANTT, AOS, UL-10A1, cx. 767; W. Stark Toller, British Consul in Guangzhou to Archibald Clark Kerr, British Ambassador to China (in Shanghai), 30 Sept. 1939, TNA FO 371/23501. Another source puts this figure at $500 (Hermann Derek Bryan, British Consul in Macau to Principal Secretary of State for Foreign Affairs, 29 Apr. 1940, TNA, FO 371/24700).

of the Zhaoqing mission and the closing of 'two or three Chinese Customs posts established in [supposed] Portuguese waters'.[19] The key unofficial motive was, however, to negotiate with Japan the recognition of Macau's outlying islands boundary claims, which will be discussed in detail later in the chapter.[20]

During his 'special mission' to Japan, Gorgulho met a number of senior government officials and, following an organised itinerary, toured ministerial buildings, military academies, factories, a warship and other places. He visited the Portuguese chargé d'affaires at Tokyo, Antero Carreiro de Freitas, where the difficult process of negotiating Timor matters came up in conversation. The strangeness of a police commander meeting ministers whilst the highest-ranking diplomat in the country was relegated to a secondary position attests to the hijacking of formal diplomatic channels by military interests. Gorgulho was contacted by officers at the Ministry of War who wanted to discuss in private the possibility of the Portuguese government allowing the establishment of a Japanese military base in Timor, to which he promptly replied that he did not have the authority to negotiate. He did, however, attend a meeting at the Ministry of War where, having treated the matters at a personal level and thus bypassing the Portuguese legation, Gorgulho presented Macau's requests regarding the disputed islands and clarified some of Japan's proposals to Macau (the railway and the Coloane harbour ideas had been abandoned, but trade deals were still desired).[21]

Gorgulho's visit to Tokyo was used as a propaganda coup, with an article in the *Asahi Shimbun* claiming that Portugal would recognise Manchukuo, sign new trade agreements with Japan and grant facilities to Japanese troops.[22] This was vehemently denied by the Portuguese Ministry of Foreign Affairs and by Gorgulho himself, who, according to the chargé

[19] Freitas to MNE, 4 Mar. 1939, AHD, 2P, A48, M217.

[20] Ibid. Also: G. O. C. Hong Kong to War Office, 8 Feb. 1939, TNA, FO 371/23501.

[21] Copy of confidential and secret report by Gorgulho to Barbosa, 20 Mar. 1939, sent by MC to MNE, 12 Sept. 1939, AHD, 2P, A48, M217.

[22] Robert Craigie, British Ambassador to Japan to Secretary of State for Foreign Affairs, 2 Mar. 1939, TNA, FO 371/23501. A clipping of the original article 'Makao seichō waga ho ni kyōryoku: Nippo teikei no ryōkai naru – Konshū made ni jitsugen sen' ('Macau Government Will Cooperate with Us: Understanding for Japanese–Portuguese Cooperation Was Established – It Will Be Implemented by This Autumn'), *Asahi Shimbun* (1 Mar. 1939) and an English translation of the article ('The Portuguese Government at Macau will Co-operate with Japan Bringing about Better Political and Economic Understandings') can be found in AHD, 2P, A48, M217. The article was mentioned in several other reports, such as 'Japan and Macao: Understanding Reached in Tokyo', *SCMP* (2 Mar. 1939); 'Co-operation of Japan and Portugal Seen', *Shanghai Times* (2 Mar. 1939); 'Un journal japonais annonce la conclusion d'un accord nippo-portugais' ('A Japanese Newspaper Announces the Conclusion of a Japanese–Portuguese Agreement'), *Le Journal de Shanghai* (2 Mar. 1939), AHD, 2P, A48, M217. A piece due

d'affaires in Tokyo, had not talked to the press.[23] The report had apparently not even been well received by the Japanese Ministry of Foreign Affairs, as it suggested Macau wanted to deal with the Japanese military authorities, excluding the ministry.[24] Scholarship on Japanese wartime propaganda has noted the existence of a 'dual system': civilian and military.[25] As this case illustrates, a peripheral territory such as Macau could easily be caught in a complex overlap. Freitas blamed Wada for the whole affair, but Gorgulho was not completely against the attention bestowed upon him. For example, he later requested permission from the Macau authorities to wear the Order of the Rising Sun (fifth class) the Japanese emperor had awarded him.[26] The material symbols of imperial prestige generated pride, not embarrassment, and the weakness of Portuguese officials for decorations provided an easy target for propaganda. Decorations would later be used effectively by the Allies in Lisbon as well.[27]

Japan's wooing of Portuguese officials was not, however, solely circumscribed to military circles, nor to East Asia. It was a transnational affair. In Brussels, the Japanese ambassador, Saburō Kuruso, visited the Portuguese legation more than once to discuss the situation in Asia. He mentioned the 'necessity of making a deal about Macau', placing Portugal's position in China with other small powers 'such as Holland or Belgium' with whom Japan wanted to keep good relations.[28] The following month, he mentioned the possibility of developing the enclave's harbour. Everything would be 'confined to private interests, simple businesses between legally constituted companies, to ease the response to any complaint by other powers'.[29] From Lisbon, Salazar wrote back recommending the chargé

to be published by the Lisbon newspapers *O Século* and *Novidades* ('Parece estar em via de conclusão um acôrdo luso-niponico que comporta o reconhecimento da Mandchuria por Portugal' ('The Conclusion of a Portuguese–Japanese Agreement That Includes Portugal's Recognition of Manchuria Seems to Be Under Way')) was cut by the Portuguese censorship.

23 The letter from the Portuguese chargé d'affaires in Tokyo to the editor of the paper ended by stating that 'such important matters . . . can only be discussed and settled between the two Governments and never between the Government of a country and the colonial Government of the other' (AHD, 2P, A48, M217).

24 Freitas to MNE, 3 Mar. 1939, ibid.

25 B. Kushner, *The Thought War: Japanese Imperial Propaganda* (Honolulu, HI, 2006), p. 32.

26 AM, MO/AH/AC/SA/01/17164, Condecoração concedida por Sua Majestade o Imperador do Japão, ao capitão Carlos de Sousa Gorgulho (Decoration Granted by His Majesty the Emperor of Japan to Captain Carlos de Sousa Gorgulho), 1939.

27 Moreli, 'The War of Seduction'.

28 António de Séves, Portuguese Chargé d'Affaires in Brussels to Salazar, 18 Feb. 1939, AHD, 2P, A48, M217. Saburō Kuruso was later appointed ambassador to Germany (1939–41), where he signed the Tripartite Pact and, afterwards, as special envoy to Washington, where he was serving when Japan attacked Pearl Harbor.

29 Séves to Salazar, 4 Mar. 1939, ibid.

d'affaires not show interest in such conversations.[30] Even before the war began in Europe, Portuguese authorities were well aware of their precarious position at the intersection of different interests.

Portuguese–Japanese cooperation did not bring tangible results, but it did generate bad publicity. With an unwanted spotlight being cast on Portuguese–Japanese relations due to Gorgulho's trip, Governor Barbosa was recalled to Lisbon to attend a colonial conference.[31] The commander of the sloop *Gonçalves Zarco*, José Carlos Rodrigues Coelho Jr, filled in as acting governor despite rumours that Gorgulho had been promised the post.[32] The Japanese personnel in Macau also changed. Wada did not return from his trip to Japan. His place was filled by Major Watanabe Giichi, an infantry officer attached to the headquarters staff of the South China Expeditionary Force. The British saw the move as due to Wada's failure to assure the peaceful surrender of Zhongshan county, which bordered Macau.[33]

Gradually, the constructive prospects of economic cooperation gave way to threats and demands over similar matters of shipping and trade. In April, Rear Admiral Sukigara, the navy chief of staff at Guangzhou, came to Macau to request the cooperation of the Portuguese authorities.[34] Sukigara wanted two motorboats detained, suspecting they were being used for contraband. Pedro Lobo, the head of the Economic Services, purportedly was their owner. The admiral also wished to establish a temporary radio station for exclusive use of the Japanese navy. The acting governor rejected the accusation, ordered Lobo to put a stop to the use of the boats and declined authorisation for the request. Next, Japanese forces threatened to detain custom launches in the waters between Macau and Lappa, an area the Portuguese considered as under sovereignty dispute with China.[35] The minister of colonies recommended the usual blend of stalling and flattering. Such requests had to be made to the Portuguese Ministry of Foreign Affairs, not to an acting governor. The minister of colonies argued, however, that it was 'useful to remind our excellent Japanese relations [of the] advantage of not changing the status quo for the moment'.[36] In other words, their de facto authority was acknowledged.

[30] Salazar to Portuguese Legation at Brussels, 11 Mar. 1939, ibid.

[31] A British intelligence report suggested that he had been recalled for consultation with the Portuguese government regarding Japanese proposals for concessions in Timor (Hong Kong Intelligence Report No. 7/39, sent from War Office to Far Eastern Department, FO, 23 May 1939, TNA FO 371/23501).

[32] Toller to Kerr, 30 Sept. 1939, ibid.

[33] 'Extract from Hong Kong Naval, Military and Air Force Intelligence Report No. 9', sent by Major D. Stansby, War Office, to FO, 3 July 1939, ibid.

[34] Coelho Jr to MC, 22 Apr. 1939, ANTT, AOS, UL-10A1, cx. 767.

[35] Coelho Jr to MC, 24 Apr. 1939, ibid. [36] Machado to Coelho Jr, 27 Apr. 1939, ibid.

The idea of exchanging high-level visits as shadow diplomacy remained under consideration and small-scale encounters did take place. After the governor's return to Macau, the Japanese consul in Guangzhou brought an invitation from the Japanese Ministry of Foreign Affairs for Barbosa to visit Japan as 'public proof of their consideration'.[37] He replied that he would accept in due course and held a dinner for Japanese officers, where Timor and Wang Jingwei were topics of conversation.

A few months later, the Japanese consul returned, accompanied by two officers. They asked for Portuguese 'cooperation' in order to prevent a campaign of some Macau Chinese newspapers against Wang Jingwei and violent actions of pro–Chiang Kai-shek Chinese. The governor assured the consul that he was doing his part, showing a 'great number of newspaper articles [that the] censorship commission had not permitted to be published because it deemed them damaging [to the Portuguese] good friendship with Japan'. The neighbouring regions did indeed receive anti-Wang pamphlets, but, he noted, the 'Macau police had been preventing their circulation'. Barbosa assured the Japanese consul that efforts were being made to curb anti-Japanese activities and punish those who did them.[38]

This rhetoric of compliance was hollowed out by the continued use of Macau for Chinese resistance efforts, as detailed in Chapter 1. Shortly after this visit, a piece in a pro-Japanese newspaper in Guangzhou declared that Macau authorities had permitted the presence of pro-Chongqing 'enemies of Japan', including members of the Blue Shirts, a secret paramilitary movement loyal to Chiang Kai-shek.[39] A few days later, Amaro Sacramento Monteiro, the new Portuguese consul in Guangzhou, discussed the accusations with his Japanese counterpart. Monteiro argued that, even though the Portuguese wished to maintain a strict neutrality in Macau and to keep 'the best and most friendly

[37] Barbosa to MC, 23 Aug. 1939, ibid. Also in AHD, 3P, A9, M128–129 and in AHD, 3P, A9, M135.

[38] Barbosa to MC, 13 Sept. 1939, ANTT, AOS, UL-10A1, cx. 767. Also in AHD, 3P, A9, M128–129.

[39] 'Aomen dangju sang xinbinkuang bi rang kangRi fenzi Rifang yanzhong kangyi fenkai yichang' ('Macau Authorities Have Gone Mad Sheltering Anti-Japanese Terrorists: Japan Protests Energetically and with Exceptional Indignation'), *Guangdong xunbao* (13 Sept. 1939), AHD, 3P, A9, M128–129. On the Lixingshe (Society for Vigorous Practice) and the Blue Shirts, see F. Wakeman Jr, 'A Revisionist View of the Nanjing Decade: Confucian Fascism', *China Quarterly*, 150 (1997), pp. 395–432; and F. Wakeman Jr, *Spymaster: Dai Li and the Chinese Secret Service* (Berkeley, CA, 2003). Wakeman noted that 'Blue Shirts' became 'common usage for two different sorts of anti-Japanese activities in the Shanghai area after the Occupation began [in 1937]: suburban guerrilla resistance movements and urban political terrorism' (Wakeman, *Shanghai Badlands*, p. 18).

relations' with its Chinese and Japanese neighbours, 'it would be difficult, if not impossible, to avoid each and every kind of manifestation by anti-Japanese elements infiltrated in Macau, a territory that was open to the Chinese'.[40] The consul was thus implicitly admitting that the Portuguese were unable to guarantee complete neutrality in Macau.

Mounting Constraints: Japanese Pressure on Macau after 1940

Japanese interactions with Macau were linked not only to military operations in South China, but also to Southeast Asia. From 1940, Japanese pressure over the enclave became less obliging. This stemmed from two different developments: at the regional level, the occupation of Zhongshan, the county that bordered Macau; at an international level, the competition over Portuguese-controlled Timor, the eastern part of an island in Southeast Asia (the other half was then part of the Dutch East Indies). Portuguese connections to the British were once again at the forefront.

The Portuguese ceded to British lobbying to grant an Australian company rights to explore for oil in a part of Timor coveted by Japan.[41] In February, the former Japanese chargé d'affaires in Lisbon stopped at Macau on his way to Japan. He hinted that a more cooperative stance regarding Timor could only be in the interest of Macau.[42] In Tokyo, he conveyed the same to the newly arrived Portuguese minister, Luís Esteves Fernandes in a private conversation. He told Fernandes that the 'Japanese government decided to exert pressure over Macau to obtain oil concessions in Timor,' something the navy and military authorities were desperate to guarantee. Fernandes noted that such intimidation was undesirable and the Japanese government had had no reason for complaint since the 'Portuguese Government [had] always [been] willing [to] acquiesce [to] Portuguese–Japanese collaboration'.[43] Soon after, the governor of Macau commented that he believed the aim of Japan's invasion of Zhongshan had been retaliation for the oil concession in Timor not having been given to them.[44] This was likely a self-deluded exaggeration, but the connection

[40] Amaro Sacramento Monteiro, Consul in Guangzhou, to Barbosa, 30 Sept. 1939, AHD, 3P, A9, M128–129.

[41] The negotiation of this concession was a lengthy affair that preceded the outbreak of an all-out war in China in 1937. For details, see G. Stone, *The Oldest Ally: Britain and the Portuguese Connection, 1936–1941* (Suffolk, 1994), pp. 183–7.

[42] Barbosa to MC, 3 Feb. 1940, ANTT, AOS, UL-10A1, cx. 767.

[43] Luís Esteves Fernandes, Minister to Japan, to MNE, 9 Mar. 1940, AHD, 2P, A48, M217.

[44] Bryan to Kerr, 24 Mar. 1940, TNA, FO 371/24700.

to Timor should not be completely dismissed as it illustrates how China's wartime experience had multiple global connections well before 1941.

Pressure over Macau came in different guises and the Portuguese resorted even more to informal diplomacy to deal with it. In March 1940, the Japanese military authorities in Guangzhou started to demand visas issued by a representative of the Japanese police for Chinese passengers travelling from Macau. This was technically illegal, but it suggests that some Japanese forces in the region used the occupation as an opportunity to challenge the authority of a small European colonial power. The governor lamented it as a 'very embarrassing situation' and again linked Japanese actions in Macau to pressure over Timor, but, as always, the immediate response was to try to talk it over.[45]

Barbosa dispatched two envoys to meet the Japanese as his 'ambassadors', Lieutenant Júlio de Montalvão e Silva and Lieutenant Botelho de Sousa. The Portuguese consul general in Guangzhou caustically condemned this initiative, revealing the tension between colonial and diplomatic representatives in their differing approaches to Japanese forces. Monteiro complained about the governor's shadow diplomacy, sending its own emissaries to directly negotiate, in a 'disastrous' manner, with the Japanese military authorities bypassing his authority.[46] The Japanese vice consul in Guangzhou also visited Macau, demanding Portuguese cooperation in suppressing anti-Japanese activities and the use of the enclave's inner harbour for Japanese vessels in transit as well as for a number of guards en route to Qianshan, near the border with Macau. As before, by insisting that everything ought to be conducted according to the existing legislation, the governor's reply was a mixture of assurance and buying time.[47] This succession of begrudged understandings can be seen as incipient forms of collaboration.

On 30 March 1940, the same day that Wang Jingwei formed a central government in Nanjing, the Japanese occupied Qianshan, a border town that is now part of Zhuhai. Chinese sources were quoted in the press listing the demands Japanese were making to the Macau government, including retreating from disputed islands, stopping supplies to Chongqing and recognising the Zhongshan 'puppet' administration.[48]

45 Barbosa to MC, 15 Mar. 1940, ANTT, AOS, UL-10A1, cx. 767.

46 Monteiro to Lima, 19 Mar. 1940, AHD, 3P, A9, M135. He insisted on denouncing this to Lisbon on other occasions, stressing that Macau's envoys had not even briefed him about what they had come to discuss with the Japanese when he could probably do it better – or at least in better English – than they could (Monteiro to Salazar, 30 Apr. 1940, AHD, 2P, A48, M217).

47 Barbosa to MC, 20 Mar. 1940, ANTT, AOS, UL-10A1, cx. 767.

48 For example, 'Colony Menaced: Japanese Demands to Portuguese', *Daily Express* (30 Mar. 1940). The British press widely reported on the pressure on Macau in late March

Although the Portuguese denied this news, Japanese pressure over Macau was reported as far away as Brazil, Chile and South Africa, countries that had important Chinese communities hailing from Guangdong.[49] Events in the region had a global audience.

Visits of Japanese military figures to Macau continued, and not only to greet the Portuguese.[50] News that Japanese officers had met with 'supporters of the new [Chinese] regime' – that is, the RNG – in a hotel in Macau, together toasting 'Asia for the Asians', alarmed the governor. Barbosa had seen some mutual colonial benefit in working together with Japan against China, but his stance changed if Japan's discourse was nominally anti-imperialist. Facing the prospect of Japanese support for Wang, he lamented to Lisbon that it seemed apparent that 'the Japanese objective is to provoke disorder and anarchy in Macau', damaging the profits of the opium and gambling monopolies and diverting wealthy Chinese residents from the enclave.[51] The governor's words are revealing of the main concerns of Macau's economy in this period.

After gaining control of Zhongshan in March 1940, the Japanese hardened their attitude towards Macau. Relations began to turn sour, to a point that the consul in Guangzhou remarked that 'Macau is a colony but it is not the first time the invader considers it a concession.'[52] A Japanese blockade of food supplies to the enclave accompanied pressure over the Portuguese occupation of Lappa island. Exploiting the potential fractures between the invading forces and local strongmen, relaxation of the strict Japanese blockade was ensured by bribing Chinese 'puppet' authorities in Lappa, who acted against the Japanese. The British consul Hermann Derek Bryan alluded to a secret financial agreement between them and the concessionary of the gambling monopoly in Macau Fu Deyin, the chairman of the Commercial Association, and Pedro Lobo. For Bryan, Japanese policy towards Macau was taking shape: blackmail.[53] The importance of Macau power holders as privileged wartime intermediaries also began to emerge clearly here, becoming more pronounced as the 1940s rolled on and a new governor took charge.

Barbosa died of illness in Macau in July 1940, shortly after being called to Lisbon to explain a controversial issue of opium smuggling from Iran

and early April, with the news appearing in the *Times, Daily Telegraph, Evening News, Sunday Dispatch, Sunday Express, Star, Scotsman* and *News Chronicle* (clippings in AHD, 2P, A48, M217).

49 Lima to Salazar, 1 Apr. 1940, news clippings, AHD, 2P, and A48, M217.

50 Barbosa to MC, 4, 12 and 23 Apr., 1940, ANTT, AOS, UL-10A1, cx. 767.

51 Barbosa to MC, 30 Apr. 1940, ibid.

52 Monteiro to Salazar, 30 Apr. 1940, AHD, 2P, A48, M217.

53 Bryan to Viscount Halifax, Foreign Secretary, 20 May 1940, TNA, FO 371/24700.

that had been presented to the League of Nations.[54] According to a post-war report in the Braga Papers, Barbosa had long been connected to a faction of opium business dominated by Lobo, Hajee Mahomed Hassan Nemazee – an Iranian merchant with agencies in Shanghai and Macau – and Bi Lüjian (Butt Lui-kim). Their activities boomed in the early years of the war. Scandal arising from this, other business activities with the Japanese and the debacle of the Lappa invasion (which will be addressed later) convinced the government in Lisbon that Barbosa was unfit to hold office.[55] His sudden death possibly prevented a humiliating dismissal.

A permanent Japanese presence in Macau took shape from mid-1940. In early August, the acting governor received a request from the Japanese army Lieutenant General Nemoto Hiroshi to station Japanese liaison officers in Macau 'in order to strengthen relations' between the Zhongshan military detachment and the Macau government. The acting governor replied that he was not authorised to answer the request, which he interpreted as reflecting 'the will to establish [in] Macau an authentic headquarters ... linked to probable attack [on] Hong Kong'.[56]

In early September, a Japanese army liaison officer, Colonel Okubo Hiroshi, came to Macau, and the Japanese consul in Hong Kong announced that a Japanese consulate would be installed in the enclave the following month.[57] This came a few months after the British sent their consul to the city, which is indicative of the British–Japanese rivalry over Macau. The Japanese consulate was established in the beginning of October, the first consul being Fukui Yasumitsu, who remained in that post until his assassination in February 1945.[58] In mid-July 1941, a new Japanese liaison officer, Lieutenant Colonel Sawa Eisaku, who had been sub-chief of Japanese intelligence in Manchuria, arrived in the enclave.[59] His previous post attests to the circulation of personnel and know-how across the Japanese imperial sphere in China. The Japanese presence in

[54] Pinto, 'Guerra em Paz', pp. 68–9.
[55] (Unsigned, most likely written by J. M. Braga), 'Economic Currents in Macao' (undated, post-war period), p. 15, NLA, MS 4300, Box 169, 8.1/27.
[56] Acting Governor to MC, 9 Aug. 1940, ANTT, AOS, UL-10A1, cx. 767.
[57] Acting Governor to MC, 9 Sept. 1940, ibid.; MC to MNE, 17 Sept. 1940, AHD, 2P, A48, M217. Also in AHD, 2P, A48, M212.
[58] G. P. Jin and Z. Wu, 'Teria Havido Acordos Secretos entre Portugal e o Japão Durante a Segunda Guerra Mundial?' ('Were There Secret Agreements between Portugal and Japan during the Second World War?'), *Administração* 14/51 (2001), pp. 239–75, at p. 244. A news report at the time of his death stated that Fukui had arrived in Macau in January 1939, as a staff member of the Japanese chancery ('Consul do Japão' ('Japan's Consul'), *VM* (3 Feb. 1945), p. 4). According to French diplomatic files, Fukui was serving as vice consul in Guangzhou in December 1938 (Philippe Simon, Consul in Guangzhou to Frédèric Knobel, French Chargé d'Affaires in Shanghai, 30 Dec. 1938, MAE, 32CPCOM/795).
[59] Teixeira to MC, 16 July 1941, ANTT, AOS, UL-10A1, cx. 767.

Macau built up, and, by the end of the war, there were several Japanese army and naval representatives and a plethora of intelligence groups, including agents supported by the army, navy and foreign ministry.[60] Hotels constituted important bases for them, namely those along Avenida Almeida Ribeiro, with the Grande Hotel Kuoc Chai – considered the tallest building in the Portuguese empire when it opened in 1941 – reportedly 'the most popular among the Japanese'.[61]

Regular interference became the new normal and Portuguese collaboration was sought for matters within and beyond Macau. Japanese officials tried to get the acting governor of Macau to convince the CMC authorities on Lappa island to accept a Japanese director. Requests were made via the Ministry of Foreign Affairs in Tokyo, the minister in Lisbon and the consul in Hong Kong. Initially, the acting governor refused.[62] Later, instructed by Lisbon, he assured Japanese officials that he would employ his services to attain the desired outcome.[63] Little by little, the Portuguese authorities began to cede more and more to the Japanese forces. Censorship over the local press became more severe. From August to October alone, the censorship commission banned the publication of 102 articles in the local Chinese press for containing passages 'offensive to Japan and the Japanese army'.[64] Signs that something bad was brewing for the British in South China began to mount as the Japanese began to transfer some of their financial assets from Hong Kong to Macau.[65]

Japanese actions towards Macau were not altered by changes in the local Portuguese administration. The new governor of Macau, naval commander Gabriel Maurício Teixeira, who arrived in October 1940,

[60] 'Japanese Installations in Macao / Hong Kong / Kwangchowan and Occupied China', NARA, RG226, UD 173, Box 9.

[61] Ibid. Also Office of Strategic Studies (hereafter OSS), China Theatre, X-2 Branch Report, 'Macao: General Intelligence', 24 Aug. 1945, p. 5, NARA, RG226, UD 173, Box 9.

[62] Acting Governor to MC, 2 Oct. 1940, AHD, 2P, A48, M217.

[63] MNE to Fernandes, 19 Dec. 1940; MNE to Japanese legation in Lisbon, 16 Oct. 1940, ibid.

[64] It also forbade 85 articles for 'alarming the population or damaging neutrality', and 38 for 'other reasons' (MC to MNE, 17 Jan. 1941, ibid.).

[65] In August, a representative of the Japanese firm Mitsui Bussan Kaisha enquired in Macau about storage space for 3,000 tons of miscellaneous cargo from Hong Kong (General Officer Commanding Hong Kong to War Office, 9 Aug. 1940, TNA, FO 371/24688). In October, the manager of the BNU Macau informed the acting governor that several Hong Kong companies had asked to open accounts there, including Mitsui, which, he added, also financed a Timor society. He warned Lisbon that 'these precautions suggest the Japanese expect something abnormal [in the] future [of] Hong Kong' (Coelho Jr to MC, 26 Oct. 1939, ANTT, AOS, UL-10A1, cx. 767). In February 1941, Mitsui deposited 10,000 patacas at the bank (Teixeira to MC, 11 Feb. 1941, ibid.).

continued to be visited by Japanese military figures.[66] An offer to exchange intelligence was made in February 1941, with the governor answering vaguely, believing a clear refusal would be inconvenient.[67]

As the war in South China dragged on, with part of Guangdong remaining unoccupied, the conduct of the Japanese in Macau worsened with several minor clashes. For example, one night in April 1941, the consul's secretary, Sakurai Hirochi, who was drunk at the time, attacked a Portuguese soldier in the street.[68] More serious attacks followed. In early May, Japanese planes returned to Zhaoqing, bombing civilian targets in the city and dropping two bombs on the Portuguese mission, again near the flagpole hoisting the Portuguese flag. A four-page long dispatch from the consul in Guangzhou to his Japanese counterpart listed the damage and protested vigorously about the five times the mission had been hit since 1938. Following the Macau bishop's reasoning that the attack might have been intentional, the consul did not hide his irony: 'Some one, in bad faith, would even say that the bombardments would have been purposely done.'[69]

Apart from bombing Zhaoqing, Japanese soldiers pillaged and looted churches and residences of Portuguese missions in Kaiping and Chikan.[70] The Portuguese kept protesting, mainly via the consulate at Guangzhou, but their pleas for compensation went unanswered until as late as 1948.[71] Portuguese Christian missions were not the only ones to be bombed. As will be addressed in Chapter 3, other foreign mission

66 Teixeira quoted in dispatch from MC to MNE, 10 Dec. 1940, AHD, 2P, A48, M212.

67 Teixeira quoted in dispatch from MC to MNE, 4 Feb. 1941, AHD, 2P, A48, M217.

68 While the fight was taking place, a second Japanese man – later identified as the vice consul, Asahina Taiki – pleaded for him not to be arrested. The soldier later declared that he had not defended himself with the pistol and sabre he carried as they 'could produce wounds that would take the matter to serious consequences' (AM, MO/AH/AC/SA/01/18210).

69 Monteiro to T. Takatsu, Japanese Consul General at Guangzhou, 21 Aug. 1941, AHD, 2P, A48, M176. Also in AM, MO/AH/AC/SA/01/17228.

70 Monteiro to Buryo Yoshioka, Acting Consul for Japan at Guangzhou, 27 Oct. 1941; Portuguese Acting Consul in Guangzhou to Japanese Consul General at Guangzhou, 18 Nov. 1941, ibid.

71 In October, the Japanese military authorities claimed clouds had been thick and low when they had flown over Zhaoqing in May and were not aware of damages done to Third Nationals' interests. They stated an investigation could not be carried out because the area was unoccupied (Takatsu to Monteiro, 31 Oct. 1941, AHD, 2P, A48, M176). In November, they stated they could not receive claims for compensation over Kaiping since the dates of the alleged looting were unknown and it was not an occupied area (Takatsu to Monteiro, 13 Nov. 1941, AM, MO/AH/AC/SA/01/17228). In January 1942, Japanese military authorities replied via the Japanese consulate that no evidence was found of looting by Japanese soldiers, suggesting it might have been done 'either by the Chinese Army ... or by the bandits'. They refused to take any responsibility (H. Oseki, Japanese Acting Consul-General at Guangzhou to Mário Horácio Gracias, Portuguese Vice Consul in Guangzhou, 20 Jan. 1942, ibid.).

compounds also suffered and some moved part of their staff to Macau. In a war of global reverberations, neutrality meant what the belligerents wanted it to mean.

Japanese interactions with other European colonial authorities became more interventionist in the 1940s, with connected effects. As the Japanese forces advanced towards French Indochina, pressure also grew on Macau. At the end of August 1941, Consul Fukui presented the governor with a note listing pro-resistance activities taking place in Macau that he wished to see suppressed. These included the smuggling of military supplies and commodities to the areas under Chiang Kai-shek's control, secret activities of its organisations and anti-Japanese propaganda. He submitted a long set of proposals that Portugal should 'find a way to accept ... at the earliest possible date in order that the Government of Macau may offer sincere cooperation in the pursuance of Japan's policy towards the Chungking regime'.

The proposals included 'prohibiting the smuggling of military supplies and transportation of commodities' to Chongqing through the enclave and allowing Japan to inspect 'all boats in the harbour of Macau ... at any time to prevent smuggling'; extending facilities to Japanese authorities' vessels and persons and granting them protection in Macau; closing Chiang's intelligence and espionage organisations in Macau 'and deportation of hostile characters designed [*sic*] by the Japanese Authorities'; 'complete suppression of anti-Japanese propaganda rumour[s], press and organisation[s]'; and 'suppression of terrorist acts and prevention of persons of this character from entering Macau'.[72] The governor replied on 3 September. He did not object to the 'doctrine' of the requests as it was integrated with neutrality duties, but certain aspects of the 'modus faciendi' were 'offensive' to Portuguese sovereignty.[73]

Stalling was no longer as easy for the Portuguese as it had been in the first years of the conflict. The Japanese consul insisted on the proposals, clarifying them in a memorandum on their execution two days later.[74] The governor accepted, only to receive an even more comprehensive list of demands handed out by liaison officers.[75] These included: stopping 'all trades [*sic*] by junks'; delivery to the Japanese authorities of a list of ships registered at the Harbour Authority; a copy of the manifests of ships and ferries travelling between Macau and Guangzhouwan, Indochina and Hong Kong; prohibition of night-time navigation within Macau's

[72] Fukui Yasumitsu, Japanese Consul in Macau to Teixeira dated 27 Aug. 1941, sent with dispatch from Teixeira to MC, 3 Sept. 1941, AHD, 2P, A48, M212.
[73] Teixeira to Fukui, 3 Sept. 1941, ibid.
[74] Memorandum from Fukui to Teixeira, 5 Sept. 1941, ibid.
[75] Teixeira to Fukui, 5 Sept. 1941, ibid.

harbour of all ships except the government and Hong Kong boats; and not only allowing men and boats of Japanese authorities to operate on land and water at any time, but also furnishing them with arms for their self-protection.[76]

This was unacceptable for the governor who, in discussion with Japanese liaison officers, refused to provide copies of the ships' manifests and grant freedom for the Japanese authorities to circulate in Macau and its waters, as it was unthinkable to presume 'the government of Macau would undertake economic espionage for Japan'. Fine words indeed, but eventually the governor consented to: suspend trade via junks for a short period; constitute a special brigade to suppress contraband; grant gun licences to six Japanese informants to be used in smuggling suppression; hand in a copy of the names of registered boats; forbid navigation for boats with combustion engines; and permit the liaison officer to have two private boats, which were not allowed to use the flag of the Imperial Japanese Navy nor do any act of inspection or policing.[77] Seen from Macau, where the Portuguese authorities largely bowed to their demands, the Japanese were certainly not 'subaltern imperialists'.[78]

To Lisbon, the governor completely downplayed what he had consented to. In his interpretation, such demands were aimed only at readjusting the 'mechanics of contraband' in the region. With China's southern coast occupied by the Japanese, smuggling 'was only possible with the complicity and profit of the pro-Japan Chinese authorities and the Japanese themselves'. The governor's conclusion of the whole affair was that there were 'some more Japanese "partners" in contraband that needed to be paid off'.[79] The Macau government was able to cash in on its compliance. Teixeira wrote to Lisbon that exports had increased and the revenue of the taxes over tobacco had gone up from the usual 25,000 patacas to 60,000 patacas in September and 70,000 patacas in October.

The anti-smuggling brigade consisted of five Chinese appointed by the Japanese who were integrated in the Portuguese police and employed by the Harbour Authority. Teixeira's dispatch to Lisbon ended by subtly upholding the advantages of Macau's own style of diplomacy. Considering that the Japanese military commands in China were 'practically independent' from the Japanese government, the governor would seek to solve any future incidents on the spot with

[76] 'Main Points of the Execution of the Proposals (A Plan)', ibid.
[77] Teixeira to MC, 27 Oct. 1941, sent by MC to MNE, 17 Jan. 1942, ibid.
[78] J. Sand, 'Subaltern Imperialists: The New Historiography of the Japanese Empire, *Past & Present*, 225/1 (2014), pp. 273–88.
[79] Teixeira to MC, 27 Oct. 1941.

them when possible, only telegraphing Lisbon about the most important cases and writing about the others via dispatch.[80]

This reveals the presence of two apparently contradictory dynamics: a high degree of autonomy on the part of Portuguese authorities in Macau, and how they were becoming increasingly constrained by Japanese demands. When analysing sources on these negotiations, two scholars have concluded that 'there was no agreement as such', but only a modus vivendi between Portugal and Japan.[81] But modi vivendi in other cases have been seen as forms of collaboration.[82] It is clear that the terms agreed by the governor amount to a degree of acquiescence to Japanese demands. Two months later, the British capitulated in Hong Kong, and, as will be seen in Chapter 4, the Macau authorities had to cede even more in order to remain nominally unoccupied.

Portugal's Occupation of Chinese Islands

Apart from the Macau peninsula, Portugal administered the islands of Taipa and Coloane as part of its 'colony of Macau'. However, the country had tried to extend its rule over part of three other islands (Lappa, D. João and Montanha) in negotiations with China at the end of the nineteenth century and the beginning of the twentieth (see Figure 2.1).[83] The Second World War provided an excuse for some hawkish actions on the matter. Under the pretext of asserting their claims over the territories, the Macau authorities sent Portuguese forces to occupy part of the islands, notably on Montanha and Lappa. These islands to the west of Macau provide an interesting case of how the expansionist designs of two different imperial powers – Japan and Portugal – intersected in the region.

As the Japanese advances in China gained momentum, the Portuguese legation in Tokyo suggested clarification of Portugal's claims over islands near Macau. To an initial cold reply from Salazar ('it is preferable to do nothing for now regarding islands'[84]), Antero Carreiro de Freitas, the

[80] Ibid. [81] Jin and Wu, 'Teria Havido', p. 266.
[82] Wasserstein, 'Ambiguities of Occupation', p. 25.
[83] For a history of these negotiations, see A. V. Saldanha, *Negociações e Acordos Luso-Chineses sobre os Limites de Macau no Século XIX* (*Sino–Portuguese Negotiations and Agreements on Macau's Borders in the Nineteenth Century*) (Lisbon, 2010). None of these islands remains today in the form it had during the war. Lappa (Wanzai, sometimes also referred to as Duimianshan) is no longer an island. It was connected to mainland China by reclamation and integrates the Xiangzhou district of the city of Zhuhai. Dom João (Xiao Hengqin) and Montanha (Da Hengqin) are now a single island, Hengqin. A bridge links it to the Macau Special Administrative Region (SAR) of the PRC. Taipa and Coloane are part of the Macau SAR, but the two have been connected by land reclamation via an artificial isthmus known as Cotai.
[84] Salazar to Portuguese Legation in Tokyo, 22 Sept. 1937, AHD, 2P, A48, M175.

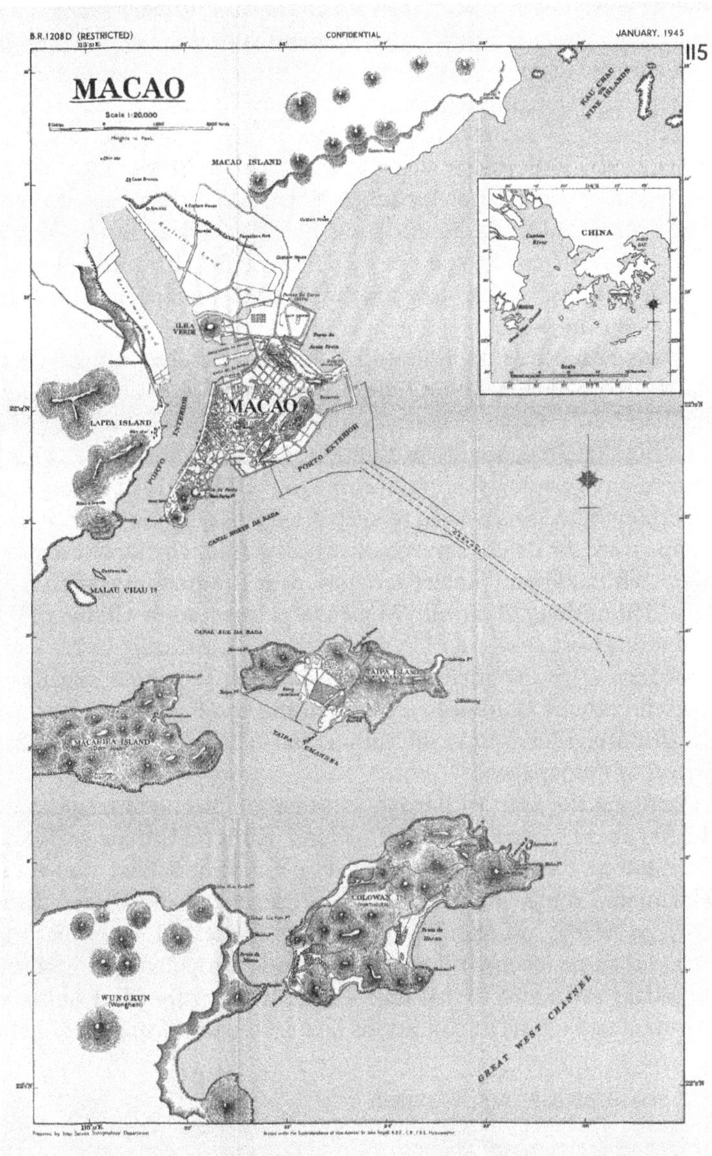

Figure 2.1 Map of Macau, 1945, showing the Portuguese-ruled Macau peninsula and the islands of Taipa and Coloane and, on the left, the islands of Lappa, Dom João and Montanha, ruled by China and occupied by Japan during the Second World War. The National Archives, ref. ADM234/670

chargé d'affaires in Tokyo, insisted on the need to clarify those claims. His reasoning was that the Japanese general staff was using a map of China made by the Chinese, which described the territories he considered under dispute as belonging to China. Therefore, Japanese military authorities could use that as an 'excuse' if they came to occupy those islands.[85] A report by a Portuguese naval commander in October 1937 further advocated Portugal's occupation of the parts it claimed if the Chinese forces retreated from these islands. He argued that 'not occupying them in the current circumstances would be giving up our rights [over the islands] forever'.[86] What exactly those rights were had been left undefined in previous decades.

The war reached the islands in 1937. By October, Chinese forces had started to open trenches in Lappa and moved on to the part of the island claimed by Portugal. Protests were made to Guangzhou and Nanjing.[87] The Portuguese embassy in London was also informed.[88] The Chinese minister in Portugal, Li Jinlun, came to the Ministry of Foreign Affairs to ascertain that China wished to keep the status quo and that the trenches in Lappa were for defence purposes against attacks by Japanese planes, and had been made on Chinese territory near the customs posts. That territory 'had nothing to do with Macau' and was 'purely Chinese'.[89] Despite Chinese assertions, on 11 November 1937, Salazar, in his capacity as president of the council, sent a dispatch approving a suggestion from the Ministry of Colonies recommending the Portuguese occupation of the disputed islands after the withdrawal of Chinese forces and before the arrival of the Japanese.[90]

Defining the islands' borders became an international affair involving the Japanese consul general in Hong Kong, Midzusawa Kosaku; the Portuguese consul, Álvaro Brilhante Laborinho; and the governor of Macau and other officials, as well as Portugal's and Japan's Ministry of Foreign Affairs.[91] From Tokyo, Freitas wrote to Lisbon that the threat of a Japanese occupation of the islands provided an opportunity to 'liquidate once and for all the old question of [border] limits between Portugal and China in conditions favourable to Portugal' as, he believed,

[85] Freitas to MNE, 23 Sept. 1937, ibid.
[86] Excerpt of Report by the Commander of the Sloop *Gonçalo Velho*, 14 Oct. 1937, AHD, 2P, A48, M176.
[87] Lima to Salazar, 1 Oct. 1937, ibid.
[88] Salazar to Portuguese Embassy in London, 3 Oct. 1937, ibid.
[89] Record of conversation between F. Calheiros and Li Jinlun at MNE, October 13, 1937, ibid.
[90] Machado, 6 Nov. 1937, and dispatch from Salazar, 11 Nov. 1937, ibid.
[91] Álvaro Brilhante Laborinho, Consul in Hong Kong to Barbosa, 27 Nov. 1937, AHD, 2P, A48, M175.

Japan would not mind the islands being occupied by a neutral country. Thinking that Japan would make Chinese collaborationist authorities agree to a Portuguese takeover of the islands, he wrote to the Ministry of Foreign Affairs led by Salazar:

Under the pretext of the threat of a Japanese occupation, and with previous establishment of a verbal and secret agreement with the Japanese Government, Portugal could occupy those islands without protests from the world and without reason for protests from the Chinese Government. In virtue of that agreement and in exchange for a well observed neutrality on the part of the Portuguese Government during the blockade, the Japanese Government would employ its influence next to the new [Chinese] Government, which will be as malleable as the Manchurian one in the hands of Japan, so that the Portuguese occupation is considered and accepted as *un fait accompli*.[92]

Negotiations between Portuguese and Japanese authorities took place at the regional level. Midzusawa returned to the Portuguese consulate in Hong Kong, where he met Gorgulho, sent by the governor of Macau with a map of the supposedly disputed territories. After the meeting, the Japanese consul handed to Laborinho a copy of a memorandum he had written to Tokyo addressing the islands. Given the sensitive nature of the matter, Laborinho travelled to Macau, where he met with the governor and several high officials of the colony's administration. Some changes to the memorandum were proposed by the governor, and the consul insisted that, when communicating this to Midzusawa, he should stress the mere informative character of such a mission, which would 'not involve obligations of any kind'.[93] Despite the jotting down of a 'Laborinho–Midzusawa memorandum', with whose content Salazar agreed, solid guarantees were not given by the Japanese government, which made clear to Midzusawa that it could not assure Portugal of prior notice should Japanese forces land on the islands because operations were often secret and only known by the government *post factum*.[94]

Indeed, the Portuguese had not been notified when, in the early morning of 28 December, Japanese troops landed on Montanha Island, with shots heard in Macau.[95] Portugal protested in Tokyo, but a local paper guaranteed that these events did not involve the neutral country in the conflict in

[92] Freitas to Salazar, 10 Dec. 10, 1937, ibid.
[93] Laborinho to Salazar, 11 Dec. 1937, ibid.
[94] Salazar to Portuguese Legation in Tokyo, 11 Dec. 1937, ibid.; Laborinho to Barbosa, 11 Dec. 1937, ibid.; Freitas to Salazar, 18 Dec. 1937, ibid.
[95] The Hong Kong press reported the affair in critical terms. The *SCMP* wrote: 'About 200 marines landed, but it is not known why the landing should have taken place, unless it was for taking the few miserable belongings, pigs and poultry of the fisherfolk on the island' ('Firing Heard at Macao: Attack on Island', *SCMP* (29 Dec. 1937), ibid.).

any way.[96] Words guaranteeing strict neutrality were often accompanied by actions indicating a murkier reality. Following the Japanese landing, the governor sent a police officer with some men to occupy Maliaohe (Manió in Portuguese), the main village on the eastern part of the island, and contacted a Japanese officer. He also sent a local administrator to inform the Chinese authorities in Zhongshan and urged for protests to be made via diplomatic channels.[97] In Hong Kong, Laborinho met Midzusawa's replacement, Nakamura Toyoichi, to express hopes that the memorandum's terms would be respected.[98] The chargé d'affaires in Tokyo presented a verbal memorandum of the Portuguese position regarding Montanha to the Ministry of Foreign Affairs.[99] Portugal's protest to Japan and the landing of Portuguese forces on the island attracted international coverage, with news clippings being sent over to Lisbon from diplomats in Paris, Rome and Havana.[100]

In the meantime, Chinese forces had gathered in the western part of Lappa. Fearing they would attack the Japanese in Montanha, the Portuguese sent an officer to meet Colonel (later Lieutenant General) Kusumoto Sanetaka in Shanghai to suggest to the Japanese forces not to land on Lappa and respect Portuguese border claims. He reserved Portugal's right to protest if that was not done. These terms were accepted, and it was stressed that understandings with the Japanese military command should be prioritised over diplomatic channels.[101] As seen earlier, diplomacy was practised via multiple means, and formal channels were but one.

The Japanese forces withdrew from Montanha one month after invading it.[102] The reason for their retreat seems less due to Portuguese protests than to the fact that Japanese soldiers posted there contracted malaria, a disease known to be prevalent on the island.[103] The Portuguese remained on the island, contrary to anything acceptable to the Chinese government. The latter made sure protests on the matter were made via proper diplomatic channels. In September 1938, Diao Zuoqian protested to the Portuguese consulate general in Guangzhou about the Portuguese occupation of

[96] 'A Ocupação da Ilha de Tai Von Cam pelo Japão' ('The Occupation of Tai Von Cam Island by Japan'), *VM* (3 Jan., 1938), p. 3.
[97] Barbosa to MC, 28 Dec. 1937, transcribed by MC to MNE, 30 Dec. 1937, AHD, 2P, A48, M175.
[98] Laborinho to Barbosa, 29 Dec. 1937, ibid. [99] Freitas to Salazar, 30 Dec. 1937, ibid.
[100] See dispatches and clippings in AHD, 2P, A48, M175.
[101] Barbosa to MC, 14 Jan. 1938, ibid.
[102] 'Retirada dos japonezes de Tai Vong Cam' (Retreat of the Japanese from Tai Vong Cam), *VM* (27 Jan. 1938), p. 4; 'Wongcam Abandoned', *SCMP* (28 Jan. 1938), AHD, 2P, A48, M175.
[103] 'Back to Wangcum', *SCMP* (15 Jan. 1938), ibid.

Montanha. This protest followed complaints by several citizens of Maliaohe to the Zhongshan county government. The villagers reported that Portuguese soldiers had beaten up three Chinese villagers and had interfered in local practices by not allowing maintenance of boats, chopping down trees and not paying for wood bought from the locals.

To guarantee respect for Chinese sovereignty, the Macau authorities were asked to withdraw their forces. Such had been guaranteed in a personal verbal note by the former chargé d'affaires at the Guangzhou consulate but had not yet taken place.[104] In fact, a *South China Morning Post* report indicated precisely the opposite. Portuguese policemen from Macau had resumed patrol of Montanha under the pretext of protecting the local population from Japanese sailors who had come to the island, robbed some residents and taken 'all available fresh water ... to cater for the Japanese warships off Chungshan [Zhongshan] county'.[105] Several months later, a vague response from Lisbon stated that the affair's resolution 'should be influenced by local conditions of the moment and largely left to the Governor's will'.[106] The Portuguese occupation was, therefore, maintained despite Chinese criticism.[107]

Of the three disputed islands, Lappa was the largest and closest to Macau. Portuguese interests in controlling at least part of the island were linked to security concerns and water provision.[108] In the absence of Governor Barbosa, the acting governor of Macau pointedly observed in May 1939 that the Portuguese occupation of Lappa 'should only be done and will have any chance of present and future success if the Chinese central government authorises it'. Contacts with the Chinese government on this issue had previously been attempted through Ling Shifen and Diao Zuoqian of the MOFA. However, their reported absence from South China, as well as of any other representatives of the central government, made it 'impossible to renew negotiations'.[109] The acting governor

104 Diao Zuoqian to Morgado, 5 Sept. 1938, ibid. The former chargé was Albano Rodrigues de Oliveira, who later served as governor of Macau from 1947 to 1951.

105 'Wang Cum Island: Portuguese Police from Macao Return There', *SCMP* (15 Sept. 1938), ibid.

106 MNE to MC, 21 Nov. 1938, ibid.

107 A Portuguese police force was still occupying Montanha in March 1939 (Barbosa, 23 Mar. 1939, AHD, 2P, A48, M176).

108 Saldanha, *Negociações*, p. 26. The idea for a project of water supply from Lappa to Macau preceded the beginning of hostilities in July 1937, and it was maintained even as they progressed. Drafts in the Braga Papers dating from January to April 1939 attest to plans for the establishment of a Sino–British company for the development of water supply from Lappa to Macau. These were to be negotiated by Zhang Huichang with the authorisation of the Chinese government (NLA, MS 4300, Box 16, 4.2/2). The plans were most likely abandoned by the subsequent occupation(s) of Lappa.

109 Coelho Jr to MC, 22 May 1939, ANTT, AOS, UL-10A1, cx. 767.

insisted on the subject of Chinese agreement in a telegram a few days later, noting that the Chinese would 'never accept our occupation of Lappa around which revolve interests of various sorts'.[110]

The situation was left idle for a while, although Japanese threats to occupy the disputed islands were used to pressure Portugal on other matters.[111] After much uncertainty, Japanese forces entered Lappa on 20 March 1940 in the midst of an attack on Zhongshan, disembarking in the north and reaching Wanzai, in the eastern part which Portugal claimed. Chinese authorities did not resist and residents from the island fled to Macau. Barbosa sent two emissaries to Qianshan to request the retreat of Japanese military from the disputed areas. They conceded and the governor sent a police force to occupy part of the island, hoisting the Portuguese flag.[112] They used the CMC station as barracks.[113] In a second informal meeting, the envoys were told that the commander of the Japanese forces had heard from the military authorities in Guangzhou that they had no information on disputed territories on Lappa. Portuguese forces were requested to leave Wanzai. The Portuguese envoys insisted the matter should be taken to the Japanese government, invoking the confidential Midzusawa memorandum.[114] Attempts at getting the Japanese to acknowledge the Portuguese occupation in this kind of back-and-forth negotiation often failed, hostage to vague commitments.

The Portuguese occupation of Lappa was done without prior notice to the Chinese government in Chongqing or even the Portuguese minister in Shanghai. Boxer was told confidentially that Portuguese advances into Lappa were made 'with the consent and approval of the local Chinese community', and the governor believed 'the matter could be settled to the mutual satisfaction of both Portuguese and Japanese by negotiation between the Foreign Office in Lisbon and Tokyo, and that the standpoint of the Chinese authorities could be safely ignored'.[115]

110 Coelho Jr [to MC], 7 June 1939, ibid.

111 In September 1939, the Japanese consul in Guangzhou, Okazaki Katsuo, came to the Portuguese consulate, where, after complaining about pro–Chiang Kai-shek activities in Macau, he stated that in the army and navy milieus in Tokyo there was an 'unfavourable environment towards Macau', the occupation of Lappa even being considered, not because it would bring Japan any added advantage, but 'as a reprisal against Macau' (Gracias to Barbosa, 11 Sept. 1939, AHD, 2P, A48, M175). Also in AHD, 3P, A9, M218–219 and AHD, 2P, A48, M212).

112 Barbosa to MC, 20 Mar. 1940, ANTT, AOS, UL-10A1, cx. 767.

113 Bryan to Kerr, 24 Mar. 1940, TNA, FO 371/24700.

114 Barbosa to MC, 22 Mar. 1940, ANTT, AOS, UL-10A1, cx. 767.

115 Report by Boxer, 26 Mar. 1940, sent from War Office to Far Eastern Department, FO, TNA, FO 371/24700.

The British consul in Macau, Hermann Derek Bryan, could certainly see Portuguese actions in Lappa for what they were: an unlawful territorial occupation accomplished by taking advantage of Japan's war on China. He wrote to the British embassy in Shanghai that the Chinese had 'been very suspicious of the policies of Macau, accusing them of intriguing with the Japanese in the hope of furthering their ambitions in regard to Lappa'.[116] The governor had assured the British consul that Portuguese manoeuvres on Lappa had been taken to safeguard Portuguese territorial waters and to 'prevent any possibility of disorder arising on Macao's doorstep'.[117] Occupying Wanzai would give Barbosa better control over Macau's inner harbour. In one of Barbosa's telegrams to Lisbon, however, the case started to take more delusional dimensions. For the governor, a possible solution for the Portuguese predicament would be stepping up colonisation efforts on the disputed island, installing 'religious, medical assistance, education and other services that would make the population respect the benefits they derive from our sovereignty'.[118] He asked for a credit of 100,000 patacas to do so. In Lisbon, the minister of colonies disagreed, fearing such initiatives would be seen as a provocation to the Japanese but – tellingly – not to the Chinese central government. 'If we have to abandon Lappa, the less we have there the less undignified it will be', he warned.[119]

A curious position in the Lappa issue was that of H. W. Bradley, CMC commissioner for the Lappa district. In April 1940, the Japanese controlled 'all the territory between the sea on one side, Shekki [Shiqi] on the upper end, the West River and the Macao frontier'. All organs of the Chinese government had withdrawn from the area, but no one had yet approached the customs authorities and they were 'formally functioning' although 'various members of the staff have been under fire from both parties'. In reality, only the Maliuzhou (Malowchow) station could make 'any pretence at actually functioning'.[120] Bryan observed that Bradley could protest over the Portuguese occupation of the customs station in Wanzai. However, timing was favourable to Macau because the only station still operating did so 'entirely at the pleasure of the Macao authorities'.[121] Bradley eventually reinstalled caretakers in the Wanzai station without objecting to the presence of the Portuguese

[116] Bryan to Kerr, 24 Mar. 1940, ibid. [117] Ibid.
[118] Barbosa to MC, 29 Mar. 1940, ANTT, AOS, UL-10A1, cx. 767.
[119] Machado to Barbosa, 1 Apr. 1940, ibid.
[120] 'Notes on the Situation in Macao', based on a memorandum by the commissioner of customs at Lappa sent by Inspector-General Frederick Maze of the CMC, to Lima, 5 Apr. 1940, AHD, 2P, A48, M217.
[121] Bryan to Kerr, 24 Mar. 1940, TNA, FO 371/24700.

police, another act of accommodation to the exceptional circumstances in the area.[122] This case provides an interesting insight on the reality of the CMC at war from the perspective of what was by then a fairly peripheral and minor station.[123]

Portuguese Withdrawal

The Portuguese occupation of Lappa in March 1940 was short-lived. Soon after, Wang Jingwei supporters took over the island. In early April, a Chinese soldier posted a notice in Wanzai advising the local people to follow Wang's policy and unite with Japan. The Portuguese did not allow it and told the soldier to leave, which he did, but it was a brief success.[124] Soon after, Chinese men, initially holding Japanese flags, took control of the north of the island and the flow of goods into Macau, demanding ever-higher amounts for supplies. The Portuguese tolerated the 'abuse' in order to 'avoid misunderstandings that may compromise the friendship relations between Portuguese and Japanese'.[125] To the minister of colonies, the Japanese strategy seemed to be one of forcing the Portuguese to leave Lappa without taking the blame, by using Chinese forces. He demanded prudence from Barbosa: '[E]ven if [we were] attacked we should retreat, avoiding any combat that is not convenient to us. If by any chance we were attacked [in] Macau, we should defend [it] to the last cartridge [and the] last man but by no means Lappa.'[126] A symbolic resistance would suffice.

Diplomatic efforts continued, however, conveyed by Portuguese officials and diplomats in Macau, Lisbon and Tokyo trying to contact Japanese military and civilian authorities, with little result. Reaction to the invading forces had gone from opportunism to frustration. Barbosa reinforced the garrison at Lappa with thirty men, and he was ready to send in twenty more, but he would not overcommit given a rumour that 'a group of around a thousand pirates [were] thinking of launching a major assault [on] Macau'.[127] The tiny peninsula, not the larger island, was his priority.

122 Bryan to Viscount Halifax, 10 Apr. 1940, ibid.

123 On the decline of the CMC presence on Lappa and neighbouring islands, see R. Nield, *China's Foreign Places: The Foreign Presence in China in the Treaty Port Era, 1840–1943* (Hong Kong, 2015), p. 154; on the predicaments of the CMC during the war, see R. Bickers, 'The Chinese Maritime Customs at War, 1941–45', *Journal of Imperial and Commonwealth History*, 36/2 (2008), pp. 295–311, and F. Boecking, *No Great Wall: Trade, Tariffs, and Nationalism in Republican China, 1927–1945* (Cambridge, MA, 2017), pp. 189–231.

124 Barbosa to MC, 12 Apr. 1940, ANTT, AOS, UL-10A1, cx. 767.

125 Barbosa to Monteiro, 24 Apr. 1940, AHD, 2P, A48, M217.

126 Machado to Barbosa, 15 Apr. 1940, ANTT, AOS, UL-10A1, cx. 767.

127 Barbosa to MC, 22 Apr. 1940, ibid.

By late April, the governor had been contacted by a man he described as a Chinese 'pseudo-officer', Lei Katchi, who claimed he had received orders from his superiors to send in troops 'to occupy and take back their territory'.[128] Given the 'usurpation of sovereign rights', Portuguese soldiers were told to retreat from the island in order to avoid a clash. Barbosa did not respond, convinced that he merely wanted money.[129] The situation escalated. Chinese forces in Lappa were reported to have risen to 200 men. Soldiers and armed civilians carrying Japanese flags opened fire on the Portuguese. At the same time, local villagers raised Chinese flags. An attack was also launched on Wanzai. An informant would later tell the Portuguese that the civilians and soldiers were from Taiwan, Xiamen and Korea, hinting that they were being used by Japan.[130] A later report also stated that the Japanese had covertly helped Wang's supporters to attack the Portuguese position.[131] After meeting a council of senior staff, the governor sent the order to retreat to Macau.[132] The entanglement of imperial spheres is also attested by the casualties on the Portuguese side. All of the men who lost their lives on Lappa were British Indian guards.

The islands' invasion(s) had been prompted by different sovereignty claims. Portuguese protests over them also faced competing authorities. Any possibility of an understanding with the Japanese military, which the Portuguese blamed for the Lappa attack, had failed. Who to protest to? In Lisbon, the minister of colonies was adamant: never to the 'Chinese government protected by Japan', as this might amount to an informal recognition of its legitimacy.[133] A protest was then submitted by the Portuguese consul in Guangzhou to his Japanese counterpart.[134] Portuguese legations in Tokyo and Washington received similar instructions to inform the Japanese and American governments of the Portuguese perspective on the incident.[135] From Shanghai, the Portuguese minister wrote to Wang Chonghui in Chongqing. He downplayed the scheming that had taken place at the Nationalists' expense, justifying that Portuguese occupation of part of Lappa was 'without any character of annexation' but served the purpose of sparing 'from the consequences of the actual hostilities a territory over which Portugal

[128] Possibly Li Jiaqi in Mandarin.
[129] Barbosa to MC, 22 Apr. 1940, ANTT, AOS, UL-10A1, cx. 767.
[130] Barbosa to MC, 26 Apr. 1940, ibid.
[131] Vasconcelos, 'Relatório', p. 25, CGD, AG-012–22–117.
[132] Barbosa to MC, 24 Apr. 1940, ANTT, AOS, UL-10A1, cx. 767.
[133] Machado to Barbosa, 25 Apr. 1940, ibid.
[134] Barbosa to MC, 26 Apr. 1940, ibid. Also in AHD, 2P, A48, M217.
[135] MNE to Portuguese Legation in Washington and in Tokyo, 1 May 1940, AHD, 2P, A48, M217.

believes she has rights which had been friendly discussed with the Chinese government'. Now that they had been ousted by 'Chinese civil and military forces, apparently directed or instigated by the Japanese', the Portuguese wished to reiterate those rights, hoping to 'resume the discussion in future date'.[136] When the war ended, the Nationalists would make sure to show that there was nothing worth discussing on the matter: the islands were Chinese territory.

Even after the retreat, Lei continued to press the Portuguese authorities in Macau. He demanded that those of his men who had been detained be set free, otherwise he would attack Macau. His request was fulfilled and the governor tried to get Japan to deal with Lei.[137]

Japanese propagandists could portray the country's wartime expansion in Asia as a project marked by racial solidarity against Euro-American colonialism, but around Macau, Japanese authorities washed their hands of the affair with an explanation that was not exactly pan-Asian. In Tokyo, the Japanese minister of foreign affairs, Nomura Kishisaburō – who would soon take up the post of ambassador to the United States – replied to a note sent by the Portuguese minister clarifying that Japanese troops were 'in no way concerned' with the incident on Lappa, stating that violent actions had been taken by local residents who, feeling 'extreme aversion to being under the control of the Moors' (meaning, presumably, South Asian policemen), had attacked them and driven them away.[138]

Shortly after, Lieutenant Colonel Oka visited the Portuguese consul in Guangzhou and hinted that the Lappa situation would be solved through diplomatic means, which the consul understood to mean the new Wang Jingwei government. To Lisbon, he reported that a definitive return of Lappa to Chinese sovereignty would give Wang a powerful political weapon by claiming that he had recovered territories Chiang's government had not taken proper care of.[139] Soon after, Lei was transferred from Wanzai and ended up being arrested in Macau for allegedly trying to mobilise some people against his replacement.[140] This episode vividly illustrates the often overlooked friction that occurred between Japanese military forces and different Chinese collaborators who had their own agenda.

Collaboration was an ambiguous practice that could shift quickly and lead to violent clashes, even amongst supposed allies. At the end of August, the Japanese began to bomb the east of Lappa, including CMC

[136] Lima to Wang Chonghui, 4 May 1940, ibid.
[137] Barbosa to MC, 26 Apr. and 18 May 1940, ANTT, AOS, UL-10A1, cx. 767.
[138] Nomura Kishisaburō to Fernandes, 20 May 1940, AHD, 2P, A48, M217.
[139] Monteiro to Salazar, 4 June 1940, ibid.
[140] Acting Governor to MC, 18 July 1940, ANTT, AOS, UL-10A1, cx. 767.

posts in Wanzai and Samei villages.[141] The pretext was to 'drive out the Chinese puppet troops', who had been breaching the Japanese-imposed blockade to Macau by supplying foodstuffs and petrol into unoccupied China, with fantastic profits.[142] The news that the reason behind the 'spectacular shelling of Lappa' had been to crack down on 'puppets' made evident to observers in Asia and in Europe that the Japanese occupation of China was marked by great tensions even with supposed collaborators.[143]

The Japanese occupation of the island was secured a few days later, according to Portuguese sources.[144] Lisbon telegraphed Tokyo to reaffirm its claims over that part of the island, 'asking for the status quo to be maintained'.[145] In September 1940, Japanese flags disappeared from Lappa and the Japanese liaison officer informed the acting governor that Japanese troops had withdrawn.[146] A complete withdrawal would only occur in early November, when the troops left to occupy neighbouring areas.[147]

Ultimately, Portuguese claims over the islands were not even acknowledged by the Japanese forces they had tried to collude with. Almost a year after the retreat from Lappa, the Japanese consul in Macau told Pedro Lobo that the Japanese military authorities did not recognise Portuguese sovereignty over Montanha, where they had had a police force since 1938. The new governor wrote to Lisbon that, although he had been verbally informed that 'there had been an agreement with the Japanese', he had found nothing about it in the archive. He then clarified his position on the disputed islands, which was different from his predecessor's: 'We have to respect the border limits question with China but we cannot use the present confusion to obtain any territorial advantage.'[148] He considered the border question suspended until 'normalcy' returned to the area.

Having tried to take advantage of the confusing situation in South China, the Portuguese ended up losing their ground, caught between the fast-changing power struggles happening around Macau and involving different collaborators and the Japanese military forces. Attempts at breaching Chinese sovereignty over the islands ended with the war. The way in which Portugal had sought to exploit China's weakness to occupy

141 Acting Governor to MC, 31 Aug. 1940, ibid.
142 Bryan to Kerr, 22 Sept. 1940, TNA, FO 371/24700.
143 'Japanese Shell Lappa Island', *NCH* (4 Sept. 1940), p. 355; 'Chronology', *Bulletin of International News*, 17/19 (1940), p. 1242.
144 Acting Governor to MC, 4 Sept. 1940, ANTT, AOS, UL-10A1, cx. 767.
145 Salazar to Portuguese Legation in Tokyo, 12 Sept. 1940, AHD, 2P, A48, M217.
146 Acting Governor to MC, 24 Sept. 1940, ibid.
147 Teixeira to MC, 7 Nov. 1940, ANTT, AOS, UL-10A1, cx. 767.
148 Teixeira to MC, 23 Aug. 1941, ibid.

territories around Macau through secret dealings with Japan is a particularly evident example of the unneutral actions that occurred in Macau during the war.

Allies of a Kind: Macau and Hong Kong

The beginnings of the British presence in China were tightly linked to Macau, but, by 1937, the Portuguese enclave's importance for the United Kingdom had become negligible.[149] When the war erupted, British interests in Macau were small, confined to the Macao Electric Lighting Company (MELCO) and Waterworks (WATCO), both managed by Frederick Johnson Gellion, a long-term resident who was also the British vice consul in the city.[150] The post had been revived in 1936, which shows that indications of Japanese competition in the enclave were not completely ignored.[151] From 1937 to late 1941, British attitudes towards Macau were marked by cautious inter-imperial cooperation through information exchange but with the avoidance of concrete commitments.

Personal networks were central to links between Macau and Hong Kong. A key figure in these was Captain (later Major) Charles Ralph Boxer, a naval intelligence officer stationed at the British colony.[152] Boxer was fluent in Japanese and Portuguese and is now best remembered as one of the most eminent historians of the Portuguese empire. He shared official documents and intelligence with the Portuguese consul in Hong Kong and the Macau authorities.[153] He also had links of personal friendship with the governor of Macau, Tamagnini de Barbosa, and figures of the Macanese elite such as Jack Braga.[154]

[149] On earlier connections, see A. Coates, *Macao and the British 1637–1842: Prelude to Hong Kong* (Oxford, 1988); R. M. Puga, *The British Presence in Macau, 1635–1793* (Hong Kong, 2013).

[150] A. P. Blunt, British Consul General at Guangzhou to Kerr, 13 Aug. 1937, TNA, FO 371/20988.

[151] 'Macau H. B. M. Vice-Consul Mr. Gellion Sets to Work', *Canton Truth* (27 June 1936), p. 23, NLA, MS 4300, Box 84, 14.2/14.

[152] Boxer was promoted to major in June 1940 ('Major C. R. Boxer', *VM* (17 May 1940), p. 5).

[153] For example, Laborinho to Salazar, 15 July 1938, AHD, 3P, A9, M128-129. Also see D. Alden, *Charles R. Boxer: An Uncommon Life* (Lisbon, 2001), p. 93.

[154] The Braga Papers held at the National Library of Australia hold letters and work drafts attesting to the long-term friendship between Boxer and Braga, who shared an interest in the history of the Portuguese presence in East Asia in the early modern period and also shared intelligence on the situation in South China. See, for example, NLA, MS 4300, Box 9, 3.2/2. Another of Boxer's informants was Lieutenant P. da Costa, the governor's

British officials were paying close attention to Japanese actions in Macau and to Portuguese responses to them. After talking to the governor about 'Japanese penetration in Macau', Boxer concluded that, whilst Barbosa 'appears to be genuinely pro-British', it was nevertheless possible for him to be 'tempted to fall in with some of the Japanese proposals' if he could not 'obtain elsewhere the necessary support for his schemes for improving Macau's economic conditions'.[155] To discourage any Portuguese perceptions of neglect by the British, A. P. Blunt, consul general in Guangzhou, visited Macau in early August 1937. One of the main goals of his trip was 'to counteract an alleged tendency towards closer relations with the Japanese'. He confirmed that attempts at Japanese penetration had been occurring since the late 1920s, but they had mostly been rejected. The governor's pro-British stance was apparent to him as well.[156]

Much like Japanese–Portuguese interactions, Anglo–Portuguese contacts about Macau were also made in Europe. The Portuguese ambassador to London, the anglophile Armindo Monteiro, discussed the situation at the Foreign Office (FO) with Deputy Under-Secretary Alexander Cadogan in September. Cadogan had been minister plenipotentiary and later ambassador to China between 1933 and 1936 and told Monteiro that Macau was not in the same danger as Hong Kong. 'If Japan wanted a footing on the Chinese coast there were a hundred other places they could choose without antagonising Portugal,' was his prescient assessment.[157] Monteiro left the conversation with the impression that British foreign policy towards Japan was marked by 'extreme caution'.[158]

The ambassador also visited the foreign secretary, Anthony Eden, a few days later to discuss the situation in East Asia. Monteiro stressed Portuguese reinforcement of its army and navy presence in Macau, but expressed the Portuguese desire for closer contacts between the governors of Hong Kong and Macau.[159] Some Macau

private secretary with 'pro-British tendencies'. It was he who told Boxer in March 1937 that the Japanese had not made any attempts to secure control in Macau after a failed scheme to establish a sugar refinery on Coloane (Minutes of Conversation between Gibbs and Boxer Sent to the British Consulate in Guangzhou, 20 Mar. 1937, TNA, FO 371/20988).

155 Boxer to Chaplin, War Office, 22 July 1937, ibid.

156 Blunt to Kerr, 13 Aug. 1937, ibid.

157 Record of conversation between Cadogan and Monteiro, 21 Sept. 1937, ibid.

158 Monteiro to Salazar, 17 Sept. 1937, AHD, 2P, A48, M176.

159 Draft of Conversation between Eden and Monteiro Sent to the British Embassy in Lisbon, 23 Sept. 1937, TNA, FO 371/20988.

officials preferred to respond favourably to Japan, but Monteiro favoured a strengthening of the old alliance. A visit by the acting governor of Hong Kong, Norman Lockhart Smith, to Macau had been prepared before the arrival of the new governor, Geoffry Northcote, and Monteiro asked for defence issues to be discussed then. In a meeting in London, British officials decided that the acting governor could discuss local defence, 'but not to appear to commit the Colony or His Majesty's Government in any way'. The Colonial Office (CO) assistant under-secretary, Henry Moore, argued that 'if the whole thing were kept vague then any further approach and request for a definite commitment could be more easily refused'.[160] The Britons' vague commitment towards their Portuguese allies was somewhat similar to their stance towards the Chinese central government.

The acting governor's visit took place in late October and nothing much came of it but a simple recommendation for enhancing commercial relations between Hong Kong and Macau. Barbosa did not raise the key question of local defences. Instead, Smith gathered a number of impressions of the governor's attitude towards China and Japan that highlight the ambiguity of Portuguese stances towards the conflict. According to him, Barbosa was more preoccupied with 'Chinese irredentism' than with Japanese penetration in Macau, being more favourable to the British than to the Japanese where foreign capital was needed.[161] The following year, in November, Governor Northcote also made an official visit to Macau.[162] These visits gave the impression of a close relationship and a coordinated strategy, although they fell quite short of a united front.

Lack of commitment did not mean lack of attention to what was happening in Macau. Evidence of this was the dispatch of a consul to replace Gellion while he was temporarily absent from the territory. Hermann Derek Bryan arrived in Macau in February, in the midst of a tense period of Japanese demands, and one day after a complaint from the governor to Gellion that he was being ignored by the British authorities.[163] The following year, Bryan took up a permanent consular post in Macau.[164]

[160] Note on Meeting, CO, 27 Sept. 1937, ibid.

[161] Norman Lockhart Smith, Acting Governor of Hong Kong to Colonial Secretary, 26 Oct. 1937, ibid.

[162] 'O Governador de Hongkong visita oficialmente Macau' ('The Governor of Hong Kong's Official Visit to Macau'), *VM* (7 Nov. 1938), pp. 2, 4.

[163] Blunt to Kerr, 14 Mar. 1939, TNA, FO 371/23501.

[164] Acting Governor to MC, 18 July 1940, ANTT, AOS, UL-10A1, cx. 767.

Boxer had been assured in a meeting with the Macau chief of police, Gorgulho, that the governor, although having come to 'some sort of modus-vivendi' with Japan, still prioritised 'closer and more friendly relations' with Hong Kong.[165] Despite the suspicious messenger, this was likely true. Nevertheless, Gorgulho's visit to Tokyo sounded alarms amongst some British observers.[166] Following the *Asahi* report, there was fear that, on Gorgulho's return, the governor would leave for Lisbon 'to undertake the final negotiations', which would include the recognition of Manchukuo. Anxieties about Portugal's stance in East Asia were very much linked to what was happening in Europe, where war broke out a few months later. The fact that Franco's Spain had recognised Japan's puppet state in the north-east was seen as possible influence over Salazar's Portugal. A report in the *South China Morning Post* emphasised the desirability of Portugal not venturing too far from its traditional ally: 'Portugal's best insurance policy is still her alliance with Britain – especially for her colonial possessions and for her trade. No other protector can offer better terms for Portugal's co-operation.'[167] The advice seems to have been heeded.

Sino–British cooperation was understood on a global scale, with actions in Asia having repercussions elsewhere. This view was particularly promoted by a few key figures. One of them was Boxer. In a 1939 report, he noted complaints over the absence of a British representative in a national holiday celebration at Macau. He stressed that such occasions should not be wasted, particularly because the German and Italian consuls at Guangzhou attended them, and given British attempts to ensure Portugal's support in Europe. He painted a perceptive picture of the Portuguese and of Macau's potential importance:

> The Portuguese are accurately described as our oldest allies, and they have also (and with equal justice) been described as our worst; but in either case it is better to treat them as friends than as potential enemies, for if they eventually do line up with the Axis Powers, Macau may well become something more than a mere nuisance to Hong Kong.[168]

165 Record of Conversation between Captain Gorgulho and the G.S.O.3 (Intelligence), Hong Kong, 1 Feb. 1939, TNA, FO 371/23501.

166 France was equally concerned. The French ambassador visited the Portuguese chargé d'affaires in Tokyo to enquire about the veracity of the report and to complain about concessions to the Japanese made by the Macau authorities (MNE to Portuguese Legation in London, 13 Mar. 1939, AHD, 2P, A48, M217).

167 'Portugal's Position', *SCMP* (3 Mar. 1939), ibid.

168 Report by C. Boxer, 4 Aug. 1939, sent by the War Office to the FO, 2 Nov. 1939, TNA, FO 371/23501.

The Hong Kong press often reported on the situation in Macau, and even the British press in Europe picked up on reports about the enclave. This was a source of tension for the Portuguese authorities who, revealing their colonial insecurities, believed that a campaign had been mounted against them. Nonetheless, relations between the two colonies remained sound. Barbosa went on an official visit to Hong Kong in March 1938, his successor returning in May 1941.[169] Whilst the press in Macau refrained from reporting anything concerning the effects of the war in China on the territory apart from the arrival of refugees and the rising cost of living, there was something far from neutral coming out in the pages of the enclave's leading Portuguese-language newspaper, *A Voz de Macau*. Particularly during 1940, pro-British articles and cartoons, as well as propaganda photos of the British war effort in Europe, were often published.[170]

In the beginning of December 1941, as the Japanese attack on Hong Kong unfolded, communications between the British colony and Macau were completely interrupted, possibly for the first time in their history. Macau businesses began to reject Hong Kong dollars, but the government worked out an agreement with the local moneychangers to continue accepting that currency. The new governor, Gabriel Teixeira, justified his pro-British decision by linking the future of the Portuguese in Macau to Hong Kong. '[I]f England loses the war, I don't believe we will stay in Macau [;] if it wins [,] our gesture would be presented as [an act of] trust [and] friendship.'[171] Veiled assistance to the British would continue during the remaining war years, when Macau became more precious to the British than ever before, as will be seen in Chapter 5.

Conclusion

Whilst China and Japan's entry into a global Second World War is often dated to 1941, the case of Macau and its surrounding areas reveals multiple connections between European and East Asian actors from the start of an all-out war in China in 1937. Macau was at the intersection of different regional, national and imperial interests and motivated manoeuvres and protests at the international level. From 1937 to late 1941,

[169] 'Visita oficial de S. Exa. o Governador a Hongkong' ('Official Visit of H. E. the Governor to Hong Kong'), *VM* (21 Mar. 1938), p. 4.

[170] The pro-British tone was so overwhelming that sometimes it could almost be read as a veiled criticism of Portugal's authoritarian regime. See, for example, the last paragraph of an article that read: 'England is rich – because England is, above all, a country of freedom' ('A Inglaterra capitalista' ('Capitalist England'), *VM* (9 July 1940), p. 1).

[171] Teixeira to MC, 10 Dec. 1941, ANTT, AOS, UL-10A1, cx. 767.

neutrality was a policy that all foreign powers (other than Japan) with interests in China adopted. As this case illustrates, however, complete neutrality was impossible to ensure. The interplay of imperial interests, projections of power and structural weaknesses dictated a course of variable degrees of accommodation by the Macau Portuguese administration. Both Portuguese officials and other key actors in the region – Japanese forces, the British authorities in Hong Kong and, as seen in the previous chapter, Chinese of different camps – also engaged in different forms of collaboration.

The progressively higher pressure Japan exerted on Macau was marked by contradictory actions. On one hand were promises of help for developing the enclave as a competitor to Hong Kong. On the other were threats over disputed territories, supply blockades and bombings of Portuguese missionary properties in South China. Sharing with them an old alliance and the common trait of being European colonialists in China, the British were regarded by the Portuguese in Macau as natural partners and protectors. Even though it soon became apparent that they could not be relied upon for significant assistance, the Portuguese refrained from actions that would antagonise the United Kingdom, and cooperation with Hong Kong was attempted whenever possible. Portuguese actions towards the two major imperial powers in China – Japan and Britain – are illustrative of the interconnectedness of foreign actors in China. Colonial powers did not exist in isolation but responded to each other, and those reactions were monitored and sometimes exploited by the Chinese authorities who themselves engaged with these powers.

The crisis in South China gave way to different opportunistic experiments around Macau, some far from the supposed inactivity suggested by its neutral status. As Chinese resistance energies focused on Japan, Portuguese authorities sought to take advantage of the situation to occupy, with Japanese consent, parts of islands they considered under dispute. However, the Portuguese were caught between power struggles that revealed the instability of Japanese relations with Chinese collaborators and the divisions amongst the latter. Collaboration was often as murky as neutrality and the last Portuguese attempt to take over those islands failed.

Three milestones marked a hardening of the Japanese position vis-à-vis Macau: the occupation of the provincial capital, Guangzhou, in 1938; the takeover of Shiqi, the capital of the Chinese county adjacent to the enclave, in 1940; and the appointment of a pro–Wang Jingwei provincial government to Guangdong in that same year. By the end of 1941, despite its neutrality, Macau was more isolated and largely under informal

Japanese control, a situation that would be aggravated after the occupation of Hong Kong.

Multiple international actors interacted in South China and neutrality created opportunities that led to forms of collaboration with different sides. Diplomatic and military manoeuvres are essential to understand the ambiguities of Macau's wartime experience, but these must be considered alongside the social changes that shaped neutrality and collaboration. The next chapter will address these in detail, considering the arrival of thousands of refugees from Shanghai and Guangdong province who came to Macau in the late 1930s and early 1940s.

3 Crisis and Opportunity

Refugees in Wartime Macau

In an anthology of oral testimonies collected by two journalists around the time of Macau's handover, Henrique de Senna Fernandes, lawyer, novelist and member of a distinguished Macanese family, recalled the war years in the enclave and the 'thousands and thousands' of Chinese refugees he had encountered:

> They came wretched, crippled, blind, sick; they came and the city was crowded with people. There was lack of supplies, lack of rice – which set the price for all other [products] –, lack of sugar, but the government policy, back then, was to let everyone in. Macau was the last refuge for all these unfortunate people coming from the most varied parts of China.[1]

Fernandes, then a young man, had been living in Guangzhou when the Japanese invasion forced him, like many Portuguese Eurasians in mainland China, back to Macau.[2] The quote hints at the challenges the arrival of so many refugees posed to the Portuguese-administered enclave: the relatively unrestrained arrival of refugees hailing from different places in China, the lack of provisions and the concentration of a large number of people in a small territory. Fernandes often evoked the war in his semi-autobiographical short stories. Acclaimed as masterpieces of Macanese literature, they capture the contradictions of the period and the diversity of refugees.[3]

This chapter explores how the exodus to Macau was both a crisis and an opportunity for the enclave's colonial authorities, local elites and refugees. It argues that refugee relief was marked by the entanglement of public and private interests. Chinese elites, Portuguese authorities and representatives of other states and institutions used welfare and charity to attain prestige and legitimacy. Whilst they tended to cater to different

[1] F. Lima and E. C. Torres, *Macau entre Dois Mundos* (*Macau between Two Worlds*) (Lisbon, 2004), pp. 71–2.
[2] J. McGivering, *Macao Remembers* (Oxford, 1999), p. 96.
[3] H. S. Fernandes, *Nam Van: Contos de Macau* (*Nanwan: Macau Short Stories*) (Macau, 1997); H. S. Fernandes, *Mong-Há* (Macau, 1998).

constituencies, their activities and modi operandi often overlapped. In fact, each of them was unable to operate entirely isolated from the others due to Macau's smallness and density. Diverse and sometimes competing relief providers came to collaborate in different ways to manage the refugee influx into neutral Macau, in however a partial way and with varying degrees of effectiveness. For many of those seeking sanctuary in Macau, the enclave guaranteed enough freedom from Japanese harassment, and a space to continue their pre-war activities, such as teaching. Many of the poorest refugees faced miserable conditions, but the positive impact of the refugee influx on Macau's financial, cultural and educational sectors before the occupation of Hong Kong in late 1941 should not be underestimated.

The Macau experience ought to be seen as part of the social history of the Second World War in China. It had striking similarities with other neutral territories that have often been regarded as exceptional, notably Shanghai's International Settlement and French Concession, where both municipal authorities and private institutions played important roles in refugee relief.[4] Shanghai was also one of the most important places of origin of the refugees who found themselves in Macau (see Figure 3.1). The mobility of displaced persons thus connected several major urban centres in China, linking occupied coastal cities to the unoccupied 'great rear area' (*da houfang*) in the interior.

This chapter will explore the role of state(s) and society in refugee relief and interrogate how they intersected in the case of the two main communities of the first wave of refugees that arrived in Macau in the 1930s: Chinese and Portuguese Eurasians from Shanghai and Guangdong province. Their growing number and multiple identities are key to understanding Macau's wartime cosmopolitanism and its challenges.

Refugees in Wartime Macau: A Comparative Perspective

China's War with Japan affected a massive number of people, the total number of refugees impossible to determine but with estimated figures ranging from 20 million to nearly 100 million.[5] Previous studies on how the Chinese central government, local authorities (sometimes foreign), civic and religious organisations and others dealt with refugees have

[4] For example, H. Zurndorfer, 'Wartime Refugee Relief in Chinese Cities and Women's Political Activism, 1937–1940', in B. K. L. So and M. Zelin (eds.), *New Narratives of Urban Space in Republican Chinese Cities: Emerging Social, Legal and Governance Orders* (Leiden, 2013), pp. 65–91, at p. 74.

[5] D. Lary, *The Chinese People at War: Human Suffering and Social Transformation, 1937–1945* (Cambridge, 2010), p. 28.

Figure 3.1 Refugees waiting to leave Shanghai, 1937. Photograph by Malcolm Rosholt. Image courtesy of Mei-Fei Elrick and Special Collections, University of Bristol Library (www.hpcbristol.net)

considered different areas of occupied and unoccupied China and have covered different actors, strategies and goals.

Studies on Shanghai have highlighted how the role of the state in refugee management was articulated with pre-existing and new networks and institutions, such as religious missions, native place associations (*tongxianghui*) and foreign authorities.[6] The challenges and limitations

[6] For example, T. Lincoln, 'Fleeing from Firestorms: Government, Cities, Native Place Associations and Refugees in the Anti-Japanese War of Resistance', *Urban History*, 38/3 (2011), pp. 437–56, at p. 439; N. Dillon, 'The Politics of Philanthropy: Social Networks and Refugee Relief in Shanghai, 1932–1949', in N. Dillon and J. C. Oi (eds.), *At the Crossroads of Empires: Middlemen, Social Networks, and State-Building in Republican Shanghai* (Stanford, CA, 2008), pp. 179–205.

of state assistance and competing government interests in reaching, mobilising and managing refugees elsewhere in China, such as in Henan and Zhejiang provinces, have also been studied.[7]

Some authors have privileged the wartime capitals of Wuhan and Chongqing and the role of the Chinese central government under the Nationalists, linking refugee management to state-building efforts and popular mobilisation, and emphasising how wartime relief provision laid the foundations for a post-war welfare state.[8] This was also observable at South China's colonial frontier. According to the China Information Committee, 'by the end of June, 1943, 994,893 overseas Chinese had registered with the Urgent Relief Commission for Overseas Chinese' in Hong Kong and Macau.[9] Although it has remained under-researched, the central government's interactions with destitute refugees in South China was certainly not negligible.

The British colony of Hong Kong, the French leased territory of Guangzhouwan and the French Concession and the International Settlement in Shanghai constitute the best comparative cases to understand the social experience of Macau during the war. These were urban spaces framed by overlapping transnational interests and actors where the desire to display colonial order and prestige faced the challenge of an unprecedented refugee influx that profoundly shaped their wartime existence and reconfigured the power of Chinese relief providers. It is estimated that, as a result of the battle of Shanghai from August to November 1937, the influx of refugees into the foreign-ruled concessions led to a population rise of 2.8 million.[10] The authorities sought to limit the arrival of refugees, regarding them as a threat to their sense of colonial order, a health hazard and an unwelcome financial burden.[11] Sending refugees 'back' to their places of origin was attempted, as was the confinement of destitute refugees in camps for 'beggars'.[12]

[7] M. S. Muscolino, 'Violence against People and the Land: The Environment and Refugee Migration from China's Henan Province, 1938–1945', *Environmental History*, 17 (2011), pp. 291–311; M. S. Muscolino, *The Ecology of War in China: Henan Province, the Yellow River, and Beyond, 1938–1950* (Cambridge, 2015); Schoppa, *In a Sea of Bitterness*.

[8] S. R. MacKinnon, *Wuhan, 1938: War, Refugees and the Making of Modern China* (Berkeley, CA, 2008); R. Mitter, 'Classifying Citizens in Nationalist China during World War II, 1937–1941', *Modern Asian Studies*, 45/2 (2011), pp. 243–75.

[9] *China Information Committee Daily Bulletin*, 1142, 13 Aug. 1945, TNA, FO 371/46224.

[10] M. C. Bergère, *Shanghai: China's Gateway to Modernity* (Stanford, CA, 2009), p. 290.

[11] Mitter, *China's War with Japan*, p. 185; C. Henriot, 'Shanghai and the Experience of War: The Fate of Refugees', *European Journal of East Asian Studies*, 5/2 (2006), pp. 215–45, at p. 220.

[12] Henriot, 'Shanghai and the Experience of War', p. 224; J. C. Chen, *Guilty of Indigence: The Urban Poor in China, 1900–1953* (Princeton, NJ, 2012), pp. 157, 161.

In Hong Kong, the arrival of refugees generated analogous responses, including concentration of poor Chinese refugees in camps outside the main urban areas and attempts to 'repatriate' them to mainland China.[13] If similar worries of imposing colonial control, particularly in the field of hygiene, can be identified in wartime Macau, there was a marked difference in the Portuguese authorities' attitude towards refugees. As will be detailed later in the chapter, guaranteeing their protection was often seen as potentially advantageous. Although analogous drives to impose colonial control and move unwanted refugees took place in Macau, there was, however, an important difference: Portuguese authorities did not attempt to prevent the entrance of refugees and used their relative openness as a shield against accusations of collaboration.

Even if British and French reluctance to accept refugees in Shanghai contrasted with Portuguese willingness to take them in Macau, relief practices were remarkably similar in both locales. In Shanghai, government institutions, civic associations and prominent individuals joined efforts to tackle the refugee crisis.[14] A prominent role was played by Chinese associations that succeeded due to the 'strength of the elite networks that helped coordinate their activities'.[15] Prominent businessmen such as Yu Xiaqing and the Green Gang boss, Du Yuesheng, assumed leading roles in philanthropic endeavours during the war in Shanghai, enhancing their influence in local and national circles.[16]

The same occurred with Chinese elites in Macau. The formation of safe havens to tackle refugee management was also emulated. In Shanghai, around 200 refugee camps were established.[17] The largest was the Jacquinot Safety Zone, devised by a French Jesuit priest.[18] This inspired the establishment of the Nanjing Safety Zone, where several foreign missionaries also played important roles in refugee management and in recording events for posterity.[19] In Macau, a refugee safety zone was also

[13] H. F. S. Lopes, 'The Impact of Refugees in Neutral Hong Kong and Macau', *Historical Journal*, 66/1 (2023), pp. 210–36, at pp. 222–6.

[14] Henriot, 'Shanghai and the Experience of War', p. 227; P. Stranahan, 'Radicalization of Refugees: Communist Party Activity in Wartime Shanghai's Displaced Persons Camps', *Modern China*, 26/2 (2000), pp. 166–93, at p. 169.

[15] Dillon, 'The Politics of Philanthropy', p. 183.

[16] Ibid.; B. G. Martin, 'Du Yuesheng, the French Concession, and Social Networks in Shanghai', in N. Dillon and J. C. Oi (eds.), *At the Crossroads of Empires: Middlemen, Social Networks, and State-Building in Republican Shanghai* (Stanford, CA, 2008), pp. 65–84.

[17] Henriot, 'Shanghai and the Experience of War', p. 236.

[18] M. R. Ristaino, *The Jacquinot Safety Zone: Wartime Refugees in Shanghai* (Stanford, CA, 2008).

[19] K. Zhang (ed.), *Eyewitnesses to the Massacre: American Missionaries Bear Witness to Japanese Atrocities in Nanjing* (New York, 2001). Other accounts of the role of missionaries can be read in D. Lary, 'A Ravaged Place: The Devastation of the Xuzhou Region, 1938', in D. Lary and S. MacKinnon (eds.), *Scars of War: The Impact of Warfare on*

envisioned at one point, camps were established to house and confine the poorest refugees, and religious groups, including Christian and Buddhist, played a part in relief activities.

Although its story is part of the complex social history of the war in China, Macau also had its own particularities. Unlike most of the aforementioned locales, it remained under foreign administration for the duration of the war. It was not ruled by the Chinese government, and so its state-building efforts through refugee management had a more indirect connection to the enclave. Macau was never under formal Japanese occupation, although Japanese control over the enclave was tightly exerted in various ways. Civil society in Macau was instrumental in ensuring the effective management and relief of those displaced, even if the Portuguese administration reaped the symbolic benefits of being seen as the protector of refugees.

In reality, a myriad of actors cooperated frequently, even if harbouring different national and political goals. These included colonial authorities, local charities, elite figures, representatives of different states and transnational institutions. Existing studies of refugees in wartime China, both the ones focusing on the unprecedented role the Chinese state played in refugee relief and those highlighting personal narratives of suffering, privilege a domestic perspective.[20] Taking a more global perspective, this book calls attention to the presence of different refugee communities that came to coexist and interact in Macau in a shared experience of displacement.

Who and How Many

'Refugee' was, and to some extent remains, a complex category.[21] Despite attempts to achieve an internationally recognised definition of refugee in the League of Nations, the one codified in the 1951 UN Refugee Convention had yet to exist during the Second World War. This book regards as refugees those who sought refuge in Macau after leaving their place of origin or domicile to flee war, external aggression or occupation. This follows the usage of the term in primary and secondary

Modern China (Vancouver, 2001), pp. 98–116, and E. J. Christensen, *In War and Famine: Missionaries in China's Honan Province in the 1940s* (Montreal, 2005).

20 For example, Lary, *The Chinese People at War*; Schoppa, *In a Sea of Bitterness*; MacKinnon, *Wuhan, 1938*.

21 A. T. Fragomen Jr, 'The Refugee: A Problem of Definition', *Case Western Reserve Journal of International Law*, 3/1 (1970), pp. 45–69; A. E. Shacknove, 'Who Is a Refugee?', *Ethics* 95/2 (1985), pp. 274–84; W. T. Worster, 'The Evolving Definition of the Refugee in Contemporary International Law', *Berkeley Journal of International Law*, 30/1 (2012), pp. 94–160.

sources that refer to those seeking refuge in Macau as refugees (*nanmin* in Chinese, *refugiados* in Portuguese), regardless of their socio-economic status, nationality or access to state assistance. When the war ended, an exodus from Macau ensued, confirming that the neutral enclave had been a temporary haven that attracted refugees fleeing war but was not seen as a final destination.

Macau's role as a place of refuge had centuries-old precedents. As a foreign-administered enclave, it had long been a haven for people – Chinese and others – escaping conflict, persecution and natural disasters. A visible example of how refugees shaped Macau in the past is the foremost architectural symbol of the territory today: the carved façade of the ruins of St Paul. This was the work of exiled Japanese Christians in the seventeenth century. However, the number of refugees entering Macau during the Second World War was unprecedented. That momentous scale had wide consequences. It framed the way that collaborative relationships were forged, kept and defended. The variety of nationalities of those who sought refuge in Macau was also striking. Often, people's identity was more fluid and plural than their citizenship, adding to the complex reality of interactions between communities and blurring the line of national interests at stake in the enclave, as will be addressed later.

The number of refugees who arrived in Macau during the war was a key factor in conditioning responses by state and non-state actors to the crisis of displaced persons. Exact figures are as impossible to ascertain for Macau as they are for mainland China.[22] Even when authorities compiled data on arriving refugees, acquiring definitive figures was an insurmountable task due to the scale of the flight, the existence of multiple administrative circumscriptions and the multiplicity of ways people found to bypass official channels. In Macau, no authority compiled systematic data on all refugees entering or leaving the territory during the war years. Available statistical records do not provide accurate figures since the flow of people and goods entering and exiting Macau was often hard to control. However, by reading official statistics alongside different references in archival documents and memoirs, it is possible to conclude that the population in Macau reached around half a million people during the war, a threefold increase from pre-war years. According to a government census in 1927, the population of Macau was 157,175, increasing to 245,194 in 1939. It was only 188,896 in 1950, at the end of the Chinese Civil War.[23]

[22] MacKinnon, *Wuhan, 1938*, p. 47; Mitter, *China's War with Japan*, p. 117.
[23] Quoted in Barreto, *Macau during the Sino–Japanese War*, p. 31.

These numbers fail to give a full picture of the refugee influx during all the war years. However, an analysis of the number of passengers who arrived in Macau in the 1940s provides approximate figures (Appendix 1). Between 1940 and 1945, there was an increase of more than 200,000 people that, if added to the total population in 1939, confirms that around half a million people were in Macau during the war. The peak of foreign arrivals in 1942 coincides with the Japanese occupation of Hong Kong, and the peak of departures in 1945 matches the end of the war, confirming that the decisive factor in the fluctuation of Macau's population in this period was the Second World War; it was a major driver for migration in and out of the enclave between 1937 and 1945, even if many of the newcomers had family connections there.

Other sources corroborate these approximate figures. During a press conference in 1946, the governor of Macau stated that, during the war, the enclave's population had been between 450,000 and 500,000.[24] Manuel Teixeira, a Portuguese missionary and local historian who lived through the war years in Macau, later wrote that the enclave's population swelled from 200,000 to half a million during the war.[25] In April 1942, the British consul listed the population at 407,300 people, and in his memoirs he stated that from 'some 150,000, the population grew during this period to 450,000', of which around 10,000 refugees (mostly from Hong Kong) were under his care.[26] A report penned by a businessman who escaped from Macau described 'a population of over 400,000 Chinese', a figure that had 'increased steadily since the Japanese occupation of Hongkong'.[27] A telegram from the Macau Red Cross to the Lisbon headquarters reported a total population of 'approximately four hundred thousand people, half of whom [are] Chinese refugees'.[28] Some authors suggest the number of people was even higher, around 600,000 people or even more than 1 million during the war years.[29] These broadly consistent

24 'Declarações do Sr. Governador de Macau à Imprensa' ('The Words of the Governor of Macau to the Press'), *Boletim Geral das Colónias (General Bulletin of the Colonies)*, 22/254–255 (1946), p. 7.

25 Teixeira, 'Macau Durante a Guerra', p. 498.

26 Reeves, 25 Apr. 1942, quoted in telegram from Embassy in Lisbon to FO, 26 Apr. 1942, TNA, FO 371/31630; Reeves, *The Lone Flag*, p. 14, p. 121.

27 Ernest Heenan, Memorandum Written in Chongqing, 27 May 1942, p. 1, sent by the British Embassy in Chongqing to the FO, 3 June 1942, TNA, FO 371/31630. Also in TNA, CO 825/30/12.

28 Fernando de Senna Fernandes Rodrigues, President of the Macau Delegation of the Portuguese Red Cross, to Portuguese Red Cross Society in Lisbon, 19 May 1943, Arquivo Histórico da Cruz Vermelha Portuguesa (Portuguese Red Cross Society Historical Archives, hereafter AHCVP), CV/3513–3514.

29 C. N. P. S. Cónim and M. F. B. Teixeira, *Macau e a sua População, 1500–2000: Aspectos Demográficos, Sociais e Económicos (Macau and Its Population, 1500–2000: Demographic,*

figures, even if slightly divergent, support the estimate of 300,000 wartime refugees in Macau. All these impressive numbers were reflected in how Macau was experienced as a lived space. An article about the housing crisis in a local newspaper vividly illustrated contemporary perceptions when the author expressed the conviction that he 'live[d] in the city with the highest population density in the world'.[30]

In Hong Kong and Guangzhouwan, the arrival of refugees in the late 1930s led to a doubling of the local population. In Macau, the smallest of these colonial territories with a combined area of only 15 square kilometres at the time, the population increase was even more dramatic. There was an almost threefold rise, an exceptional case even by today's standards, as the number of refugees rarely surpasses the pre-existing population in any given host territory. It became a temporary city for hundreds of thousands of displaced persons fleeing the brutality of the Japanese invasion. The number of refugees who passed through Macau during the Second World War largely dwarfs the figures of those transiting via Portugal, who have merited more attention by historians.[31]

The two cases were also connected: a great number of war refugees who came to Portugal were Jews fleeing the horrors of the Holocaust, many hoping for a safe passage to the United States; Macau also hosted a few Jewish refugees, although they largely lacked the protection of the support organisations that they could seek in Lisbon or, in the case of China, in Shanghai.[32] However, unlike in Lisbon, most of the people who sought

Social, and Economic Aspects) (Macau, 1998), p. 188; Botas, *Macau 1937–1945*, p. 127; Cannon, 'Experience, Memory', p. 7.

30 'A crise de habitações' ('The Housing Crisis'), *Renascimento* (2 Mar. 1945), p. 2.

31 It is estimated that around 100,000 European refugees passed through Portugal during the war (I. F. Pimentel, 'Refugiados' ('Refugees'), in F. Rosas and J. M. B. Brito (eds.), *Dicionário de História do Estado Novo* (*Estado Novo History Dictionary*), vol. 2 (Lisbon, 1996), pp. 823–5, at p. 823; F. R. Meneses, *Salazar: A Political Biography* (New York, 2009), pp. 236–7. The most comprehensive studies on the passage of Jewish refugees through Portugal during the war are I. F. Pimentel, *Judeus em Portugal durante a II Guerra Mundial: Em Fuga de Hitler e do Holocausto* (*Jews in Portugal during World War II: Fleeing Hitler and the Holocaust*) (Lisbon, 2006), and Pimentel and Ninhos, *Salazar, Portugal e o Holocausto*.

32 In contrast to the vast scholarship on Jewish refugees in Shanghai, there has been a dearth of studies on Jews in wartime Macau. However, a few works of fiction based on true stories shed some light on their experiences in the enclave. See R. Shaplen, *A Corner of the World* (London, 1950), pp. 184–262; R. L. Carvalho, *A Mãe* (*The Mother*) (Macau, 2001); P. French, *Strangers on the Praia: A Tale of Refugees and Resistance in Wartime Macao* (Hong Kong, 2020). On Jewish refugees in wartime Hong Kong, see A. Allsop, 'A Borrowed Place: Jewish Refugees in Hong Kong, 1938–1949' (PhD thesis, King's College London, 2022); C. H. R. Sun, 'More Than a Transit Port, but Less Than a Refuge: Hong Kong and Jewish Refugee Transmigration, 1938–1941' (MA thesis, University of British Columbia, 2019); and C. H. R. Sun, 'The Holocaust and Hong Kong: An Overlooked History', *Holocaust Studies* (2022), pp. 1–21. doi.org/10.1080/17504902.2022.2057118.

refuge in Macau were not from Europe but from Asia. This chapter centres on Chinese and Portuguese Eurasians, the largest communities in the first main wave of refugees that came to Macau fleeing the Japanese occupation of Shanghai in 1937 and of parts of southern China, particularly in Guangdong province, from 1938. Although these might seem to constitute two clearly demarcated groups, there was also some overlap between those described as 'Chinese' and those described as 'Portuguese'.

It may seem odd that one of the most significant communities of refugees in Macau was the Portuguese. After all, wasn't Macau governed as a Portuguese colony? Theirs is one of the several migration histories that came to intersect in the territory during the war. In the context of 1930s China, 'Portuguese' did not primarily refer to a Europe-born citizen of the Republic of Portugal. Most Portuguese then in China were Eurasians, had never set foot in Portugal, spoke little or no Portuguese and were sometimes citizens of other countries, notably of the United Kingdom. Most of their families had ancestral links to Macau. Either them or their forefathers had left the small enclave in search of employment opportunities and a better life in neighbouring Hong Kong or the main Chinese treaty ports. Their specific ethnic origins have been the focus of some scholarly debate, and data on marriage patterns reveals links to numerous other communities, such as the Chinese, Indians, British, Japanese, Filipinos or Russians.[33] Nowadays, the former Portuguese community in China, the members of which have since dispersed even further with many living in Australia, Great Britain or the United States, is often referred to as Macanese.[34] In documents from the 1930s and 1940s, members of this community are invariably described as 'Portuguese'.

For the Portuguese colonial authorities in Macau, the Macanese were not regarded as a separate Eurasian group with a particular identity but as fully Portuguese, recognisable by family relations, surnames and the practice of the Roman Catholic faith. For the authoritarian Estado Novo regime governing Portugal, unlike most people in the Portuguese African colonies whom it considered 'indigenous' (*indígenas* – used as a derogatory term) or 'uncivilised natives' subject to legal discrimination,

[33] See, for example, A. M. Amaro, 'Sons and Daughters of the Soil', *Review of Culture*, 20 (1994), pp. 16–67; J. P. Cabral, 'The "Ethnic" Composition of Macao', *Review of Culture*, 20 (1994), pp. 229–38; M. Teixeira, 'The Origin of the Macanese', *Review of Culture*, 20 (1994), pp. 157–67.

[34] This is clearly observable in the community associations and projects established around the world such as the Macanese American Union (União Macaense Americana) or the Macanese Association (Associação dos Macaenses) in Macau, not to mention the several Macau Houses (Casas de Macau) in various countries.

the Macanese had a 'special status', like the people of Cape Verde and the Portuguese State of India, and were considered 'full citizens'.[35]

That, however, did not mean that they could aspire to the highest official posts in the colonial administration: governors and other senior posts were the privilege of white European Portuguese, most of whom only served in Macau for a short period and none of whom spoke or read Chinese. Nevertheless, it should be noted that different perceptions towards the Portuguese in China help to explain how so many of them found refuge in Macau during the war. Outside of Macau, they lived and worked mostly in the British-dominated colonial spaces of the treaty ports and in Hong Kong, where 'racial or ethnic segregation and discrimination' were 'both tolerated and encouraged'.[36] Even though it was argued that the British discriminated less against the Portuguese than against other Eurasians, the Portuguese were regarded as inferior to white Europeans and did not escape the portrayal that British popular culture reserved for Eurasians as misfits or criminals.[37] As the anthropologist João de Pina-Cabral noted, however: if an 'English *mestiço* was called *half-cast*', a 'Portuguese *mestiço* was called Portuguese'.[38] The Portuguese refugees who came to Macau during the war received privileged treatment from the local authorities, who prioritised them over the Chinese in evacuation efforts and in housing allocation. Portuguese Eurasians could also take on other nationalities or assume other identities such as British and Chinese, especially outside of Macau.

Portuguese authorities were far from anti-racist. In Macau, some Portuguese subjects were the object of racialised forms of discrimination, notably the African troops serving in the armed forces, most of whom were from Mozambique. An informal hierarchy of treatment also existed amongst the victims of the war. The legal protection extraterritoriality offered led many Chinese, even long before the war started, to obtain

[35] G. Clarence-Smith, *The Third Portuguese Empire* (Manchester, 1985), p. 138; P. F. Matos, *As Côres do Império: Representações Raciais no Império Colonial Português* (*The Colours of the Empire: Racialized Representations in the Portuguese Colonial Empire*) (Lisbon, 2012), pp. 63, 66.

[36] J. M. Carroll, 'Chinese Collaboration in the Making of British Hong Kong', in T. W. Ngo (ed.), *Hong Kong's History: State and Society under Colonial Rule* (London, 1999), pp. 13–29, at p. 14.

[37] Yap, 'Portuguese Communities', p. 208; R. Bickers, *Britain in China: Community, Culture and Colonialism, 1900–1949* (Manchester, 1999), pp. 46–9. For a concrete example, see G. Collins, *Chinese Red* (London, 1932).

[38] J. P. Cabral, 'A Composição Social de Macau' ('Macau's Social Composition'), in F. Bethencourt and K. Chaudhuri (eds.), *História da Expansão Portuguesa, Volume V: O Último Império e Recentramento (1930–1998)* (*History of the Portuguese Expansion, Volume V: The Last Empire and Recentring (1930–1998)*) (Lisbon, 1999), pp. 275–301, at p. 278.

foreign nationalities, sometimes more than one, as ways of minimising business risks and enjoying new opportunities or freedoms.[39] Portuguese nationality was a popular choice, even for Chinese figures never associated with Portugal or Macau, such as the famous Shanghai gangster Du Yuesheng.[40]

Although they were legally Portuguese citizens entitled to the same treatment as others, in practice they were regarded as aliens. For example, Portuguese authorities commented negatively on the claims of a Portuguese national called John Tong who complained about the damage Japanese soldiers caused to his residence in Guangzhou in 1938. His English name and Chinese surname were seen as proof of his 'un-Portugueseness'.[41] Similarly, members of the Club Lusitano in Fuzhou (Fuzhou Puqiao gonghui) asked for Portuguese consular protection in 1939 as the war in South China raged on. However, their nationality claims were contested in diplomatic correspondence and, one year later, their ballots confirming them as Portuguese citizens were not renewed because 'the photographs attached to the ballots, with some garments and the typical Chinese cap and the names of the applicants attest that these are 100% Chinese'.[42] As these examples show, discrimination, positive or negative, could be highly arbitrary and have serious consequences in a conflict.

Intersecting national, linguistic and other identities offered different paths for security in an ambiguous neutral territory – as well as other neutral or unoccupied territories beyond it to where many could try to escape in the middle of a massive conflict. This is evident in the communities considered in this chapter, as well as in those addressed in Chapter 5, which will focus on refugees arriving from Hong Kong.

Portuguese Refugees from Shanghai and Guangzhou

The literature on refugees during the first years of China's War of Resistance usually focuses on Chinese citizens. Foreigners in China are assumed to be uniformly in a position of privilege and not directly affected by the conflict. During the war, at least until the Japanese attack on Pearl Harbor in December 1941, foreigners in China are cast as relief providers,

39 M. H. Lin, 'Overseas Chinese Merchants and Multiple Nationality: A Means for Reducing Commercial Risk (1895–1935)', *Modern Asian Studies*, 35/4 (2001), pp. 985–1009, at p. 993.

40 B. G. Martin, '"The Pact with the Devil": The Relationship between the Green Gang and the Shanghai French Concession Authorities, 1925–1935', in F. Wakeman Jr and W. H. Yeh (eds.), *Shanghai Sojourners* (Berkeley, 1992), pp. 266–304, at p. 270.

41 Freitas to Salazar, 22 Mar. 1939, AHD, 2P, A48, M176.

42 Monteiro to Lima, 1 Aug. 1940, AHD, Arquivo do Consulado de Portugal em Cantão, No. 199–203. The decision appears to have been reversed in 1941.

not as beneficiaries of charity. The case of the Portuguese challenges this assumption. It demonstrates how the effects of the war were international from the onset and highlights similar relief practices across communities. As will be made clear later in this chapter, refugees' escape to Macau and maintenance in the territory was guaranteed by different entities. These included not only state representatives, but also local associations and charities – that is, representatives of civil society – at the point of departure and in Macau (Appendix 2). Although their target audience for relief differed, these associations provided a crucial intermediary link between the refugees and the local authorities. Without this grassroots, often translocal, mobilisation for assistance, the local colonial authorities would have had a much harder task of managing the refugee influx alone. However, support for Portuguese refugees was not a mere local story but one where several local dimensions interact with national, imperial and global links.

The Portuguese were one of the most numerous foreign communities in Shanghai.[43] Their relatively low socio-economic standing and the difficulty in writing them into the narratives of Euro-American white privilege and prejudice in China likely explain their absence from the existing literature on foreigners in treaty ports in China.[44] According to the consul general in the city, António Alves, the Portuguese community counted 1,938 people in 1937, fewer than the British but more than the French.[45] That year, with the beginning of an all-out war between China and Japan, foreigners in Shanghai faced their fate with apprehension. The Portuguese were no exception. Diplomatic correspondence reveals the dilemmas faced by a small imperial power concerned with saving its own citizens whilst not showing its weakness in relation to the major players in the region.

Plans for taking some of the Portuguese out of Shanghai began in the summer of 1937. In August, Consul Alves telegraphed the Ministry of

[43] In 1900, the Portuguese were the second largest foreign community in Shanghai's International Settlement after the British (A. G. Dias, *Diáspora Macaense: Macau, Hong Kong, Xangai (1850–1952)* (*Macanese Diaspora: Macau, Hong Kong, Shanghai (1850–1952)*) (Lisbon, 2014), p. 170). One estimate for 1939 placed them as the fifth largest community of foreign nationals, after the Japanese, Jewish refugees, Russian and British (C. Henriot, Shi L. and C. Aubrun, *The Population of Shanghai (1865–1953)* (Leiden, 2019), p. 178).

[44] Few exceptions include Dias, *Diáspora Macaense*; A. G. Dias, 'The Origins of the Macao Community in Shanghai: Hong Kong's Emigration (1850–1909)', *Bulletin of Portuguese–Japanese Studies*, 17 (2008), pp. 197–224; A. M. P. J. Silva, *The Portuguese Community in Shanghai: A Pictorial History* (Macau, 2012); C. S. Chan, 'Macau Martyr of Portuguese Traitor? The Macanese Communities of Macau, Hong Kong and Shanghai and the Portuguese Nation', *Historical Research*, 93/262 (2020), pp. 754–68.

[45] António J. Alves, Portuguese Consul in Shanghai to Marcel Baudez, French Consul in Shanghai, 16 Aug. 1937, AHD, 2P, A48, M175.

Foreign Affairs reporting that 'a great number of Portuguese had abandoned the threatened district [Hongkou]' and that he had 'nominated a commission responsible for transportation, housing [and] relief of refugees'.[46] Two days later, a 'Portuguese relief group managed to evacuate under fire 70 people [from a] zone [of] hostilities' and the consul informed Lisbon he had 'protested [the] bombing reserving right to ask compensation'.[47] The Portuguese consulate in Shanghai published – in English, for the local Portuguese had become predominantly English-speaking – notices in the local press asking for Portuguese nationals to register their address and for those who had had properties destroyed to 'collect immediately all the available evidence of such destruction, damage or looting, whenever possible with the aid of the Police authorities'.[48] Without means to transport them – a fact that pointedly illustrates the limitations of Portugal's actual power in China – the consul requested the American and British governments to guarantee the evacuation of the Portuguese. He also asked for the Ministry of Foreign Affairs to support his request to the Macau authorities to prepare to host 2,000 refugees.[49]

The Portuguese consulate in Shanghai, and Portuguese embassies abroad, contacted British, American and French representatives to request assistance in a potential withdrawal of the 'Portuguese colony' in Shanghai, but such appeals were usually met with a lukewarm response. Even major colonial powers in China seemed unsure of the necessity to evacuate all their citizens and of their ability to pull them out.[50] The Portuguese ambassador in London, who had also made enquiries on the subject, cautioned against the bad image such requests could generate. He wrote to the minister of foreign affairs, the dictator Salazar, that 'to maintain our prestige in the Pacific it would be advantageous not to place ourselves in a situation of strict dependence on other countries'.[51] Facing financial and logistical barriers, and generating unease in terms of projecting 'imperial prestige', the evacuation of Portuguese refugees became possible only through a collaborative effort of local associations and consular representatives and engagement with different authorities.

[46] Alves to MNE, 13 Aug. 1937, AHD, 3P, A9, M132-133.
[47] Alves to MNE, 15 Aug. 1937, ibid. Also in AHD, 2P, A48, M175.
[48] Newspaper clippings in appendix no. 8 to the report on Sino–Japanese hostilities in Shanghai, 15 Oct. 1937, AHD, 3P, A9, M132-133.
[49] Alves to MNE, and Alves to Barbosa, 16 Aug. 1937, ibid.
[50] Several telegrams and dispatches in AHD, 2P, A48, M175.
[51] Monteiro MNE, 17 Aug. 1937, ibid. Also in AHD, 3P, A9, M132–133.

In war, as in peace, the experience of the Portuguese community in China was marked by triangular links between Shanghai, Hong Kong and Macau. This meant connections with different sets of colonial authorities and with multinational populations.[52] In 1937, preparations began in Hong Kong and Macau to receive refugees from Shanghai. As Portuguese authorities and diplomats debated whether to completely evacuate the Portuguese in the city, members of the Portuguese community in Hong Kong established a Relief Commission (Comissão de Socorros) in August 1937 to deal with the refugees coming from Shanghai. The idea came from Leo d'Almada e Castro. A British citizen who was a distinguished figure of the Hong Kong Portuguese community, d'Almada was a member of Hong Kong's Legislative Council and the president of the Club Lusitano, a Portuguese club that still exists.[53]

On 17 August, a meeting in that club between members of the community and the Portuguese consul in Hong Kong, Álvaro Brilhante Laborinho, finalised the establishment of the Relief Commission, in which the consul acted as president. The remaining members of the commission were all male and, with one exception, were all presidents of associations that catered to the Portuguese community in Hong Kong. Portuguese residing in Hong Kong were requested to offer housing to the refugees and the destitute would be housed in the premises of Portuguese associations. The consul expected financial subsidies to be needed and he did not know what could be given by the local community 'who, in its great majority, is poor'.[54] Relief models anchored on public–private collaboration had parallels. Laborinho remarked that the British organised 'their commissions' and prepared housing in hotels, associations and hospitals. The Portuguese were paying close attention to how other nations were handling relief. Efforts in refugee relief had many translocal and transnational similarities.

Fleeing for safety was sometimes arranged between state agents and civil society but could also be an individual endeavour, bypassing government-backed schemes. The consul in Shanghai noted that, apart from the refugees sent via the consulate, 'others depart, of unknown number, who buy tickets directly from the Messageries Maritimes company, mostly

[52] On Portuguese in Shanghai and Hong Kong see, Dias, *Diáspora Macaense*; V. Kong, 'Exclusivity and Cosmopolitanism: Multi-ethnic Civil Society in Interwar Hong Kong', *Historical Journal*, 63/5, (2020), pp. 1281–1305; C. S. Chan, *The Macanese Diaspora in British Hong Kong: A Century of Transimperial Drifting* (Amsterdam, 2021).

[53] There was also a Club Lusitano in Shanghai, but it was a different institution from the one in Hong Kong.

[54] Laborinho to Salazar, 20 Aug. 1937, AHD, 2P, A48, M175.

first-class passengers'.[55] As in other places in China, the wealthy were usually the first to leave. As for those Portuguese without the means to seek refuge on their own, the Portuguese authorities – from consular representatives in China to the Macau government – strove to guarantee their safe departure in coordination with local associations and different authorities. Taking care of the Portuguese refugees was perceived as a useful way of fostering their reconnection with their Macau family origins and their attachment to Portugal – a country many had never been to but whose state reach was more present in Macau than in the treaty ports. Many of the Portuguese in China were native English speakers and worked for foreign companies, so fears of 'denationalisation' were sometimes voiced. The Second World War provided a temporary reversal of their detachment from a Portuguese identity, which for many became a ticket to survival. This will also be evident in Chapter 5, which covers the experience of refugees who came to Macau during the Japanese occupation of Hong Kong.

The arrival of refugees in Macau from Shanghai was usually preceded by an important stopover in Hong Kong, demonstrating the profound links between these urban centres. The first contingent of Portuguese refugees from Shanghai arrived in the British colony on 24 August 1937: 199 people on the French ship *Aramis*. The second batch departed from Shanghai on the following day aboard the British ship *Empress of Canada*. These vessels also carried many evacuees of other nationalities. The exodus of Shanghai was a transnational endeavour, as news reports of the time attest.[56]

Met with fierce Chinese resistance, the invasion of Shanghai was far from the quick victory expected by Japanese forces, and hostilities dragged on for months. More and more people fled the city as the weeks passed, and many amongst them were Portuguese. In September, the consul in Shanghai noted: 'Situation very serious ... Evacuation of Portuguese continues as circumstances allow.'[57] From August to October 1937, several groups of Portuguese refugees were evacuated from Shanghai in foreign boats, a fact that illustrates the diminished naval capacity of the Portuguese in treaty-port China as well as the multiple global connections forged, even if unintended, through shipping.[58] According to a report compiled by the Portuguese consul in

[55] Alves to Laborinho, 21 Aug. 1937, ibid.
[56] For example, 'First Refugee Groups Leave Shanghai', *NCH* (25 Aug. 1937), p. 302; 'Evacuation of British Complete', *CP* (26 Aug. 1937), p. 3.
[57] Alves to MNE, 11 Sept. 1937, AHD, 3P, A9, M132–133.
[58] Apart from the aforementioned two ships, they arrived in the *Conte Verde* (Italian), the *Tjinegara, Tjisondari* and *Tjasalak* (Dutch) and the *Chenonceaux* (French).

Hong Kong, from August to November, 603 refugees arrived in Hong Kong from Shanghai, of whom 335 went straight to Macau and 268 remained in Hong Kong. Of the latter, 27 left later for Macau fully funded by the consulate.[59] Thus, most Portuguese refugees ended up in Macau and, as the correspondence between the Shanghai consulate and the Macau government indicates, many were 'without any resources'.[60]

Communal efforts to deal with the Shanghai refugees were taking place not just in Shanghai and Macau, but also in Hong Kong. The Relief Commission there worked with the Portuguese consulate in order to receive the newly arrived.[61] A group of volunteers accompanied the commission's representatives to take care of the sorting and transport of luggage and to assist elders, women and children.[62] Lists were made of those who were to stay with their families in Hong Kong and those who would follow by boat to Macau. To deal with the refugee influx from Shanghai, the Macau government transferred funds to the Portuguese consulate in Hong Kong.[63] It also sent the consul a list of instructions concerning assistance to refugees, who were to be examined by a doctor on arrival in Macau and had to be vaccinated against cholera. To those without means, the government would distribute a small cash sum for daily food, housing to those 'without family or friends in Macau who wish to receive them' and a modest subsidy for personal expenses for all refugees.[64] The refugees were not simply an object of charity. For some of the locals, their presence represented an opportunity for profit – for example, through overpriced housing rentals.[65]

Many Portuguese were sent to Macau partly because it was deemed cheaper to assist them there than locally in Shanghai. In September 1937, the consul noted the growing number of destitute and unemployed in Shanghai, suggesting that it would be preferable to send them to Macau, 'where their maintenance is much cheaper and accommodation easier'.[66] Destitute refugees were regarded as a 'problem' and their relocation was planned as a way to 'solve' it. Alves stressed that those unable to earn their living in Shanghai should not be permitted to return. With discriminatory considerations, he suggested that more elderly refugees and those with disabilities should be kept in Macau.[67] Refugee management was also a process of delegating unwelcome tasks and costly decisions to others.

[59] 'Refugiados Portuguese de Shanghai' ('Portuguese Refugees from Shanghai'), report by the Portuguese consul in Hong Kong, Álvaro Brilhante Laborinho, Nov. 1937, p. 21, AHD, 2P, A48, M175.
[60] Alves to Barbosa, 8 Sept. 1937, ibid. [61] Laborinho to MNE, 27 Aug. 1937, ibid.
[62] 'Refugiados Portugueses de Shanghai', p. 17, ibid. [63] Ibid., p. 22.
[64] Ibid., pp. 34–5.
[65] 'Noticias de Hongkong' ('Hong Kong News'), *VM* (8 July 1940), p. 4.
[66] Alves to Barbosa, 8 Sept. 1937, AHD, 2P, A48, M175. [67] Ibid.

Due to the overlapping national and imperial identities at play, the relocation of refugees was an international affair. Portuguese authorities were keen to ensure the British paid their share because some of the Portuguese refugees were British citizens. The consul in Shanghai considered it acceptable for Portuguese who held British nationality to be helped by the consulate. However, he believed 'a certain distinction should be made between the people who became British subjects for reasons other than their own, continuing always to maintain contact with the Portuguese, and those who, having acquired British nationality spontaneously and voluntarily, have ostentatiously drifted apart from their race brethren [*irmãos de raça*]', who, he argued, should be taken care of by the British authorities.[68] 'Race' was being used to denote nationality. With nationality allowing a passage to safety and access to relief, those deciding on these matters had, in times of war, a heightened power over the lives of individuals. Despite discussions on who would be 'deserving' of support, there was, in reality, a considerable degree of flexibility. For example, the Relief Commission in Hong Kong decided to make no distinction between Portuguese refugees who were British subjects seeking help from the commission and those who were only Portuguese citizens.[69]

Evacuation procedures were repeated in 1938 during the occupation of Guangzhou, where a small community of Portuguese resided. In one of his wartime reports to the Ministry of Foreign Affairs, the consul general, Vasco Martins Morgado, explained that he had warned the 'Portuguese colony' in the city to prepare for the evacuation of women and children.[70] Like his counterpart in Shanghai, he was taking note of the attitudes of the British, French and American consuls, although he was unable to count on British assistance, whose ships were either defending Shamian – the island in Guangzhou where foreign concessions and most consulates were located – or evacuating their own citizens.[71] Without foreign assistance, he had acquired the services of a Portuguese-owned 'half abandoned' motorboat which he had had repaired for the purpose and arranged an evacuation to Macau with the governor there.[72] Most of the Portuguese women and children had left for Hong Kong and Macau by October 1938, when Guangzhou fell to the Japanese forces after months of heavy bombing. As in Shanghai, the evacuation from Guangzhou to Macau was a collaborative

68 Alves to Barbosa, 9 Sept. 1937, ibid.
69 'Refugiados Portugueses de Shanghai', p. 68, ibid.
70 Morgado to MNE, 30 Sept. 1938, in *A Guerra vista de Cantão*, p. 191.
71 Morgado to MNE, 30 Nov. 1938, AHD, 2 P, A 48, M175.
72 Morgado to MNE, 2 Nov. 1938 in *A Guerra vista de Cantão*, p. 234.

endeavour that involved diplomats, the Macau administration and civilian efforts, and for which the assistance of foreign nations was sought, even if it did not always correspond to expectations.

How to manage housing, healthcare and food provision for the newcomers became prime concerns for the Portuguese authorities in Macau. The commission set up in Hong Kong sought to mobilise family members and friends that the refugees might have in the neighbouring enclave. The Macau government published appeals in a local newspaper for those who could take some refugees into their houses or provide them with food to sign up at the civil administration bureau.[73] The Portuguese refugees, first from Shanghai and Guangzhou and later from Hong Kong, were the top priorities. No such moves were undertaken to assist Chinese refugees, who were left to fend for themselves, to count on family members or Chinese charities or, if destitute, moved to camps and asylums. The Portuguese, on the other hand, were offered accommodation in several locations, including hotels, clubs, schools, a theatre and even the Canidrome (greyhound racing stadium).[74] Documents produced in 1942 by the Macau senate list twelve locations, the most iconic of which was perhaps the Bela Vista Hotel.[75] Spaces of modern urban culture were repurposed to house the victims of a modern war.

Willingness to accept refugees did not mean financial capacity to support them whilst in Macau. The contours of a major crisis became apparent in the first few months of the war, with the governor of Macau labelling the refugee influx a potential 'problem without solution'.[76] Different authorities pushed the financial responsibilities of caring for refugees onto others. Telegraphing the Ministry of Colonies in October, the governor of Macau, Artur Tamagnini de Barbosa, requested that the Ministry of Foreign Affairs instruct the Portuguese consul in Shanghai not to send more refugees without first solving funding issues, which he considered should come out of the Ministry of Foreign Affairs' budget.[77]

[73] 'Repartição Central de Administração Civil: Aviso' ('Central Division of the Civil Administration: Notice'), *VM* (21 Jan. 1942), p. 2.

[74] Teixeira, 'Macau Durante a Guerra', p. 501.

[75] Club de Macau, 3 Praia Grande, Caixa Escolar, Clube Recreativo 1° de Junho, 7 Rua do Barão, 54 Rua de S. Paulo, 56 Rua de S. Paulo, Escola Municipal Luso Chinesa, Hotel Bela Vista, Vila Leitão, Estrada Ferreira do Amaral (Carlos da Silva Carvalho, Administrative Commission President, Leal Senado, to the Manager of the Electric Lighting Company, 18 July 1942, AM, AH/LS/184); M. Teixeira, *Bela Vista Hotel* (Macau, 1978), p. 9. Recollections of one of the refugees housed in the hotel can be read in A. P. Silva, 'Life and Learning in Wartime Macau', *UMA News Bulletin* (2009): www.uma-casademacau.com/files/9212/9669/0353/UMA_News_Bulletin__All_Summer_2009.pdf.

[76] Barbosa to MC, copy sent by MC to MNE, 29 Oct. 1937, AHD, 2P, A48, M175.

[77] Barbosa to MNE, 7 Oct. 1937, ibid.

Such squabbling over funding became even more evident after 1941, as will be seen in Chapter 5. Even with some help from the Portuguese state, the prospects for refugees' livelihoods in Macau were complicated.

Lack of employment opportunities had motivated many Macau-born Portuguese to leave for the treaty ports since their opening in the mid-nineteenth century. Now the same problem led several refugees to cut their Macau exile short and go back to their homes in Shanghai. In April 1940, the governor wrote to inform Lisbon that some of the Shanghai refugees funded by the Ministry of Foreign Affairs wished to return to the city and asked that the ministry pay for their travel fares.[78] As with most financial support requests, the situation was not immediately solved. In October, the Portuguese consul noted the precarious situation of many of the Shanghai Portuguese in Macau, where the local Charity and Relief Commission had not been able to help them since May.[79] The financial limitations of relief schemes are evident in official correspondence. In January 1941, several Portuguese refugees appealed individually to the Macau government to be provided with funds to return to Shanghai. Their stories highlight the difficulties many refugees faced in finding a job in Macau during the war.[80] Their will to return to Shanghai plainly reveals the limitations of Macau's assistance and the reality that the benefits of a safe refuge could be almost meaningless without adequate means of subsistence. Refugees who fled to Macau did not necessarily stay there, and many continued to circulate between the enclave and other cities.

The 'lone island' period in Shanghai (1937–41) still afforded some guarantee of survival for the local Portuguese community, as intensive associative endeavours suggest.[81] No wonder, then, that some of those who had fled to Macau in 1937 wanted to return to the city. Those who did so would soon face a far worse situation, however. Because they mainly worked for British and American companies, after Japan declared war on the Allies and took over the International Settlement and French Concession in 1942–3, the livelihood of the Portuguese became severely

78 Barbosa to MC, 29 Apr. 1940, ibid.

79 José A. Ribeiro de Melo, Portuguese consul in Shanghai to MNE, 14 Oct. 1940, ibid.

80 For example, Humberto Vasco Colaço to Teixeira, 19 Jan. 1941; Roberto Jesús Xavier to Teixeira, 22 Jan. 1941, Administração Civil, No P-18040, Cx. 337, AM, MO/AH/AC/SA/01/18103.

81 The Organisation of the Portuguese Community (Organização da Colónia Portuguesa), a branch of the youth organisation Mocidade Portuguesa and a food-retail cooperative were founded in 1940 and new buildings were opened by the Club Lusitano and the Association of Portuguese Ladies (Associação das Senhoras Portuguesas) in 1941 (Silva, *The Portuguese Community in Shanghai*, pp. 61–74). A radio station, Radio Portugal, was also set up in 1940 ('Pela Patria' ('For the Homeland'), *VM* (29 July 1940), p. 4).

threatened. Once again, the strategy the Portuguese diplomatic representatives adopted was to join forces with the local community to ensure a degree of assistance. The Portuguese minister to China, who remained in the occupied city throughout the war, called for the creation of a 'central association' congregating representatives from all the local associations. This umbrella association represented the Portuguese community and dealt with its needs. The association and the consulate were the main funders of 'the Camp', a slum in the French Concession where those who were completely destitute lingered.[82] Those who could leave returned to Macau or went there for the first time. A Macau newspaper reported in February 1942 that 'many Portuguese, without jobs or means of subsistence' would be 'arriving shortly' from Shanghai, showing how the late 1930s plans to shift the most destitute to Macau was partly implemented.[83] Others remained in Shanghai and their situation deteriorated significantly in the mid-1940s as the war approached its end. At the time, appeals to assist the Portuguese community in Shanghai, notably through public subscriptions, were a constant presence in newspapers published in Macau.[84]

The translocal efforts of the Portuguese community in China played a crucial role in assisting their members in need, regardless of where they were, working concertedly with the Portuguese – and sometimes other – state representatives. Portuguese nationals sought to ensure government support but also demonstrated resilience and initiative in stepping up when official means were lacking.

Chinese Refugees from Shanghai and Guangdong Province

The intersecting role of state and society in refugee relief is even more evident in the case of the Chinese refugees who came to Macau. Although the colonial authorities were primarily concerned with assisting Portuguese refugees, a much greater number of Chinese also moved to Macau during the war. Chinese refugees who fled to Macau came from all socio-economic backgrounds. Many brought to the enclave a new-found prosperity in the fields of finance, education and the arts. Others were as poor as the Portuguese refugees, but often ended up much worse off due to lack of support from the colonial authorities.

82 Silva, *The Portuguese Community in Shanghai*, pp. 92, 94–5.

83 'Refugiados portugueses de Hongkong e Shanghai' ('Portuguese Refugees from Hong Kong and Shanghai'), *VM* (10 Feb. 1942), p. 3.

84 'Os portugueses em Shanghai' ('The Portuguese in Shanghai'), *Jornal de Notícias* (hereafter *JN*) (8 July 1945), p. 2.

Chinese refugees in Macau came mostly from the Cantonese community in Shanghai and from Guangdong province. Some arrived in evacuation drives coordinated by the Guangdong Native Place Association Council for Refugee Relief, which ensured the evacuation of thousands of members of the Cantonese community in Shanghai, with around 10,000 people taken by boat to Guangzhou, Hong Kong and Macau in several groups.[85] In August 1937, the Portuguese consul in Hong Kong observed the arrival of 'numerous refugees, coming particularly from Canton, of Chinese nationality, and from Shanghai'.[86] Their number was perceived as problematic by the governor of Macau, who blamed them for 'making life expensive' in the city.[87]

Fears for the economic impact of Chinese refugees were soon joined by concerns for their impact on public health. In mainland China, images of poor refugees also 'stirred up anxieties about chaos and public health', but these compelled the central government to take up an active role in refugee management and relief.[88] In Macau, perceptions of destitute refugees were inextricable from discriminatory colonial hierarchies that placed poor Chinese at the bottom of the social scale. Facing a cholera epidemic in the territory in 1938, the governor blamed it on the arrival of 'thousands of Chinese refugees'.[89] These hygienic scares usually targeted the poorest Chinese. In a newspaper article reporting positively about the official efforts to ensure street cleanliness – a not-so-subtle praise for the colonial authorities' 'civilising' actions – the authors describe how they visited 'the shadiest neighbourhood where the most dense and miserable population lives, in its largest majority constituted by the thousands of poor Chinese refugees that have come to take shelter here due to the circumstances'.[90] The association of dirtiness and disease with poor Chinese refugees is a common trope found in reports written at the time and accounts penned decades after the events, which often lack any critique of the local authorities' dire record of welfare provision.

Destitute Chinese refugees in Portuguese sources are usually described in collective and vague terms, as an embodiment of extreme misery and, sometimes, as a symbol for China's weakness. The short stories of the writer and journalist Deolinda da Conceição, who lived in Macau during

85 Lincoln, 'Fleeing from Firestorms', p. 453.
86 Laborinho to MNE, 20 Aug. 1937, AHD, 2P, A48, M175.
87 Barbosa to MC, transcribed in letter from MC to MNE, 20 Aug. 1937, ibid.
88 L. Liu, 'Imagining the Refugee: The Emergence of a State Welfare System in the War of Resistance', in J. A Cook et al. (eds.), *Visualizing Modern China: Image, History, and Memory, 1750-Present* (Lanham, 2014), pp. 165–83, at p. 167.
89 Barbosa to MC, 21 Oct. 1938, Arquivo Histórico Ultramarino (Overseas Historical Archives, hereafter AHU), 157, 1A, MU, GM, MÇ, 1938.
90 'A limpeza de Macau' ('Macau's Cleanliness'), *VM* (11 May 1942), p. 3.

the war, are often gendered accounts of the conflict's social impact. In one, entitled 'Hunger' ('Fome'), she contrasted the violence in China with the situation in Macau through the story of a nameless Chinese mother who succumbs to disease when she gets to the enclave, portrayed as 'an oasis of peace'.[91] Although this story focused on gendered Chinese victimhood with an emphasis on hopelessness and not on resistance or survival, the decision of many refugees to move to neutral Macau reveals agency and endurance.

As the Japanese advanced through South China, the number of Chinese refugees in the territory increased. The numbers were already significant before the Japanese occupation of Guangzhou in October 1938. In one of his lengthy reports to the Ministry of Foreign Affairs, the Portuguese consul in the city reported that many Chinese were seeking refuge in Macau animated by a perceived lack of strict neutrality, notably a favourable treatment of Portugal by Japan.[92] In a later report, he estimated that some 10,000 people, mostly women and children, were leaving Guangzhou daily.[93] The Macau newspaper *Huaqiao ribao* (*Jornal Va Kio*) – founded in November 1937 – wrote that the number of refugees who had fled to Macau had reached more than 40,000 and that a Refugee Relief Commission (Nanmin jiuji weiyuanhui) had been organised to provide assistance to them.[94] The occupation of Guangzhou in October 1938 brought about a major exodus. It was estimated that 13.76 per cent of people in China who had to leave their homes between 1937 and 1945 were from Guangdong province.[95] Around a million people reportedly moved to Hong Kong and Macau in the late 1930s, including the president of the Cantonese Residents' Association in Shanghai, who lived in Macau through the 1940s.[96] A high number of refugees in Macau came from Zhongshan county.

In Macau, as elsewhere in China, refugee relief was often linked to a general grassroots mobilisation to support efforts to resist Japan. This involved the participation of women in patriotic social welfare activities. It was the case of the Macau Chinese Women's Support Association

[91] D. Conceição, *Cheong-Sam – A Cabaia* (Cheongsam) (Macau, n.d.), p. 129.
[92] *A Guerra vista de Cantão*, p. 36. [93] Ibid., p. 108.
[94] 'Comissão de Assistência aos Refugiados' in Portuguese. *Huaqiao ribao* (16 June 1938), cited in Guangdong Provincial Archives, *Guangdong Aomen dang'an shiliao xuanbian* (*Selected Historical Materials about Macau from Guangdong*) (Beijing, 1999), p. 380.
[95] H. S. Ch'i, 'The Military Dimension, 1942–1945', in J. C. Hsiung and S. I. Levine (eds.), *China's Bitter Victory: The War with Japan 1937–1945* (Armonk, NY, 1992), p. 180. Data based on a 1946 KMT survey.
[96] S. MacKinnon, 'Refugee Flight at the Outset of the Anti-Japanese War', in D. Lary and S. MacKinnon (eds.), *Scars of War: The Impact of Warfare on Modern China* (Vancouver, 2001), pp. 118–34, at p. 124; J. K. Choy, *My China Years 1911–1945: Practical Politics in China after the 1911 Revolution* (San Francisco, CA, 1974), p. 194.

(Aomen Zhongguo funü weilaohui), which was visited by Shi Liang, one of the leaders of the National Salvation Movement, which was close to the CCP.[97] Like other charities, the Macau Chinese Women's Support Association participated in joint initiatives contributing to the Chinese war effort, in and beyond Macau. For example, in June 1938, it sent bags of medical supplies to a campaign run by Sun Yat-sen University in Guangzhou.[98] A 1939 article documented how Macau was seeing an 'enthusiastic movement of women' who came together to make clothes and first-aid articles for those fighting in China.[99]

Chinese women were also involved in the Macau Four Circles Assistance Association.[100] Its activities in Macau included fundraising, propaganda mobilisation and relief.[101] From 1937 to 1940, Chinese patriotic associations in Macau, including of singers and sex workers, carried out more than 100 fundraising activities.[102] The enclave's Chinese civil society continued to organise fundraising events until the end of the war.[103] The magnitude of the social effects of the war allied to the relative weakness of the colonial state capacity led to an outburst of grassroots civic mobilisation in Macau, with many similarities with what happened in pre-1941 Hong Kong and Shanghai.[104]

[97] On Shi Liang, see MacKinnon, *Wuhan, 1938*, pp. 55–9; on her visit to Macau, see 'Shi Liang zai Aomen' ('Shi Liang in Macau'), *Funü shenghuo* (20 Jan. 1938); Guo, 'Shilun Aomen', p. 100; Zhang, 'Aomen tongbao', p. 107. On the mobilisation of women in China, see Y. Pan, 'Feminism and Nationalism in China's War of Resistance against Japan', *International History Review*, 19/1 (1997), pp. 115–30; R. Cheung, 'Wartime Feminists in the City of Ram: Women's Movement in the City of Guangzhou during the Second World War', UCLA Center for the Study of Women (2009): eprints.cdlib.org /uc/item/77k5j421; H. H. Schneider, 'Mobilising Women: The Women's Advisory Council, Resistance and Reconstruction during China's War with Japan', *European Journal of East Asian Studies*, 11/2 (2012), pp. 213–36.

[98] 'Zhongda fuwutuan, chou zhen jiangquan jiexiao, gai tuan jin shouji yaowu shen duo' ('National Sun Yat-sen University Service Group, Lottery Tickets Announced, Group Has Recently Collected a Lot of Medical Drugs'), *Shenbao* (1 June 1938), p. 4.

[99] 'Aomen fuyun' ('Macao Women Movement'), *Yuandong*, 8 (1939), p. 21.

[100] Barreto, *Macau during the Sino–Japanese War*, pp. 147–53.

[101] Zou, 'Qianxi kangzhan', p. 146. On the fundraising activities undertaken by sports teams associated with this association see K. J. Tang, 'Os Desportos Modernos de Macau no Período Republicano: Formação e Desenvolvimento' ('Macau Modern Sports during the Republican Period: Formation and Development'), *Administração*, 68 (2005), pp. 800–3.

[102] Barreto, *Macau during the Sino–Japanese War*, p. 110; Guo, 'Shilun Aomen', p. 100; Zhang, 'Aomen tongbao', p. 109; Zhang, 'Kangzhan qianqi', p. 89.

[103] For example, in 1945, the Tung Sin Tong organised theatrical performances and the Chinese Women Association organised a flower sale ('Em prol dos necessitados' ('For Those in Need'), *JN* (4 May 1945), p. 4; 'Venda de flores' ('Flower Sale'), *JN* (16 June 1945), p. 4).

[104] Y. Lu, 'Together with the Homeland: Civic Activism for National Salvation in British Hong Kong', *Modern China*, 40/6 (2014), pp. 639–74; Chan Lau, *China, Britain and Hong Kong*, pp. 267; Parks M. Coble, 'The National Salvation Movement and Social

From the beginning of the conflict, the Portuguese authorities coordinated with local Chinese personalities and associations in order to assist many of those coming to the enclave. That cooperation served both parts: it ensured a level of autonomy to local Chinese elites whilst the Portuguese authorities offloaded any responsibility for devising specific relief schemes aimed solely at Chinese refugees. Although such collaboration with Chinese associations was not unheard of, its strengthening during the War of Resistance was particularly significant.[105] These associations acted as mediators between the colonial administration and the majority of the population.

To these local arrangements, one should add the role of the Chinese central government, a major relief provider during the war. Chiang Kai-shek's government was directly informed of some of the activities taking place in Macau to deal with the refugee crisis. For example, in September 1937, Cui Nuozhi,[106] an influential figure of the Chinese community in Macau, wrote to the central government in Nanjing to report that, to tackle the growing number of refugees, fifteen people, including himself, had decided to form a committee and were hoping to establish a long-term fundraising service to help the refugees: the Macau All Circles Relief Organisation (Aomen gejie jiuzaihui).[107] This institution comprised the Chinese Commercial Association, the Kiang Wu Hospital, the Tung Sin Tong Charitable Society (Tongshantang) and the Macau Chinese Education Association (Aomen Zhonghua jiaoyuhui).[108] These were influential Chinese elite institutions, some of which dated back to the late Qing.[109] Amongst the names in the

Networks in Republican Shanghai', in N. Dillon and J. C. Oi (eds.), *At the Crossroads of Empires: Middlemen, Social Networks, and State-Building in Republican Shanghai* (Stanford, CA, 2008), pp. 110–30.

105 S. Lou, 'Acerca das Características do Corporativismo de Macau' ('On the Characteristics of Macau's Corporatism'), *Administração*, 65 (2004), p. 818.

106 Often identified by his Portuguese name, Joel José Choi Anok, in Western sources. A Catholic with Portuguese nationality, he had served in the Portuguese navy in his youth and was president of the Tung Sin Tong and the Kiang Wu Hospital for several stints (C. Jorge and R. B. Coelho, *Roque Choi: Um Homem Dois Sistemas* (*Roque Choi: A Man Two Systems*) (Macau, 2015), pp. 108–15). His son, Cui Leqi (Roque Choi) was an important intermediary figure after the war.

107 AH, Guomin zhengfu (National Government), 001000004794A, Gang'Ao huashang juankuan jiuzai (yi) (Relief Contributions from Hong Kong and Macau Chinese Businessmen (I)). This association was still running in August 1939, when it reported to Chongqing that it had collected 4,000 yuan to help the local refugees in a fundraising drive on the anniversary of the Marco Polo Bridge Incident (AH, Guomin zhengfu, 001000004795A, Gang'Ao huashang juankuan jiuzai (san) (Relief Contributions from Hong Kong and Macau Chinese Businessmen (III)).

108 Lou, 'Acerca', p. 800.

109 The King Wu Hospital was founded in 1871, the Tung Sin Tong in 1892 and the Commercial Association in 1911.

committee was Gao Kening, a local tycoon who was one of the most important Chinese figures in Macau during the war and whose activities will be addressed in Chapter 4.

The involvement of elite figures in wartime relief has been noted at length in studies focused on Southeast Asia, where new forms of 'Chinese bourgeois nationalism' were articulated through transnational links between, amongst others, British-ruled Singapore, Hong Kong and Guangdong.[110] The developments in Macau had clear similarities; like Hong Kong, it too connected Chinese authorities on the mainland to Chinese resident overseas, including eminent community leaders able to provide financial and other support.

In May 1938, the Macau government established the Charity and Relief Commission (Comissão de Assistência e Beneficência).[111] This new organisation linked together old charitable institutions, supporting their services to tackle the new challenges that the arrival of many wartime refugees posed to the local authorities. The people and charities involved in this commission are a vivid example not only of the interplay of state and non-state actors for relief during the war years, but also of some of their wider connections. The president of the Charity and Relief Commission was the *provedor* (president) of the Holy House of Mercy (Santa Casa da Misericórdia), a centuries-old Portuguese charity that has operated in Macau since 1569. Of the commission's governing body, only one member was a representative of the Chinese community, Liu Yulin (Lew Yuk Lin), who died in 1942. Liu had been one of the first Chinese students in the United States and had a distinguished diplomatic career under the Qing and the Republic, having been minister in London and Washington. Amongst other ventures, the commission subsidised Chinese institutions, particularly the Kiang Wu Hospital and the Tung Sin Tong. Starting from 1938 and continuing after the end of the war, the government supported these institutions with both regular and extraordinary donations.[112] Institutions such as these, as well as other civic and religious charities, provided shelter, meals and medical care to many Chinese refugees.[113] By delegating to these charities a significant share of responsibility for caring for vulnerable members of society in general, and refugees in particular, the government

[110] H. Y. Kuo, *Networks beyond Empires: Chinese Business and Nationalism in the Hong Kong–Singapore Corridor, 1914–1941* (Leiden, 2014), pp. 130–65.

[111] 'Comissão de Assistência e Beneficência' ('Charity and Relief Commission'), *VM* (28 May 1938), p. 4.

[112] Lou, 'Acerca', p. 789.

[113] For example, in 1945, the Tung Sin Tong was giving around 600 free medical appointments per day ('Um apelo' ('An Appeal'), *JN* (21 June 1945), p. 4).

indirectly recognised its inability to manage refugee relief on its own. Such 'public–private partnerships' to deliver assistance were also evident in Shanghai and in Hong Kong.[114]

The Safety Zone Project

Following models being tried elsewhere in China, plans were devised to house refugees in a special type of neutral territory: a safety zone outside of Macau's borders. Similarly to what happened in Shanghai, Nanjing and other Chinese cities, some in Macau tried to establish a refugee zone in Qianshan in cooperation with the local Chinese authorities, a project that ultimately did not materialise. Writing two decades after the events he had witnessed, news correspondent and liaison figure Jack Braga attributed the failure to a lack of response by the Chinese government.[115] However, documents from his private collection at the National Library of Australia and from the Portuguese National Archives tell a slightly different story and reveal the ambiguities surrounding the politics of refugee relief in Macau.

Initially, the Macau governor seemed to have had doubts about such a project, particularly if it involved other foreign powers. A refugee zone under international jurisdiction with British, American and French intervention near Qianshan 'will in no way be convenient to us', he wrote in November 1938, showing how imperial competition and the desire to preserve national prestige could trump humanitarian concerns. Barbosa was not enthusiastic about a safety zone, which he believed would make impossible to expel 'communist elements near Macau'. His preference was for Japanese forces to 'clean up' the region and, if needed, the Macau authorities would attend to refugees in Coloane or, if that did not work, they could occupy nearby Lappa island.[116]

Despite this, the project for a Qianshan refugee zone took shape and the political advantage of providing help to the Chinese refugees won over the governor's mind: 'When the conflict is finished we cannot consider Chinsan [Qianshan] as a territory attached to Macau,' but 'the services we provide' will bring 'recognition from both parts and prestige to Portugal', having the potential 'to make disappear custom posts near Macau and forces that disturb us so much with their nearness'.[117] He

114 N. Dillon, 'Middlemen in the Chinese Welfare State: The Role of Philanthropists in Refugee Relief in Wartime Shanghai', *Studies in Comparative International Development*, 46 (2011), pp. 22–45; Lopes, 'Impact of Refugees'.

115 J. M. Braga, *Hong Kong and Macao* (Hong Kong, 1960), p. 119.

116 Barbosa [to MC], 15 Nov. 1938, ANTT, AOS, UL-10A1, cx. 767.

117 Barbosa [to MC], 22 Nov. 1938, ibid.

waited for the Chinese central government and the Zhongshan county magistrate (whom he referred to as the 'governor of Seaki [Shiqi]') to approve his request to establish the zone.[118]

Barbosa sent a police force to occupy the area previously designated by local Chinese authorities for the refugee zone in December 1938. The men were greeted with bombs. The Zhongshan magistrate tried to convince the Portuguese to enter as unarmed civilians, but the governor of Macau gave up the project altogether. He thanked the Japanese 'for their good will' and 'protested energetically' to the magistrate for having 'subjected us to such great risks when we were only going for humanitarian motives and to his and the Chinese population's request'.[119] Humanitarian motives were certainly not the sole purpose of the occupation and refugee relief was seen as potentially useful to extend the Portuguese sphere of influence beyond the borders of Macau. Unsurprisingly, the Chinese authorities resisted this.

The Qianshan Refugee Relief Committee was not a Portuguese colonial initiative, however, but a truly transnational one. Formed in Macau, it included figures from the Macau administration, Chinese elites and the Catholic Church, amongst others. Minutes of a meeting held in January 1939 at the Episcopal House and chaired by the bishop of Macau, José da Costa Nunes, also list as attendees Dai Ensai (brother-in-law of Sun Yat-sen who lived in Macau), T. H. Bannister, Pedro José Lobo, Liang Houyuan (representative of the Macau Chinese community), Jack Braga and Father Serafim Brum Amaral (superior of the Catholic mission in Zhongshan). The British and German consuls in Guangzhou were also consulted (with little result), as was the governor of Macau. The last had told the bishop that he 'could not provide protection for an unlimited number of refugees, because of financial considerations', arguing that the Macau government was already funding a very large number of refugees. Barbosa eventually conceded that the territory could receive about 10,000 refugees from Qianshan.[120]

At the committee's third meeting, held the following month, Father Amaral reported on his talks with the Japanese consul general in Guangzhou.[121] He tried to secure the consul's authorisation for the refugee

[118] Barbosa to MC, 29 Nov. 1938, AHU, 157, 1A, MU, GM, MÇ, 1938. Also in ANTT, AOS, UL-10A1, cx. 767.

[119] Barbosa to MC, 5 Dec. 1938, ANTT, AOS, UL-10A1, cx. 767.

[120] Minutes of Meeting of the Tsinshan [Qianshan] Refugee Relief Committee, 9 Jan. 1939. NLA, MS 4300, Box 52, 8.1/14.

[121] Minutes of the Third Meeting of the Tsinshan Refugee Relief Association, 14 Feb. 1939, ibid. The meeting was arranged via the Portuguese consulate (Morgado to Salazar, 13 Feb. 1939, AHD, Arquivo do Consulado de Portugal em Cantão, No. 199–2013).

zone. This was denied, but some vague concessions were outlined: 'Missions may receive refugees within their properties, but they must prevent the admission [of] any form of anti-Japanese elements, individual or associations, and in case the Japanese are informed by spies that there are anti-Japanese elements within such property, the Japanese forces will take such steps as they consider necessary to clear out such elements, without consideration for anybody.'[122] This sort of demand was not uncommon and mirrored similar constraints placed upon other safety zones in China.

Committee members were divided on how to proceed. The bishop wanted to know whether 'the [Refugee Relief] Committee could count on the financial help from the Chinese Government, through the organisations established for the purpose' if the Japanese invaded Zhongshan.[123] Dai explained how he was in touch with Chinese officials, having played a crucial role in securing two contributions for the Macau government-controlled Refugee Centre in Coloane on two occasions. He stated that '$10,000 [Chinese dollars] had been handed over only a few days ago, through Ambassador Hsu [Xu Shiying]', China's representative in Tokyo until the start of the war. He would seek to approach 'the same people again, asking them to reserve a sufficient sum of money, to be available in case the Committee should require the money at any time'.[124]

An idea for the establishment of a refugee centre on Lappa island was put forward by Father Amaral, but the committee agreed that it would need the authorisation of both the Chinese and the Portuguese authorities. Lappa had been claimed by Macau Portuguese authorities but it was, de jure and de facto, governed by China, as the presence of a CMC station there attested.

During the meeting, it was also decided that Pedro Lobo would try to obtain the Macau government's consent to transfer the Coloane refugee centre to the committee. This reference is one of many that illustrated the important role Lobo played as a transnational intermediary. An undated document on a meeting of the Macau Refugee Relief Committee stated that it had been decided to round up the Coloane refugee camp and transfer the 'inmates' to a new camp to be established at Lappa.[125] However, confrontations on that island put such plans to rest. The aborted plan for a safety zone near Macau highlights some of the difficulties in managing conflicting interests in wartime Macau, including the pursuit of territorial control and prestige through humanitarian assistance.

[122] 'Summary of the Reply of the Japanese Consul General in Canton [to Father Amaral]', NLA, MS 4300, Box 52, 8.1/14.
[123] Minutes of the Third Meeting of the Tsinshan Refugee Relief Association. [124] Ibid.
[125] 'Macao Refugee Relief Committee', Undated Minutes, NLA, MS 4300, Box 52, 8.1/14.

Camps for the Poor

The Macau colonial government had a more indirect contact with Chinese refugees than it had with the Portuguese. Still, poor refugees were not free from a considerable degree of government intervention. Similarly to the steps taken by authorities in mainland China and in Hong Kong, the poor in Macau were sent to designated areas where they could be contained and controlled, especially on Taipa and Coloane, the two outlying islands ruled by the Macau colonial government. The Chinese government, however, was not overly keen on Portuguese managing Chinese refugees on those islands. Diao Zuoqian, MOFA special commissioner for Guangdong and Guangxi, was informed by the consul in Guangzhou of the Portuguese plan to set up shelters (*binansuo*) in Taipa and Coloane. Reporting to MOFA after investigating the matter, Diao noted that the Chinese government did not recognise Portuguese control over those islands. Therefore, he replied to the consul that Chinese authorities should ensure the management of a Chinese refugee shelter, although he thanked the governor for his generosity. Diao also stressed to MOFA that the matter should not be reported in the press.[126]

Even though the Chinese central government was anxious to safeguard its position and was interested in being a prime actor in refugee relief for state-building purposes, the extent of its authority in the two islands governed as part of the 'Macau colony' was limited. Yet a refugee camp was in fact set up on Coloane by the colonial government and was run by the local authorities in coordination with the Refugee Relief Commission. In December, the first batch of 600 Chinese refugees was moved to what a local paper called the Coloane 'concentration camp' in order to 'decongest' the city of Macau.[127]

Conditions in the camp were dire. In April 1939, concerns were raised about the quantity and quality of the food provided.[128] After visiting the camp, the Islands Council administrator reported in shock to the head of civil administration services in the Macau government:

> The shack where the kitchen is located can be said to be little less than filthy. The shack that hosts the refugees is a constant threat to their lives, if a cigarette tip starts a fire that will rapidly make that container a brazier ... It has around 600 refugees amongst men, women and children, and the sick aspect of most, without any medical assistance, with shortage of quinine that has been lacking for some

[126] Diao Zuoqian to MOFA, 28 June 1938, AH-IMH, Waijiaobu, 312.8/0001.
[127] 'Refugiados Chineses' ('Chinese Refugees'), *VM* (30 Dec. 1938), p. 4.
[128] Islands Council Administrator to President of the Refugee Relief Commission, 28 Apr. 1939, AM, MO/AH/AC/AC1/35/13.

time, and with the frightening number of hospitalised sick and deceased, with orphaned children, has wounded my humanitarian feelings.[129]

Despite this description, which vividly illustrates the extreme misery poor refugees faced, the authorities did provide some medical assistance, as other documents in the Archives of Macau reveal. Refugees were taken to the Hospital Conde São Januário when sick and were vaccinated against smallpox.[130] However, the island continued to be treated as a dumping ground for those deemed undesirable. In December 1941, the local government decided to intern beggars 'in an appropriate place in Coloane island where they will be provided with housing and food'.[131] Even in their material destitution, refugees still had agency, however. A local paper reported that the Macau government's 'kindness' in designating an unused factory building on Green Island (Ilha Verde) to harbour Chinese homeless refugees was repaid with 'the theft of all the factory's equipment: taps, pipes, bulbs, lampshades, lamps and cleaning material'.[132] Amidst the moralistic tone of the report, one glimpses the small, but real, efforts that refugees made to survive. By using materials that did not belong to them to presumably sell or exchange, possibly for food or money, they were not so far removed from the wartime reality in the enclave, where the authorities engaged in similar activities on quite a different scale, as will be addressed in Chapter 4.

After the occupation of Hong Kong and the arrival of more refugees, efforts to contain the urban poor were heightened through a combination of public and private initiatives to relocate people to spaces that were reinvented during the war but where the goal of state control was evident in the involvement of police officers. The Beggars' Refuge (Refúgio dos Mendigos), for example, was an institution funded by government funds, subscriptions and charity events that the numerous philanthropic institutions of Macau organised, as well as donations from private individuals, particularly Chinese.

Initially located in terrible conditions on Green Island, the refuge was moved to an old firecracker factory, which a local newspaper reporter described as a proper, clean place where 'everybody worked, except the elderly and children', and where there was no lack of food. The Beggars' Refuge was run by a lieutenant and two guards from the Public Security

[129] Islands Council Administrator to Head of the Civil Administration Services, 8 Sept. 1939, ibid.

[130] See files in AM, MO/AH/AC/ACI/35/13.

[131] 'Nota Oficiosa' ('Unofficial Note'), *VM* (26 Dec. 1941), p. 3.

[132] 'Por bem fazer' ('By Doing Good'), *VM* (19 Jan. 1942), p. 3.

Police, and one male nurse. It housed 840 people, including criminals (155 men, 283 women, 213 children and 189 detainees serving various sentences).

Another place to which destitute refugees were sent was the Poorhouse (Casa dos Pobres), located in the same place where racing dogs used to live before the war. It housed 200 people who, according to a positive news report, benefitted from 'clean cubicles, schools for the children, an admirably kept little garden, chicken, ducks, goose and pork raising, etc.'.[133] The institution was run by the police commissioner, a sergeant, three guards and a male nurse. It was funded by the Macau government and by private donations. Named after the governor, an asylum 'for the internment of 150 poor children' was also founded in October 1942 and included a children's infirmary.[134] The involvement of security forces in these spaces is also telling of the colonial state's militarised control of refugee camps, in contrast to most camps in Hong Kong and Shanghai, for example, where civilian groups were largely in charge.[135] Although the camps were publicly promoted as humanitarian projects, those confined there experienced dire poverty conditions and, at least in the case of one camp, were victims of indiscriminate violence, such as beatings.[136]

As in the case of the Portuguese refugees, willingness to provide relief, however small, clashed with financial constraints to do so and with the inability to manage its implementation. As late as May 1944, the Macau government nominated a commission of four Chinese figures, amongst whom were Gao Kening and the president of the Kiang Wu Hospital, Liu Xutang, to investigate the conditions of the Chinese refugees in Macau, implying the local authorities were unable to do so themselves effectively.[137]

These cases illustrate how management of the poorest refugees involved the collaboration of local colonial authorities (including military and police officers), local elites of different nationalities and religious figures. Their activities evidence the ambiguous links between humanitarian assistance and discipline measures against the most vulnerable refugees.

[133] 'Uma extraordinária Obra de Assistência' ('An Extraordinary Work of Assistance'), *VM* (24 Apr. 1943), p. 2.

[134] 'Asilo Governador Gabriel Teixeira' ('Governor Gabriel Teixeira Asylum'), *VM* (6 Apr. 1943), p. 3.

[135] For example, Ristaino, *Jacquinot Safety Zone*.

[136] 'Some Preliminary Observations on the Macao Refugee Camps', 26 Oct. 1945, NLA, MS 4300, Box 169, Series 8.1/27.

[137] 'Refugiados chineses' ('Chinese Refugees'), *VM* (27 May 1944), p. 2.

Commercial and Cultural Golden Era

The massive refugee influx into Macau was a crisis, but it was also an opportunity – and not just for the colonial authorities. Some of those who sought refuge in Macau had a considerable impact on the enclave's economic, artistic and educational sectors. The 'boom' caused by the arrival of refugees was observable in different parts of China such as the first wartime capital of Wuhan or the British colony of Hong Kong.[138] In Macau, which was deemed a relative backwater, the effects were tremendous, and heightened by its nominal maintenance of neutrality until the end of the war.

Several financial institutions and companies moved to Macau, leading to an ambivalent period of new-found economic prosperity. Fei notes how some of the newcomers brought 'huge amounts of gold, silver and foreign currency with them' and the financial market in Macau boomed, with as many as 300 banking institutions set up in the enclave.[139] The financial prosperity of Macau in the early stages of the war derived from Macau's role as an exchange station between the interior and Hong Kong, a situation that ended with the occupation of the British colony in 1941.[140] One Chinese scholar called it Macau's financial 'golden era'.[141] Throughout the war, money exchange brokers were some of the main private philanthropists to donate to refugee relief. Amongst the newcomers was a man who would become the most powerful Chinese figure in Macau after the war, Ho Yin (He Xian). In 1938, he left Guangzhou for Hong Kong, and then moved to Macau where he excelled in financial activities, later branching out to other sectors. In the post-war period, he consolidated his position as a gold trade magnate and, as a prominent 'red capitalist', he became the key intermediary between the Portuguese administration and the communist authorities across the border.[142]

The movement of people and capital to Macau during the war was accompanied by the relocation of providers of commodities and services. The enclave became a key transfer station between the Chinese interior, Hong Kong and occupied areas, with many transport companies moving to the enclave.[143] The China Travel Service, a commercial agency

[138] MacKinnon, *Wuhan, 1938*; Lopes, 'Impact of Refugees'.
[139] Fei, *Macau 400 Years*, p. 345.
[140] K. Deng and X. Lu (eds.), *Yue Gang Ao jindai guanxi shi* (*Modern History of Guangdong–Hong Kong–Macau Relations*) (Guangzhou, 1996), pp. 291–2.
[141] Zhang, 'Kangzhan qianqi', p. 86.
[142] 'He Xian', in *Gang'Ao dabaike quanshu*, p. 804; Jorge and Coelho, *Roque Choi*, pp. 38–41.
[143] Zhang, 'Kangzhan qianqi', pp. 83–4.

founded by the Chiang Kai-shek ally Chen Guangfu, set up offices in Macau to serve international travellers, including Chinese students going overseas.[144] Several Chinese companies opened branches or relocated activities to Macau. One of them was the herbal tea brand Wong Lo Kat (Wang lao ji), which still exists today.[145] Neutrality enticed refugees fleeing the war, and their presence provided a new pool of consumers who were embraced by Chinese medicine businesses from Guangdong or clothes and furniture shops.[146]

The impact of refugees on the enclave's artistic scene was also significant. Many musicians and Cantonese opera singers and troupes – whose main audiences had previously been found in Shanghai, Guangzhou and Hong Kong – moved to Macau, especially after the occupation of Hong Kong, contributing to the cultural 'golden era' of wartime Macau.[147]

The visual arts also experienced an unusual prosperity in Macau with the arrival of individuals such as Gao Jianfu, a leading figure of the Lingnan school of painting.[148] Like the other artists of the Lingnan school, Gao had a close relationship with the KMT and had travelled widely before reaching Macau. He had become a member of Sun Yat-sen's Tongmenhui whilst studying in Japan in the early twentieth century and had travelled to several parts of Asia, including to India, Persia and Egypt, in the 1930s.[149] In 1936, he had been appointed professor of fine arts at the National Central University in Nanjing, having left the capital for Guangzhou when the Japanese invaded. When Guangzhou was occupied, he left again, this time for Macau, where he stayed in the Puji Buddhist Temple and re-established the art studio he had in Guangzhou, the Chun Shui Studio.[150] In Macau, Gao and his disciples, such as Guan Shanyue, supported the Chinese resistance through art.[151]

[144] P. M. Coble, *China's War Reporters: The Legacy of Resistance against Japan* (Cambridge, MA, 2015), p. 92; Y. Mo, *Touring China: A History of Travel Culture, 1912–1949* (Ithaca, NY, 2021), p. 145.

[145] Zhang, 'Kangzhan qianqi', p. 86.

[146] Ibid., pp. 84, 86–7.

[147] M. B. Ching, 'Itinerant Singers: Triangulating the Canton–Hong Kong–Macau Soundscape', in E. Tagliacozzo, H. F. Siu and P. C. Perdue (eds.), *Asia Inside Out: Itinerant People* (Cambridge, MA, 2019), pp. 244–70, at pp. 261–2; N. L. Lam, '"The Song of Selling Olives": Acoustic Experience and Cantonese Identity in Canton, Hong Kong, and Macau across the Great Divide of 1949', *China Perspectives*, 3 (2019), pp. 9–16, at p. 12.

[148] Barreto, *Macau during the Sino–Japanese War*, p. 87.

[149] D. Nash, 'Gao Jianfu', Grove Art Online (2003). doi.org/10.1093/gao/9781884446054.article.T030631.

[150] *The Art of Kao Chien-Fu* (Hong Kong 1978), pp. 12, 14.

[151] W. Chen, 'Guan Shanyue', Grove Art Online (2002). doi.org/10.1093/gao/9781884446054.article.T097478.

In July 1939, Gao and his students exhibited more than 200 works at the Commercial Association, drawing the attention of the public. Ralph Crozier notes that 'large crowds, reportedly over ten thousand people in five days, flocked to what must have been one of the biggest cultural events in the history of the tiny Portuguese colony'. Gao and his disciples produced paintings in the Lingnan style that addressed the effects of the war on Chinese civilians.[152] That such an exhibition could have been held in Macau highlights the relative freedom of expression that still graced Chinese opponents to Japan in the territory. Until 1941, like other refugees, Gao moved between Macau and Hong Kong. When the latter was occupied, he relocated with his family and several of his students to the Portuguese-administered enclave for the remainder of the war. He refused to have any association with Wang Jingwei's collaborationist government, despite the deteriorating living conditions in wartime Macau and the fact that he had once been close to Wang's left KMT faction.[153] Gao Jianfu's case is also significant because it illustrates how certain dynamics of the wartime refugee experience were replicated during the Chinese Civil War that followed the conflict with Japan. Gao returned to Guangzhou in 1945, but after the communist victory he moved to Macau, remaining there until the end of his life.[154]

The cases of financiers, traders and artists who came to Macau during the war attest to the relative openness enjoyed in the territory. They also show how, instead of being passive receivers or spectators, some of those seeking refuge took the initiative to help themselves and other refugees through their professions, philanthropy or fundraising activities. As observed in other colonial spaces in China in earlier time periods, neutral Macau offered many Chinese 'considerable freedom, choice, agency and economic prosperity, without denying the hierarchical power relations of imperialism'.[155] Macau's relevance had declined with the rise of the treaty ports. By the late 1930s, when the free-market cosmopolitanism of the treaty ports was succumbing to Japanese military might, Macau benefitted from the transfer of people, ideas, activities, material goods and funds, regaining some of the importance that it had lost in the nineteenth century.

[152] R. Croizier, *Art and Revolution in Modern China: The Lingnan (Cantonese) School of Painting, 1906–1951* (Berkeley, CA, 1988), p. 153.
[153] Ibid., pp. 144–5.
[154] M. Sullivan, *Art and Artists of Twentieth-Century China* (Berkeley, CA, 1996), p. 57.
[155] B. Goodman and D. S. G. Goodman, 'Introduction: Colonialism in China', in B. Goodman and D. S. G. Goodman (eds.), *Twentieth-Century Colonialism and China: Localities, the Everyday and the World* (Abingdon, 2012), pp. 1–22, at p. 11.

Relocation of Schools

One of the aspects that best demonstrates the impact Chinese refugees had on Macau was the relocation of several Chinese schools and tens of thousands of students from mainland China, particularly from Guangdong province.[156] Apart from Catholic clergy training, Macau was far from being a renowned education centre in China, but the war created an opportunity for a significant enhancement of its education sector.

The relocation of schools is a clear example of how neutral Macau was very much part of the social experience of China's War of Resistance. The wartime relocation of Chinese schools to unoccupied areas was a monumental government-supported undertaking.[157] The smaller-scale relocation of schools to foreign-ruled neutral territories has received less scholarly attention, but it was significant in illustrating the interplay of state and non-state responses to wartime displacement.

Portuguese colonial indifference to the education of Chinese people in Macau was, until the late 1980s, a key characteristic of its administration. Chinese residents of Macau mostly attended private schools or those run by the Catholic Church, with Chinese as the main medium of instruction.[158] Figures for 1933 – which may already reflect a rise in the number of students after the 1932 conflict in Shanghai – show around 7,600 students attending around 98 Chinese private schools in Macau.[159] The war was significant in strengthening both Christian and secular private schools, enhancing the enclave's educational opportunities and blurring the lines between foreign and Chinese providers.

In the late 1930s, the schools that relocated to Macau hailed predominantly from different parts of Guangdong province, such as Jiangmen, Zhongshan or Guangzhou.[160] Even before the last was occupied, the transfer of schools was already being noted in official correspondence. In August 1938, Barbosa informed the minister of colonies in Lisbon of a rise in the number of Chinese schools transferred from Guangzhou.[161] By 1939, there were 36 middle and secondary schools in Macau with

[156] I cover this in greater detail in H. F. S. Lopes, 'Wartime Education at the Crossroads of Empires: The Relocation of Schools to Macao during the Second World War, 1937–1945', *Twentieth-Century China*, 46/2 (2021), pp. 130–52.

[157] For example, J. Israel, *Lianda: A Chinese University in War and Revolution* (Stanford, CA, 1998); J. Liu, 'Defiant Retreat: The Relocation of Middle Schools to China's Interior, 1937–1945', *Frontiers of History in China*, 8/4 (2013), pp. 558–84.

[158] X. Yan, 'The Language Situation in Macao', *Current Issues in Language Planning*, 18/1 (2017), pp. 1–38, at p. 18.

[159] Zheng, *1940 niandai de Aomen jiaoyu*, p. 54.

[160] AM, AH/EDU/3174 and AM, AH/EDU/3187.

[161] Barbosa to MC, 9 Aug. 1938, ANTT, AOS, UL-10A1, cx. 767.

more than 30,000 students, and more than 140 primary schools with 30,000 to 40,000 students.[162] Relocated Chinese schools reached more than 100. The number dropped after 1941, reaching about 50 (of which 35 were private) in 1943, and it rose again in 1945.[163] That year, there were almost 90 schools, more than 900 staff, and around 16,300 students in Macau, most of whom were attending middle school.[164] The dynamism of Chinese education in Macau is well illustrated by the plethora of school advertisements found in the enclave's press during the war.[165]

The number of schools operating in Macau during the war grew, but there was fluctuation, reflecting wartime developments in surrounding areas. Some schools expanded, but others seemed to have decided to leave Macau, notably after the relative consolidation of the RNG, which made some in Macau consider the possibility of a safe return to the mainland. The occupation of Hong Kong in late 1941 also affected the educational landscape as it disrupted the flow of remittances from Chinese overseas. Starved of funding, several Chinese schools closed.[166] Still, other students and teachers continued to flee to Macau, notably from occupied Hong Kong. Overall numbers increased markedly in the final years of the war, when many left Guangdong and Hong Kong to flee Allied bombing announcing the impending defeat of Japan and the RNG.

Files held at the Archives of Macau demonstrate the similarities between the neutral enclave and wartime China's better-known 'lone islands', namely Shanghai's foreign concessions. Several authorisation requests for the (re-)establishment of Chinese schools often start by noting that the school had come to flee the war.[167] Reasons for fleeing included the material destruction of schools' premises, danger to students and staff and disruption caused by supplies, including remittances, being cut off. The schools' relocation to Macau was often marked by financial instability and dependency on lengthy bureaucratic approvals. Archival records reveal a continuous increase in the number of students, especially

[162] Tan, *Aomen zhuquan wenti shimo*, p. 223. Similar data are stated in Deng, *Aomen lishi*, pp. 412–13, which includes a list of most of the relocated schools.

[163] Z. Zheng, '1941–1945 nianjian Aomen jiaoyujie dui jiaoshi he xuesheng de jiuji gongzuo' ('Macau Education Circles' Relief Work for Teachers and Students in the 1941–1945 Period'), *Minguo dang'an* (*Republican Archives*), 3 (2013), pp. 134–41, at p. 141.

[164] Table 'Huashi xuehui 1941–1945 nian Aomen xuexiao ziliao' ('Inspectorate of Chinese Schools Materials on Schools in Macau, 1941–1945'), in Zheng, *1940 niandai de Aomen jiaoyu*, p. 82.

[165] See examples from the *Huaqiao ribao* reproduced in Barreto, *Macau during the Sino–Japanese War*, p. 73, and in Lin and Wang, *Gudao yingxiang*, p. 14.

[166] Zheng lists a series of schools that ceased operating around 1943 (Zheng, *1940 niandai de Aomen jiaoyu*, p. 79).

[167] AM, AH/EDU/3174; AM, AH/EDU/3180; and AM, AH/EDU/3194.

Figure 3.2 Staff and children of the Tak Kei Primary School in Macau, June 1941. P-A1.37-128a. Courtesy of Archives Research Centre of the Presbyterian Church of Aotearoa New Zealand

through the late 1930s. This required flexible responses: the sharing of premises, delivery of some classes at night or the merger of different schools into a single institution, such as the Zhongshan Lianhe Middle School.[168] Schools classified as 'middle school' often offered several other teaching levels, including kindergarten. Some also set up free classes for poor children.

Schools with foreign missionary connections are particularly fitting examples to explore the multiple regional and international entanglements framing the relocation of schools to Macau. The Presbyterian Church of New Zealand transferred to Macau two of the schools it supported in Guangdong: the Union Normal and High School for Women, known as the Union Normal School (Guangzhou shi xiehe zhongxue), in late 1937, and the Tak Kei School (Deji nüxiao), in 1938 (see Figure 3.2). In the enclave, the Tak Kei School enrolled a record

[168] AM, AH/EDU/3187; Zheng, *1940 niandai de Aomen jiaoyu*, p. 77.

number of students and the Union Normal School also saw a steady rise in the number of students attending its normal, middle, junior and primary schools, and kindergarten; in 1940, it had 801 pupils.[169] In a report written in September 1941, the Union Normal School principal, Liao Fengling, who had overseen the school's relocation, mentioned the activities undertaken by the students to support Chinese resistance. They fundraised for relief and organised a performance of the patriotic play *Put Down Your Whip* (*Fangxia ni de bianzi*), which was a major work in wartime popular culture.[170]

As Liao noted, when it became impossible 'to raise money publicly for patriotic work' in 1939, students attempted to save privately for 'soldiers and refugees'.[171] The school engaged directly with charity work for the urban poor in Macau. Students assisted in a free school run by the Young Women's Christian Association (YWCA), about 100 girls contributed to a 'Women Labourers' Night School', and volunteers helped in refugee camps.[172] The Union Normal School played an important role in maintaining connections to the Guangzhou YWCA, facilitating the founding of a branch office in Macau, of which Liao Fengling became chairwoman. The YWCA was actively engaged in refugee relief, especially to women, cooperating with the Macau Chinese Women's Association to provide affordable meals.[173] This case illustrates the similarities between the schools that moved to neutral Macau and unoccupied China, including a prominent role played by women's and Christian institutions, and the mobilisation of students in support of the Chinese war effort.[174]

169 Archives Research Centre of the Presbyterian Church of Aotearoa New Zealand (hereafter ARC-PCANZ), 'South China Mission of the Presbyterian Church of New Zealand Annual General Report, 1939–1940', in *Proceedings of the General Assembly of the Presbyterian Church of New Zealand* (Dunedin, 1940), pp. 110–12.

170 C. T. Hung, *War and Popular Culture: Resistance in Modern China* (Berkeley, CA, 1994), pp. 55–64; X. Tang, 'Street Theater and Subject Formation in Wartime China: Toward a New Form of Public Art', *Cross-Currents – East Asian History and Culture Review*, 18 (2016), pp. 30–5.

171 'Principal's Report 1937–1941', Sept. 1941, p. 2, ARC-PCANZ, AA11/6, Union Normal & Middle School Canton (1937–1948), Missions Committee-Subject Files.

172 Ibid., p. 4.

173 W. Y. C. Wong, 'Shifting Memories: An Oral Study of the Canton Young Women's Christian Association in the 1940s', *Social Sciences and Missions*, 33 (2020), pp. 157–89, at pp. 163, 165.

174 Y. F. Wu, 'Women in the War', *Chinese Recorder and Educational Review*, 71/6 (1940), pp. 369–73; Schneider, 'Mobilising Women', pp. 213–36; M. M. Tillman, *Raising China's Revolutionaries: Modernizing Childhood for Cosmopolitan Nationalists and Liberated Comrades, 1920s–1950s* (New York, 2018), pp. 79–130; A. W. Moore, 'Kunming Dreaming: Hope, Change, and War in the Autobiographies of Youth in China's Southwest', in T. Lincoln and T. Xu (eds.), *The Habitable City in China: Urban History in the Twentieth Century* (New York, 2017), pp. 43–70.

Personal links, therefore, also played a role in the process of transferring schools. Sometimes, family ties connected different institutions. The Union Middle School principal, Liao Fengling, was one of the daughters of Liao Deshan, an associate of Sun Yat-sen who had founded the Pui Ching [Peizheng] Middle School in Guangzhou, which also relocated to Macau. The number of students increased considerably, with dormitories spreading over different locations, including in the Lou Lim Ieoc Garden, next to the present-day school buildings.[175] Initially, the school expected to enrol 250 students, but it ended up with some 450.[176] As the war went on, the Pui Ching Middle School played an important role in securing relief for its most vulnerable pupils. For example, in 1944, the school directors undertook a fundraising campaign with the support of Governor Teixeira to assist poor children attending the school.[177]

Archival files on Pui Ching and other schools, containing requests for expanding their premises, highlight the growth of the student population in Macau, fuelled by the continuous arrival of refugees. Their presence was quite visible in the everyday life of the city, as attested by the recollections written by the British consul and by the Portuguese missionary and local historian Manuel Teixeira.[178] The refugees included not only students but also education professionals such as teachers and administrators. Pre-existing institutions hired some of them and expanded their activities due to rising demand. For example, St Joseph's College (Colégio de São José), a Catholic school set up in Macau in 1931, hired many refugee teachers from China.[179] Another Catholic school, the Yuet Wah [Yuehua] College – which had moved from Guangzhou in 1928 – set up free classes for around 300 poor refugees. In 1942, facing an economic crisis due to disruption of its overseas funding and the growing number of students, one of the school's founders, Liao Fengji – elder sister of Liao Fengling – asked for the assistance of the Salesians (a Catholic institute with a significant international presence), who took over the school. Yuet Wah's wartime

[175] 'Guangzhou Pei Zheng zhongxuexiao wen' ('Guangzhou Pui Ching Middle School News'), *Jiaoyu jikan* (*Education Quarterly*), 14/4 (1938), p. 84 (the garden is mentioned here as the 'Lu family garden' (*Lu jia huayuan*). The Lou Lim Ieoc Garden is named after Lu Lianruo (Lou Lim Ieoc, 1878–1927), a Macau philanthropist, supporter of Sun Yat-sen.

[176] Zheng, *1940 niandai de Aomen jiaoyu*, p. 62.

[177] 'Campaign to Raise Funds for Free Education', *Macau Tribune* (26 Mar. 1944), p. 6.

[178] Reeves estimated that the number of Chinese students relocated to Macau was 20,000 (Reeves, *The Lone Flag*, p. 44); Teixeira put the number at 30,000 (Teixeira, 'Macau Durante a Guerra', p. 515).

[179] M. Teixeira, *A Educação em Macau* (*Education in Macau*) (Macau, 1982), p. 262.

expansion also included a women's branch.[180] The Liao family's connections to different schools further exemplifies the importance of personal relations to wartime education and relief.

The expansion of education in Macau benefitted the student-refugees and the children of pre-existing residents. In fact, scholars have argued that this period witnessed an unprecedented flourishing of Chinese education in Macau.[181] The arrival of the relocated students and teachers brought an influx of expertise. Theatre performances became relatively frequent, echoing developments in mainland China, where children's theatre experienced spectacular growth during the war.[182] Physical education also expanded, leading to a lively period for sports competitions of various kinds in the enclave.[183]

The refugee students were not only regarded as important for Chinese resistance to Japan, but also featured in Portuguese ideas of colonial prestige, two concerns that were not necessarily compatible as they had very different rationales regarding imperial power. Governor Gabriel Teixeira in particular sought to convey to authorities in Lisbon that the influx of Chinese students could hold the key to the territory's future development. The model for this reasoning was likely Hong Kong, whose prosperity under British rule was a permanent source of anxiety for the Portuguese authorities, who partly resented how Hong Kong had overtaken Macau as a major node for maritime trade between China, Southeast Asia and Europe.

Teixeira remarked on the overseas connections of some of the schools' staff and students and was no doubt aware that assisting them meant, implicitly, closer links to affluent people. According to Robert Culp, most students attending secondary schools in pre-war Nationalist China hailed from families with an income in the top 10–15 per cent of the urban national average.[184] The Portuguese authorities believed that their willingness to host these students who required relief could lead to future partnerships beneficial for the territory. Their knowledge and family connections would bring social and human capital to develop Macau as had happened in neighbouring Hong Kong.

[180] Teixeira, *A Educação em Macau*, p. 377. Similar data are reproduced in the Yuet Wah College website. www.yuetwah.edu.mo/86/yw.php?read=int&lang=CHT&type=history.
[181] Li, 'Lunxian qian guomin zhengfu zai Xianggang de wenjiao huodong', p. 455; Tan, *Aomen zhuquan wenti shimo*, p. 223; Deng, *Aomen lishi*, p. 413.
[182] L. Xu, 'Little Teachers: Children's Drama, Travelling, and Ruptured Childhoods in 1930s and 1940s China', *Twentieth-Century China*, 42/2 (2016), pp. 180–200, at p. 182.
[183] Tang, 'Os Desportos Modernos', p. 783.
[184] R. Culp, *Articulating Citizenship: Civic Education and Student Politics in Southeastern China, 1912–1940* (Cambridge, MA, 2007), pp. 26–7.

Even though Teixeira noted the political advantages of refugee relief, he was conscious of Portugal's limited capacity to provide it and suggested transnational solutions. In early 1942, he reported to Lisbon on a meeting with the directors of Chinese schools in Macau, who had explained that more than one third of the students were children of Chinese residents abroad affected by the lack of communications with Hong Kong, through which their family's allowances had been remitted.[185] The governor recommended notifying the Chinese ambassadors in Britain, the United States, Canada and Australia so that the students' parents would be instructed to transfer their funds to BNU in Lisbon, which would then send them to the bank's Macau branch.[186] Strategies for funding schools in Macau, therefore, highlight an often overlooked global dimension of the conflict.

As in Shanghai's French Concession and International Settlement before 1941, relief to the most destitute refugees in Macau owed much to non-state actors and local elites, whose activities colonial authorities allowed as they helped ensure a semblance of public order.[187] By allowing Chinese schools to operate in Macau, local authorities could boost colonial prestige by presenting themselves as generous protectors to distraught Chinese at a time of crisis. This image was essential to placate critiques of Portuguese rule over Macau. The supposed benevolence of colonial authorities offered an argument against probes into Portuguese collaboration with Japan by Chiang's representatives as well as against attempts by the RNG to increase control over Macau.

Incoming students enjoyed minimum governmental supervision and were only occasionally involved in joint activities intent on highlighting vague notions of 'Sino–Portuguese friendship'. In general, apart from granting authorisation for the running of the schools and inspecting their premises, the Portuguese authorities do not appear to have had any influence over the relocated Chinese schools' curriculum. This relative lack of oversight had advantages for all those involved: for the many teachers and students who moved to Macau, the enclave tended to guarantee them enough freedom to continue their activities, including the fostering of nationalist and revolutionary ideas. The fact that their major target was Japan and not, at the time, Portuguese colonialism, was important, but so was the Portuguese authorities' lack of means to fully control resistance activities. These circumstances allowed, inadvertently, for Chinese resistance to develop in Macau.

185 Teixeira to MC, 23 Jan. 1942, ANTT, AOS, UL-10A1, cx. 767. 186 Ibid.
187 Mitter, *China's War with Japan*, pp. 184–5.

In this unregulated and diverse environment, Chinese nationalism and Portuguese imperial nationalism managed to coexist and sometimes even collaborate. The presence of so many Chinese students led to new joint initiatives. In April 1940, a local paper reported on the activities of the Chinese Student-Refugees in Macau Relief Association, which provided lodging (including on boats), food and medical care. Like similar institutions set up during the war, this was a transnational endeavour, counting on the support of both Chinese and Portuguese benefactors, including the governor.[188]

Regardless of Portuguese designs, Chinese schools in Macau were, as elsewhere in China, linked to the nurture and spread of nationalistic and revolutionary ideas, and wartime education pursued a dual goal: 'support the war and prepare for national reconstruction'.[189] Indeed, support for the war effort and relief activities for victims was part of schools' wartime experience in Macau.[190] Some of the relocated schools 'advocated enthusiastically anti-Japanese patriotic education', teaching students 'to sing anti-aggression songs' and printing 'patriotic slogans ... on students' stationery'.[191]

The links between schools and resistance are also clear in Chinese Ministry of Foreign Affairs files pertaining to Macau. For example, in September 1939, under increasing Japanese pressure to curb resistance activities, the local Portuguese authorities sent the police to raid (among other locations) the Chong Tak Middle School, which was closely linked to the KMT.[192] This private school from Guangzhou was founded in 1914 as a Sino–German School and, in 1938, KMT luminaries such as Wu Tiecheng initiated its Macau branch. Student numbers increased considerably such that, by September 1943, the school had more than 400 students starting from kindergarten. Like other relocated schools, it also ran classes for refugee children.[193] Despite the rise in student numbers, overt actions supporting the Chinese resistance were toned down under tightening Japanese control and were, after 1941, largely confined to refugee relief.

[188] 'Socorros aos estudantes chineses refugiados' ('Relief to Chinese Refugee Students'), *VM* (24 Apr. 1940), p. 5; 'Festa de Caridade' (Charity Fête), *VM* (7 Aug. 1944), p. 4.

[189] T. C. Ou, 'Education in Wartime China', in P. K. T. Sih (ed.), *Nationalist China during the Sino–Japanese War, 1937–1945* (Hicksville, NY, 1977), pp. 89–123, at p. 90.

[190] On Hong Kong, see B. H. K. Luk, 'War, Schools, China, Hong Kong: 1937–1949', in James Flath and Norman Smith (eds.), *Beyond Suffering: Recounting War in Modern China* (Vancouver, 2011), pp. 36–58, at pp. 45–6.

[191] Barreto, *Macau during the Sino–Japanese War*, p. 75.

[192] Military Affairs Commission to Wang Chonghui, 20 Sept. 1939. Later reports dating from Barbosa's governorship indicate that Portuguese authorities continued to search the schools in order to curb anti-Japanese activities in Macau ('Japanese Threats to Macao', *NCH* (3 Apr. 1940), p. 8).

[193] Zheng, *1940 niandai de Aomen jiaoyu*, pp. 71–2.

The relocation of Chinese schools to Macau allows us to understand how some of the regional and transnational networks engaged in refugee relief operated in the enclave. For Chinese students and teaching staff, Macau's neutrality was convenient as it provided them with a space both to continue their teaching activities and to foster a politically conscious youth that could be used for patriotic mobilisation. For the Portuguese authorities, the influx of educated and potentially influential Chinese figures was seen as a source of colonial prestige, reflecting positively on their 'openness' to assist them at a time of need. In the eyes of some Portuguese officials, the newcomers provided potentially useful connections that were considered advantageous for Macau's future development under colonial rule. The experience of the relocated schools and of the educators and student-refugees in Macau during the war expands and complicates the narrative of wartime education in China, highlighting the interplay of nationalists and imperial interests, relief providers and transnational encounters. It also attests to the ambivalences of neutrality that allowed for expressions of Chinese anti-imperialist nationalism in territories under foreign colonial rule.

Conclusion

The collaborative practices brought about by the experience of neutrality in Macau were indissociable from the influx of refugees into the territory since 1937. The arrival of around 300,000 displaced persons was a central feature of the territory's wartime experience, conditioning political, diplomatic and economic connections at local, regional and international levels. This chapter has shown how the flight of displaced persons to Macau represented both a challenge and an opportunity to different authorities, local elites and the refugees themselves. Responses to the refugee crisis sprang from interconnected top-down and bottom-up efforts. Without popular mobilisation for assisting refugees, it would have been impossible for the Portuguese authorities to manage the influx on their own. However, the territory's neutrality sprang from the fact that it was under the rule of a neutral foreign country. Colonial authorities had the power to control (most) arrivals and to facilitate the allocation of relief funds. Regardless of how partial that power was, collaboration with the local government was sought by different actors to manage the circulation or the relocation of multinational groups of refugees.

The first wave of refugees to reach Macau mostly comprised Chinese and Portuguese from Shanghai and Guangdong province. Neutrality made Macau a feasible option for many fleeing the war on the mainland. Contrary to other foreign authorities elsewhere in China, the Portuguese did not limit the number of those allowed to enter. Welcoming refugees was used as a strategy to enhance colonial prestige even though, in practice, Portuguese authorities had limited means for relief provision. Evacuation plans often included requesting assistance from other countries and were only set in motion with significant involvement from local associations. Chinese elite figures and charities acted as indispensable intermediaries between the majority of the population and the Macau government. They also played a key role in liaising with occupation authorities beyond Macau to provide livelihood supplies to a significantly swollen population. The following chapters will demonstrate how Portuguese authorities cited assistance to refugees as a defence of their wartime conduct against accusations of collaboration with Japan and the Wang Jingwei government. Although not the only reason, it helped to prevent serious inquiries on wartime collaboration and guaranteed the continuity of the Portuguese administration in Macau after the conflict.

Responses to the refugee influx were marked by various forms of collaboration involving different state and civil society representatives. The unrealised project to establish a refugee safety zone outside of Macau's borders is particularly illustrative of the interactions of different national, political and religious entities in refugee management.

The ambiguity of Macau's neutrality is also discerned in the unintended opportunities the war created in the enclave by and for the newcomers. Refugees brought financial and human capital that revitalised the socio-economic and cultural life of the territory. For the hundreds of thousands who came to Macau during the war, the enclave guaranteed enough freedom from the Japanese occupation and opportunities to pursue their activities. They could still trade, paint, teach and mobilise for resistance, although the last became more difficult from 1942 onwards. This relatively open environment resulted from the powerlessness of the Portuguese authorities, who would not have been able to enforce more thorough control without the risk of being overpowered by the Chinese forces (either of the central government or of collaborationist authorities in Guangdong) or by the Japanese forces.

Nevertheless, Macau's neutrality did not isolate it from the effects of the war as they were felt in other areas of China. Many refugees faced unemployment, poverty and a growing problem of food scarcity, which will be detailed in the next chapter. The challenge of a swollen and deprived population created further needs for collaboration.

The Japanese occupation of Hong Kong in late 1941 prompted a second wave of refugees to seek shelter in Macau. The know-how acquired during the first wave was of paramount importance, with similar actions deployed and some common individuals and institutions involved. However, there were also some important differences, including the emergence of the British consulate as a major player in refugee management, as we will see in Chapter 5.

4 The Last 'Lone Island'

Pressure, Profits and Philanthropy

In May 1942, a letter sent to Sydney from C. H. Cheng, a Chinese man in Macau, was intercepted by the Investigation Section of Australian customs. With an associate, Cheng had set up an office to 'take care of communications and sustenance money sent home by friends in Australia and New Zealand for their families'. Counting on the ability to send communications by cable from Macau to other parts of the world via Lisbon, he also noted that it was possible to transfer money to occupied Guangzhou, Zengcheng and Zhongshan without difficulty.[1] As this letter and several requests from Chinese Australians to send remittances to relatives in Macau found in Australian archives indicate, Macau's neutral status was an oddity that both facilitated the flow of information and funds at a time of disruption and confused government officials. Indeed, the Department of the Treasury in Canberra requested the comptroller-general of customs in July 1942 to 'advise urgently whether the Portuguese settlement of Macao is regarded as enemy territory or not for the purposes of the Trading with the Enemy Act'.[2] At a time when other commercial centres – most notably Hong Kong – were temporarily cut off by the conflict, Macau offered new prospects and motivated new suspicions to different people.

The diplomatic tensions and the challenges and opportunities springing from a growing number of refugees in Macau reached a peak between the occupation of Hong Kong in late 1941 and the end of the war. This period, when Macau came to be the last 'lone island' of neutrality in China, brought to the forefront old and novel needs for collaboration between different sides. Despite being the extant foreign-ruled territory in

[1] Translated extract from letter from C. H. Cheng to Ah Yen, 20 May 1942, sent from H. B. Cody, Investigation Section of the Customs and Excise Office, New South Wales, to the Comptroller-General, Canberra, National Archives of Australia (hereafter NAA), Series no. A1539, 1942/W/2712, National Security (Exchange Control) regulations – Trading with the Enemy Act 1939–1940 – Remittances to Portuguese Macao.

[2] Department of the Treasury to Comptroller-General of Customs, Canberra, 17 July 1942, NAA, Series no. A1539, 1942/W/2712.

China still technically neutral and formally unoccupied by Japan, Macau remained connected to different locales in China and beyond (see Figure 4.1). It was the last *gudao*, but a porous one. This chapter explores the uses of Macau's neutral status by a series of actors whose interests both clashed and intersected: the Chinese central government, the collaborationist RNG, Japanese military, naval and diplomatic agents, the Macau Portuguese authorities, the Portuguese government and local elite figures in Macau. Macau was at the crossroads of these competing forces struggling for political, economic and social leverage.

Channels of communication between Chiang Kai-shek's government in Chongqing and Macau were kept open despite growing Japanese control. State-to-state relations between China and Portugal were also conducted in Lisbon. The Nationalists closely monitored what was happening in the enclave. Despite the monumental challenges it faced in terms of military resistance and governance in unoccupied China, the central government did not overlook diplomacy during the war – quite the contrary – and their scrutiny of Portuguese actions attests to their longer-term, post-war vision for a sovereign China that included Macau.

In parallel, unofficial relations were conducted between the Macau authorities and Wang Jingwei's RNG, notably with the provincial government in Guangdong. This chapter provides a pioneering analysis of this relationship, which lasted until the end of the war. This was a clear example of the centuries-old parallel diplomacy between Macau and Guangzhou that bypassed formal state-to-state channels. Events in Macau made evident the tense interplay between the RNG authorities and Japanese forces, especially regarding the former's aspirations for greater sovereignty over colonial territories in South China, something little acknowledged in studies of wartime collaboration.

The struggle for control over the enclave is further explored through the analysis of the social impact of the war in Macau. The previous chapter has shown how this was severe and comparable to other occupied areas in China; this chapter will delve further into the most challenging period of the conflict, showing how lack of food supplies due to blockades led to starvation. The need to ensure the import of foodstuffs and other essential products exposed the limitations of the Portuguese colonial administration, unable to guarantee the most basic provisions of those living under their nominally neutral rule. New opportunities for collaboration emerged from this livelihood crisis and led to the rise of powerful local economic elites who acted as intermediaries between the Portuguese administration, Japanese and collaborationist forces, and other actors.

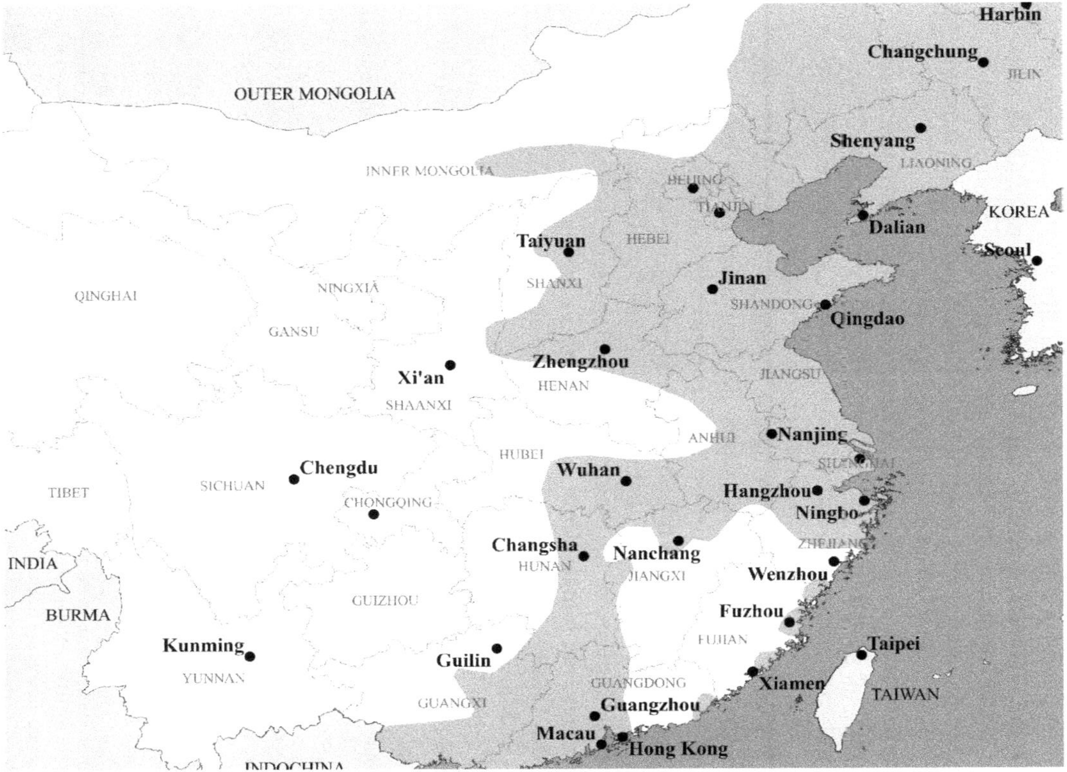

Figure 4.1 Partial map of wartime China, showing Macau surrounded by Japanese-occupied areas in 1945 (shaded). Map by Rui Teixeira Alves (based on a US Army map in the public domain via Wikimedia Commons)

An International Affair: The Nationalists and the Portuguese in Lisbon, Macau, Timor and Chongqing

It has been stated that the Nationalists had no official contact with Macau from January 1941 until the end of the war.[3] However, archival sources reveal a string of contacts and the flow of information between the Chinese wartime capital of Chongqing, Macau and Lisbon. What happened in Macau and to Chinese in the territory mattered to the Nationalist government resisting Japan and was monitored by their agents, officially and underground.

Whilst in Macau, as in Shanghai, Chinese resistance operated under life-threatening constraints, in Lisbon, official contacts were maintained with relative safety and regularity.[4] The Chinese central government kept its legation fully functioning throughout the war and it played a role well beyond Portuguese borders. In July 1941, the Chinese ambassador in Berlin, Chen Jie, and thirty of his collaborators moved to the Portuguese capital to return to China from there after Chiang's government relations with Germany broke down.[5] The legation in Lisbon was also contacted to obtain Spanish transit visas for Chinese diplomats in Switzerland.[6] After German pressure to expel Chinese diplomats from Vichy France, Lisbon received the staff of the Chinese legation and consulates, and of the KMT branch in Paris in March 1943.[7]

The French legation was led by Wellington Koo, one of the more renowned Chinese diplomats of the twentieth century. He had been

[3] G. C. Gunn, 'Introduction', in G. C. Gunn (ed.), *Wartime Macau: Under the Japanese Shadow* (Hong Kong, 2016), pp. 1–24, at p. 15.

[4] On Shanghai, see, for example, W. H. Yeh, 'Urban Warfare and Underground Resistance: Heroism in the Chinese Secret Service during the War of Resistance', in Y. H. Yeh (ed.), *Wartime Shanghai* (London, 1998), pp. 111–32.

[5] Robert de la Baume, French Ambassador do Berne, to François Darlan, Vichy Minister of Foreign Affairs, 12 July 1941, MAE, 3GMII/94.

[6] Victor Hoo, Washington, to Chinese Minister in Lisbon, 17 Apr. 1942, TNA, HW 12/275.

[7] On the journey from Vichy to Lisbon via Spain, see files in MAE, 3GMII/93 and MAE, 3GMII/94; Kuomintang Central Committee, *Zhongguo Guomindang zai haiwai* (*The KMT Overseas*) (Taipei, 1961), p. 148; M. Bastid-Bruguière, 'Les Relations entre l'Indochine de Decoux et le Gouvernement de Wang Jingwei Pendant la Deuxième Guerre Mondiale' ('Relations between Decoux's Indochina and the Wang Jingwei Government during the Second World War'), in L. Cesari and D. Varaschin (eds.), *Les Relations Franco-Chinoises au Vingtième Siècle et leurs Antécédents* (*Sino–French Relations in the Twentieth Century and Their Antecedents*) (Arras, 2003), pp. 233, 239. Likewise, when the French (Vichy) embassy in Chongqing was closed in March 1943, its staff moved to Lisbon ('A embaixada de França em Chungking foi fechada' ('The French Embassy in Chongqing Was Closed'), *VM* (9 Mar. 1943), p. 1).

part of the Chinese delegation to the Paris Peace Conference in 1919, China's first representative to the League of Nations, minister of foreign affairs and premier, and would go on to serve as ambassador to the United Kingdom and to the United States. Koo went to Lisbon more than once during the war. In April 1941, he travelled to the Portuguese capital to meet the new Chinese minister of foreign affairs, Guo Taiqi, who was on his way to Chongqing after leaving his post as ambassador in London, which Koo took over.[8]

Earlier, in 1940, Koo had attended the Portuguese World Exhibition, a massive imperial propaganda event under the pretext of celebrating 800 years since Portugal's 'foundation' and 300 years of independence from Spanish rule. Koo's wife, Java-born Oei Hui-lan (Huang Huilan), a global figure in her own right, accompanied him to Lisbon on that occasion and left a lively account of her experience, where the contrast between the drama of recently occupied France and the festive elite atmosphere she experienced in neutral Lisbon is striking. The Chinese minister, Li Jinlun, and the Portuguese authorities gave them a warm welcome. There is an interesting gendered dimension in Oei Hui-lan's recollections. Although she describes Salazar as 'charming' and 'very good looking', she also notes that he 'was amused when I talked politics', suggesting that a highly educated and cosmopolitan Chinese woman puzzled Salazar.[9]

She was quick to notice that, at a state dinner she attended, 'there were no Germans or Japanese', and she guessed that 'duplicate dinners must have been given'.[10] Even if not on display, the Portuguese attempts to be on good terms with opposing sides were easily assumed. Like Macau, Lisbon was a global intersection in World War II, an important stopover and haven for many people: Chinese diplomats participated in the wartime cosmopolitanism of the Portuguese capital much as the underground KMT agents participated in Macau's.

The smooth running of the Chinese legation in Lisbon contrasted with the shambolic Portuguese diplomatic presence in China that, as noted in Chapter 2, was concentrated in occupied areas. A particular point of contention was the presence of the Portuguese minister to China

[8] Note from the Political Direction of the Vichy Ministry of Foreign Affairs, 15 Apr. 1941, MAE, 3GMII/94; 'Gu Weijun wang Pu wu Guo Taiqi' ('Wellington Koo Goes to Portugal to Meet Guo Taiqi'), *Shenbao* (18 Apr. 1941).

[9] H. L. Koo, *An Autobiography As Told to Mary Van Rensselaer Thayer* (New York, 1943), pp. 343–4.

[10] Ibid., p. 344. When Wellington Koo moved to Lisbon after the exodus of the Legation in Paris, Hui-lan Koo initially stayed behind, only returning by car later. Her border-crossing adventure through France and Spain before finding a temporary refuge in the Portuguese seaside town of Estoril – a centre of international exile and intrigue with some parallels to Macau – closes her 1943 memoir (ibid., pp. 361–4).

accredited to Chiang's government, João de Lebre e Lima, in occupied Shanghai, throughout the war. He remained in Shanghai because Portuguese authorities believed that to move him to Chongqing would create difficulties with Japan.[11] Even so, Lima was indeed forced to experience 'difficulties' in Shanghai. Japanese authorities had prevented him from communicating with Lisbon in cypher since July 1942, ensuring that all of his communications were monitored and, in practice, compromising their content.[12]

In January 1943, the Chinese minister to Portugal, Li Jinlun, wrote to Chongqing about the problematic issue of Lima's geographical base. The Portuguese justified not moving him there by alleging difficulties in transportation. Li informed Chongqing that the Portuguese authorities had written to Lima urging him to leave Shanghai for Chongqing, but it had not been possible until then because Portugal did not have diplomatic relations with Russia and so Lima could not travel via that country. It was an odd justification given all the other routes still open to him, including via French-ruled Guangzhouwan.[13]

The excuse for not transferring Lima is even more unconvincing if we consider that several foreign diplomats facing arguably harder challenges got to Chongqing during the war: the Norwegian minister came after being interned by the Japanese in Bangkok, and the Belgium ambassador had been in Hong Kong and in Shanghai and got to Chongqing through an exchange.[14] After some attempts to clarify the situation with the Portuguese government, it was concluded in June 1943 that it was impossible for Lima to move to Chongqing. The Chinese legation was told that another diplomat would be dispatched to the Nationalists' wartime capital, although Lima would continue to be minister to China.[15] There was an aborted attempt to dispatch a replacement for Lima, but the appointee resisted placement in China.[16] Only in 1945, at the end of the war, did a Portuguese envoy reach Chongqing.

[11] MNE to Ambassador in Rio de Janeiro, 9 Apr. 1942, TNA, HW 12/275.
[12] Henri Cosme, French Ambassador in Beijing to Vichy Ministry of Foreign Affairs, 10 Nov. 1943, MAE, 3GMII/93; also in MAE, 3GMII/122.
[13] Lima to MOFA, 7 Jan. 1943, AH, Waijiaobu, 020000023906A.
[14] British Embassy in Chongqing to FO, 7 Dec. 1942, TNA, FO 371/31679.
[15] Li Jinlun to MOFA, 17 June 1943, AH, Waijiaobu, 020000023906A.
[16] Zhang Qian to MOFA, 22 Dec. 1945, AH, Waijiaobu, 020000006303A, Putaoya zhu Hua gongshi Lima Feileila rennei (Portuguese Ministers in China: Period in Office of Lima and Ferreira da Fonseca). Alberto da Veiga Simões, a former Portuguese ambassador to Berlin recalled in 1940 for being too critical of Nazi Germany, considered the China post a demotion and tried to escape his appointment by invoking health reasons. The refusal cost him his career in the diplomatic corps (Fernandes, *Confluência de Interesses*, p. 42; L. A. Madeira, 'Introdução' ('Introduction'), in *Correspondência de um*

Although Sino–Portuguese diplomatic contacts could not be kept in Chongqing, that did not mean they were wholly absent. The Nationalist government found ways to send messages to the Macau Portuguese authorities, whether via the Portuguese consulate in occupied Guangzhou or through its men in Macau. The Japanese invasion of Hong Kong was accompanied by a temporary freeze in travel between the two territories, which also affected the flow of food supplies. By the early 1940s, as Macau started to face serious food shortages, a representative of the central government hidden in Hong Kong sent a delegate to the governor of Macau offering to smuggle wolfram (tungsten), tin and other minerals that could even be sold to the Japanese to buy rice, justifying his move by thanking the local authorities for the 'protection' given to Chinese residents.[17]

That acknowledgement can also be read as a warning: China, now formally part of the Allies, was paying attention to the fate of its citizens. Contacts were also made via the Portuguese consulate in Guangzhou to keep the Portuguese actions towards the local Chinese in check. For example, in November 1942, the MOFA special commissioner for Guangdong and Guangxi telegraphed the Portuguese consul in order to ask the Macau authorities to hand back to China a man who had been arrested in 1940 and sentenced to exile.[18]

Despite the maintenance of some communications, the occupation of Hong Kong made life more difficult for Nationalist agents in Macau. The British colony had been a germane location of Chinese resistance and, now that it was almost sealed off, Macau became a more important escape route. Zhou Yongneng, the head of the local KMT branch, left the enclave for Chongqing in early 1942. Those who stayed in Macau to carry on with his work faced mounting difficulties and some lost their lives in the process.[19] Liang Yanming, the principal of Chongshi Middle School and the head of the Macau Chinese Education Association, was killed on Christmas Eve 1942, shot in the street by a hidden assassin. He had been involved in setting up a variety of initiatives for 'national salvation' (*jiuguo*) and refugee relief activities, including free classes for refugee children. Post-war KMT sources celebrated Liang as a national martyr.[20]

Diplomata no III Reich (*Correspondence of a Diplomat in the Third Reich*) (Coimbra, 2005), pp. 15–33, at p. 30).

[17] Teixeira to MC, 23 Feb. 1942, ANTT, AOS, UL-10A1, cx. 767.

[18] MOFA Delegate of Guangdong and Guangxi to Monteiro, 18 Nov. 1942, Copy Sent by Gracias to Teixeira, 11 Dec. 1942, AHD, 2P, A48, M221.

[19] Zhou, *Zhou Yongneng*, p. 155; Li, 'Lunxian qian guomin zhengfu zai Xianggang', p. 461, Deng, *Aomen lishi*, p. 88.

[20] Kuomintang Branch in Hong Kong and Macau, *GangAo kangzhan xunguo lieshi jiniance* (*Album of Martyrs from Hong Kong and Macau during the War of Resistance*) (Hong Kong,

The blame for his murder would be pinned on a notorious Chinese traitor (*hanjian*), Huang Gongjie (Wong Kong Kit), whose complex journey will be addressed in Chapter 6.

Another KMT figure linked to wartime education in Macau, Lin Zhuofu, was assassinated in 1943. Lin was from nearby Zhongshan, had worked for the Guangdong province educational department, had served as secretary for the Zhongshan county KMT branch and, since the invasion of Hong Kong, had been a committee member of the Macau KMT. In February 1943, he fell victim to five bullets from a sniper as he was on his way home.[21] Both Liang and Lin attest to the links between the relocation of schools from occupied China and resistance by the Nationalists from their places of temporary exile.

Different groups of Nationalist intelligence operated in Macau during the war years. According to a post-war report, the Blue Shirts' man was Zhao Ping, who reportedly controlled '86 agents and about 200 informers'.[22] Another group was linked to the Academia Sinica president, Zhu Jiahua, at the time serving also as minister of communications. In Macau, the main figure in this group was Chen Shaomu, who worked with the collaboration of Hawaii-born Chinese Warren Wong (also known as Warren Wong Achuck or Warren Achuck), and later Xu Weimin. Smaller in number than the Blue Shirts, it reputedly controlled the KMT agents in the enclave and was in constant contact with the British consulate.[23] With an even smaller staff and pool of informers was a group under Luo Chun reporting to the Department of International Affairs in Chongqing.[24]

There was also a presence of military intelligence that reported to General Yu Hanmou, and guerrillas under Colonel Qu Renze (Watt Yuen-chat). Their men in Macau were Zhang Xinzhi and He Weihan, said to have the capacity to multiply their circa 200-strong membership

1946), p. 2; H. Guo and Z. Luo (eds.), *Liang Yanming lieshi jinianji* (*Martyr Liang Yanming Memorial Collection*) (Beijing, 1946).

[21] Kuomintang, *Gang'Ao kangzhan*, p. 1. [22] 'Economic Currents in Macao', p. 33.

[23] Ibid. A post-war OSS report based on information provided by 'Chinese, Portuguese, and British officials' lists Warren Wong as a spokesman of the 'counter-espionage agencies' of the KMT Secret Service in Macau and of the 'Magistrate of Chungshan [Zhongshan] District' (OSS, China Theatre, X-2 Branch Report 'Counter Espionage Activities in Macau', p. 2, 28 Nov. 1945, NARA, RG226, UD 173, Box 9). Another OSS report, based on 'confidential informants', lists Warren Wong (spelling his Chinese name as 黃金令 Huang Jinling, instead of 王金鈴 Wang Jinling) as representative of Dai Li's Juntong (OSS, China Theatre, X-2 Branch Report 'Political Situation in Macau', p. 3, 16 Apr. 1946, ibid.).

[24] 'Economic Currents in Macao', p. 33.

into 'as many as 2,000 within 5 or 6 hours'.[25] Although Qu Renze was given a title by the Nationalists ('deputy commander of the Third Regiment of the Seventh War Zone'), he was a 'local boss' whose smuggling network with his cousin Yuan Dai boomed during the war. They transported a variety of commodities, including opium, between Macau, Hong Kong and other parts of the Pearl River Delta.[26]

A surprising point of contact for all of these groups was Hong Kong–born British–Portuguese Jack Braga, a figure who was relatively close to Governor Teixeira and other Portuguese officials and who was also involved with British intelligence. He likely also was connected to American intelligence.[27] On good terms with a variety of local elites, Braga and his associates were engaged in intelligence, trading with the interior, contacts with Hong Kong, escapes and, not of small importance, in running a Chinese transmitting station connected to Chongqing.[28]

The Nationalists in Macau were a composite of diverse people, several of whom were part of pre-war Cantonese revolutionary circles with ambivalent postures towards Chiang Kai-shek. An example of this is Tang Liu, who would become the first MOFA commissioner in Macau after the war. He was the eldest son of Tang Shaoyi, a Zhongshan native who had been the first prime minister of the Chinese Republic.[29] In 1936, his father sided with Chiang against the Cantonese leader Chen Jitang, but later retired from politics and moved to Shanghai's French Concession, where he was killed by Chiang's agents in 1938 at a time when the Japanese were approaching Tang about becoming the president of the Nanjing collaborationist government.[30]

British intelligence files from 1939, translations of documents caught in a raid on wireless transmissions of Nationalist agents in Hong Kong, list Tang Liu as a 'traitor', noting that he was vying to become the

[25] Ibid., p. 34.
[26] H. F. Siu, *Tracing China: A Forty-Year Ethnographic Journey* (Hong Kong, 2016), p. 282.
[27] Information on Allied intelligence in Macau in the Braga Papers bears striking similarities with the content of some OSS reports in the US National Archives. On Braga's possible connections to US intelligence see Jorge and Coelho, *Roque Choi*, p. 78.
[28] Charles M. Knaggs, 'Information about Macau and the Macau area', 11 June 1942, TNA, FO 371/31630.
[29] 'Tang Liu', in *Baidu baike*. baike.baidu.com/item/唐榴.
[30] Wakeman, *Shanghai Badlands*, p. 48. Tang Shaoyi, who had chaired the Zhongshan County Administrative Committee from 1929 to 1934, was acquainted with Jack Braga, as attested by several photos in the Braga collection (NLA, MS 4300, Photographs, Box 14).

'puppet governor' of Guangdong.[31] That did not happen. Tang Liu, who had served as consul in Surabaya, Nagasaki, Singapore and Calcutta, ended up in Macau, claiming to have been the first Chinese to escape by junk from Hong Kong in early January 1942.[32] By 1943 – the year his brother-in-law Zhang Qian began serving as minister to Portugal – he was acting as representative to the central government, fostering good relations with the governor and guaranteeing him that 'Chongqing repudiates any action against Macau,' the only territory it did not claim given the 'antiquity' of Portuguese occupation.[33]

The Chinese minister to Lisbon gave similar assurances to Luís Teixeira de Sampaio, secretary general at Portugal's Ministry of Foreign Affairs. He stated that, despite rumours to the contrary, the Nationalist government did not claim Macau and 'completely recognised Macau as a Portuguese colony'.[34] Such assurances, given in 1943, when Japanese control over Macau was tight, can easily be interpreted as a way of buying time, which ran out once the conflict with Japan ended. Regardless of protestations of friendship, Chinese representatives continued to monitor Portuguese actions deemed problematic, including their dealings with the collaborationist authorities, be they in Macau or in Shanghai.

Emboldened by their diplomatic gains in early 1943, with treaties with Britain and the United States abolishing extraterritoriality, the Nationalists also took on ambitious propaganda initiatives to expose the extensive power of Japanese forces in Macau. Reports of Japanese takeover of the enclave were sometimes reproduced internationally, seemingly credible to faraway audiences.[35] Arguably, the incident that attracted the most international attention was the takeover of the British ship the SS *Sai-On* (*Xi'an*). Around 2 a.m. on 19 August 1943, a group of people, initially described as pro-Wang Jingwei, landed in Macau and towed away the *Sai-On* with all of its passengers (around seventy people), amongst whom were many Filipinos and British, including three British children.[36] Instead of confronting the attackers, Portuguese troops were ordered to remain inside the barracks. The governor was informed that 'pirates' from Zhongshan

[31] 'Translations from Card Index. Nos. 17–1741', TNA, CO 129/579/11/2. The British raid led to the expulsion from Hong Kong of David Kung (Kong Lingkan), son of H. H. Kung and Song Ailing.

[32] Tang Liu, Macau, quoted in telegram from the Chinese Legation in Lisbon to MOFA, 18 Aug. 1945, AH, Waijiaobu, 020000023906A.

[33] Teixeira to MC, 27 Feb. 1943, ANTT, AOS, NE-10A2, cx. 768. Zhang Qian was married to Tang Baozhang (Isabel Tong Chang), second daughter of Tang Shaoyi and Tang Liu's sister.

[34] Note on Conversation with the Chinese Minister, 27 May 1943, AHD, 2P, A48, M212.

[35] For example, 'Portuguese Disarmed', *San Francisco Chronicle* (6 July 1943), p. 14.

[36] Reeves, *The Lone Flag*, p. 98.

had been paid 150,000 military yen to do the job, which, he later learnt, had been planned by a Japanese navy sector whose commanders, as well as the Japanese army, had disapproved.[37] The incident constituted a clear case of 'external violation of neutrality' given that a belligerent – Japan – used the territorial waters of a neutral state to act against its enemies.[38]

The Nationalists capitalised on the propaganda value of the episode. Inflating the numbers, the Central News Agency reported that 'more than 20 Portuguese armed guards and policemen' had been killed when 'Japanese naval authorities ... forcibly commandeered the British river boat' out of Macau with 'more than 100 refugees' and large quantities of merchandise on board.[39] Reports from Chongqing about the incident had a global reach, reproduced in national and local newspapers from Dundee, Scotland, to Wilmington, North Carolina.[40] Despite the exaggerated figures, Japanese responsibility for the attack was obvious to Portuguese authorities and to the British. The aftermath of the attack saw some protests voiced, only to be quickly muted. International contacts for the return of the refugees aboard the *Sai-On* were made through specific individuals, notably the Japanese consul in Macau, Fukui Yasumitsu, who played a helpful role in the process, earning him praise from the governor and criticism from fellow Japanese. The background negotiations were only partially successful. The advantages of Macau's neutrality were carefully weighed by those involved.[41] The threat of losing that neutral space loomed large, offering a good topic for Chinese propaganda.

With the highest-ranking Portuguese diplomat in China living in occupied Shanghai, the only official channel of communication between the Portuguese and the Chinese governments during the war was via the Chinese legation in Lisbon. The Chinese minister there informed his government on Portuguese attitudes towards China, on the country's foreign relations (namely with Japan), on the domestic situation in Portugal and on matters of overseas Chinese in the Portuguese empire. Around 1,200 Chinese were residing in Portugal at the start of the war.[42]

[37] Teixeira to MC, 20 and 23 Aug. 1943, ANTT, AOS, NE-10A2, cx. 768.

[38] On external violations of neutrality, see Karsh, *Neutrality and Small States*, pp. 22–3.

[39] Central News Agency, 'Japanese Forcibly Seize British Ship in Macau', 29 Aug. 1943, AH, Waijiaobu, 020000023906A.

[40] 'British Ship Seized by Japanese: Portuguese Neutrality Violated', *The Times* (30 Aug. 1943), p. 4; 'Japs Shoot Portuguese: British Steamer Seized at Macao', *Dundee Courier and Advertiser* (30 Aug. 1943), p. 2; 'Japs Take Small Ship from Portuguese Force', *Wilmington Morning Star* (30 Aug. 1943), p. 8.

[41] Several files in ANTT, AOS, NE-10A2, cx. 768, TNA, FO 371/35735, TNA, FO 371/35736, TNA, FO 371/41620, TNA, HW 12/293, and AH, Waijiaobu, 020000023906A.

[42] *The Chinese Year Book 1936–37* (Shanghai, 1937), p. 199.

They fundraised for the resistance in Lisbon and participated in events such as the anniversary of the Marco Polo Bridge Incident or the obsequies for President Lin Sen.[43]

In May 1943, Li Jinlun informed Chongqing that the Japanese minister to Portugal had attempted to pressure the government into relinquishing municipal rights in Shanghai and to hand them over to the collaborationist administration. The Portuguese Ministry of Foreign Affairs had assured him that Portugal could not take any ambivalent action towards the RNG, which it did not recognise.[44] Li warned that if Portugal signed any such agreement with Japan the Chinese government would not recognise it and would protest. In another move that attests to the global entanglements of Chinese wartime diplomacy, the American minister to Portugal affirmed his government's support for Chiang's through a note dispatched a few days later. He expressed the hope that 'no action tend to give recognition support to the Puppet regime at Nanking [Nanjing] and against the interest of China will be taken by the Portuguese Government'.[45] Actions such as these served to remind the Portuguese government that the central government in Chongqing had powerful allies and to discourage any temptation to engage with the RNG in an official capacity.

The presence of the myriad foreign dignitaries in Lisbon also allowed for formal and informal exchanges of information between them. For example, Li was informed of the Azores agreement in 1943 – by which Portugal ceded basing rights to Britain in the Atlantic archipelago – by the British ambassador who had come to see him.[46] He reported on the 'increasingly bitter antagonism against Japan', but concluded that it would be unlikely for Portugal to declare war. Amongst other reasons, Portugal had 'no effective means for offensive war' and a 'declaration of war against Japan would probably cause immediate seizure of Macao and internment of Portuguese in Japanese occupied areas'.[47] The Chinese minister also monitored the heavily censored Portuguese press and reported back to Chongqing on what he read. Zhang Qian, who replaced Li Jinlun in November 1943, reported on the American bombing of Macau based on a local paper in early 1945.[48] News about

[43] MNE, 10 Ago. 1943, ANTT, AOS, NE-2A2, cx. 422, Pt. 5; Yang Xianceng, Lisbon to MOFA, 7 July, 1944, AH, Waijiaobu, 020000023906A; Kuomintang Central Committee, *Zhongguo Guomindang zai haiwai*, p. 147.

[44] Li Jinlun to MOFA, 14 May 1943, AH, Waijiaobu, 020000023906A.

[45] Li Jinlun to MOFA, 15 May 1943, ibid.

[46] Li Jinlun to MOFA, 13 and 16 Oct. 1943, ibid.

[47] Li Jinlun to MOFA, 13 Oct. 1943, ibid. Also in AH, Waijiaobu, 020000039817A.

[48] Zhang Qian to MOFA, 11 Jan. 1945, AH, Waijiaobu, 020000023906A. Zhang Qian, also known as Henry Kunghui Chang, presented credentials in December 1943 and

Timor was of particular interest due to the large Chinese community residing there.[49]

At the beginning of the war, Timor counted the largest number of Chinese residents in the Portuguese empire after Macau: 3,500 people.[50] A KMT branch in the territory was established in 1911, the first year of the Republic of China (ROC). In 1934, it was involved in founding a Chinese Chamber of Commerce and its members had made contributions towards anti-Japanese resistance since the early 1930s. By 1937, more than 800 party members lived on the island and, although the number diminished (possibly due to migration elsewhere, including to fight Japan in China), they still surpassed 300 in 1941. The Japanese occupation left a trail of destruction for the Chinese in Timor, including to the KMT headquarters, as can be assessed by post-war requests for compensation.[51]

When assessing the global connections framing neutrality and collaboration in Macau, it is necessary to consider how Chinese diplomacy towards Portugal had a far more wide-ranging scope of concerns beyond local events in Macau. The Japanese takeover of the Portuguese colony of Timor served as a warning to Macau about what could happen if Japanese forces moved to a formal occupation. It also linked Chinese government concerns over Macau with those over the brutal treatment of Chinese communities in Southeast Asia.[52]

remained in Lisbon until January 1947. A native of Guangdong, his father had been ambassador to the United States during the Qing–Republican transition. Zhang graduated from American universities and before coming to Portugal was consul general in New York, minister to Chile and director of the MOFA American Affairs Department. After his post in Lisbon, he served in the Netherlands and, in August 1948, he was assigned to the Xiangxiang county court in Hunan province as judge and president. He retired in 1950. Like Li Jinlun, he died in New York, in 1977 (Chinese Ministry of Information, *China Handbook 1937–1945* (New York, 1947), p. 633; *Zhongguo zhu wai ge gong/dashiguan liren guanzhang xian mingbiao* (*Chronological List of Chinese Embassies/ Legations Abroad*) (Taipei, 1989), p. 132; G. Liu (ed.), *Zhongguo Guomindang bai nian renwu quanshu* (*Book of 100 Years of KMT Figures*) (Beijing, 2005), p. 1149; W. Bamberger, 'Henry K. Chang, 92; Chinese Nationalist Held Envoy Posts', *New York Times* (hereafter *NYT*) (23 Feb. 1977), p. 17).

49 For example, Zhang Qian to MOFA, 27 Nov. 1943, AH, Waijiaobu, 020000023906A; Zhang Qian to MOFA, 21 Jan. 1944, ibid.

50 *The Chinese Year Book 1936–37*, p. 199.

51 Kuomintang, *Zhongguo Guomindang zai haiwai*, pp. 304–6; AS-IMH, Waijiaobu, 063.1/001.

52 Research Department, FO, 'Portuguese Possessions in Asia and Oceania', 5 June 1944, p. 12, TNA, FO 371/46199; Teixeira to MC, 7 June 1944, ANTT, AOS, NE-10A2, cx. 768; W. Levi, 'Portuguese Timor and the War', *Far Eastern Survey*, 15/14 (1946), pp. 221–3, at p. 222; J. M. Ferreira, 'Timor', in F. Rosas and J. M. B. Brito (eds.), *Dicionário de História do Estado Novo* (*Estado Novo History Dictionary*), vol. 2 (Lisbon, 1996), pp. 974–6, at p. 974; Meneses, *Salazar*, p. 273; N. Tarling, 'Britain, Portugal and East Timor in 1941', *Journal of Southeast Asian Studies*, 27/1 (1996), pp. 132–8, at p. 132; Telo, *Portugal na Segunda Guerra*, vol. 1, p. 61, and vol. 2, p. 209. On massacres of

Japan occupied Timor in February 1942 after an unauthorised Allied landing. Whereas the population received Australian and Dutch troops with open arms, the Japanese arrival marked the start of years of brutality and active resistance, itself marked by transnational cooperation, notably with Australian guerrillas.[53] The Japanese kept Timor's governor under virtual house arrest and cut off direct communications with Portugal. One of Portugal's leading historians of World War II has synthesised what happened de facto: from October 1942, 'the Portuguese administration ceased to exist'.[54] One colonial administration was replaced with a military occupation by another imperial power. The parallel to what could happen in Macau was evident. Salazar himself – interested in the maintenance of the Portuguese empire in the post-war period – saw Macau and Timor as 'pieces of the same game'.[55]

Even if Macau's neutrality was much preferred to the fate of Timor, the Chinese legation in Lisbon continued to probe Portuguese practices deemed problematic up to the end of the war. Information reached the Chinese government not only from Macau, but also from Nationalist military forces in Guangdong province. The Macau government had allegedly handed over guns and ammunitions to a major collaborationist criminal, Huang Gongjie.[56] Those materials had come from Chinese soldiers previously disarmed and interned in Macau. The first secretary of the Chinese legation urged the Portuguese government to deny the veracity of the report so that he could reassure the MOFA in Chongqing.[57] The governor of Macau later explained to Lisbon what had taken place. He had indeed lent 60 Mauser rifles and 5,000 cartridges to 93 Chinese under deposit of 30,000 patacas guaranteed by a commission which included an (unnamed) unofficial representative of the Chinese Ministry of Information. A representative of the Allied command in China had been told of the arrangement and had approved it,

Chinese communities in Southeast Asia, see, for example, H. Hayashi, 'Massacre of Chinese in Singapore and Its Coverage in Postwar Japan', in A. Yoji and Y. Mako (eds.), *New Perspectives on the Japanese Occupation in Malaya and Singapore, 1941–1945* (Singapore, 2008), pp. 234–49; O. K. Gin, 'Cash and Blood: The Chinese Community and the Japanese Occupation of Borneo, 1941–45', in C. de Matos and M. E. Caprio (eds.), *Japan As the Occupier and the Occupied* (London, 2015), pp. 152–71.

53 Timor was a penal colony and amongst its European settler community were people convicted for supposed 'crimes' of a political nature, including leftists who opposed the Estado Novo regime.

54 Telo, *Portugal na Segunda Guerra*, vol. 1, p. 60.

55 'Communiqué de la Présidence du Conseil Publié dans les journaux portugais du 7 Octobre 1945' (Presidency of the Council Communiqué Published in Portuguese Newspapers on 7 October 1945), p. 9, MAE, 125QO/7.

56 Yu Hanmou to MOFA, 15 May 1945, AH, Waijiaobu, 020000023906A.

57 Note on Conversation with the First Secretary of the Chinese Legation, 1 June 1945, AHD, 2P, A48, M212.

and in turn lent 12 Mauser pistols to the Macau police. The governor attributed the incorrect report to factionalism amongst the Nationalists and recommended that 'relations with other Chinese official departments' should not be mentioned to the Chinese minister in Lisbon as they did not get along. He recommended he reply that only a few rifles without military value had been lent for protection of food supplies in Macau.[58]

Minister Zhang Qian transmitted these assurances to Chongqing in November 1943.[59] The Portuguese later explained that a small number of weapons had been given to a group of overseas Chinese (*huaqiao tuanti*) in order to protect the transportation of food. Their leader was a supporter of the central government and the guns provided were so old they could not be used in aggression.[60] This episode illustrates the overlap of official and unofficial diplomatic communications channels between China and Portugal and the misunderstandings that could arise.

In Macau, the governor was well aware that many Nationalist secret agents operated in the enclave and their actions were seen as part of a series of collaborative resistance endeavours. Teixeira believed them to be working in connection with agents of the British consul, as RNG agents collaborated with the Japanese. Although the governor ensured Lisbon he had his own agents amongst each of the factions, different sources attest to overlapping intelligence penetrations, making it hard to clarify with absolute certainty who was infiltrating whom at any given moment.[61]

The ambiguities of neutrality in Macau, as in other neutral territories, contributed to making it fertile ground for propaganda operations. In October 1943, Radio Chongqing announced that the Japanese had assassinated the governor of Macau, yet another piece of overblown news released during the war, which the Japanese decried as attempts to harm Portugal's relations with Japan.[62] Later that month, the Nationalists sent word to (a very much alive) Teixeira offering the help of guerrillas to fight the Japanese if they attempted anything against Macau and proposing to send an officer to devise a plan. The governor declined, explaining to Lisbon that even if Macau could benefit should they expel the Japanese from neighbouring areas, they would exert reprisals against innocent Chinese villages and he could not bear the

[58] Teixeira to MC, 5 June 1945, ANTT, AOS, NE-10A2, cx. 768. British intelligence intercepted the message, which can be found translated in TNA, HW 12/319.
[59] Li Jinlun and Zhang Qian to MOFA, 15 Nov. 1943, AH, Waijiaobu, 020000023906A.
[60] Zhang Qian to MOFA, 12 June 1945, ibid.
[61] Teixeira to MC, 22 Apr. 1943, ANTT, AOS, NE-10A2, cx. 768.
[62] Teixeira to MC, 14 Oct. 1943, ibid.

thought of it. However, they would keep in touch and exchange information.[63] By issuing such reports through official channels and maintaining contacts through private ones, the Nationalists made different uses of Macau's neutrality: they kept Japanese actions in the enclave in check whilst ensuring a smooth, mutually beneficial relationship with the Portuguese governor.

Refugee welfare was at the centre of Nationalist–Portuguese contacts in Macau. Any assistance – or facilitation thereof – the Portuguese authorities provided to a largely Chinese refugee population in Macau became an asset to be cited when doubts arose about Portugal's collaboration with the RNG and the Japanese. In March 1944, Portugal's Ministry of Foreign Affairs sent a memorandum to the Chinese legation in Lisbon listing Portuguese actions supportive of the Chinese in Macau. Somewhat ironically, some of the achievements included there had not been led by the colonial authorities but had been organised by local charities or had resulted from ambiguous endeavours with links to collaboration with the 'enemy', such as the policy of a controlled rice market. Other accomplishments listed included the establishment of soup kitchens, the setting up of public works employing Chinese refugees, the free distribution of land for cultivation and special protection offered for the disabled, abandoned and poor children cared for in asylums and refuges, to whom food was provided.

A critical view of some of these practices – such as the deployment of refugee labour or confinement of destitute people – will find them far from benevolent. Yet they were proudly listed as Portuguese achievements. Continuing to take credit from local Chinese institutions, the memorandum also mentioned that the Macau government had helped the Kiang Wu Hospital and the Tung Sin Tong, which distributed free meals and supplied rice at minimum prices to the schools run by the charity attended by refugee children. The document ended by affirming that, in all the relief work done, the Portuguese authorities had sought the 'collaboration and suggestions of the most qualified representatives of the Chinese community'.[64]

Later that year, in a letter to the then Chinese minister of foreign affairs, T. V. Soong (Song Ziwen), Tang Liu – signing as 'consul general' (*zonglingshi*) – informed on the difficulties that had arisen in Macau due to population influx.[65] He credited the governor for letting the Chinese live a peaceful life in Macau, including establishing asylums for the young,

[63] Teixeira to MC, 20 Oct. 1943, ibid.
[64] MNE to Chinese Legation in Lisbon, 13 Mar 1944, AH, Waijiaobu, 020000023906A.
[65] Tang Liu to T. V. Soong, Chinese Minister of Foreign Affairs, 24 Aug. 1944, AH, Waijiaobu, 020000023906A. Also in AH, Waijiaobu, 020000003315A.

old and poor. Amongst the initiatives he mentioned was a system of distributing food twice a day, although such initiatives were at risk as funds were drying up. A Sino–Portuguese juvenile association (ZhongPu lianhe qingnianhui) had been created as well.[66] Tang also mentioned the important role of the Tung Sin Tong in poverty relief. The charity would ask some of those destitute but in good health to do certain jobs, such as work on road pavements, in exchange for better meals. He also reported he intended to invite Captain Silva Costa to be the secretary general of a Refugee Survey Committee (Nanmin diaocha weiyuanhui), showing how forging close relations with the local colonial authorities was a strategy pursued by different sides. In the meantime, local businessmen, including Gao Kening, had been asked to contribute.[67] It is interesting to note that some of these initiatives involved figures and institutions, Chinese and Portuguese, which had links to both the Chinese government resisting Japan and the collaborationist authorities on whose goodwill the flow of food supplies to Macau depended.

If multiple, at times confusing, communications were a feature of the relationship between Chiang's Nationalists and Portuguese authorities, unofficial contacts were also taking place between the communist guerrillas and the Macau government, and between the latter and the collaborationist RNG led by Chiang's rival, Wang Jingwei.

Communist Guerrillas

In the complex web of Chinese agents in Macau, one must not overlook a key player in underground resistance in South China: the CCP. Some important CCP figures in post-war Macau started to operate there during the war. Groups such as the now famous East River Column (Dongjiang zongdui) operated in Guangdong province and the Hong Kong New Territories and recruited some of its members in Macau.[68] Ke Zhengping was one of them. Brother to Ke Lin, a medical doctor at the Kiang Wu Hospital who went on to be the first secretary of the Macau

[66] This is referred to in Portuguese sources as the Macau Youth Association (Associação dos Jovens de Macau). Its establishment involved several figures, including a Hong Kong Portuguese, the honorary president of the Pui Ching and Pui To schools and the governor ('As comemorações do 28 de Maio' ('The 28 May Commemorations'), *VM* (31 May 1944) p. 3; 'Sino–Portuguese Juvenile Association', *VM* (26 June 1944), p. 2).

[67] Tang to Soong, 24 Aug. 1944.

[68] G. Y. M. Chan, *The Chinese Communists' East River Column, Guangdong, 1937–1945* (Leeds, 1998), p. 41; G. Y. M. Chan, 'Hong Kong and Communist Guerrilla Resistance in South China, 1937–1945', *Twentieth-Century China*, 29/1 (2003), pp. 39–63, at p. 47; S. J. Chan, *East River Column: Hong Kong Guerrillas in the Second World War and After* (Hong Kong, 2009), p. 10.

branch of the CCP, Ke Zhengping was sent from Hong Kong to Macau to undertake underground activities to help the column.[69] He remained in Macau for the rest of his life, becoming a key CCP operative in Macau after 1949.

Like the Nationalists, communist guerrillas found ways to contact the Portuguese authorities and to make their official neutrality in Macau work to their advantage. In late 1943, Father Amaral, a Portuguese missionary based in Shiqi, came to Macau after reportedly being kidnapped by communists nearby but then freed by other guerrillas.[70] A Chinese author stated that the Zhongshan guerrillas used Amaral, referred to as Father An (his Chinese name was An Puling), as an intermediary to get in touch with the Macau government.[71] A few months later, in the spring of 1944, the Zhongshan Volunteer Brigade (Zhongshan yiyong dadui) contacted the enclave's authorities directly. It intended to send agents to operate in Macau (e.g. to raise funds), to send their wounded for treatment in the enclave as well as to buy cartridges and medicine, and to set up a transmitting station to send messages to Yan'an, capital of the main communist base area in China, where Mao Zedong spent the war years. In exchange for these facilities, they offered to attack the collaborationists who menaced the safety and public order in Macau. According to Chinese historians, the Portuguese agreed.[72] In October, Governor Gabriel Teixeira reported to Lisbon that he had struck up good relations with the leader of the communist guerrillas in Zhongshan.[73] Yet he considered this special relationship as one amongst his broad range of good links to different factions of the Chinese resistance.

Teixeira was also strengthening relations with the 'Chongqing people' (i.e. pro-Chiang Nationalists), and was well aware that resistance in South China was quite heterogeneous: Nationalist and Communist guerrillas fought against Japan but independently from one another whilst pro-Japanese Chinese groups connected to the navy or army fought each other with the support of elements in the Japanese navy or army, some pondering a switch to Chiang's side. The governor also wrote of

[69] M. S. Fernandes, 'How to Relate to a Colonial Power on Its Shore: Macau in the Chinese Foreign Policy, 1949–1965', *Bulletin of Portuguese–Japanese Studies*, 17 (2008), pp. 225–50, at p. 229; Barreto, *Macau during the Sino–Japanese War*, p. 163.

[70] Teixeira to MC, 30 Oct. and 20 Nov. 1943, ANTT, AOS, NE-10A2, cx. 768.

[71] Guo, 'Shilun Aomen', p. 103.

[72] K. S. Deng, J. M. Lu and R. F. Yang, *Aomen shihua* (*A Brief History of Macau*) (Beijing, 2011), p. 293. Jin and Wu and Mo attribute an identical account to the memoirs of Ou Chu, who directed the Chinese resistance at the No. 9 zone in Zhongshan (Jin and Wu, 'Teria havido', p. 274; Z. Wu, *Segredos da Sobrevivência: História Política de Macau* (*Secrets of Survival: Political History of Macau*) (Macau, 1999), p. 304; Mo, 'Kangzhan qijian', p. 53).

[73] Teixeira to MC, 18 Oct. 1944, ANTT, AOS, NE-10A2, cx. 768.

competing 'groups of pirates' – that is, organised underground groups without a clear political affiliation – a topic that remains virtually unexplored by historians. Governor Teixeira saw Macau as the place where elements of all of these factions chose to rest. 'Rare is the group chief that does not have a house in Macau as a refuge in case of a setback', he noted. Collaboration caused unease, but it was indispensable. The governor 'trusted no one' but 'depended on all of them for supplies'.[74] Imports were needed to sustain a large refugee population and its presence underpinned the multiple layers of collaboration in Macau.

Avoiding Occupation: Macau's Relations with the Reorganised National Government and Japanese Authorities

Macau's neutral status and strategic location made it a site of interest for the collaborationist RNG that governed the enclave's surrounding areas and to the Japanese forces with whom they were supposed to be allied. The territory's dependency on imports, particularly rice, led the local Portuguese authorities to constantly engage with Japanese occupation forces as well as in unofficial relations with the RNG authorities in Guangdong province, taking the shadow diplomacy moves discussed in Chapter 1 to a deeper level. Furthermore, Macau continued to provide a relatively safe space for RNG agents to communicate with Chongqing representatives.

After months of growing food scarcity, in April 1942, Pedro Lobo, the influential head of the Macau Economic Services, was sent to Guangzhou, where he met the RNG provincial governor, Chen Yaozu, and Japanese economic advisers. He tried to guarantee the regularisation of rice supply to Macau, enquired about the possibility of importing minerals from unoccupied China and sought assistance with repatriating Chinese refugees.[75] Displaced persons were central to these contacts. The Macau authorities intended to send 200,000–300,000 Chinese refugees to mainland China in order to 'relieve' the pressure on the enclave.[76] In 1942, an organisation was set up to help Chinese return to their homes in the countryside: the Macau Overseas Chinese Association for Assisting Refugees to Return Home (Aoqiao xiezhu nanmin huixiang hui).[77] By the end of that year, it had repatriated 12,000 people.[78] Although sending

[74] Teixeira to MC, 19 Sept. 1944, ibid.
[75] Teixeira to MC, 24 Apr. 1942, ANTT, AOS, UL-10A1, cx. 767.
[76] Gracias to Lima, 16 Apr. 1942, AHD, 2P, A48, M221.
[77] Guangdong Provincial Archives, *Guangdong Aomen*, p. 383.
[78] 'Vida Social Chinesa' ('Chinese Social Life'), *VM* (29 Dec. 1942), p. 3.

unwanted refugees 'back' to their home towns was something that other authorities – including the Shanghai Municipal Council and the French Concession's Conseil Municipal – also did, it is noteworthy that the only refugees the Portuguese authorities sought to send away were Chinese.

The level of contact between the RNG and the Macau government was considerably elevated when, in June 1942, the RNG Guangdong provincial government requested the Portuguese to post a liaison officer in Macau. Governor Teixeira considered this potentially useful despite not looking favourably at the possibility of the agent promoting pro-Wang political activity. Under the circumstances, he thought it 'impolitic to refuse' and said that, if the minister of colonies approved, he would agree to the 'private arrangement' (*combinação particular*) between the Macau and the Guangzhou governments.[79] The proposed deal was announced in the Cantonese press. The provincial government set up an office (*shengzhengfu banshichu*) in Macau. The commissioner of foreign affairs of Guangdong, Zhou Bingsan, served concomitantly as special representative (*tepai jiaosheyuan*) and Geng Tingzhen, the head of the second section of the foreign affairs special commission, would double as secretary. Only the latter resided in Macau.[80] The office began operating in early July. Amongst the guests at the welcome banquet in the Hotel Riviera were the governor and a number of Japanese figures, including the consul, Fukui Yasumitsu.[81]

Although the Portuguese did not consider these relations official, the RNG authorities, for whom displays of legitimacy were paramount, appear to have treated them as such. However, throughout the 1940s, relations in Macau remained tense. On one hand, there were attempts to forge trade and other agreements; on the other, there were repeated rumours that pro-Wang groups were preparing an occupation of the enclave, which kept Portuguese authorities suspicious of their motives. Attempts to control supplies to Macau had been engendered before 1941, but RNG moves became more daring after the occupation of Hong Kong.

In August 1942, Teixeira got wind of a plan to allegedly take over Macau, with the threat of fire to be used as a decoy to keep the police busy. To avoid this, the governor tried to play the Japanese against the collaborators and approached the former for assistance to keep Macau neutral.[82] He made enquiries with Colonel Sawa Eisaku, the Japanese army liaison officer in

[79] Teixeira to MC, 11 June 1942, ANTT, AOS, UL-10A1, cx. 767.

[80] 'Guangdong shen zhengfu zai Aomen sheli banshichu' (Guangdong Provincial Government Sets Up an Office in Macau), *Guangdong xunbao* (4 June 1942), AHD, 2P, A48, M221.

[81] Gracias to Lima, 15 July, 1942, ibid.

[82] Teixeira to MC, 22 Aug. 1942, ANTT, AOS, UL-10A1, cx. 767.

Macau (who had replaced Okubo). Sawa also sought to turn the rumour to his advantage, suggesting that the conspirators might have accomplices inside the police. The Macau police were believed to be infiltrated by all the major belligerents in the region, so they could easily be used as a scapegoat by all parties.

In his frequent telegrams to the Ministry of Colonies in Portugal, the governor continued to refer to the takeover threat. He was convinced that the Japanese were not involved and speculated that it could be a maverick plan engendered by Chinese and Taiwanese agents.[83] The Macau authorities published a note in a local paper that denied rumours of 'external danger' and guaranteed the means to clamp down on any attempt of creating 'internal disorder'. Should the latter occur, the population was advised to stay indoors to facilitate the government's 'repressive actions, which will be immediate and exerted with the utmost violence'.[84] These confident proclamations of ability to ensure Macau's neutrality – through the maintenance of its colonial rule – masked great private uncertainty, evident in the governor's communications to Lisbon.

Apprehension did not preclude openness to continuous engagement with RNG authorities. In September, Chen Yaozu visited the enclave for two days before heading to nearby Zhongshan. He came with a number of other provincial government officials, but the visit was not granted official status as Portugal still recognised Chiang's government.[85] Teixeira hosted Chen for an 'intimate dinner' where Lobo, the harbour master, the chief of staff and the police commissioner were present. In 1942, cracks in the Japanese–RNG alliance were already evident as Consul Fukui and Sawa, who had been invited, both failed to show up, alleging illness. Teixeira was confident that Chen's visit had been useful and advocated that, henceforth, relations with Guangzhou should be treated 'personally' between the two governors, without Japanese interference if at all possible.[86]

Intimate conviviality had its limits, however, and when Chen was invited for lunch by a group of local elite figures such as Gao Kening and Liang Houyuan, the Portuguese governor declined to attend. Still, Teixeira later went for a car ride alone with Chen, asking for assistance in obtaining rice, wood and cement supplies.[87] It is unclear what language was spoken, but

[83] Teixeira to MC, 26, 29 and 31 Aug. 1942, ANTT, AOS, UL-10A1, cx. 767.
[84] 'Nota Oficiosa' ('Unofficial Note'), *VM* (9 Sept. 1942), p. 1.
[85] Gracias to Teixeira, 25 Sept. 1942, AHD, 2P, A48, M221.
[86] Teixeira to MC, 20 Sept. 1942, ANTT, AOS, UL-10A1, cx. 767.
[87] Teixeira to MC, 22 Sept. 1942, ibid. See also 'Visita de Sua Exa. O Governador da Província de Kwantung' ('Visit of His Excellency the Governor of Guangdong Province'), *VM* (23 Sept. 1942), p. 3.

Chen Yaozu's father had been a prominent businessman in British Malaya, so it was probably English. This kind of elite rapprochement, making use of local notables and fostering personal connections, continued throughout the conflict, but did not provide solid assurances of a smooth relationship between the RNG and the Portuguese.

Less than a year had passed before rumours of an RNG takeover of Macau resurfaced in early 1943. Some commentators considered the possibility that the Portuguese government might ditch neutrality and enter the war. The popular Shanghai newspaper *Shenbao* noted in February that Portugal was preparing for war.[88] At the end of the month, as if to qualm such rumours, the pro-Japanese *Hongkong News* stressed that the position of the governor of Macau remained stable. A report based on an interview with Teixeira asserted that Macau's position towards Japan 'was one of the fullest co-operation and friendship'.[89]

Portugal's perceived closeness to Japan was not necessarily synonymous with closeness to the RNG, however. The British consul, John Reeves, reported that the previous month a meeting had taken place in Macau between Japanese and Wang Jingwei representatives where Wang's men exhorted Japan, without success, to take over Macau, challenging them to act in accordance with their professed policy of 'Asia for the Asians'.[90] Similar information, probably passed on by Reeves, reached the Macau governor. The Japanese consul assured Teixeira that his government had not altered his promise of respecting the enclave's neutrality. The governor was not convinced that the Japanese were innocent, but believed that, if he obtained an official Japanese denial that they had no connection to any activities threatening the enclave's neutrality, the Chinese collaborators would feel unsupported and give up on their supposed plans.[91]

Teixeira then proceeded to have representatives of Japan and the RNG distance themselves from the invasion rumour. He invited Zhou Bingsan and encouraged him to dissociate the RNG from such 'adventurous speculators'. Zhou reassured Teixeira that Wang Jingwei did 'not hold any intentions against Macau' and that General Yazaki Kanju, an intelligence chief in Guangzhou, would never allow them.[92] Assurances of Guangzhou–Macau friendship and of good relations were given at a tea and dinner party, where the omnipresent businessman Gao Kening made

[88] 'Putaoya zhanshi zhunbei, banbu chanye dongyuanling' ('Portugal Wartime Preparations, Promulgation of Industrial Mobilisation Order'), *Shenbao* (19 Feb. 1943), p. 3.

[89] 'Governor of Macao Voices Friendship', *Hongkong News* (21 Feb. 1943), AHD, 2P, A48, M221.

[90] Ride, *BAAG*, p. 214.

[91] Teixeira to MC, 27 Feb., 4 and 14 Mar. 1943, ANTT, AOS, NE-10A2, cx. 768.

[92] Teixeira to MC, 20 Mar. 1943, ibid.

a speech.[93] Entertaining collaborationist authorities was deemed a success by the Macau governor. It exposed the RNG's weaknesses by having Japanese figures dissociate themselves from plans for a Macau takeover. It also laid bare the tensions underlying the Japan–RNG relationship. Japanese claims of supporting Asian liberation against Western colonialism were, after all, mere self-serving rhetoric. Having Macau under the rule of a small neutral power such as Portugal served Japanese interests just fine without the need for violent decolonisation. The governor boasted to Lisbon that he had 'liquidated' what he regarded as the biggest offensive against Macau, and reiterated his belief that there was great 'convenience in keeping good relations with these people', particularly the provincial governor, given that he was a relative of Wang Jingwei.[94]

The RNG was unable to decolonise Macau, but it came to deal with the Portuguese authorities there as de facto rulers of Guangdong. Relations between the RNG and the Macau government were also framed by different international connections, especially with Japan. Those also included the RNG's Axis allies, notably Germany and Italy. A high point in the enclave's parallel diplomacy with the RNG occurred in late April 1943, when the governor of Macau visited Chen Yaozu in Guangzhou; another informal visit that was treated very much as an official one. Teixeira travelled with his chief of cabinet, Captain Silva e Costa, his aide-de-camp, and Sawa, staying at the Portuguese consulate in Shamian as the hotel initially proposed by the Cantonese authorities was without working lifts or satisfactory water supply – a subtle reminder that Macau's shortages were not that far removed from the difficulties felt in Guangdong province.[95]

Despite the publicity it generated for Chen, the visit made clear who was really in charge, as Teixeira's schedule included encounters with Japanese representatives. The governor informed Lisbon that the Chinese and Japanese had showered him with attention and accounts of the visit list a succession of lunches, cocktail parties and dinners organised by the Japanese, Chinese and the Portuguese consulate.[96] Lieutenant General Tanaka Hisakazu offered a lunch in Teixeira's honour in the presence of several Japanese officers and the consul, and toasted Portuguese–Japanese friendship, guaranteeing he would assist

[93] 'Cativante homenagem' ('Captivating Tribute'), *VM* (25 Mar. 1943), p. 3.

[94] Teixeira to MC, 20 and 22 Mar. 1943, ANTT, AOS, NE-10A2, cx. 768.

[95] Gracias to Lima, 16 Apr. 1943, AHD, 2P, A48, M212.

[96] Gracias to Lima, 20 Apr. 1943, ibid.; 'Cativantes homenagens a Sua Exa. o Governador da Colónia em Cantão' ('Captivating Tributes to H. E. the Governor of the Colony in Guangzhou'), *VM* (22 Apr. 1943), p. 3.

with supplies to Macau.[97] General Yazaki welcomed him to a Japanese-style lunch, and the Japanese consul, Ishikawa Minoru, invited to a cocktail party all Portuguese in Guangzhou – presumably a community much smaller than it once had been given the refugee flight that had accompanied the city's invasion.

Chen Yaozu took Teixeira sightseeing and organised a dinner for him with Cantonese officials. The German and Italian consuls also visited Teixeira. He left with a good impression, describing Yazaki as a 'good element we have on our side' and Chen as a 'person of superior culture' and a 'man of good will'.[98] The visit made for great propaganda and was reported in several newspapers in occupied Guangzhou, Hong Kong and Singapore.[99] In the last, the Japanese propaganda newspaper *Syonan Shimbun* went as far as to describe Macau as a member of the *Dai Tōa Kyōeiken* – that is, the Greater East Asia Co-Prosperity Sphere – a term used to refer to Japanese-dominated Asia in the 1940s. The news report used the expansion of Japanese-language education in Macau as a sign of the 'increasing zeal and enthusiasm of Macao citizens towards all-out collaboration with members of Kyoeiken'.[100]

Fraternisation over meals was also happening in Shanghai, where the Portuguese minister mingled in Axis circles. For example, in early May, Lima informed Lisbon that he and his wife had hosted a dinner at the Portuguese legation. Amongst the guests were the Italian ambassador, the Spanish minister, the German consul general and two Imperial Japanese Army officers.[101] RNG–Portuguese informal relations can be understood in a particular context of fascist diplomacy, which also included a close relationship between Wang's government and Franco's Spain.

If Chiang Kai-shek's agents kept tabs on Portuguese (mis)uses of neutrality in Macau, the RNG authorities also sought to keep in check actions perceived as beneficial to their rivals. In June 1943, Zhou Bingsan came to Macau to present to the governor a long protest about an attack on the Zhongshan magistrate. Accusing the Macau police of having pro-Chiang elements, he demanded that RNG agents replace those elements and that all 'Chongqing terrorists' be expelled or

[97] Tanaka Hisakazu was the last Japanese governor of occupied Hong Kong. After the war, he was sentenced by an American military tribunal for war crimes and was later handed to the Nationalists, who also tried him. He was executed in 1947.

[98] Teixeira to MC, 22 Apr. 1943, ANTT, AOS, NE-10A2, cx. 768.

[99] Clippings in AHD, 2P, A48, M212.

[100] 'Macao Showing Enthusiasm, Zeal As Member of Kyoeiken', *Syonan Shimbun* (23 Apr. 1943), p. 2. On the expansion of Japanese-language teaching in Macau during the war, see Lopes, 'Wartime Education at the Crossroads of Empires', pp. 147–8.

[101] Lima to Salazar, 4 May 1943, AHD, 2P, A48, M212.

arrested. Teixeira skirted responsibility, pointing out that the RNG side also had assassins in Macau and that the best option would be for them to agree on a truce.[102] In other words, the governor was well aware that Macau's neutrality was being disrespected by all sides.

Despite the Portuguese pushback, RNG attempts to exert economic control over Macau became evident from 1943, sometimes involving Japanese agents. Proposals from the pro-Wang camp expose the wish to control food supplies to the enclave and curb pro-Chiang activities there. In June, the Guangdong government sent a commissioner for supplies to Macau to propose an agreement: it would supply 10,000–12,000 bags of rice to a syndicate of merchants they considered financially sound, the Macau Import-Export Traders Syndicate, set up that month.[103] The supply would have to be ensured through the syndicate because the RNG authorities feared their emissaries would be killed by guerrillas, as had occurred in the past. In exchange, RNG authorities asked for rice imports by smugglers to be forbidden and for their merchandise to be handed over to the provincial government. They also asked for pro-Chiang elements and propaganda not to be allowed in Macau, which suggests their presence remained relatively strong. The political consequences of such a deal were high on the governor's mind. It could suggest that the government was freeing itself from the responsibility of feeding the population and relying instead on the collaborationist authorities across the border. Still, Teixeira knew that such promises of legal trade were probably empty and estimated that the Japanese navy would 'be the first to break the monopoly'.[104]

Such neutrality-bending schemes blurred national boundaries and personal connections played a key role in them. Anonymous information in English found amongst the governor's papers details that the plan to monopolise the rice supply in Macau involved the Japanese, the former Zhongshan magistrate and some of his relatives. The façade of legal trade was also linked to intelligence and propaganda. Zhou Bingsan brought from Guangzhou twenty-five special workers, including agents 'trained for anti-British work' to operate in Macau.[105] Yet things did not quite go to plan due to the 'passive resistance' of traders in Macau, whose capital was necessary to finance the venture. Consenting to such stifling control by the RNG authorities was not a desired scenario, especially as spectacular profits could be made through smuggling.

[102] Teixeira to MC, 18 June 1943, ANTT, AOS, NE-10A2, cx. 768.
[103] 'Comerciantes de importação e exportação' ('Import–Export Merchants), *VM* (8 June 1943), p. 3.
[104] Teixeira to MC, 26 and 29 June 1943, ANTT, AOS, NE-10A2, cx. 768.
[105] Unsigned typed information, 9 July 1943, AHU, Espólio Gabriel Maurício Teixeira.

Still, more supplies had to be ensured as the living conditions in Macau kept deteriorating. As an alternative, the governor proposed to the provincial authorities setting up a non-profit cooperative in order to supply the population with rice. Chinese elite figures in Macau, of different political persuasions, agreed. The former syndicate would cede its share and integrate the cooperative. To guarantee Zhou's compliance, he was made a member of the board of directors at the new cooperative.[106] The Public Association for the Purchase of Foodstuffs was founded in August, with its provisional headquarters at the Chinese Commercial Association. The Guangdong government supply department deputy chief came to Macau to discuss the matter and the representatives of the Macau Chinese community and charities managed to get him to cancel rice import tariffs.[107] The Macau Chinese elites aptly played the RNG and ensured their own interests came out on top. As this scheme reduced the scale of the capitulation of the Portuguese authorities to RNG directives, the colonial rulers were satisfied with the outcome.

The arrangement was not, however, sufficient to make rumours of an eventual RNG invasion disappear. These resurfaced in August 1943, the same month as the *Sai-On* takeover.[108] Various informants warned the governor that there were people in Macau ready to execute a large-scale plan to take over the enclave. Sawa told the governor that some of the names of the alleged involved pointed towards the 'Nanjing people' – that is, pro-Wang Jingwei agents. The governor reported to Lisbon that he had co-opted the gambling concessionaire (he did not specify who, but it was likely to have been Fu Deyin) to get information. The concessionaire brought Teixeira a list of thirteen groups in Macau with connections to Nanjing and Japan, and proposed to have his spies infiltrate these groups to be forewarned if a coup was planned.[109] Different layers of cooperation were activated in times of crisis; the governor could count on trusted businessmen to gather useful intelligence. What he provided in return can only be speculated on, but neutrality did offer its own set of economic advantages.

106 Teixeira to MC, 10 Aug. 1943, ANTT, AOS, NE-10A2, cx. 768.
107 'Governor and Merchants Discuss Rice Problem', *Macau Tribune* (15 Aug. 1943), p. 1; 'Associação Publica para Aquisição de Géneros Alimentícios' ('Public Association for the Purchase of Foodstuffs'), *VM* (17 Aug. 1943), p. 3; 'Associação Publica de Auxilio Mutuo para Aquisição de Generos Alimenticios' ('Public Association of Mutual Assistance for the Purchase of Foodstuffs'), *VM* (20, 21 and 27 Aug. 1943), p. 3; 'Cantão atendeu o pedido de cancelamento dos direitos sobre o arroz' ('Guangzhou Accepted the Request for Cancelling Tariffs on Rice'), *VM* (11 Sept. 1943), p. 3.
108 Teixeira to MC, 22 Aug. 1943, ANTT, AOS, NE-10A2, cx. 768.
109 Teixeira to MC, 4 and 8 Sept. 1943, ibid.

Beyond relations with Portuguese authorities, the RNG also used Macau as a site for contacts with Chiang's side. In September 1943, Chu Minyi, the RNG minister of foreign affairs, and Wang Jingwei's wife, Chen Bijun, passed through Macau incognito. The governor sent a message saying he would not greet them in order to respect their anonymity, but should they need anything he would be glad to be of service. Before they left, Chu sent Teixeira a card and he reciprocated.[110] According to the governor, Chen's visit to Macau had been an attempt to co-opt Sun Yat-sen's widow – his first wife, Lu Muzhen – and eldest daughter, Sun Wan, but her efforts were unsuccessful.[111] Other reports on negotiations between Wang and Chiang's men reached the governor in October. The talks, which had led to nothing, had included the president of the rice cooperative in Macau (a former finance minister in Sun Yat-sen's government), Chu Minyi, Chongqing's 'minister of publicity' (it is unclear who this referred to), and the Hong Kong chief of staff.[112]

The encounter was confirmed by the Japanese minister in Lisbon, who received a telegram from Macau stating that Chen Bijun had visited Macau and mentioning her meeting with Feng Zhuwan and the existing rumours of a Japanese occupation of Macau.[113] The contents of such a meeting generated international attention. The French military mission in Chongqing also wrote to the Free French Forces in Algiers that Chen met Chongqing emissaries in Macau, with Japan supposedly accepting that they would evacuate Manchuria and hand over Indochina to China.[114] This was a far-fetched possibility that suggests a carefully mounted propaganda move. Indeed, for the Nationalists, making overtures to a peace settlement has been interpreted as representing a bargaining chip to convince the United States and Britain to offer more assistance to Chiang's resistance.[115] The consequences of China willing to give up resistance were not in the interests of the other Allies.

[110] Teixeira to MC, 17 and 20 Sept. 1943. [111] Teixeira to MC, 30 Sept. 1943, ibid.
[112] Teixeira to MC, 11 and 20 Oct. 1943, ibid.
[113] Morishima Morito, Japanese Minister in Lisbon to Shigemitsu Mamoru, Japanese Minister for Foreign Affairs, 1 Oct. 1943, TNA, HW 12/293. Feng was an associate of Li Jishen, a military commander who had been governor of Guangdong and was a rival of Zhang Fakui, having an uneasy relationship with Chiang Kai-shek. Feng had taken part in the Liangguang Incident in 1936, a confrontation between Cantonese military warlords and the central government to fight Japan, after the failure of which he had moved to Macau.
[114] French Military Mission in Chongqing to Fighting French in Algiers, 19 Oct. 1943, TNA, HW 12/293.
[115] Huang and Yang, 'Nationalist China's Negotiating', p. 73.

By 1944, the RNG began to disintegrate from within. American bombings over Guangzhou and increased guerrilla activity with the support of regular troops loyal to Chiang were hitting Japan hard. Wang Jingwei died in November 1944, but rumours of his death began circulating in South China in April. The governor of Macau informed Lisbon that Guangzhou was in turmoil, with everyone trying to get rid of the RNG's Central Reserve Bank (CRB) currency.[116] Wang's centrality in the RNG has been noted by historians, who have stressed how Wang was 'essential to the survival of his government'.[117] The mere idea of his departure was enough to make the RNG apparatus in Guangdong stumble. From Macau, the governor noted that more Wang supporters were defecting. He deemed it likely that the RNG collapse would lead to a new influx of refugees from Guangzhou as the 'situation there is that of a volcano that everyone feels can erupt at any moment'.[118] Indeed, by 1944, many high-profile figures of the Wang government secretly switched sides. Some had had channels open with unoccupied China for years, the most notable case arguably being Vice President and Minister of Finance Zhou Fohai, who was in contact with Chiang's spymaster, Dai Li.[119]

In May, the RNG governor of Guangdong, Chen Yaozu, was murdered in Guangzhou. Some sources attribute the killing to a 'local bandit general', Li Fuqun, following orders from Chiang's intelligence agency, the Bureau of Investigation and Statistics (Juntong).[120] The governor of Macau wrote to Lisbon that, although he did not know who the perpetrators were, he had heard that Chen had begun conversations with Chongqing and was preparing to change sides.[121] Shortly after, Teixeira reported to Lisbon that Wang's people blamed his death on the Japanese.[122] A few months later, a summary of intelligence handed to the governor of Macau claimed that an informer had said Chen Yaozu had not been killed for political reasons or by Nationalist agents, but because he had tried to control rice matters, together with Madame Wang and her faction who were 'making a lot of money [whilst] harming the growers'.[123]

116 Teixeira to MC, 20 and 25 Mar. 1944, ANTT, AOS, NE-10A2, cx. 768.
117 D. P. Barrett, 'The Wang Jingwei Regime, 1940–1945: Continuities and Disjunctures with Nationalist China', in D. P. Barrett and L. N. Shyu (eds.), *Chinese Collaboration with Japan, 1932–1945: The Limits of Accommodation* (Stanford, CA, 2001), pp. 102–15, at p. 104.
118 Teixeira to MC, 12 and 27 July 1944, ANTT, AOS, NE-10A2, cx. 768.
119 Martin, 'Collaboration within Collaboration'.
120 Yick, '"Self-Serving Collaboration"', p. 225.
121 Teixeira to MC, 6 Apr. 1944, ANTT, AOS, NE-10A2, cx. 768.
122 Teixeira to MC, 12 Apr., 1944, ibid.
123 'Notícias soltas' ('Loose Reports'), 19 July 1944, AHU, Espólio Gabriel Maurício Teixeira.

Some of the charges brought against Chen Bijun in her post-war trial did mention her interference in the flow of goods, namely how she had used 'her authority to cut off the supply of goods and [military] assistance' provided by nations 'friendly' to Chiang's government and sent via Hong Kong and Macau.[124] The RNG's control over areas of Guangdong province bordering Macau meant that Wang's regime had enormous power over essential food supplies to the enclave, especially rice. It could yield that power by stopping those supplies, or enabling them to suit its own interests. Even though areas under RNG control in Guangdong experienced famine in the 1940s, rice could be exported to Macau at premium prices, with Chen Bijun's faction reportedly using the profits to purchase gold and other things in Macau.[125]

The Guangdong provincial government continued to be a family business after the death of Chen Yaozu. Illustrating the weight of Madame Wang's influence in the south, Yaozu's replacement was another of her relatives, Russia-educated Chen Chunpu. Interactions with Macau also proceeded. Even as Guangzhou experienced shortages of coal and water, Chen Chunpu agreed to supply Macau with rice.[126]

Between 13 and 26 July 1944, Captain Silva e Costa, the new president of the Macau Imports Regulation Commission, came to Guangzhou to negotiate an agreement for rice supply from Zhongshan. The Guangdong government wanted to buy some railway track and locomotives in the possession of the Netherlands Harbour Works (NHW) in the enclave. Costa replied that the Macau government could indeed cede the small number of railway track it possessed in the public works but, regarding Dutch company property, he could only try. Knowing the leverage their control of food supplies had over Macau, the provincial authorities, represented by the director of public works, Zhang Youyun, made the amount of rice supplied dependent on acquiring what they wanted.

Nonetheless, these deals were not merely bilateral. As negotiations stalled, the Portuguese approached General Yazaki Kanju, the intelligence chief the governor had met during his visit to Guangzhou, to help guarantee that Macau would not be left without rice. The intervention worked, further attesting to the RNG's subaltern position in relation to the Japanese military. The provincial authorities agreed to provide 15,000 catties of rice to Macau (a previous agreement had been 30,000, a quantity they argued was impossible to maintain given the supplies

[124] C. D. Musgrove, 'Cheering the Traitor: The Post-war Trial of Chen Bijun, April 1946', *Twentieth-Century China*, 30/2 (2005), pp. 3–27, at p. 9. Also mentioned in Yick, '"Self-Serving Collaboration"', p. 227.

[125] 'Economic Currents in Macao', p. 14.

[126] Teixeira to MC, 27 July 1944, ANTT, AOS, NE-10A2, cx. 768.

required by the Japanese navy).[127] In exchange, the Macau government agreed to provide some railway track it owned (as soon as they were no longer being used by the entity to which they had been lent), 20–30 tonnes of stakes and a launch, and it would try to guarantee that railway track and locomotives of the NHW stored in Macau would be sold to Chinese traders there, presumably to be transferred to the control of the provincial government.[128]

The RNG justified coming to an agreement with the Portuguese in a way that legitimised their regime, arguing that they were supplying rice to Macau in order to provide for the Chinese residents there facing difficult subsistence conditions. Provincial authorities reserved the right to reduce or suspend the amount agreed if Guangdong experienced scarcity, or production decreased due to a calamity.[129] They also wanted the Macau government to prevent individuals or news articles that 'disturbed peace' in the enclave, a repeated request evidencing that resistance continued unabated. By expressing their concern over the Chinese population in Macau, RNG authorities were competing directly with Chiang's government for recognition as the legitimate political representative overseeing the livelihood of Chinese nationals.

In Macau, Portuguese interactions with the RNG authorities remained functional until the end of the war, as the governor kept trying to negotiate rice supplies. As late as July 1945, the Macau authorities sent an envoy to Guangzhou to negotiate a contract with the Cantonese government, whilst the Japanese military, on whom the imports depended, was also approached. It was believed that a food crisis could be averted if RNG authorities kept their promises – otherwise there would be only four days' supply of rice for Macau residents.[130]

The following month, the governor informed Lisbon that the living costs in Macau were so high 'that officials and even high-ranking officers' were 'suffering from hunger'.[131] Now, even the relatively shielded Portuguese colonial apparatus was starting to feel the scarcity that most Macau residents had been battling for years. By 1945, the only rice coming into the enclave, Teixeira reported, did so through smuggling. This food dependency, which will be further

[127] A catty (*jin* in Mandarin) is a Chinese unit of measurement equivalent to 500 grams.
[128] Gracias to Lima, 29 July 1944, AHD, 2P, A48, M221.
[129] Point 8 and 9 of the agreement signed in 22 July 1944. A copy of the Portuguese version can be found in AHD, 2P, A48, M221.
[130] Teixeira to MC, 20 July 1945, TNA, HW 12/325.
[131] Teixeira to MC, 3 Aug. 1945, TNA, HW 12/327.

analysed in the following section, was the key factor in the collaborative attitude the Portuguese authorities in Macau had towards the Japanese forces and the RNG in Guangdong. Collaboration, even if under duress, was a dangerous game, however.

It was not solely the Wang Jingwei regime that began to turn on itself but also the Japanese in Macau. By 1944, the governor had already noted sharp divisions amongst the main Japanese representatives in Macau: Consul Fukui, the military liaison officer, Sawa, and naval forces. Teixeira sought to capitalise on these to ensure food supplies, guaranteeing that Macau was useful to Japan then and after the war.[132]

Divisions amongst the Japanese in Macau were brought to the fore when the Japanese consul was shot twice on 2 February 1945, dying in hospital the following day, arguably the highest-profile murder to occur in the enclave during the war. Fukui had been a well-regarded presence in Macau, an example of how some Japanese diplomats sought to mitigate the abuses of the military.[133] British and Portuguese accounts attribute responsibility to the Japanese military that resented Fukui's cordial relations with the Allies in Macau, notably his role in facilitating prisoner of war (POW)–related communications.[134]

British Army Aid Group (BAAG) documents state that Fukui was assassinated by a Formosan for personal revenge.[135] Publicly, the Japanese blamed Chinese resistance. Dōmei, the official Japanese news agency, reported the assassination as having been perpetrated by 'enemy terrorists' and the Japanese ambassador in Lisbon demanded an apology.[136] Two months later, a Japanese naval officer named Shibayama was also assassinated in Macau. He was believed to be of the naval special branch and was reportedly killed by his Chinese assistants.[137] Even if these were inside jobs, the immediate result was the imposition of Japanese blockades on Macau. Blackmailing the Portuguese into compliance by threatening to withhold food supplies

132 Teixeira to MC, 6 Sept. 1944, ANTT, AOS, NE-10A2, cx. 768.
133 Teixeira to MC, 2 Feb. 1945, ibid.
134 Reeves to FO, 3 Feb. 1945, TNA, FO 371/46199; Reeves, *The Lone Flag*, p. 22; Roger Lobo quoted in McGivering, *Macao Remembers*, p. 76; Teixeira, 'Macau Durante a Guerra', p. 533.
135 Kweilin Intelligence Summary No. 87, 28 Feb. 1945, University of Hong Kong Libraries Special Collections (hereafter HKU), MF 2530701, Roll 19.
136 Dōmei, 4 Feb. 1945, TNA, FO 371/46199; Morishima to Salazar, 23 Mar. 1945, ANTT, AOS, NE-7B, Pt. 40.
137 Reeves to FO, 9 Apr. 1945, TNA, FO 371/46199; Morishima to Salazar, 25 Apr. 1945, ANTT, AOS, NE-2F1, pt. 41; 'Economic Currents in Macao', p. 32.

was a fairly common occurrence, but its effects grew more serious from 1943 onwards as the ability to get supplies through alternative channels dwindled.

In any case, terror did not bow the local population into submission. Governor Teixeira noted that the Japanese resented the atmosphere of hatred towards them by the Chinese, but they were 'unable to understand that that was the result of their actions [in] China'.[138] He observed that, in Macau, no assistance was given when the police investigated attacks against Japanese. Eventually, the blockade ended through decisive démarches of enterprising intermediaries after Lobo got a 'Chinese commission' to ask Sawa to cancel it.[139]

Lobo continued to play an important role, liaising with Fukui's replacements, Iwai Eichii and Yodogawa Masaki (who had previously served as consul in Timor).[140] Although Portuguese–Japanese diplomatic relations were not broken, they deteriorated considerably in 1945. Despite this, Japan's Ministry of Foreign Affairs deemed it necessary to keep Portugal neutral, especially as relations with Spain deteriorated to the point of rupture.[141] Portugal itself remained for Japan an important intelligence collection outpost, whilst Macau became a safe haven for Japanese women and children when Allied bombs fell over Guangzhou and Hong Kong, in a curious echo of the movement of other refugees who Japanese bombs had driven towards Macau in the previous years.[142]

The end of the war in September 1945 caught several people connected to the Japanese and the RNG in Macau by surprise. Several figured in lists of war criminals and traitors sought after by both the Nationalists and the British. As will be seen in Chapter 6, their presence in the enclave created a new set of problems for the Portuguese authorities, whose vulnerability to supply blockades did not end with the war.

138 Teixeira to MC, 9 Apr. 1945, ANTT, AOS, NE-10A2, cx. 768.

139 Teixeira to MC, 12 Apr. 1945, ibid.

140 Tōgō Shigenori, Japanese Minister of Foreign Affairs to Morishima, 2 May 1945, TNA, HW 12/315; Tōgō to Morishima quoting Iwai's telegram from Macau, 7 May. 1945, TNA, HW 12/316; Teixeira to MC, 8 and 21 May 1945, ANTT, AOS, NE-10A2, cx. 768.

141 'Japanese–Portuguese Relations and the "Macao Problem" (February–May 1945)', pp. 4–6, p. 11, NARA, RG38, A1 27, Box 59.

142 They started to come in 1942, but the move intensified in later stages of the war (Knaggs, 'Information'; G. A. MacKaskie, 'Report on conditions in Macau', 18 June 1942, TNA, FO 371/31630; Ride, *BAAG*, p. 171; Teixeira to MC, 15 Sept. 1943 and 27 July 1944, ANTT, AOS, NE-10A2, cx. 768).

Starvation, Intermediaries and Philanthropy

Relations with the RNG often revolved around food supplies because the issue was, literally, a matter of life and death to Macau's significantly swollen population. As seen in Chapter 3, the arrival of hundreds of thousands of refugees had a profound effect on everyday life in the enclave. The social impact of the war was comparable to occupied areas in China, not only in what pertained to displacement, but also on wartime food shortages and associated mortality. Studies on wartime Shanghai, for example, reveal identical dynamics: growing destitution, ineffective policies, smuggling dependency and the use of food as 'an economic weapon for political purposes'.[143] As in the case of Shanghai, the misery of the many contrasted with the opulence of a few. Resentment towards unnamed profiteers transpired in newspapers at the time and in memoirs written later.[144] This long-lasting emotional response illustrates the ambivalence of neutrality as a lived experience of scarcity, poverty and inequality.

Macau had always been dependent on food imports and with sea and land transport often disrupted by Japanese blockades, everyday life became marked by shortages and inflation. In August 1937, the Macau government fixed the price of rice sales.[145] However, this early measure did not prevent a spiralling price rise, which grew more dramatic as the war dragged on. The price of rice in Macau in 1945 was thirty-three times greater than the price in 1939.[146]

In December 1941, the local government started rationing some products, including bread, olive oil and coal.[147] Rice was arguably the most important commodity, and the government continually sought to control access to it, with some degree of success, though that control was built on different forms of collaboration.[148] In early 1942, it announced that all people who had more than two bags of rice for their own consumption

143 C. Henriot, 'Rice, Power and People: The Politics of Food Supply in Wartime Shanghai (1937–1945)', *Twentieth-Century China*, 26/1 (2000), pp. 41–84, at p. 69.

144 'Macau e a Guerra' ('Macau and the War'), *Renascimento* (23 Mar. 1945), p. 4; F. T. O. Li and T. Harrison, *Much Beloved Daughter* (London, 1985), p. 35.

145 'Portaria nº 2:359', *Boletim Oficial da Colónia de Macau* (*Official Bulletin of the Macau Colony*), no. 33, 17 Aug. 1937, p. 1.

146 The price rose every year. In 1939, it was 0.08 patacas per catty and in 1945, it was 2.70 patacas per catty (Repartição Central dos Serviços de Administração Civil – Secção de Estatística, *Anuário Estatístico de Macau. Ano de 1949* (Macau Statistical Yearbook. Year of 1949) (Macau, 1950), p. 154).

147 *Boletim Oficial da Colónia de Macau*, no. 50, 13 Dec. 1941, p. 868. Examples of rice rationing coupons dated from the last year of the conflict can be seen in NLA, MS 4300, Box 52, Series 8.1/11.

148 For a positive assessment of the Portuguese colonial authorities' intervention in the supply and distribution of rice after the fall of Hong Kong, see V. Viana and K. Y. Kim,

needed to register with the police.[149] Milk was also rationed, and it was announced that it would only be sold to sick children and the elderly, and with a medical prescription. Lists of the places where ration coupons could be exchanged were constantly published in the local papers. These coupons were also distributed to the 'floating population' (those who lived on boats).[150]

The Macau authorities also took steps to regulate the use of rationing coupons as people exploited existing loopholes and lax enforcement to access extra food.[151] From April onwards, exiting Macau without handing in rationing coupons was forbidden.[152] Queues for rice, bread and sugar were sizeable and methods and amounts of distribution were reported as unclear.[153] Complaints were voiced in the press about the queues to exchange ration coupons, about the cheaters who sold fake coupons or empty bags to naïve people, and about the hoarders.[154] Whatever the steps the colonial authorities took – which mirror similar policies in Shanghai – they did not ensure enough food was available to all Macau residents. Smuggling continued to be not only common but absolutely indispensable.

During the war, the enclave revived its centuries-old vocation as a smuggling entrepôt, one of the dimensions where the porosity of its *gudao* experience is most evident. Petrol, petrol tins, rubber, scrap metal, leather, cloth and toilet articles were smuggled into China in exchange for rice and sometimes wolfram (tungsten) ore. An early post-war list of 'puppets' in Macau provided to the American Office of Strategic Studies (OSS) by a Portuguese agent named a few merchants who had obtained gun powder, wolfram and other commodities for the Japanese, as well as several companies collaborating with the military and intelligence.[155]

Philip Thai, who has demonstrated the prevalence of tungsten smuggling in wartime China, describes one of these entrepreneurial middlemen: Zhang Wendong, from Guangdong province. Having worked for

'Rice Scarcity in World War II Macao: The Local Experience Revisited', *Urban History*, 46/3 (2019), pp. 518–41.

149 'Comissão Reguladora das Importações – Anuncio' ('Imports Regulation Commission – Announcement'), *VM* (3 Mar. 1943), p. 2.

150 For example, 'Administração do Conselho de Macau – Aviso' (Macau Council Administration – Notice), *VM* (30 Jan. 1942), p. 3.

151 'Administração do Conselho de Macau – Edital' ('Macau Council Administration – Proclamation'), *VM* (27 Feb. 1942), p. 3; 'Abutres' ('Vultures'), *Renascimento* (18 May 1945), p. 1; Viana and Kim, 'Rice Scarcity in World War II Macao', p. 535.

152 'Administração do Conselho de Macau – Edital', *VM* (27 Mar. 1942), p. 3.

153 MacKaskie, 'Report'.

154 'Mais uma exploração' (One More Exploitation), *VM* (27 Feb. 1942), p 3.

155 OSS, China Theatre, X-2 Branch Report, 'Puppets in Macao', 3 Jan. 1946, NARA, RG226, UD 173, Box 9.

Mitsui in Hong Kong, Zhang then managed the Jincheng Company in Macau and his supplies of wolfram, grains and other materials to the Japanese drew the attention of the Nationalist authorities, who sought his arrest as a traitor after the war.[156] Wolfram was also a key trading commodity in Portugal, where its supply to Germany was significant and controversial.[157]

As with most activities in the neutral enclave, smuggling was a transnational affair. Major players included Chinese and Japanese, with patrol boats and troops stationed along the West and Pearl rivers in places such as Shiqi, Tangjia, Sangchuan island or Doumen controlling the amounts in circulation.[158] Alberto Barros Lopes, a Macau resident who lived through the war years, recalled in a testimony collected decades after the events: '[W]e could get things from Hong Kong . . . as long as we had a good contact amongst the Japanese.'[159] Smuggling involved food, energy supplies, military products and even entertainment, such as looted American films that, challenging wartime enmities, were being shown by the Japanese.[160] As we shall see in Chapter 5, smuggling people across enemy lines was also common.

The increased scarcity of foodstuffs and other materials, the intervention of colonial authorities by commandeering stocks from businesses and civilians (including, controversially, removing a small amount of rice from the residence of Sun Yat-sen's first wife) and the growing influence of well-connected smugglers eroded popular trust in the colonial government. Portuguese authorities were seen as enablers of collaboration with Japanese forces and their allies, who were thought to be involved in a number of these businesses. According to a post-war report:

> The feeling against the Government extended therefore to all sections of the populace, excepting those who were benefited from this business by reason of the fact that they were collaborating with the Japanese, and the talk went round that the Portuguese were favouring the traitors by taking away any merchandise from the patriotic and giving the traitors an opportunity, thereby, of helping the Japanese. It will never be possible to eradicate from the minds of the Chinese people generally that the Portuguese were really on the side of the Japanese.[161]

[156] P. Thai, *China's War on Smuggling: Law, Economic Life, and the Making of the Modern State, 1842–1965* (New York, 2018), pp. 199–200.
[157] Reginbogin, *Faces of Neutrality*, pp. 128–9.
[158] Knaggs, 'Information', TNA, FO 371/31630.
[159] Lima and Torres, *Macau entre Dois Mundos*, pp. 34–5
[160] Reeves, 19 Jan. 1943, quoted in telegram from Ronald Campbell, British Ambassador to Portugal to FO, 28 Jan. 1943, TNA, FO 371/35731.
[161] 'Economic Currents in Macao', p. 13.

Shortly after the occupation of Hong Kong, a precarious situation quickly deteriorated and the human toll soon became evident. Of the 27,000 people estimated to have died of starvation in 1942, 1,007 died in February.[162] Observers at the time blamed Japanese blockades. The governor praised the 'admirable resistance' of the population and assured Lisbon that the local government was not being criticised for the scarcity of rice.[163] Despite Teixeira's words, some in Macau did wonder why the Portuguese government was not more proactive in shipping food and other supplies to Macau.[164]

By April, the local situation had escalated. The British consul reported to the FO that deaths from starvation were numbering fifty-five a day. Weeks went on without rice, prices skyrocketed and robberies increased.[165] That month, Teixeira informed Lisbon there had been three cases of cannibalism amongst Chinese refugees. A group of seven people involved in the incident that included sale of human flesh was caught, but the governor decided not to put them on trial. Instead, he sent them away in a smuggling junk and spread the rumour that they had been executed to discourage others.[166]

By the end of the month, the average number of deaths by starvation per day was sixty, with another two cases of cannibalism reported.[167] A censored letter sent by a woman in Macau to her fiancé in the navy in Lisbon vividly described cannibalism cases in Macau, including references to the cooking and selling of human flesh at the Hotel Central, one of Macau's main hotels.[168] Other accounts mention cannibalism and go as far as to indicate that premeditated killings were perpetrated to harvest human flesh.[169] Although references to cannibalism did not usually pertain to cases witnessed directly, their frequency in accounts of the period points towards a probable veracity, and the practice is often mentioned in secondary sources on wartime Macau.[170]

[162] Reeves, *The Lone Flag*, p. 14; Governor of Macau to MC, 23 Feb. 1942, ANTT, AOS, UL-10A1, cx. 767.
[163] Teixeira to MC, 23 Feb. 1942, ANTT, AOS, UL-10A1, cx. 767.
[164] 'Economic Currents in Macao', p. 30.
[165] Reeves, 25 Apr., 1942, quoted in telegram from British Embassy in Lisbon to FO, 26 Apr. 1942, TNA, FO 371/31630. Also in TNA, CO 825/30/12.
[166] Teixeira to MC, 1 Apr. 1942, ANTT, AOS, UL-10A1, cx. 767.
[167] Teixeira to MC, 29 Apr. 1942, ibid.
[168] Censorship transcript dated 18 Dec. 1942 of letter from D. M. Sousa Afonso to Augusto Souto Silva Cruz, 23 July 1942, ibid.
[169] For example, Pinto, 'Guerra em Paz', pp. 80–2; Ana Maria Amaro's testimony in Lima and Torres, *Macau entre Dois Mundos*, p. 141.
[170] For example, Silva, *Eu estive em Macau*, p. 91; G. C. Gunn, 'Hunger amidst Plenty: Rice Supply and Livelihood in Wartime Macau', in G. C. Gunn (ed.), *Wartime Macau: Under the Japanese Shadow* (Hong Kong, 2016), pp. 72–93, at pp. 80–2.

South China was a highly connected region, even in times of conflict, and Macau's food supplies were vulnerable to military operations outside of its borders. In February 1943, Japanese forces took de facto control of the French leased territory of Guangzhouwan, which had been the major supply line into Macau.[171] The effects were immediately felt, with rising prices and diminishing supply. To try to find a solution for the supply problem, the governor met with rice merchants and charity representatives, including Gao Kening, then president of the Commercial Association, Liu Xutang, the president of the Kiang Wu Hospital, and Liang Houyuan, the representative of the Chinese community.[172] Similar meetings were held several times, but the problem persisted.

As the year went on, the governor reported that the number of those who starved to death had increased. The famished robbed people with food parcels on the street and deliberately let themselves get caught, pleading to be taken to jail where they would have something to eat.[173] In a detailed post-war report to the bank's headquarters in Lisbon, Carlos Vasconcelos, the BNU manager in Macau, described the moral breakdown in the enclave in vivid terms, with 'streets infested with cadaveric beggars', and the city's cemetery having no more space for the dead, who were sent to Taipa island piled on a boat, 'a macabre spectacle' to which people became accustomed.

He also mentioned the 'not few' cases of cannibalism, the mutilated corpses of children with missing limbs found in a beggars' asylum in the morning and the 'almost weekly' murders on the street.[174] Other observers penned identical accounts. António de Andrade e Silva, who was harbour master in Macau from 1941 to 1945, also described in his unfinished memoirs shocking scenes of famine and inequality witnessed during the war, including the sight of two famished boys rushing to devour the vomit left by drunken Japanese on the street.[175] Chinese American Jun Ke Choy (Cai Zengji), who had held official posts in China prior to the war and served as vice president of the Cantonese Residents Association in Shanghai, lived 'underground' in Macau in the 1940s and recalled in his memoir:

> Thousands of refugees lived out in the open in Macao and many died every day from starvation. Corpses lay unburied by the side of the streets for days. Flies fluttered above, and the stench from the corpses was nauseating. It was a terrible

[171] Teixeira to MC, 23 Feb. 1943, ANTT, AOS, NE-10A2, cx. 768.
[172] 'Uma reunião no Palacio do Governo' ('A Meeting at the Government Palace'), *VM* (24 Feb. 1943), p. 3; 'O problema do arrôs' ('The Rice Problem'), *VM* (2 Mar. 1943), p. 3.
[173] Teixeira to MC, 29 June 1943, ANTT, AOS, NE-10A2, cx. 768.
[174] Vasconcelos, 'Relatório', p. 66. [175] Silva, *Eu estive em Macau*, p. 142.

sight. Sometimes the stronger starving refugees would snatch food from certain carriers and run for safety. The police usually ignored these petty pilferings. It was a hopeless situation.[176]

A case in the Chinese Ministry of Foreign Affairs archives demonstrates the dire situation reached in wartime Macau at the same time as it reveals the challenges of information flow between those in Macau and their family members overseas. In 1944, a Chinese Canadian requested news about his family in Macau, only to hear later that his relatives had died of hunger.[177] Even with delays, news of the horrors taking place in the neutral enclave travelled far, via personal or via official communications, or the overlap between the two. As many of the dead went unaccounted for, statistics remain as flawed as those for the total number of refugees. Some estimates do exist, however. The number of deaths due to starvation and disease in Macau during the war was estimated to have surpassed 50,000.[178] The everyday visibility of starvation made a strong impression on those who lived in wartime Macau. Macanese lawyer and writer Henrique de Senna Fernandes said that when he came across news footage of the survivors of concentration camps in Europe at the end of the war, it reminded him of what he had seen in the enclave.[179]

Wartime Elites

The urgency to get supplies and the colonial state's inability to provide them to the extent necessary was an opportunity for the business figures residing in the territory. The need for food generated needs for compromise, and collaboration thrived. Portuguese authorities gave in to demands to cede vessels and other materials in exchange for foodstuffs or access to food markets. The occupation of Hong Kong precipitated extraordinary measures that reinforced the power and influence of local elites who acted as intermediaries for the colonial authorities. Some, like the gambling concessionaries Gao Kening and Fu Deyin, were already prominent figures in Macau's business circles before the war. Others, such as Stanley Ho (He Hongshen), were newcomers from Hong Kong. Others still were part of the Portuguese administration, most notably the head of the Economic Services, Pedro José Lobo (see Figure 4.2).

[176] Choy, *My China Years 1911–1945*, pp. 193–4.
[177] Chinese Consul in Winnipeg to MOFA, 21 Aug. 1944; Chinese Legation in Lisbon to MOFA, 14 Oct. 1944, AH, Waijiaobu, 020000023906A.
[178] Tan, *Aomen zhuquan wenti*, p. 228.
[179] McGivering, *Macao Remembers*, p. 95. Similar comparisons were made by Cannon's interviewees in Cannon, 'Experience, Memory and the Construction of the Past', p. 15.

Figure 4.2 Pedro José Lobo, head of the Macau Economic Services, 1950. Photograph by Harrison Forman. From the American Geographical Society Library, University of Wisconsin-Milwaukee Libraries

The rise of business philanthropists was, of course, not wholly new and bears striking similarities with cases in Shanghai and elsewhere in the Pearl River Delta that also involved government and international connections.[180] However, in contrast with occupied areas where private elite charity was either constrained by the Japanese occupation or saw its legitimacy eroded by collaboration, in Macau the war period was one of virtually unbridled ascendancy of powerful business intermediaries, and the prominence they gained lasted long after the war ended.

The Macau authorities' dependency on business elites became particularly evident after the occupation of Hong Kong. At the beginning of the Japanese invasion, the Macau government's funds in the British colony became inaccessible and the flow of material goods was temporarily

[180] Dillon, 'The Politics of Philanthropy'; H. Liao, '*Shang* and *Shan*: Charitable Networks of the "Four Great Department Stores" and Their Associated Chinese–Australian Families 1900–1949' (PhD thesis, Swinburne University of Technology, 2018).

suspended. The Portuguese authorities decided to seize contraband material they knew existed in the enclave. According to the BNU manager, who played an important role in these operations, a great quantity of stocks was destined to be smuggled by boat to the Nationalists. The local authorities 'requisitioned petrol, oil, flammable oils, cotton yarn, raw materials and others from the stockists, shut down grocery stores and bought basic necessities'.[181] To ensure the supply of rice, Lobo negotiated with a representative of the Japanese navy, and from then on supplies were paid to the Japanese in silver and Hong Kong dollars.

The Imports Regulation Commission that had been created in November 1941 took on a new role after the occupation of Hong Kong: it gathered existing stocks in Macau under the pretext of distributing them to different sectors and of creating reserves for an uncertain future. Distribution of these supplies was not, however, a purely humanitarian gift. Initially, the BNU manager was also the commission's president, and began a process of manipulating prices by selling rice faster to those who paid in the currency needed at a particular time.[182]

Despite the local government's attempts to manage supplies, its financial capacity was limited and, at first, it was largely powerless in the face of the machinations of money exchangers, who speculated in everything, particularly silver.[183] The British consul reported to London 'speculation on a vast scale' in several currencies, with a black market that was believed to include Hong Kong, Indochina, Shanghai and unoccupied China. Profits were easily made by starting rumours.[184] Both British and Portuguese sources decry the action of the men involved in wild currency trading, who were seen to have 'exploited everything to get rich, despoiling the population'.[185] However, expressions of contempt coexisted with some of admiration for their financial power, which ensured that supplies, however meagre, reached the enclave.

The BNU manager went as far as to conclude that these businessmen's actions could be seen as 'beneficial' and nothing short of essential: '[I]f the Colony was able to survive, it owed it to them, to their connections with the Japanese and to their influence in the neighbouring regions, [as well as] to the cooperation they provided the Government regarding supplies.'[186] Collaboration between colonial administration and business elites was neither new nor exclusive to Macau. However, its wartime

[181] Vasconcelos, 'Relatório', p. 54. [182] Vasconcelos, 'Relatório', p. 60.

[183] Heenan, Memorandum, p. 2; Reeves, 21 June 1943, quoted in telegram from British Embassy in Chongqing to FO, 22 June 1943, TNA, FO 371/35733.

[184] Reeves, 21 June 1943. [185] Vasconcelos, 'Relatório', p. 63.

[186] Ibid., p. 78. Also quoted in Braga, *Macau Durante a II Guerra Mundial*, p. 79, and Botas, *Macau 1937–1945*, p. 255.

manifestations in the neutral enclave saw key developments. Collaboration came to involve predominantly Chinese elites, and major intermediaries during the conflict went on to dominate Macau's economy in the post-war period and for many decades to come.

There was a material dimension to wartime collaboration and it too was marked by different global connections. Japanese military forces and their collaborators approached the Portuguese authorities to acquire vessels, including several that were foreign property, such as Dutch dredgers or the Panamanian ship *Masbate*. Incidents involving these were reported to Lisbon, London and Chongqing, but if protestations and excuses were able to stall some of the sales, not all were successful.[187]

Compliance was certainly not enthusiastically given. Governor Teixeira was wary of Japanese demands and, unlike his predecessor, he saw no future silver lining in these delicate wartime businesses. It soon became clear that collaboration with Japan was eroding the legitimacy of Portuguese colonial rule in the eyes of both the majority of the Chinese population – who opposed the Japanese invasion of China – and of the Portuguese old allies, the British, whose presence in Macau had become quite significant after the fall of Hong Kong. According to the BNU manager, the Portuguese felt 'diminished and vexed' in relation to the Chinese population who, he sensed, regarded them 'with an expression of contempt and mockery'.[188] The loss of colonial prestige was a major worry for the Portuguese authorities.

The war also provided opportunities to try to disentangle the bonds of 'subaltern colonialism', which tied them to the British. That was particularly evident in the little-known case of the British-owned MELCO. The company had a monopoly on the supply of electric energy to Macau and the majority of its shares were owned by the General Electric Company of China, a subsidiary of the General Electric Company. In late 1941, the chief of staff of the Japanese navy in Hong Kong visited the Macau governor and informed him that no more coal would be supplied given that it was intended for use by a British company.[189] At the start of 1943, the senate, Macau's municipal council, unilaterally took over MELCO's concession, generating an Anglo–Portuguese crisis evident in lengthy diplomatic files. Only in July 1945 did the Portuguese formally settle an agreement that recognised the wartime takeover as a temporary measure

[187] See various files in ANTT, AOS, NE-10A2, cx. 768, TNA, FO 371/31630, TNA, FO 371/35731, TNA, FO 371/35732, TNA, FO 371/35733, TNA, FO 371/35734, TNA, FO 371/35736, and AH, Waijiaobu, 020000023906A; Fernandes, *Confluência de Interesses*, pp. 39–40.

[188] Vasconcelos, 'Relatório', p. 65.

[189] Teixeira to MC, 4 Dec. 1942, ANTT, AOS, UL-10A1, cx. 767.

and return the electric services provision rights to the original company in December 1945.[190]

The sharp decline of British power in South China following the occupation of Hong Kong pushed the Portuguese colonial authorities to strengthen their ties with Chinese elites and Japanese forces in the region. In 1942, Pedro Lobo founded the Macau Cooperative Company. Its official responsibilities were 'commerce, industry and shipping (cargo and passengers) between Macau and other ports'.[191] Set up in order to guarantee supplies to Macau, it worked closely with Japanese and Chinese partners. The Imports Regulation Commission gave the Cooperative Company metal bars and coins in exchange for foodstuffs.[192] The company's secretary was a young refugee from Hong Kong who was to have a major role in post-war Macau: Stanley Ho.

In an anthology of Macau-related recollections, Ho noted that the company's main purpose was 'to provide food' for the enclave, and to achieve it the government supplied the company 'with all the surplus they could afford to give away'. He also gave English lessons to Sawa, the Japanese liaison officer.[193] He remembered Macau as a site of opportunity during the conflict ('Macau was paradise during the war'), a place where one could lead an enjoyable life with 'excellent food' if one 'had the money'.[194]

The war period was a decisive one for Stanley Ho's business career and he always acknowledged that in later interviews. Virtually all of his obituaries in 2020 included references to his professional beginnings in wartime Macau.[195] Other figures who became prominent in the post-war period, such as Ho Yin, also first became noted as intermediaries in Macau during the war.[196]

[190] See various files in TNA, FO 371/35731 and TNA, FO 371/46199; 'Diploma legislativo nº 899', *Boletim Oficial da Colónia de Macau*, no. 50, 15 Dec. 1945, p. 467.

[191] 'Nova companhia' ('New Company'), *VM* (11 May 1942), p. 3.

[192] Vasconcelos, 'Relatório', p. 70.

[193] McGivering, *Macao Remembers*, pp. 107–8; J. Studwell, *Asian Godfathers: Money and Power in Hong Kong and South-East Asia* (London, 2007), p. 19. Studwell listed as source for his section on Stanley Ho the notes of an interview that Ho had given Philip Snow in 1995.

[194] McGivering, *Macao Remembers*, p. 108

[195] For example, J. Kandell, 'Stanley Ho, Who Turned Macau into a Global Gambling Hub, Dies at 98', *NYT* (26 May 2020), www.nytimes.com/2020/05/26/business/stanley-ho-dead.html; I. Chaiça, L. Botelho and L. Villalobos, 'Stanley Ho, o magnata que "não sabia dizer que não a Portugal"' ('Stanley Ho, the tycoon who "didn't know how to say no to Portugal"'), *PÚBLICO* (26 May 2020), www.publico.pt/2020/05/26/economia/noticia/morreu-stanley-ho-magnata-jogo-macau-1918092; P. French, 'Stanley Ho's escape to Macao in World War II laid the foundation for his fortune. But it wasn't without controversy', *CNN* (1 June 2020), edition.cnn.com/2020/05/30/china/stanley-ho-macau-hnk-intl/index.html.

[196] Jorge and Coelho, *Roque Choi*, pp. 66–7.

The public face of Macau's wartime business opportunities intersected directly with the livelihood crisis generated by the conflict through philanthropy. If the tightly censored press kept potentially controversial business activities out of the limelight, it often reported the charitable donations of the 'generous capitalists' in town. These brief reports provide a who's who of pre-war and post-war tycoons in the region: Gao Kening, Fu Deyin, Robert Ho Tung, Ho Yin and even the Tiger Balm boss Aw Boon Hwa (Hu Wenhu) and his son, amongst several others, were often mentioned as contributing to charitable relief of the poor in Macau.[197] Whilst some of these figures are now fairly well known, and some had been prominent contributors to the Chinese resistance cause in the late 1930s, others have been largely forgotten.

The closest to the Portuguese administration was Pedro Lobo, head of Macau's Economic Services bureau. Lobo's role in shadow diplomacy with all belligerents in the region was recognised at the time and has been ever since. Portuguese sources highly praise his shrewd negotiation skills, often remarking on the 'profound knowledge' of the 'Oriental soul'. [198] This can also be read as a veiled discriminatory remark on Lobo's Eurasian origins that, by emphasising his difference from the white Portuguese in the administration, deviated to Lobo potential criticism from their own acts of collaboration.

The governor's dependency on Lobo cemented the latter's position, which continued to be of great influence in the post-war gold trade in Macau that later inspired Ian Fleming's *Goldfinger*.[199] Cui Nuozi's son, Cui Leqi, who would become a key intermediary figure in his own right in the post-war period (as secretary to Lobo and Ho Yin), remembered Lobo's role during the conflict as being 'a sort of minister of foreign affairs' for the Macau government.[200] Lobo was also in close contact

[197] For example, 'Sir Robert Ho Tung', *VM* (17 Aug. 1942), p. 3. 'Mais uma benemerencia do sr. Kou Hó Neng' ('One More Charitable Act by Mr Gao Kening'), *VM* (28 Sept. 1942), p. 3; 'Donativos á Beneficencia' ('Charitable Donations'), *VM* (23 Dec. 1942), p. 3; 'Donativo aos Pobres' ('Donation for the Poor'), *VM* (13 Feb. 1943), p. 3; 'Corações Generosos' ('Generous Hearts'), *VM* (17 Feb. 1943), p. 3; 'Bem Fazer' ('Doing Good'), *VM* (11 Oct. 1944), p. 4; 'Gestos Filantropicos' ('Philanthropic Gestures'), *Renascimento* (8 May 1945), p. 2.

[198] For example, Vasconcelos, BNU Macau Manager to BNU Lisbon Manager, 15 Oct. 1941, ANTT, AOS, UL-5A, cx. 750, pt. 7; Governor of Macau to MC, 6 Feb. 1945, ANTT, AOS, NE-10A2, cx. 768; M. Teixeira, '"A Alfandega Roubada" e "O Barco Roubado"' ('The Stolen Customs Station' and 'The Stolen Boat'), *Boletim Eclesiástico da Diocese de Macau*, 885 (1978), p. 526; Alberto Barros Lopes' testimony in Lima and Torres, *Macau entre Dois Mundos*, p. 35.

[199] P. Pons, *Macao*, trans. S. Adams (London, 2002), p. 121. For Ian Fleming's account of 1960s Macau, see *Thrilling Cities* (London, 2013), pp. 25–49.

[200] Lima and Torres, *Macau entre Dois Mundos*, p. 97.

with British and American intelligence. His son Roger, who had a remarkable career in Hong Kong after the war, was, by his own admission, 'involved with British intelligence' through his father.[201] After the war, the elder Lobo was invited to join a commission for Hong Kong's economic reconstruction as well as to be T. V. Soong's agent in the British colony, which demonstrates how he had gained the trust of both the British and the Nationalists.[202]

Although Stanley Ho and Ho Yin are more often mentioned in studies of Macau's economy in the twentieth century, two other names figure prominently in sources of the 1930s and 1940s: Gao Kening and Fu Deyin. Their company Tai Heng (Tai Xing) had been granted a lucrative gambling monopoly and owned one of the main hotels in the territory, the Hotel Central, a key entertainment venue in wartime Macau, patronised by clients of all sides.

Gao had been previously connected to an opium processing business in Macau and had founded a currency exchange house that later expanded into a bank. During the war, he served as president of the Commercial Association and was also connected to the two leading Chinese charities in the territory, the Kiang Wu Hospital and the Tung Sin Tong. In 1942, Gao was decorated by the Portuguese government with the title of *comendador* (commander), a testament to his good relations with the colonial administration.[203] His dealings with the Japanese were well known, but the governor was willing to vouch for him politically, asking Reeves to convey that to the Nationalists in 1943.[204] As will be seen in Chapter 6, the Chinese government had Gao on a list of 'economic traitors' (*jingji hanjian*), although, like his business partner, he was never convicted of anything.

After the war, the governor tried to clean up the image of some alleged collaborators. He wrote to the British consul (copies reached the Chinese Ministry of Foreign Affairs) declaring that, during the war, he had the names of several Chinese citizens in Macau – Gao and Fu amongst them – falsely announced as traitors on Radio Chongqing. His idea was to use this information to persuade the Japanese to lift their blockade and allow some food supplies into Macau.[205]

201 McGivering, *Macao Remembers*, p. 75.
202 Vasconcelos to BNU Lisbon, 30 Ago. 1945, CGD, AG-011–7–185.
203 'Ordem de Benemerencia' ('Charitable Order'), *VM* (10 Dec. 1942), p. 3.
204 Reeves quoted in dispatch from the British Consulate in Guilin to Chancery, 28 Jan. 1943, TNA, FO 371/35731.
205 Teixeira to Reeves, 27 June, 1946, copy from MOFA delegate in Macau, 7 Ago. 1946, AH, Waijiaobu, 020000003314A.

Gao and Fu's names were also mentioned in a particularly revealing letter from the British consul detailing the Allied sinking of the cargo ship *Wing Wah* (also known by the Japanese name *Eika Maru*) in late May 1943. The steamer was travelling under a Portuguese flag but with a Japanese charter and was torpedoed and sunk near Haiphong by an American submarine. Reeves' account is indicative of how food supplies and military smuggling were tightly linked. The Japanese had allowed the *Wing Wah* to make occasional voyages, for example to Guangzhouwan and Xiamen, for supplies.[206] When it was sunk it was bringing rice and coal (required for water supply) from Indochina, both of which were desperately needed in Macau.[207]

That was not all that the ship had on board: amongst the more than 300 passengers (of whom only fifteen survived), eleven were Japanese officers who were going to take up military positions in Haiphong. Two million worth of wolfram, copper, iron bars and gold bars also went down with the ship.[208] The cargo suggests that Japan was using a neutral port, Macau, for military supplies, which can be considered a case of external violation of neutrality.[209]

Allied military operations disrupted some of the wartime trade involving Macau, but other murky economic activities continued. Also in 1943, the BNU found an entry point into the lucrative market of currency exchange, one that further connected Macau to other parts of China. After a meeting in Macau with the Guangzhou branch manager of the Deutsch-Asiatische Bank (DAB), Vasconcelos discovered the bank was interested in Swiss francs. In exchange, the DAB sold the BNU military yen and CRB dollars, both of which could be used to buy rice. The profits for the Portuguese bank were considerable.[210] The economic opportunities of the war in Macau were a peculiar mirror image of what was going on in Portugal, where the conflict is regarded as having 'allowed the accumulation of public and private capital, via fabulous "war businesses"'.[211] The BNU's connection with the DAB demonstrates how the enclave was connected to Axis financial interests in East Asia.

Portuguese authorities and their associates in Macau justified their dealings with Japanese and Chinese collaborators as necessary moves to ensure food and energy supplies to feed Macau's population, comprised

206 Heenan, Memorandum, p. 3.
207 Teixeira to MC, 12 June 1943, ANTT, AOS, NE-10A2, cx.768.
208 Extract from Macau letter to Guilin, p. 9, 14 June 1943, sent with dispatch from Seymour to FO, 8 Sept. 1943, TNA, FO 371/35736. The currency unit is not stated.
209 Karsh, *Neutrality and Small States*, p. 23.
210 Vasconcelos, 'Relatório', p. 80.
211 Rosas, 'Portuguese Neutrality', p. 281.

mostly of refugees, and protect the territory from an invasion. It was, however, precisely the spectre of collaboration that brought about the only direct military attack on Macau during the conflict.

The enclave was bombed by American aircraft on five occasions in 1945: in January, February, April, June and July.[212] The air strikes were later deemed a mistake and the US government paid compensation to Portugal.[213] Just as the maintenance of Portugal's nominal neutrality was important for Japanese policymakers, it was also the overall policy of the American military authorities vis-à-vis Macau. A draft report by the State-War-Navy Coordinating Subcommittee for the Far East recommended that the United States 'should avoid military operations in Macao whether or not Japan respects Portuguese neutrality in regard to the colony'.[214] Yet the 1945 bombing targets were strategic: the former Pan American Airways hangar, where 250 fifty-gallon drums of petrol belonging to the local government were stored; the radio and power stations; the apron where a malfunctioning Japanese military plane was parked; the Panamanian ship *Masbate* about to be used for cargo shipping; and a tugboat. The different bombings caused several civilian casualties.

At the time of the second bombing, a note from Salazar in the Lisbon newspaper *Diário da Manhã* lamented the event and stated that neutrality had been perfectly maintained despite the presence of Japanese forces in Chinese territories contiguous to Macau, and that was evident since none of the Allied nations had made diplomatic protests over the conduct of the local Portuguese authorities.[215]

These claims are not corroborated if one reads through different sources on wartime Macau, where suspicions and complaints over the (ab)uses of neutrality were voiced by different sides. In fact, some accounts have considered the bombings a premeditated action against the Macau Portuguese authorities' 'pro-Japanese neutrality'.[216] Although

[212] Fernandes, *Sinopse de Macau*, pp. 27–32; Kweilin Intelligence Summary No. 83, 26 Jan. 1945, HKU, MF 2530701, Roll 18; Files in ANTT, AOS, NE-10A2, cx. 768, ANTT, AOS, PC-2D, cx. 587, pt. 25, and TNA, FO 371/46199.

[213] Garrett, *The Defences of Macao*, p. 116; S. K. Bailey, 'Briefing Failure in Ready Room 4: The Question of Culpability for U.S. Navy Air Strikes on Macau, 16 January 1945', *Journal of the Royal Asiatic Society Hong Kong Branch*, 58 (2018), pp. 30–54.

[214] State-War-Navy Coordinating Committee, 'Politico-Military Problems in the Far East: Treatment by United States Occupation Forces of Special Areas: Macao', 11 July 1945, NARA, RG165, NM84 421, Box 37.

[215] 'Macau foi de novo bombardeada por um avião americano' ('Macau was Bombed Again by an American Plane'), *Diário da Manhã* (26 Feb. 1945), ANTT, AOS, PC-2D, cx. 587, pt. 25.

[216] Fernandes, *Sinopse de Macau*, p. 27; Braga, *Macau Durante a II Guerra Mundial*, pp. 57–8. See also 'Economic Currents in Macao', p. 26.

the situation on the ground was a lot more complex and involved multiple layers of cooperation with different actors, the bombings do indicate that abuses of Macau's neutrality were not without consequences.

Conclusion

The flexible uses of neutrality in Macau and the different layers of collaboration that marked them reached a critical point during Macau's 'lone island' phase, between the fall of Hong Kong and the end of the war. In those years of heightened – but not total – isolation, Macau became an arena where different actors competed for political legitimacy, economic control and social influence. It was a period marked by some continuities and key changes.

Nationalist resistance remained active in Macau, even if operating under increased risks. Chiang Kai-shek's government was also able to play with the ambiguities of Portuguese neutrality on the international stage, be it through official diplomatic channels or by exposing the growth of Japanese control over the territory through propaganda operations. Perceived breaches of neutrality were attentively followed by the Nationalists. The Chinese central government remained interested in Macau's situation and kept contacts with Portuguese authorities there through its agents in the territory and in Lisbon via its legation. Its concern for the impact of the war on the Chinese population was directed not only towards Macau and Lisbon, but also towards the Portuguese colony of Timor, which remained under Japanese occupation from 1942 until the end of the war.

A major change occurring in this period was the consolidation of CCP presence in Macau. Guerrillas operating in the enclave's neighbouring Zhongshan county established contacts with the Portuguese authorities as they too found Macau a useful place to acquire materials, receive medical care and gather and transmit intelligence.

With the arrival of a new wave of refugees from Hong Kong, the social crisis that Macau had experienced since 1937 intensified. The pressures imposed by Japanese and RNG authorities often manifested themselves in supply blockades. Lack of foodstuffs led to hunger and increased mortality. Neutrality turned Macau into a haven for many, but it also fuelled a rampant inequality that raged in the absence of a colonial government able to fully support all of those it ruled over. Many had to resort to charity, which was often dispensed by philanthropists enriched by the conflict.

Still, concern for the fate of refugees in Macau was part of state-building goals beyond the Portuguese. In fact, it was an arena for legitimacy competition and the RNG authorities in Guangdong tried to use it to their advantage. Their partial control over rice supplies to Macau meant that the enclave's authorities had to engage with them in what ended up being regular, if unofficial, relations, attested by visits and attempts to forge local supply agreements. The dealings of RNG officials with Macau exposed divisions between them and the Japanese forces they were allied with, as well as within the Japanese representatives. The Macau authorities sought to exploit these perceived disagreements to ensure the import of much-needed supplies, as well as to safeguard their own position as colonial rulers. In times of great need, multiple forms of collaboration were attempted or redesigned; they kept (some) food on the table, bought safety and time, and kept Portuguese colonialism in place since the major belligerents had more pressing worries than overthrowing an accommodating small power governing a territory where all sides could gather intelligence, make handsome profits and project their influence.

The links between politics, diplomacy and refugees had been apparent before 1941 but became even more critical after the occupation of Hong Kong. The lack of food was a crucial feature of Macau's wartime experience in the 1940s. It had devastating effects on the increased population and was used to justify concessions to Japanese and collaborators. Old and new elite figures involved in businesses and money exchange enhanced their economic power and political influence, being co-opted by the government as key suppliers. Some of these wartime economic elites came to assume an even greater importance in post-war Macau. The war was a major turning point in their fortunes.

Neutral territories are often sites of competing interests and intense pressure, as agents of the belligerents keep each other in check and seek to ensure the local authorities are not benefitting their enemies. As the war entered its final year, the Allied counter-attack in South China did not always look the other way from what was being permitted in Macau. Consequently, Macau's shipping was disrupted by Allied attacks in the Pacific and the territory itself was bombed by American planes several times in 1945. The incidents were clear reminders that, for all its risks and advantages, neutrality did not mean being completely sealed off from the war or from the consequences of collaboration.

The intersecting presence of Chinese resistance, Chinese collaborators, Japanese forces and Portuguese colonial authorities in Macau was also connected to another major actor in the region: the United Kingdom. The role the British consulate played in managing a multinational community of refugees, intermediaries and informants will be detailed in the next chapter.

5 Colonial Transplantation

Hong Kong in Macau

In his post-war memoir, John Pownall Reeves, the enterprising British consul in Macau, recalled the 'double life' he led in the enclave after Hong Kong was occupied:

> There were times when I was, as it were, half buried; that is to say that part of my activities were underground while the rest were open for all to see. There was quite an atmosphere of espionage and counter-espionage in Macao, some of it purely comic opera and the rest in deadly earnest.[1]

Reeves and his global network of contacts are central to understanding the importance of Macau for Allied resistance in South China. His consulate was a meeting place whose wartime experience attests to one of the enclave's most germane links: Hong Kong, a territory often seen as the complete opposite of Macau. Narratives of Macau and of Hong Kong's respective exceptionalism tend to overlook the profound connections between these territories. In no period were these more crucial than the 1940s, when Hong Kong was occupied by Japan and the sole British consular representation in the region was located in Macau.

From 1942 to 1945, Macau resumed the key role in British activities in South China that it had lost after the First Opium War in the mid-nineteenth century. As seen in Chapter 1, Macau and Hong Kong were united by geographical proximity, colonial status and an international alliance. They were also connected through an important human dimension embodied in the thousands of people who moved between Macau and Hong Kong, with personal and professional engagements in both territories. Even more than the displaced persons who had come to Macau in the late 1930s, the Hong Kong refugees formed a global community encompassing not only British, but also Chinese, Portuguese, Indians, Filipinos, Norwegians, Russians and others. Personal connections and relatively flexible understandings of nationality became

[1] Reeves, *The Lone Flag*, p. 91.

important assets when the temporary loss of Hong Kong led to a colonial transplantation to Macau. This second wave of refugees was too a product of neutrality and enabled by different forms of collaboration, particularly Anglo–Portuguese collaboration.

During the occupation of Hong Kong, the Portuguese-administered enclave became the nearest – and arguably the safest – possible point of refuge for thousands of people who fled Hong Kong through open or underground means. In Macau, the British consulate not only guaranteed relief to multinational refugee communities, but it also became a node in intelligence and escape networks that used Macau to get people, goods and information in and out of Hong Kong, Guangzhouwan and unoccupied China. In Macau, assistance to the British was provided by a number of people and institutions, of which the Macau Delegation of the Portuguese Red Cross, re-established in 1943, is a prime example. Ongoing connections to Hong Kong illustrate the porosity of Macau's neutrality; even in its 'lone island' phase, the territory was not truly isolated.

This colonial transplantation was to have long-lasting consequences. Macau was important in assisting Great Britain's reoccupation of Hong Kong in 1945. Hongkongers' wartime refuge in the neighbouring enclave no doubt buttressed British connivance in the maintenance of Portuguese colonial rule in Macau. Neutrality in Macau contributed to the post-war maintenance of two remnants of colonialism that escaped the fate of other foreign-ruled territories in China fully decolonised by the end of the Second World War, such as French-ruled Guangzhouwan, the other main European colonial territory in the Guangdong region.

Escapes from Hong Kong: States and Individuals

Like the first wave of refugees who had entered Macau when an all-out Sino–Japanese war erupted in 1937, the exodus that followed the fall of Hong Kong in late 1941 was enabled by the efforts of state and non-state actors. Personal relations and transnational interactions were common denominators before and during the escape. Many refugees reached Macau through evacuation drives set up in the immediate aftermath of the British defeat. These were not formally planned in Lisbon, but they nevertheless had a certain official capacity since they were organised by the Macau government through contacts with the Portuguese consulate and the Japanese authorities in Hong Kong. There, procedures were coordinated by the Portuguese vice consul, Francisco Paulo de Vasconcelos Soares, who opened his house in Kowloon to some 400 refugees whom he fed with the help of a Chinese merchant.[2]

Soares was himself a Portuguese Hongkonger affected by the war, having had two sons taken as POWs by the Japanese.[3] In 1942, he registered more than 1,100 people as Portuguese, possibly illegally, so they could flee to Macau with third-country nationals' passes issued by the Japanese authorities.[4] Stuart Braga estimated that more than 90 per cent of the Hong Kong Portuguese went to Macau during the war and described Soares as 'Hong Kong's Schindler'.[5] Soares' actions were not unanimously well received at the time, even being criticised by Leo d'Almada e Castro, who represented the Hong Kong Portuguese refugees in the neighbouring enclave.[6]

In early February 1942, the first batch of Hong Kong refugees, 950 people, whose transport had been arranged by the Macau governor, arrived in Macau. At the time, it was expected that the number would rise to 2,800, but it greatly surpassed it.[7] The Macau government requisitioned clubs and other buildings to house them and set up an 'economic kitchen'. Portuguese-language classes were offered to those newcomers who did not speak it well, which was most of them.[8]

For the Macau authorities, the Portuguese community in the neighbouring colony was their main priority, but, as had happened with refugees from Shanghai and Guangdong province, they were dependent on private generosity to tackle the challenges of refugee relocation. At the end of January, the Macau government opened applications for those who could provide housing, food or furniture for Portuguese affected by the war.[9] Having initially put forward 50,000 patacas for

[2] Koo, *The Portuguese in Hongkong and China*, p. 127; S. Braga, 'Nossa Gente (Our People): The Portuguese Refugee Community in Wartime Macau', in G. C. Gunn (ed.), *Wartime Macau: Under the Japanese Shadow* (Hong Kong, 2016), pp. 116–40, at p. 118.

[3] A. G. Dias, 'Os Refugiados de Hong Kong (1942)' ('The Hong Kong Refugees (1942)'), *Revista de Cultura* (*Review of Culture*), 34 (2010), pp. 117–28, at p. 125.

[4] For example, he provided some Filipinos and Dutch with Portuguese papers (Álvaro da Fontoura, Ministry of Colonies, to Secretary General of MNE, 13 Oct. 1942, AHD, 2P, A49, M115).

[5] Braga, 'Nossa Gente', pp. 119–20.

[6] L. A. Sá, *The Boys from Macau: Portugueses em Hong Kong* (*The Boys from Macau: Portuguese in Hong Kong*) (Macau, 1999), p. 141.

[7] Teixeira to MC, 6 Feb. 1942, ANTT, AOS, UL-10A1, cx. 767.

[8] Teixeira to MC, 18 Feb. 1942, ibid.; Reeves, *The Lone Flag*, pp. 37–8; Sá, *The Boys from Macau*, pp. 161–2; Silva, 'Life and Learning in Wartime Macau', p. 9; R. E. Xavier, 'The Macanese at War: Survival and Identity among Portuguese Eurasians during World War II', in G. C. Gunn (ed.), *Wartime Macau: Under the Japanese Shadow* (Hong Kong, 2016), pp. 94–115, at pp. 107–8; Braga, 'Nossa Gente', pp. 127–9.

[9] 'Repartição Central de Administração Civil – Aviso' ('Civil Administration Bureau – Notice'), *VM* (21 Jan. 1942), p. 2.

a relief fund to assist destitute Portuguese in Hong Kong and Guangzhou, Governor Gabriel Teixeira requested the Japanese consul, Fukui Yasumitsu, to back him up by sending a ship to bring those who wanted to come to Macau, where assistance was cheaper.[10] Fukui is often praised in accounts of the period for facilitating such moves, though it was also in his country's interests to reduce the population of Hong Kong, which Japan had no means to feed.

After a few weeks of being cut off from Hong Kong, ships started to arrive in Macau towards the end of January. Teixeira noted that they were full of Chinese and that not many Portuguese were coming, so he stepped up efforts to attract them.[11] We can see here an informal selection of refugees, with one's 'compatriots' – even if they were British citizens – preferred over Chinese refugees. Those who arrived told of 'acts of altruism of Japanese soldiers in favour of the Portuguese' and the governor conveyed this praise to military authorities in the hope that they would ease the pressure on him.[12]

Other accounts by non-Portuguese also refer to individual acts of kindness by Japanese in Hong Kong that demonstrate the importance of personal connections and transnational solidarity, including around a shared Christian faith. Patrick Yu, a University of Hong Kong (HKU) student who went on to work for British naval intelligence and for the Chinese Nationalist army during the war, mentioned in a later testimony that a Japanese Christian, a former school headmaster who had known his father when he was senior inspector of schools, escorted his family on their departure to Macau after providing them with rice in Hong Kong.[13] Ellen Field, an Englishwoman who pretended to be Irish and moved to Macau in June 1945, was helped by a Japanese army interpreter who was a Lutheran minister.[14] These cases reveal how the practice of humanitarian relief in the Second World War in South China often implied direct engagement with the occupation forces.

In parallel to these relocations, but sharing with them the transnational character of the parties involved, some escapees fled to Macau undetected by Japanese forces. Their accounts provide details of the routes taken to unoccupied China through Macau as well as features common to

[10] Teixeira to MC, 9 and 13 Jan. 1942, ANTT, AOS, UL-10A1, cx. 767.

[11] Teixeira to MC, 25 Jan. 1942, ibid.

[12] Teixeira to MC, 26 Jan. 1942, ibid. See also 'Os Portugueses de Hongkong são afavelmente tratados pelas autoridades japonesas' ('The Hong Kong Portuguese Are Warmly Treated by the Japanese Authorities'), *VM* (7 Feb. 1942), p. 4.

[13] P. Yu, 'Wartime Experiences in Hong Kong and China (Part 2)', in C. Matthews and O. Cheung (eds.), *Dispersal and Renewal: Hong Kong University during the War Years* (Hong Kong, 1998), pp. 313–34, at p. 316.

[14] E. Field, *Twilight in Hong Kong* (London, 1960), pp. 75, 135–8, 217–25.

different escapes. The key similarity was the role Chinese agents and intermediaries played in arranging the logistics of the escape. Their names were often left out of the published testimonies, but it is clear that several networks were mobilised for the undertaking, including Communist, Nationalist and secret societies.

Regarding the secret societies, an OSS report on Chinese leaders in South China mentioned Lin Jinghun (Lum King-hwen), leader of the triad society Hong Bang, who was said to be able to arrange safe passage from Hong Kong, Macau and Guangzhou, having personally escorted some of Sun Yat-sen's relatives safely out of Macau at the request of the Portuguese governor.[15] Smugglers who facilitated escapes to, through or from Macau were 'service providers' who were remembered by those whom they assisted as saviours, akin to the nuanced accounts of smugglers as 'criminal heroes' included in a study of the role of smugglers in refugee journeys in the twenty-first century.[16]

Whilst many refugees stayed in Macau, others sought to continue their journey into Free China or to find a route further afield to India or to Europe in order to continue to fight for the Allies. Escapes from Macau were made by land or by boat. The land route, via Shiqi, was easier for Chinese who had connections in neighbouring areas. Boat escapes were the most commonly cited in Western accounts. The quickest way was to sail from Macau via Taishan and Sanbu, using the same route as that of boats that smuggled goods into unoccupied China.[17]

There were also other routes, including via Guangzhouwan, which was nominally under French rule until March 1945. This was the route chosen by Phyllis Harrop, an Englishwoman who had been the assistant secretary to the secretary of Chinese affairs in Hong Kong, and who claimed to have been the first person to escape from the British colony. Through the advice and contacts of a Chinese acquaintance in Hong Kong, Harrop used in her favour the German passport she had acquired when she got married. She prepared her escape to Macau through a network of friends and acquaintances of different nationalities. On arrival, she was met by a Portuguese naval officer who took her ashore without security checks and registered her as a Portuguese subject. In Macau, she met the British consul, the governor and a number of other personalities. She also got a 'spare neutral passport'. After being

15 OSS Report, 'Kwangsi–Kwangtung Leaders', 26 Feb. 1944, p. 15, sent from the British Embassy in Washington to FO, 25 Mar. 1944, TNA, FO 371/41662.

16 P. Tinti and T. Reitano, *Migrant Refugee Smuggler Saviour* (London, 2018), pp. 4–5, 31.

17 MacKaskie, 'Report'; Knaggs, 'Information', TNA, FO 371/31630.

given letters to the governor at Guangzhouwan's capital, Fort Bayard, by a Chinese government official with connections there, she left Macau on a steamer chartered by the Portuguese authorities to bring supplies to Macau. From Guangzhouwan, she went by land to Chongqing.[18]

Harrop's case, told in her 1943 memoir, clearly exemplifies the web of personal and international connections that made these trips possible, the fluidity of one's nationality and, as Robert Bickers observed, the 'strangeness of the South China front', marked by a geography of connected colonial remnants offering peculiar opportunities.[19]

Whilst it is easy to frame escapes from Hong Kong as a purely British story, arguably no escape was undertaken without Chinese collaboration. The experience of the journalist Israel Epstein, who had moved to Hong Kong from North China earlier in the war, is a case in point. His account reveals how a range of figures were involved in the escapes, including communists, local bosses and missionaries. After failed attempts to remove him from Hong Kong with the assistance of Liao Chengzhi, the CCP representative in Hong Kong, Epstein evaded Stanley Internment Camp in a multinational group that included two seamen, a former CMC staff member, F. W. Wright, and Elsie Fairfaix-Cholmeley, whom Epstein would later marry in 1944.[20]

Using an abandoned boat, the group left Stanley in March 1942, were helped by a group of fisherman on Lantau Island and then taken to Macau.[21] On arrival, the group was welcomed by Father Paulus, an American member of the Maryknoll mission who took them to the British consulate, where they were met by Consul Reeves.[22] Later, Epstein contacted a physician named Tang, who had been recommended by Sa Kongliao, a Chinese journalist associated with the Democratic League and sympathetic towards the CCP. Tang's 'brother', Chen, arranged for the group's escape in

[18] P. Harrop, *Hong Kong Incident* (London, 1943), pp. 130–52.

[19] R. Bickers, *Out of China: How the Chinese Ended the Era of Western Domination* (London, 2017), p. 227.

[20] Heenan, Memorandum, p. 1. Wright appeared on a list of BAAG agents and runners dated 23 July 1942 as being 'in charge of Macao if required' (Ride, *BAAG*, p. 312).

[21] The escape is also briefly described in another memoir, which does not mention Epstein (G. Wright-Nooth and M. Adkin, *Prisoner of the Turnip Heads: Horror, Hunger and Humour in Hong Kong, 1941–1945* (London, 1994), p. 112).

[22] Epstein did not remember him as the consul but simply as a consulate 'functionary' he had met in Wuhan (Reeves had been posted in Hankou before arriving in Macau). Reeves did not recognise Epstein at all, perhaps because he was travelling under the name of Alec Stevenson. I. Epstein, *My China Eye: Memoirs of a Jew and a Journalist* (San Francisco, CA, 2005), pp. 150–1.

the same smuggling boat that would take the former Dutch consul in Guangzhou and his wife into Free China at Reeves' request.[23] The fee for the undertaking was provided by Father Paulus and his colleagues.[24] To escape Macau safely, an arrangement was made with collaborationist guards outside Macau, and Epstein reached Guilin via the West River.[25]

Epstein would discover many years later that the leader of the organisation who had put together his escape, Zhao Qixiu, was a merchant turned smuggler and organiser of a local anti-Japanese militia. Contacts between Chen and Zhao had been made through the latter's secretary, Zhong Hua, who was an underground communist.[26] During the war, Zhao was involved in smuggling from Macau to Nationalist-controlled areas in north-western Guangdong, as well as in escapes. He was given the title of adviser by both Zhang Fakui, who commanded the Fourth War Zone, and Yu Hanmou, commander of the Seventh.[27] Also prominent in the smuggling of people and goods between Macau and Free China was a group of three brothers surnamed Wong, whose opium business gave them useful contacts with the Japanese in Guangdong. The Wongs were also involved in transmitting intelligence to Chinese and Portuguese contacts.[28] These cases illustrate how global these escapes were, from the diversity of the people involved through the crossing of territories under different jurisdictions, to the confluence of different motivations and backgrounds of those moving to or via Macau.

By cross-referencing different records, it becomes clear not only that Chinese facilitators were involved in all escapes but also that some of them were frequent go-betweens. Zhao Qixiu's name comes up more than once, and so does that of Patrick Wong, a *Dagongbao* reporter from Hong Kong who had left for Guilin. He assisted Ernest Heenan, the Far Eastern representative of the Royal Insurance Company in Liverpool who escaped to Chongqing in April 1942 after being left stranded in Macau in early December 1941.[29]

[23] In one of his telegrams to Lisbon the governor of Macau mentioned hearing about the Dutch consul in Guangzhou coming to Macau and then leaving. At the time he had sent Lobo to meet him and enquire on the possibility of selling the Dutch dredger *Hankow* to the Japanese (Teixeira to MC, 13 May 1942, ANTT, AOS, UL-10A1, cx. 767).

[24] Epstein, *My China Eye*, pp. 152–3. [25] Ibid., p. 155. [26] Ibid., p. 156.

[27] After an uneasy relationship with the Nationalists due to his involvement in a peasants' association, Zhao fled to Indonesia in the late 1920s before returning to Macau. After the war, he got into trouble with the Nationalists again and provided escort for a pro-communist shipping company operating between Macau and Kaiping after 1949, ending up in Hong Kong, where he was decorated by the British for helping refugees (H. F. Siu, *Agents and Victims in South China: Accomplices in Rural Revolution* (New Haven, CT, 1989), pp. 96–7).

[28] 'Economic Currents in Macao', pp. 18, 27. [29] Heenan, Memorandum, p. 5.

Wong was also acknowledged as a key intermediary by G. A. MacKaskie and C. M. Knaggs, two Malayan service cadets who departed from Macau, where they had been studying Cantonese, in May 1942.[30] Wong put them in touch with Zhao. The Nationalist military forces were also involved, however, and some of these escape masterminds had close links with KMT authorities. The commissioner of the Guangdong First Division had informed the British he would 'give all possible help to those who wish[ed] to leave the colony and enter China', and sent two of his men to enable the escape.[31]

The cadet party included twelve other foreigners. Amongst them were, once again, customs staff and missionaries: the American former commissioner in Jiangmen and two fathers of the Maryknoll mission, who were on friendly terms with Zhao. In pre-war times, both CMC staff and missionaries were some of the foreigners in China most knowledgeable of Chinese affairs, in part because they were often fluent in Chinese languages. Their prominent role in wartime escapes is, therefore, hardly surprising. MacKaskie's party left Macau in May, after bribing an Indian policeman, and travelled via a small junk, a sampan and a heavily armed motor junk sailing under a Japanese flag. They were taken to Sanbu, from there to Guilin and finally by plane to Chongqing in early June.[32] Whilst travelling across Guangdong, their expenses were paid by the provincial government in unoccupied China, which also provided official escorts.[33]

Despite the role of Nationalist authorities in guaranteeing the safe passage of people to Chongqing, the contribution of intermediaries such as Zhao Qixiu was paramount because, although the provincial government could aid escapees when they reached Free China, it was unable to guarantee passages from Macau. This pattern of multinational groups of escapees, their dependency on Chinese intermediaries and the role played by Chinese guerrillas supported by the Nationalist military is also evident in the account written by Marjorie Fletcher, wife of the MELCO accountant, whose escape from Macau was organised by the BAAG.[34] Escapes stemmed from the collaboration of state and non-state actors and benefitted both Chinese and British resistance.

30 Already in February 1942 the FO had told Reeves that if they had the chance to make their way to a place where their services would be more effectively employed, they should do so (FO to British Embassy in Lisbon, 20 Feb. 1942, TNA, CO 825/30/12).
31 Knaggs, 'Information'.
32 Reeves, 25 May 1942, quoted in message from Campbell to FO, 27 May 1942, TNA, CO 825/30/12; MacKaskie, 'Report'.
33 Knaggs, 'Information'.
34 Imperial War Museum, London (hereafter IWM), Private Papers of Mrs Fletcher, 97/40/1.

Organising escapes into Free China from Macau was a service offered by several figures and involved an economic dimension alongside more patriotic goals. Costs differed, from free to 6,000 patacas per party. Portuguese middlemen were also involved in establishing contacts with local merchants and others involved in this 'trade' – amongst them Jack Braga, addressed later in the chapter – for those who wanted to escape.[35] Although several successful escapes took place during the war, the majority of Hongkongers who came to Macau remained there until the end of the war, and the British consulate played a key role in managing their relief.

The British Consulate in Macau and Different Refugee Communities

Upon arrival, the usual first stop for all Hong Kong escapees was the British consulate, headed by John Reeves (see Figure 5.1). Reeves was fluent in Chinese, having begun his diplomatic career in 1933 as a student interpreter in the British Foreign Service at the legation in Beijing. He later served as acting consul general in Hankou and in Shenyang.[36] Although Reeves belonged to the China Consular Service, the consulate in Macau reported to the British embassy in Lisbon, not to the one in Chongqing, even though, during the war, Reeves occasionally wrote directly to the latter given that his activities were, naturally, connected to the conflict in China. His professional circumstances are suggestive of Macau's ambiguous position: enmeshed in China's politics whilst kept institutionally apart due to its colonial status.

In December 1945, a few months after the war had ended, 5,650 people were drawing relief from the British consulate in Macau.[37] Lists of thousands of names waiting to return in late 1945 and early 1946 stored at the Hong Kong Public Records Office (HKPRO) provide individual portraits of the refugee communities in wartime Macau.[38] British, Portuguese, Chinese, Indians and others from all walks of life came to Macau in an extraordinary case of temporary colonial transplantation.[39] The consulate

[35] Knaggs, 'Information'.

[36] D. Calthorpe, 'About *The Lone Flag* and John Pownall Reeves', in J. P. Reeves, *The Lone Flag*, ed. C. Day and R. Garrett (Hong Kong, 2014), pp. 167–80, at pp. 169, 173.

[37] Hong Kong Civil Affairs Administration, Refugee Relief in Macao, Summary of Discussions with HBM Consul, 19 Dec. 1945, Hong Kong Public Records Office (hereafter HKPRO), HKRS 170–1–333. A report from January 1946 estimated that of amongst those there were about 2,000 Chinese, 700 Indians and 500–1,000 Europeans.

[38] See files in HKPRO, HKRS 170–1–334 and HKPRO, HKRS 170–1–359.

[39] The links between the Portuguese and British imperial spheres in China are evident in the case of Indian men from villages in Punjab employed as police officers in Macau (TNA, FO 371/41620; BL, IOR/L/PJ/8/334). During the war, a branch of the pro-Japanese Indian Independence League was established in Macau under the title 'Japanese

Figure 5.1 The British consul in Macau John Reeves (right) shaking hands with Admiral Chan Chak (left), who escaped from Hong Kong into Free China in 1941, while observed by the acting governor of Macau, Samuel Vieira, early post-war period. J. M. Braga Collection. Courtesy of the National Library of Australia

also took care of individuals of other nationalities, including 940 Americans, mostly from the Philippines or Hawaii, amongst whom were many Chinese Americans.[40] Clerks, workers, civil servants, policemen, musicians, teachers, homemakers and countless others registered at the consulate. Their names, age, arrival date and conduct during the war were methodically registered. The lists also show how a time believed to be of

Independence League India (Macao branch)'. The consul asked 'loyal Indians' to join and report back to him (TNA, FO 371/31630).

40 Reeves, *The Lone Flag*, p. 71.

isolation was actually marked by considerable mobility.[41] People came and went from Hong Kong to Macau, from Macau to occupied and unoccupied China and along other routes. The British consulate was informed of their movements and of their misdemeanours, from cheating the system for extra allowances to working for the enemy.

Detailed lists of persons who had moved to Macau compiled by the British consulate attest to the multiple imperial, professional and personal networks that framed the experience of those who came to Macau.[42] These individual cases reveal how the war was marked by the movement of very diverse people and their agency whilst striving to survive. These records also demonstrate the extent to which the British consulate was able to monitor even the private lives of those in Macau. Inclusively, Reeves set up a team of 'gambling inspectors' who reported on any refugees caught gambling, which was an attempt to impose notions of morality that wartime privations had rendered inadequate.[43] These acts of surveillance were likely the genesis of the consulate's local intelligence networks, addressed later in the chapter.

Much like the role played by Portuguese authorities in Macau – with whom they interacted closely – the British consul came to support a large number of Hong Kong refugees, not as a result of a pre-devised plan, but as an ad hoc response, decided locally and only later approved by policymakers in Europe, often as a fait accompli. Reeves' management of a global community of refugees did not, however, escape discussions at the bilateral level over who should be paid, who should pay and how much should be spent on those who found themselves in need of assistance in Macau.

By April 1942, a few months after the first batch of government-backed arrivals, the governor of Macau had realised many of the Hong Kong Portuguese refugees were British subjects, and discussions began with the British consul on who should shoulder the relief costs.[44] Haggling over costs also took place in Europe, at a high level. Salazar, who held the post of minister of foreign affairs, contacted the ambassador in London to enquire about the matter.[45] The FO agreed to cover expenses for Hong Kong refugees of Portuguese descent if their British nationality could be proven.[46]

[41] This is also revealed by a number of requests made to the Macau Civil Administration showing how several refugees travelled to Guangzhou as late as 1944, for example, to take care of personal businesses (AM, MO/AH/AC/SA/01/25738).
[42] See note 38. [43] Reeves, *The Lone Flag*, p. 34.
[44] Teixeira to MC, 4 Apr. 1942, ANTT, AOS, UL-10A1, cx. 767.
[45] Salazar to Monteiro, 2 Apr. 1942, TNA, HW 12/275.
[46] MC to Salazar, 18 Apr. 1942, TNA, FO 371/35734.

The matter was of interest to both the Portuguese authorities and the refugees themselves. According to a report by a British escapee, the pecuniary relief the Portuguese refugees received was very low and did not allow large families to afford the soaring living prices. This caused many to 'reclaim and substantiate their British nationality' in order to receive assistance from the consulate.[47] Reeves was instructed to 'admit liability for relief of British subjects only' and decline responsibility for those of dual nationality.[48] As the war progressed and living conditions deteriorated in Macau, the issue of deservedness resurfaced periodically. In January 1944, Reeves requested to examine the records of the Portuguese consulate in Hong Kong, which had been transferred to Macau, in order to ascertain if some of the refugees receiving allowances from the consulate were Portuguese citizens.[49] Some did not know for sure and others 'for reasons of their own, supress[ed] their nationality'.[50] Flexible approaches to citizenship could mean the difference between life and death and those who could, used that to their advantage.

In June 1942, the governor asked Lisbon for authorisation to open an extraordinary credit of 800,000 patacas for refugee relief in order to meet the payments for British subjects of Portuguese descent.[51] After smaller remittances in previous months, from June 1942 the British embassy in Lisbon committed to transferring the equivalent of 60,000 patacas per month in order to reimburse the Macau government of sums advanced to the British consulate.[52] Reeves had insisted on the fact, arguing that the Macau government had 'voluntarily undertaken military protection and maintenance' of many British subjects. The amount was higher than had been calculated per person, but the remainder would be left for the governor and Reeves to spend on the 'hardest cases irrespective of nationality'.[53] The US government also reimbursed the Portuguese authorities, via the Ministry of Foreign Affairs in Lisbon, for any relief provided to American refugees in Macau.[54]

47 Heenan, Memorandum, p. 2.
48 FO to British Embassy in Lisbon, 22 May 1942, TNA, CO 825/30/12.
49 Cases in which British consuls in China questioned the British nationality of non-white subjects had several precedents. See, for example, E. Whewell, *Law across Imperial Borders: British Consuls and Colonial Connections on China's Western Frontiers, 1880–1943* (Manchester, 2020), pp. 158–9.
50 Reeves to Luíz da Câmara Meneses Alves, Head of the Civil Administration Services, 7 Jan. 1944, AM, MO/AH/AC/SA/01/25726.
51 Teixeira to MC, 15 June 1942, ANTT, AOS, UL-10A1, cx. 767.
52 Files on dozens of payments made until May 1946 can be found in AHD, 2P, A49, M115.
53 Reeves, 5 June 1942, quoted in telegram from Campbell to FO, 8 June, 1942; Reeves, 20 July 1942, quoted in message from Campbell to FO, 29 July 1942; Campbell to Reeves and FO, 4 Aug. 1942; Campbell to FO, 5 Dec. 1942, TNA, CO 825/30/12.
54 See files on American refugees in AHD, 2P, A49, M115.

Despite its British flag, Reeves' consulate came to be a nexus for a much wider pool of people, as cosmopolitan as Hong Kong had been in pre-war years. In January 1943, Reeves enquired about the possibility of being put in charge of Allied interests in Macau by individual governments.[55] The FO replied that, although it 'had no objection to his taking charge of United States and Dutch interests', the smallness of Allied interests in Macau did not justify him taking care of all of them for the time being.[56] Yet, in practice, Reeves did end up looking after a truly global community. This included Norwegians and Polish who reportedly arrived in Macau in 1942.[57]

An American Citizens Committee was established to request relief for American nationals, many of whom were Filipinos and Chinese Hawaiians who wanted to leave for China 'to join the fighting forces'.[58] From the 1942–3 New Year's greetings transmitted via the British consulate, we also learn of a community of 'Fighting French' and Russians.[59] Amongst the applications to return to Hong Kong after the war were men with Portuguese surnames who arrived in Macau in 1944 in charge of consular affairs for the Dominican Republic, Nicaragua, El Salvador, Panama, Mexico, Ecuador, Brazil and Argentina.[60] Several Chinese Mexicans fleeing exclusionary policies in North and South America had also come to Macau in the 1930s.[61]

Chinese Hongkongers were fundamental elements in this international refugee community. In May 1942, Reeves enquired how he should treat them and was instructed to assist those who were government pensioners, civil servants and their wives, and volunteers and others who had taken part in the defence of Hong Kong.[62] Reeves also gave small relief subsidies to Chinese from Malaya, New Zealand, Canada and other places.[63]

Relief funds to those in Macau were remitted not only by the UK and US governments, but also by the refugees' former employers and, in

55 Reeves, 19 Jan. 1943, quoted in telegram from British Embassy in Lisbon to FO, 28 Jan. 1943, TNA, FO 371/35731.
56 FO to Embassy in Lisbon, 14 Feb. 1943, ibid.
57 MacKaskie, 'Report'.
58 Draft to the Associated Press Correspondent in Chongqing, 18 Nov. 1942, NLA, MS 4300, Box 52, 8.1/10; Reeves, 29 July 1942, quoted in telegram from Campbell to FO, 8 Aug. 1942, TNA, FO 371/31630.
59 Reeves, 28 Dec. 1942, quoted in telegram from British Embassy in Lisbon to FO, 6 Jan. 1943, TNA, FO 371/35731.
60 HKPRO, HKRS, 170–1–359.
61 J. M. S. Camacho, *Chinese Mexicans: Transpacific Migration and the Search for a Homeland, 1910–1960* (Chapel Hill, NC, 2012), pp. 114–15; K. Lopez, *Chinese Cubans: A Transnational History* (Chapel Hill, NC, 2013), p. 177.
62 FO to British Embassy in Lisbon, 23 May 1942, TNA, CO 825/30/12.
63 FO to British Embassy in Chongqing, 26 Sept. 1942, ibid.

typical colonial fashion, Chinese were sometimes singled out as an unwanted financial burden. Correspondence between Guy C. Clarke from Shell Petroleum Company, the British subsidiary of Royal Dutch Shell, and the FO is revealing of some of the discussions. When asked for permission to do so by Reeves, Clarke had decided that Chinese evacuees would receive the same rate of subsistence as the Portuguese because 'any rate of racial discrimination would be fatal' and could 'mean starvation or semi-starvation'. However, facing high numbers of Chinese requesting assistance in Macau, where they were unlikely to find work, he proposed some limits to the scheme. Chinese would be able to go to Macau only in transit and after four months would cease to receive relief there. He considered it preferable to get Chinese from Hong Kong directly into Free China where they could be paid in Chinese national dollars instead of sterling, as well as find work and 'assist to some extent at any rate in the war effort'.[64]

Eventually, Reeves himself requested permission to refuse relief to Chinese who arrived in Macau after September 1943 as he believed these people had only chosen to leave Hong Kong then 'for purely selfish reasons'.[65] In early February, the CO confirmed that there were no grounds 'on which such relief could be made a charge on Hong Kong funds'.[66] For British subjects with no record of anti-British activities, however, relief would not be withheld. Despite obvious caps imposed on relief to Chinese refugees, Reeves' support was high enough to be resented by other British officials in unoccupied China. Facing claims of discriminatory treatment by the chairman of the Hong Kong Chinese Civil Servants Association in Shaoguan when compared to practices in Macau, the acting consul general at Guilin lamented that Reeves had 'undertaken to support completely large numbers of Hongkong refugees, who should rather, if of Chinese race, have been encouraged to come to Free China', accusing him of fostering a 'dole mentality' costly to the British government.[67] Despite occasional bureaucratic protestations on the costs of refugee relief, it is evident that Reeves was willing to stretch the limits of what he was able to do with the funds he had access to. He comes across in the existing records as willing to bend the rules if a person's basic livelihood was at stake irrespective of their background

64 Guy C. Clarke to Ashley Clarke, FO, 7 June 1944, TNA, FO 371/41620.

65 Reeves, 17 Jan. 1944, quoted in telegram from British Embassy in Lisbon to FO, 19 Jan. 1944, TNA, FO 371/41619.

66 CO to FO, 7 Feb. 1944, TNA, ibid.

67 Lau Wing Shum to Secretary of State for the Colonies, 12 Apr. 1944; British Consulate in Guilin to Horace James Seymour, British Ambassador to China (in Chongqing), 21 Apr. 1944, TNA, FO 371/41564.

and was regarded by contemporaries as the 'great champion' of Hong Kong refugees.[68]

New Cosmopolitanism

Stranded in Macau for the foreseeable future, the Hong Kong refugees, together with the British consul and, often with direct support from the supposedly neutral Portuguese authorities, organised a number of activities to get on with their lives with a degree of normality. At times, these activities also served to support the Allies. Programmes and invitations to various charitable events can be found in the Braga Papers and in the everyday news reported in the English-language supplement *Macau Herald*.[69]

Some of those who lived through the period remember it as pretty joyful, with regular sports and dancing.[70] The 'cultural shock' between the refugees from Hong Kong and their Macau hosts had an immediate social impact. Hong Kong refugees, notably the women, were perceived as more open-minded and less conservative.[71] With the refugees from Hong Kong, as indeed with those who had come before them from Shanghai and Guangzhou covered in Chapter 3, Macau benefitted from new cosmopolitan everyday experiences, in areas from education to sports, including a boom in the entertainment sector.[72] Some of the short stories by Henrique de Senna Fernandes, who lived through the period, capture the extremes and opportunities of wartime Macau as a city of international encounters and how these affected a variety of people and had transformative effects on the young.[73]

Nevertheless, accounts of the period reveal how local resentment, built upon decades of rivalry between Macau and Hong Kong, was present alongside the most publicised solidarity. 'Refugees' became a term 'of scorn rather than of pity', and the Anglicised Portuguese were an easy target, with pieces in the local papers even pointing out that they were now learning what their 'true' nationality was.[74] In March 1943,

[68] 'Economic Currents in Macao', p. 24.

[69] For example, NLA, MS 4300, Box 52, 8.1/15; 'Refugee Topics', *Macau Herald* (21 Mar. 1943), p. 7.

[70] For example, Sir Roger Lobo's testimony in *Macao Remembers*, p. 74.

[71] For example, José Silveira Machado's testimony in *Macau entre Dois Mundos*, p. 42.

[72] For example, Henrique de Senna Fernandes' recollections in *Macao Remembers*, p. 96; Sá, *A História na Bagagem*, p. 117; Braga, *Macau Durante a II Guerra Mundial*, p. 71.

[73] For an illustrative example of this, see the short story 'Candy' on the experience of a female Portuguese Eurasian refugee from Hong Kong (Fernandes, *Nam Van*, pp. 69–102).

[74] Reeves, *The Lone Flag*, p. 18; 'Portugueses de Hongkong' ('Hong Kong Portuguese') *VM* (28 Feb. 1942), p. 2; Braga, 'Nossa Gente', p. 123.

a Refugee Club set up by Portuguese from Hong Kong was shut down about one month after having been founded. The pages of the local daily gave account of opposing views on this case, which reflect the conflicting attitudes towards the newcomers and hint at deeper issues such as pressure to curb open expressions of support for the Allies.[75]

Even so, a good deal of Macau's society mobilised itself to provide relief to refugees and the urban poor. These initiatives became more varied and frequent as the number of those needing assistance increased in the 1940s. Old and new charitable institutions such as those noted in Chapter 3 continued to be of great relevance to the wave of Hong Kong refugees. Football matches, dance contests, concerts, exhibitions, bridge tournaments, lotteries and other events were used to fundraise for charities and associations operating in Macau.[76] The local paper *A Voz de Macau*, which often reported on these events, hailed the enclave as the largest 'centre of charity' in South China.[77]

The social impact of the Hong Kong refugees in Macau was multifaceted. Whilst the arrival of thousands of people further strained local services, some refugees also made a significant contribution to relief activities. Hong Kong doctors provided medical care to fellow refugees and teachers contributed to pre-existing and new-found educational institutions.[78] Religious personnel who had worked in Hong Kong also provided refugee relief and spiritual support. This was the case of missionaries such as the Maryknoll Sisters, an American Catholic group. Of the twenty-eight Maryknoll Sisters in Hong Kong when the Japanese invaded, four came to

[75] 'Muito Sensato' ('Very Wise'), *VM* (16 Mar. 1943), p. 3; 'Refugee Club', *VM* (19 Mar. 1943), p. 3; 'Tribuna do Leitor' ('Reader's Tribune'), *VM* (27 Mar. 1943), p. 4.

[76] Articles in *A Voz de Macau* such as 'Encontro de Futebol Portugal–China' ('Portugal–China Football Match') (12 Feb. 1942), p. 3; 'Exposição' (Exhibition) (9 Dec. 1942), p. 3; 'Recita de Beneficência' ('Charitable Performance') (18 Jan. 1943), p. 3; 'Futebol' ('Football') (22 Jan. 1943), p. 3; 'Concurso de Dança' ('Dance Contest') (27 Feb. 1943), p. 3; 'Lotaria de Caridade' ('Charitable Lottery') (8 May 1943), p. 3; 'Exposição de Pintura e Caligrafia' ('Painting and Calligraphy Exhibition') (2 Mar. 1944), p. 3. For a detailed description of some of the cultural activities organised in Macau during the war, see Braga, *Macau Durante a II Guerra Mundial*, pp. 88–95.

[77] 'Ainda o Torneio de Bridge' ('Still the Bridge Tournament'), *VM* (23 Apr. 1943), p. 3.

[78] Such were the cases of doctors António Guterres, Joseph Barnes, Eddie Gosano, Horacio P. Luis Ozorio or G. A. V. Ribeiro, whom Reeves highly praised (Reeves, quoted in dispatch from the British Consulate in Guilin to Chancery, 28 Jan. 1943, TNA, FO 371/35731; 'Anúncio' ('Announcement'), *VM* (20 May 1944), p. 4; 'M.S. Refugee Clinic', *VM* (5 June 1944), p. 3; Reeves, *The Lone Flag*, pp. 36, 61; Wordie, 'The Hong Kong Portuguese Community', pp.169–70; IWM, *Hong Kong Farewell*, p. 25). On teachers see Lopes, 'Wartime Education at the Crossroads of Empires', pp. 149–51.

Macau between 1942 and 1943.[79] They made front-page news in the Lisbon daily *O Século* in January 1944, when more than 400 refugee children were entrusted to their care by the authorities.[80]

The sizeable Anglican community of Hong Kong refugees was welcomed by Florence Tim Oi Li (Li Tian'ai), whose experience in wartime Macau is also revealing of the new opportunities the conflict opened up for women. Li was sent to Macau in 1940, after witnessing the devastating effects of the war in Guangzhou. After six months in charge of the Anglican parish, she went to Hong Kong to be ordained deacon, and then returned to Macau where she held services for the Anglican community until the end of the war. Not only was she the first Chinese woman to be ordained deacon, later she was also the first woman to become an Anglican priest. Her community work went beyond religion – for example, vouching for Hong Kong refugees at the British consulate when they arrived in Macau, which led her to being watched by the Japanese.

As Macau did not have a resident Anglican priest, Deacon Li was allowed to baptise, marry and bury, but not to celebrate communion. As the war left Macau progressively more isolated and the visits from the Anglican priest in Shiqi stopped, Li was authorised to celebrate communion and, later, Bishop Ronald Hall from Hong Kong wrote to the Archbishop of Canterbury from his refuge in Chongqing in order to ordain her, something 'totally unprecedented in the Anglican Church'. They both made dangerous journeys to Xingxing in unoccupied Guangdong for the ceremony. After being ordained a priest in an Anglican church in Zhaoqing in 1944, Li returned to Macau via Guilin and Guangzhou.[81] The archbishop did not approve of this, but his reply to Bishop Hall's request arrived after the ordination.[82] Li's pioneering accomplishments are a telling example of wartime contingencies and the unintended new possibilities opened up by neutrality.

[79] C. Y. Y. Chu, *The Maryknoll Sisters in Hong Kong, 1921–1969: In Love with the Chinese* (New York, 2004), pp. 51–9.

[80] 'Centenas de crianças vitimas da guerra que se refugiaram em Macau estão a ser tratadas por irmãs de caridade' ('Hundreds of Children Victims of the War Who Took Refuge in Macau Are Being Looked After by Sisters of Charity'), *O Século* (10 Jan. 1944), p. 1. A translation was sent from the British Embassy in Lisbon to the FO, 27 Jan. 1944, TNA, FO 371/41619.

[81] Li and Harrison, *Much Beloved Daughter*, pp. 28–48.

[82] In 1946, the Chinese House of Bishops decided that she could not continue to exercise priestly functions. She later refrained from using the title of priest in order to avoid creating problems for Bishop Hall. She left Macau for a new post in China in early 1947 (ibid., pp. 49–52, 58).

The Macau Delegation of the Portuguese Red Cross

The crossover between refugee relief in Macau and cooperation with the British is particularly well illustrated in the case of the Macau Delegation of the Portuguese Red Cross Society.[83] A short-lived Red Cross branch had existed in Macau earlier in the twentieth century, but a new one was set up from 1943 to 1946.[84] The connection to the Allies is evident from its 'POW service' (*serviço de prisioneiros de guerra*), when Portugal, as a neutral country, was not supposed to have such a thing.[85] Filling the empty space left by the constraints imposed by Japan on Red Cross activities in East Asia and by the failures of negotiating a British–Japanese civilian exchange that included those in Hong Kong, the Red Cross in Macau enacted global connections at a time of disruption of communications, linked people in Macau to those in occupied Hong Kong and Shanghai, and was a very subtle way of aiding the British.[86]

As with other relief initiatives considered earlier, the Macau Red Cross resulted from the collaboration of state and non-state actors. The first discussions for establishing a branch in Macau took place in 1942 in its articulation with the International Committee of the Red Cross (ICRC) in Hong Kong, led by delegate Rudolf Zindler. It was pushed by the Portuguese colonial authorities in Macau and by Reeves.[87] When the Macau Delegation of the Portuguese Red Cross was formally (re-)established in January 1943, its presidency was ensured by Fernando de Senna Fernandes Rodrigues, a local merchant who appears to have played a decisive role in setting up and running this wartime branch.

The Red Cross in Macau was therefore simultaneously: a local entity (springing from the personal efforts of its president); a national and colonial body (belonging to the Portuguese Red Cross); an inter-imperial structure (due to its close links to the British authorities); an

[83] H. F. S. Lopes, 'Inter-imperial Humanitarianism: The Macau Delegation of the Portuguese Red Cross during the Second World War', *Journal of Imperial and Commonwealth History*, 46/6 (2018), pp. 1125–47.

[84] A branch of the Portuguese Red Cross Society had been established after the First World War, but it closed down in 1922 (Minutes of the Macau Delegation of the Portuguese Red Cross, 23 Apr. 1922, AHCVP, Delegação de Macau, 1ª Pasta (1915–1974)).

[85] For example, Rodrigues to the Head of the Macau Civil Administration Services, 28 Apr. 1944, AM, MO/AH/AC/SA/01/25736.

[86] On the failed exchanges, see K. Fedorowich, 'Doomed from the Outset? Internment and Civilian Exchange in the Far East: The British Failure over Hong Kong, 1941–45', *Journal of Imperial and Commonwealth History*, 25/1 (1997), pp. 113–40; R. Ward, 'The Asia-Pacific War and the Failed Second Anglo–Japanese Civilian Exchange, 1942–45', *Asia-Pacific Journal*, 13/12/4 (2015), apjjf.org/2015/13/11/Rowena-Ward/4301.html.

[87] Teixeira to MC, 12 Aug. 1942, AHU, 236, 1E, MU, GM, MÇ, 1942.

organisation with international connections (linking those in Macau to their relatives, employers and acquaintances all over the world); and, given the Red Cross label, a transnational institution.[88]

The Macau Red Cross case shows how private and public dimensions were interlocked in relief provision during the war. Its headquarters were established in the commercial house of its president that – in a telling example of the overlapping connections in the enclave – shared the same building as the Macau branch of the Yokohama Specie Bank.[89] Having received so many information requests about POWs, Rodrigues put his company staff to do some work for the Red Cross as well.[90] Since the beginning, the Macau government sought to guarantee that it was informed of relevant Red Cross correspondence, asking the president to remit copies of the replies to enquiries forwarded by the government to stay in its archives.[91]

The key figures in the institution further stress the branch's colonial dimension: the president, the secretary, the treasurer and the board members were all Portuguese and Macanese men living in the enclave, some of them serving officers.[92] However, the public emphasis on the Macau delegation as part of the Portuguese Red Cross Society was somewhat paradoxical. Its nationalistic outward presentation contrasted with the fact that a significant part of its activities benefitted citizens of other nations and that some of its key local donors were Chinese businessmen, such as Gao Kening.[93]

The activities of the Macau delegation dealt mainly with communications between Macau, Hong Kong and Shanghai by citizens of different nationalities who happened to be (or were thought to be) in these cities during the war. However, several messages, transmitted

[88] Lopes, 'Inter-imperial Humanitarianism'; H. F. S. Lopes, 'The Red Cross in Wartime Macau and Its Global Connections', in N. Wylie, M. Oppenheimer and J. Crossland (eds.), *The Red Cross Movement: Myths, Practices and Turning Points* (Manchester, 2020), pp. 264–81.

[89] OSS, China Theatre, X-2 Branch Report 'Macao – General Intelligence', 24 Aug. 1945, p. 4.

[90] Rodrigues to the Secretary General of the Portuguese Red Cross, 5 June 1943, AHCVP, CV/3513–3514.

[91] Head of the Macau Civil Administration Services to Rodrigues, 12 Mar. 1943, AM, MO/AH/AC/SA/01/18566.

[92] Respectively, Fernando de Senna Fernandes Rodrigues, Navy First Lieutenant José Peixoto de Lima, Infantry Lieutenant Manuel Gedeão, Captain José Joaquim da Silva e Costa, Alberto Pacheco Jorge, João Correia Pais Assunção and retired Lieutenant Augusto Teixeira (Cruz Vermelha Portuguesa, *Boletim Oficial 1943*, 1st semester (1943), p. 23; 'Delegação da Cruz Vermelha Portuguesa' ('Portuguese Red Cross Delegation'), *VM* (29 Feb. 1943), p. 3).

[93] Macau Delegation to Secretary General of the Portuguese Red Cross, 12 May 1955, AHCVP, Delegação de Macau, 1ª Pasta (1915–1974).

to Macau via the ICRC in Geneva or the Portuguese Red Cross headquarters in Lisbon, came from all corners of the world. More than 1,000 telegrams from Macau were relayed to the Lisbon headquarters alone.[94] This relative ease in transmitting messages was probably aided by the fact that the post office in Macau was mostly pro-Allies and 'never took steps to suppress pro-Allied wireless stations'.[95]

One of the most important activities of the Macau Red Cross during the war was the transmission of correspondence, money transfers and parcels to and from Japanese POW and civilian camps in Hong Kong and Shanghai.[96] By October 1944, the Macau Red Cross was listed the second-largest source of remittances (35 per cent) to the ICRC in Hong Kong between January and September.[97]

The most demanding endeavours between the ICRC in Hong Kong and the Macau Delegation of the Portuguese Red Cross pertained to the Rosary Hill Red Cross Home, a centre for civilian internees' dependants set up by Zindel in Hong Kong in 1943 (see Figure 5.2). Initially, it housed 670 people, most of them women and children of various nationalities.[98] In the last two years of the war, rising living costs and the suspension of rice rations forced the ICRC delegate to encourage the relocation of the inhabitants. Hundreds of them came to Macau, where they were received by the Portuguese Red Cross.[99] The British consulate funded most of the Rosary Hill evacuees, the money having been sent by British agents in Lisbon to the governor of Macau via the Portuguese Ministry of Foreign Affairs.[100] Those who were not initially deemed 'legitimate dependants of the British prisoners of war or internees' were

[94] 'Elementos estatísticos da acção da Cruz Vermelha Portuguesa durante a Guerra de 1939 –1945' ('Statistical Elements of the Actions of the Portuguese Red Cross during the 1939–1945 War'), AHCVP, CV/4742–4805.

[95] 'Economic Currents in Macao', p. 24.

[96] Edouard Egle, ICRC Delegate in Shanghai to Rodrigues, 24 Jan. 1944, International Committee of the Red Cross Archives (hereafter ICRC), D AO CHINE1 01–086.

[97] Zindel, ICRC Delegate in Hong Kong to ICRC Tokyo Office for ICRC in Geneva, 19 Oct. 1944, ICRC, B G 017 07–068. However, later that same month he asked Geneva for assistance because the Hong Kong authorities had stipulated that 'future Macau remittances to us must pass via Geneva/Tokyo' (Zindel to ICRC Tokyo Office for ICRC in Geneva, 24 Oct. 1944. ICRC, B G 017 07–068).

[98] Zindel to ICRC, Dec. 20 1943. ICRC, B G 017 07–063.

[99] For example, between January and November 1944, more than 200 dependants left Rosary Hill and, in May 1945, 281 dependants left for Macau (Zindel, 'Memorandum on Proposed Measures to Ensure the Future Maintenance of the "Rosary Hill" Red Cross Home', 30 Apr. 1945; Zindel to ICRC, 20 June 1945, ICRC, B G 017 07–063).

[100] M. C. M. Kerr-Pearse, British Vice Consul in Geneva to D. Mouravieff, ICRC, May 28 1945, ICRC, B G 017 07–077; Note from FO to CO, 16 Aug. 1945, TNA, FO 369/3267.

Figure 5.2 Rosary Hill Red Cross Home, Hong Kong, October 1944. Reference: V-P-HIST-E-01199. Copyright: International Committee of the Red Cross

taken care of by the Macau delegation, to whom expenses were later reimbursed by the British authorities.[101]

The wartime Macau Red Cross was an institution built on transnational cooperation. It was highly vulnerable to attacks and its activities were significantly affected when its president was shot dead in a Macau street after returning from a funeral on 10 July 1945. Although the exact reasons for his murder are unclear, it is possible that Rodrigues' tragic death had something to do with other 'collaborations', notably his association with smuggling networks, in particular with a pro-RNG group that had switched to Chiang's side.[102]

As the Macau Red Cross delegation case shows, relief and support for the Allies could be tightly linked. Neutrality offered some cover but,

[101] Jean Cellérier, London Delegation of the Central Agency for Prisoners of War of the International Committee of the Red Cross to CO, 5 July 1945, TNA, FO 369/3267.

[102] Teixeira to MC, 14 July 1945, NE-10A2, cx. 768.

ultimately, its flexible practice exposed its connections to wartime dynamics and its vulnerability to the conflict's violence.

Intelligence Networks

Collecting and transmitting intelligence were key activities in neutral territories during the Second World War. Macau was an arena for both Allied and Axis networks and, from 1942 onwards, its place as the intersection of different Allied networks became particularly pronounced. Amongst the individuals who straddled different national and imperial spheres was Consul Reeves, whose paths crossed with different intelligence groups. The BAAG and the Special Operations Executive (SOE) are the best known, although their remit in Macau overlapped and interacted with the activities of other Allied groups, such as the OSS.

Created in 1942, the BAAG was led by Lieutenant Colonel Lindsay Tasman Ride, an Australian veteran of the First World War who had taught at HKU and served in the Hong Kong Volunteer Defence Corps before the Japanese occupation. He escaped to Chongqing in early 1942, was appointed MI9 representative in China and worked under instructions of the military attaché at the British embassy. All BAAG activities had to be carried out with the knowledge of the Chinese authorities. Macau became a node in the operations in South China largely because the enclave housed 'several thousand British subjects', most of whom were refugees from Hong Kong.[103]

The consulate supervising them had a variety of secret contacts at its disposal. In May 1942, Reeves informed the FO that he was 'in direct touch' with agents of the Guangdong Political Affairs Committee with credentials. He proposed to 'use them exclusively' and send messages to Chongqing.[104] That same month, SOE agents were sent to enquire on the potential for activities in Macau and Guangzhouwan to try to establish contact with Hong Kong. The operation was named 'Vodka'. Macau's location and Portuguese neutrality made it an asset for intelligence gathering. The hypothesis that Macau could be used to interfere with enemy shipping in the region or to create incidents that could bring Portugal into the war on the Allied side was, at one point, on the table, but, eventually, plans for using the enclave as a sabotage base were left dormant until a potential Japanese occupation of the enclave.[105] Operation Vodka

[103] War Office report, 'British agencies in China', pp. 1–2, copy sent by War Cabinet Offices to FO, 27 Mar., 1945, TNA, FO 371/46196.
[104] Reeves, 7 May 1942, quoted in message from Campbell to FO, 9 May 1942, TNA CO 825/30/12.
[105] 'The Portuguese Colony of Macao', 5 Mar. 1942, TNA, HS 1/176.

seems to have been offered to the Secret Intelligence Service instead, and it was likely never carried out.[106]

One month after the SOE probe, Ride established contact with Reeves via William Chong, a Chinese Canadian who had lived in Hong Kong before the occupation. Another telling example of how the war generated new opportunities for women was when Joy Wilson, who worked for the British consulate, was appointed the official BAAG representative in Macau. Her husband, Police Superintendent Geoffrey Wilson, was in a POW camp in Hong Kong. She was put 'in charge of all codes and communications and was the main point of contact for the various agents in the colony'.[107] Joy Wilson was soon approached by the SOE as well. In August, F. A. Olsen, a Danish operative, reported unfavourably on Reeves' lack of discretion with a code he had given him and ended up entrusting a second code to Wilson.[108]

Olsen also engaged Karl P. Fletcher from MELCO and Jean Fay, a 'very Anti-Vichy' Frenchman from the CMC station on Lappa, as well as two Chinese men, one of whom with contacts in Guangzhouwan and Hainan. According to Olsen, Reeves was 'very friendly' with the governor and 'apt to confide too much' with him. He was also described as giving out information that he should have kept to himself.[109] Olsen made arrangements for carrying written messages via the crews of ships plying between Macau, Guangzhouwan and Hong Kong. In Macau, a 'compradore shop' was used as their underground post office. Transfers of funds could be made through CMC, from the Norwegian commissioner in Guangzhouwan to Fay.[110] After visiting Macau, Olsen managed to smuggle funds used to set up a wireless station to communicate directly with Chongqing.[111] As this network suggests, Macau's place in Allied networks in South China is best understood as a connected nexus, whose relevance derived from its links to Hong Kong, French-ruled Guangzhouwan and other occupied and unoccupied locales in Guangdong province.

[106] TNA, HS 1/176. [107] Ride, *BAAG*, p. 211.

[108] P. Elphick, *Far Eastern File: The Intelligence War in the Far East, 1930–1945* (London, 1997), pp. 369–70.

[109] Report by F. A. Olsen, 4 Aug., 1942, TNA, HS 1/176.

[110] Ibid. Fay had arrived in Macau in October 1941 and retired from his post in July 1944. Before that, he wrote a letter to the governor thanking him for his hospitality and expressed the will to remain an intermediary between the Macau authorities and the CMC (Fay to Teixeira, 9 June, 1944, AHU, Espólio Gabriel Maurício Teixeira). In June 1945, he was still residing in Macau and in dire straits financially due to difficulties in receiving his pension in sterling (Zinovi Pechkoff, French Ambassador in Chongqing to Ministry of Foreign Affairs of the Provisional Government of the French Republic, 29 June 1945, MAE, 125QO/6).

[111] Elphick, *Far Eastern File*, p. 370.

The exodus of Hongkongers to Macau provided a vast pool of informers to the British consulate that enabled it to reach out to intelligence operatives in China and beyond. The scale of Reeves' intelligence activities would only become evident in London in mid-1943, when one of his letters reached the British ambassador in Chongqing, Horace James Seymour, via Guilin. In it, Reeves alluded to the tight Japanese surveillance over his activities, with sentries posted at intervals outside the consulate and cars tailing him and his family. More intriguing for Seymour, Reeves provided intelligence he had received to be passed on to the BAAG about the situation in Hong Kong and information about specific people there.[112]

Reeves' consular post meant that he reported to the ambassador in Lisbon, not to the one stationed at the Chinese capital. The fact that he also contacted Seymour is illustrative of Macau's real place in the war: as much, if not more relevant to China as it was to Europe. Reeves also provided information on Japanese and collaborationist actions and men in South China and Macau, passed by one of his agents who was a student in the local Japanese school.[113] According to Reeves, he had three groups working in intelligence: one predominantly Portuguese and the others composed of Portuguese, Indians and Chinese, with the last the majority. They only received 'small amounts for expenses' and the consul had promised that 'their names will be reported to our people at the end of the war'. Reeves estimated that some 100 people were reporting to him, including an agent whom he did not trust completely, who covered Wang Jingwei and his 'peace movement'. Reeves also mentioned the existence of radio communications with Free China, corroborating information about that from other sources.[114]

After enquiries were made, it became apparent that Reeves' intelligence activities had not been directed by London or Lisbon and were considered a potential liability that could compromise British organisations operating in China. The SOE confirmed that Reeves occasionally used its cyphers, but it had 'no other interest in him'.[115] Replying to the FO, Reeves stated that he had asked some people receiving relief from the consulate to gather information, including on 'enemy politics and trading activities' in Macau. He noted the potential usefulness of these reports for a post-war British government in Hong Kong and stated that the intelligence he had gathered had been welcomed by different constituencies: he had served the Macau governor 'in domestic affairs', it had served

112 Seymour to FO, 8 Sept. 1943, TNA, FO 371/35736; Extract from Macau letter to Guilin, p. 2, ibid.
113 Extract from Macau letter to Guilin, p. 5. 114 Ibid., pp. 7–9.
115 Ministry of Economic Warfare to FO, 6 Nov. 1943, TNA, FO 371/35736.

Chongqing 'politically' and 'over smuggling', and had been useful to the BAAG when their means had not been sufficient to deal with Macau.[116]

The FO ordered him to stop collecting such reports and acting as a channel of communication for the BAAG as the Japanese were fully aware of his activities.[117] Jack Braga took over this local 'independent secret service' from him, and amongst his personal papers are several relating to intelligence, including files from the final years of the war and the early post-war period that were declassified only in 2017.[118] Still, like his flexible approach to the allocation of relief to the refugees under his care, Reeves continued to assume a complex role in intelligence activities in Macau despite not being officially sanctioned by his bosses in Whitehall.

The British Army Aid Group and Escapes

The activities of the BAAG in Macau went much beyond Reeves and did not simply pertain to intelligence collection. In October 1943, the BAAG organised the successful transfer of HSBC records to Chongqing (from where they were dispatched to London), duplicates of which had been moved to the BNU in Macau before the Japanese invasion.[119]

The BAAG also set up an escape route from Hong Kong into Free China via Macau, which was used by around 100 people during the war, including Wilson herself.[120] In 1943, she entrusted the leadership of the Macau branch to her physician, Eddie Gosano. Born in Hong Kong to a Portuguese family, according to his memoirs, Gosano was legally classified as Chinese. Trained as a doctor, he had volunteered to serve in Argyle and Sham Shui Po POW camps before arriving in Macau in 1942, where he became Reeves' attending physician. Personal and professional relationships were key to establishing intelligence networks. When she escaped from Macau, Wilson also left behind three Chinese associates in Macau, including Y. C. Liang (Liang Runchang), whom Gosano described as 'a rice merchant with a small shop' in central Macau.[121] When Gosano later stepped down from the leadership of the Macau

[116] Reeves, 28 Oct. 1943, quoted in telegram from British Embassy in Chongqing to FO, 10 Nov. 1943, ibid.

[117] FO to Embassy in Chongqing, 10 and 19 Nov. 1943, ibid.

[118] 'Economic Currents in Macao', p. 34.

[119] F. H. H. King, *The History of the Hongkong and Shanghai Banking Corporation, Volume III – The Hong Kong Bank between the Wars and the Bank Interned, 1919–1945: Return from Grandeur* (Cambridge, 1988), p. 615; Gunn, 'The British Army Aid Group (BAAG) and the Anti-Japanese Resistance Movement in Macau', in G. C. Gunn (ed.), *Wartime Macau: Under the Japanese Shadow* (Hong Kong, 2016), pp. 141–65, at p. 153.

[120] Ride, *BAAG*, p. 212.

[121] IWM, *Hong Kong Farewell*, p. 27.

BAAG, he appointed Liang as his successor.[122] Y. C. Liang, a naturalised Portuguese citizen, would become particularly prominent after the conflict, making a fortune from buying the cheap assets of people fleeing the Chinese Civil War and being involved in Macau's booming gold trade.[123]

The people involved in the BAAG activities in Macau reveal how personal trust was a key element in the establishment of intelligence operations during the war. They also confirm my argument that resistance in wartime Macau was often a global endeavour involving figures of different nationalities, socio-economic strata and interests who came together in the small enclave due to the extraordinary circumstances of its neutrality.

Amongst the major escapes the BAAG coordinated were those of the number two in the Macau administration, Luíz da Câmara Meneses Alves, and of a group of American airmen shot down near the enclave. The quasi-defection of the head of the civil administration services – Macau's equivalent of colonial secretary – in April 1944 remains a matter of some speculation, compounded by his sudden death after being interviewed about the affair in the 1990s. Described in British sources as a 'staunch supporter of the Allied Cause', Alves left Macau disguised as a peasant and was smuggled by Chinese agents into unoccupied China.[124] He arrived at the BAAG post in Sanbu en route to Guilin.[125] From Guilin he was transported by the US Air Force to Kunming, and from there he travelled to Portugal via India, Egypt and Gibraltar. When he reached Lisbon after globetrotting for months, Alves called at the British embassy to thank the Royal Air Force and the British Overseas Airways Corporation for their assistance with his return to Europe.

Alves also provided information about the circumstances in Macau. Japanese morale had been deteriorating and their shipping resources were being depleted. Alves believed that if Portugal toughened up its attitude regarding Timor, the Japanese would seize Macau at once, 'probably not directly but by employing puppet Chinese and disclaiming all responsibility'. For Alves, one of the reasons that Japan had not seized Macau was

[122] They remained friends until Gosano migrated to the USA in 1960. In his memoir, Gosano wrote that Liang named the first hydrofoil in Hong Kong (belonging to a company he founded) 'Phoenix' after Gosano's BAAG code name (ibid., p. 37). E. Ride stated that 'Phoenix' had been Liang's own code name (Ride, *BAAG*, p. 211), but Y. C. Liang's papers in the HK PRO confirm he was not 'Phoenix', whom he replaced (HKPRO, HKRS 30-1-1).

[123] Jorge and Coelho, *Roque Choi*, pp. 75–7.

[124] BAAG Guilin, quoted in telegram from British Embassy in Chongqing to FO, 27 Apr. 1944, TNA, FO 371/41620.

[125] Ibid.

to use it as propaganda 'to refute the charge that they were making war on the white race as such'. He praised Reeves as having done 'magnificent work for British interests'.[126] In a later conversation with a member of staff of the British embassy, Alves offered more praise for the consul, stating that he was 'treated with respect by the bulk of the population, who are convinced of eventual allied victory'. He also provided further details about his escape and the local authorities.

Alves' name had been on the Japanese blacklist, and he had travelled as a private person to prevent a diplomatic incident if he were killed. Although criticising the governor, whose 'isolation from Portugal for three years had put him into a position of independent power which he is not completely qualified to occupy', he believed him to be honest and trying his best, reserving a harsher judgement for other unnamed 'elements in the Government who have been assisting the Japanese to an unnecessary extent'.[127]

A few months later, Alves' assessment of the governor's performance had hardened considerably. In a conversation with the British embassy's third secretary, he 'stated that the Governor was definitely pro-Japanese and took the Japanese side in every question that arose to a greater extent than was necessitated by his admittedly difficult position'. He believed 'a little firmness on the part of the Governor would have avoided the infestation of Macau by numbers of Japanese gendarmerie in plain clothes, who were able to assassinate and kidnap prominent Chinese with impunity'. Alves considered that during the war, 'the Portuguese in Macao have lost much face in Chinese eyes by their attitude'.[128]

Alves' accounts, together with critical Chinese reports, were considered to have altered Salazar's opinion of the governor.[129] Although the fact that Teixeira kept his post contradicts the British perception of a loss of trust by the Portuguese dictator, the more critical tone Alves adopted towards the governor remained the same when he was interviewed decades later. There, he stated that his opposition to the sale of vessels and materials to the Japanese had damaged his relations with the governor and his co-workers to a point where he got anonymous death threats, and finally decided to leave.[130] Despite Alves contrasting

[126] Campbell to Anthony Eden, 28 July 1944, ibid.

[127] Memorandum from Embassy in Lisbon to Eden, 27 Oct. 1944, ibid.

[128] Minute by Third Secretary John Noel Ormiston Curle, 24 Nov. 1944, sent with dispatch from Ashley Clarke to J. C. Sterndale Bennett, Far Eastern Department, FO, 25 Nov. 1944, ibid.

[129] Ibid.

[130] R. Pinto, 'A Grande Evasão' ('The Great Escape'), *Macau*, 43 (1995), p. 93.

himself – a friend of Reeves and well connected with a clandestine network of pro-Chongqing Chinese refugees from Shanghai – with a pro-Japanese governor, other primary sources make clear that Teixeira was equally close to the British and not favourably disposed towards the Japanese, whose abuses he constantly decried in his telegrams to Lisbon but with whom he had to interact to avoid an actual occupation.

In fact, the governor's name appears to be linked to what is considered one of the highlights of Portuguese–Allied cooperation in Macau during the war: the escape of US Navy Reserve airmen George Clark, Donald Mize and Charles George Myers.[131] The operation involved Y. C. Liang from the BAAG and the Chinese agent Wong Kau.[132] It counted on the cooperation of Pedro Lobo and the Macau chief of police, Captain Ribeiro da Cunha.[133] As with all escapes from Macau, Chinese intermediaries were crucial; their voices are often absent from the surviving records, but a rare exception can be found amongst the Braga Papers in the National Library of Australia. An English-language draft signed by Pang Meng and probably handwritten by Braga details the heroic deed of a 'poor fisherman' and bears witness to the neglect that many of those who had helped the Allies around Macau suffered after the war.

In early 1945, Pang was on his junk when he saved the three American airmen as their plane was sinking. Although a passenger on his boat had suggested handing them over to the Japanese for a reward, he took them to Macau and asked for help at the British consulate. Reeves set up a plan with Chinese guerrillas, and the airmen (disguised as Chinese fishermen) were taken into Free China on the same junk. Reeves paid Pang Meng for his services and paid the other passengers to keep quiet. Later, Pang was warned that the Japanese had found out about his deed, and he escaped with his family to unoccupied China, having to borrow to survive.

131 Ride thanked the governor for his assistance after the war and said he would propose Ribeiro da Cunha for a decoration, Gosano mentioned the episode in his memoir and Jack Braga's nephew celebrated it in a newsletter of a Macanese association in Australia (Ride to Teixeira, 22 Oct. 1946, AHU, Espólio Gabriel Maurício Teixeira; IWM, *Hong Kong Farewell*, p. 33; S. Braga, 'Rescued from Certain Death', *Casa Down Under Newsletter*, 23/4 (2011), pp. 1–4, casademacau.org.au/wp-content/uploads/newsletters/11_4CasaOct2011.pdf). George Clarke's surname appears spelled as Clark in other sources (e.g. L.C. Cooper, BAAG, to American Consul-General in Hong Kong, 5 Dec. 1945, NARA, RG226, UD 140, Box 54).

132 Likely Wang Jiu in Mandarin, one of the Wong brothers.

133 Gunn, 'The British Army Aid Group', p. 153.

After the war, he returned to Macau and asked Reeves for help finding work. Reeves sent him to the American consulate in Hong Kong. The matter was referred to more people until he was notified that he had already been 'sufficiently rewarded'. He sought Reeves' help again, but Reeves had by then been replaced and the new consul did not even receive him. Pang did not want money but work to be able to pay the debts he had incurred for saving the airmen. He appealed to them to plea for him, if they were still alive, via the United Press News Service.[134] It is unclear if they ever received the message. The airmen's adventurous escape elucidates the nuances of collaboration in neutral Macau: not only Allied collaboration between Chinese, Americans and British taking place in the frontlines, but also the active support that those in Macau could give them in the shadows.

Multiple Connections

Several of those involved in intelligence in Macau had links to different powers. The case of an OSS agent, whose information may have triggered one of the American bombings over Macau discussed in Chapter 4, illustrates the complex overlap of neutrality, collaboration and global connections. Bernard Felix Xavier had worked for the Shanghai Municipal Police before going to Hong Kong, where he joined the Royal Navy as a signalman in 1940.

When Hong Kong was occupied, he went to Macau (helped by Francisco Soares) and, later, reached Guilin by junk. After being recruited by the OSS at the BAAG headquarters, Xavier (who spoke Cantonese) was sent back to Macau, pretending to offer information on the Guilin air base to Japanese officers. His contact in Macau was Jack Braga, whom Xavier recalled as 'the man in charge of the British intelligence in Macau'.[135] Because Braga was aware that the Japanese knew of his activities, he told Xavier that his new contact would be Pedro Lobo. Xavier described him as 'a very, very rich man' and 'very pro-British'.[136] Lobo paid Xavier for his services and passed the information to Braga. At one time Xavier was advised to 'disappear' or 'hide', and he hid for three months under a bed in his mother's house – an interesting element revealing the importance of family relations in survival strategies in wartime Macau.

Later, Braga arranged for Xavier to join the Macau police force. All the Chinese agents knew him and tipped him off that the Japanese were

[134] Undated handwritten draft by Pang Meng, NLA, MS 4300, Box 52, 8.1/11.
[135] IWM, Catalogue no. 19926, Interview with Bernard Felix Xavier (1999). [136] Ibid.

'buying petrol from the Portuguese government in exchange for rice'. He reported this to Braga, who then informed American intelligence, and, a few hours later, 'American planes came over and bombed it'. Pedro Lobo was very angry, telling Xavier that he had not expected him to have 'tipped [off] the Japanese [to the Americans] so soon'. Lobo warned Xavier that the Japanese would shoot him if they knew, and recommended he stay hidden on Coloane. Xavier remained on the island until the end of the war, never returning to the Macau peninsula. He was picked up by a British vessel, rejoined the navy and eventually moved to Britain. He left behind his Chinese wife 'from a very rich family', whose father opposed her going with him and who migrated to San Francisco instead. Xavier stated he never received thanks for the help he had given the Allies.[137]

Xavier's extraordinary account was candidly narrated for an interview preserved in the Imperial War Museum. The extent to which the American bombings of Macau were deliberate remains unclear, but, regardless, Xavier's testimony is a valuable source describing the multiple layers of cooperation that existed in wartime Macau. He was a Hong Kong-born Portuguese who had served in the Royal Navy and had been an American intelligence agent who reported not only to a Hong Kong Portuguese (who spied for the British), but also to a Eurasian Portuguese (who was a key intermediary between different sides). The fate of his Chinese family also reveals the intimate relations (and their difficulties) between members of different communities during the war.

A person who crossed over different intelligence agencies was Jack Braga, truly one unsung hero of the Allied war effort in South China. Hong Kong-born Braga had been living in Macau since the 1920s and was a close friend of many Cantonese elite figures. During the war, he liaised between the British consulate, Nationalist agents, the governor of Macau and several intelligence operatives. Most of his efforts appear to have sprung from his own initiative. The Braga Papers in Australia hold documents written in late 1945 and early 1946 about Chinese and others who had assisted the Allies, notably the Nationalists' and British agents, in information gathering, propaganda and escapes during the war, including files attesting to their wartime service to help them find work after the conflict.[138]

These people had helped the Allies, but in the post-war period, neither the British nor the Chinese government acknowledged them officially or were willing to assist them financially. A poignant letter

[137] Ibid. [138] NLA, MS 4300, Box 53, 8.1/18.

shows Braga was helping some of these people out of his own pocket whilst he himself had to borrow money.[139] Before leaving his post in Macau, Reeves wrote him a reference acknowledging the services he had rendered to the Allies.[140] In June 1947, when articles in the Chinese press were criticising Macau, Braga wrote to Robert Ho Tung: 'We know that the Macao authorities were not only sympathetic, they were actually helping the Allied agents.'[141] Neutrality allowed, in practice, for extensive collaboration with the Allies. Braga's efforts for British–Chinese–Portuguese cooperation did not have enduring results, but these contacts on the ground helped preserve Macau's nominal neutrality through very unneutral ways.

The considerable scale of these local, bottom-up efforts is confirmed by nervous diplomatic correspondence that resurfaced in 1945 about Reeves' involvement in intelligence activities. British documents declassified only in 2013 reveal the extent to which Reeves' actions went beyond London's control. News reached the FO via the British consulate general at Kunming, which had received telegrams from Reeves containing messages for OSS representatives. The OSS, however, believed that 'the author of the messages is working for the Japanese' and that Reeves had compromised himself by sending them. London decided that Reeves should stop sending such messages in the interests of his safety as he would be 'in serious danger if and when the Japanese take over Macao'.[142]

At the end of April, Supreme Allied Command South East Asia telegraphed the British embassy in Chongqing asking if messages regarding future operations had been sent to Reeves for transmission to Teixeira.[143] A few days later, the Portuguese ambassador in London also asked if the FO had seen the note Reeves had addressed to the governor.[144] After making enquiries, the FO wrote to Chongqing that it had learnt 'from a most secret source which must on no account be quoted or compromised' that Reeves had communicated a message to Teixeira upon instructions from 'the Allied Command in the Interior of China'. The message reassured the governor that the Allies were aware of Japanese pressure on him, but a landing was forthcoming in April near Macau, in French Indochina and at another point on the Chinese coast,

139 Unsigned to Cheung Tsz-wai, 11 Dec. 1945, ibid.
140 Reeves to J. M. Braga, 24 July, 1946, NLA, MS 4300, Box 52, 8.1/11.
141 Unsigned to Sir Robert Hotung, 9 June 1947, NLA, MS 4300, Box 26, 4.7/1.
142 Seymour to Government of India, 3 Apr. 1945, TNA, FO 371/46199.
143 Supreme Allied Command Southeast Asia to British Embassy in Chongqing, 20 Apr. 1945, ibid.
144 Record of Visit of Portuguese Ambassador to Sir Orme Sargent, 2 May 1945, ibid.

so he should 'play for time'.[145] The governor did not think anything seemed odd and informed Lisbon he had been doing just that, as advised by Lobo.[146]

Who had sent such a message to Reeves in the first place? The message had been an item of strategic deception and British intelligence was keen on knowing the source.[147] Reeves could not be asked directly because there was no safe, confidential way of reaching him. The ambassador in China, Horace Seymour, and General Carton de Wiart, Churchill's representative in Chongqing, made enquiries and concluded that the message had not been sent to any British organisation in China and that the Americans had not sent it either.[148] The possibility was raised that 'some Chinese organisation may have sent it without the knowledge of General Wedemeyer's headquarters'.[149] Seymour did not believe it likely that 'any official Chinese organisation *with which British Organisations have contact* would have sent the message' (my italic) and suggested it could have been orchestrated by the Japanese.[150] His choice of words, however, hinted that it could have been done by other Chinese agents.

Eventually, Reeves reported back to London via the governor of Macau and then the Portuguese embassy in London that the message had been conveyed by 'an individual who was in possession of credentials from the Chungking Government'. Reeves had passed it to Teixeira as 'a duty of friendship' to him without 'accepting responsibility as to its authenticity'.[151] As this case shows, Reeves was engaged with multiple Allied agents, as well as in constant contact with the governor, appearing immune to rivalries between agencies and countries.

It is known that Chinese agents of the OSS had been sent to Macau and other places to spread disinformation in order to damage Japanese morale, and it is possible that Reeves got caught up in the middle of this.[152] The variety of his connections makes it difficult to demarcate specific allegiances beyond the vaguely defined 'Allied cause', but

[145] FO to British Embassy in Chongqing, 27 Apr. 1945, ibid.
[146] Teixeira to MC, 16 Apr. 1945, TNA, HW 40/84.
[147] D Division Weekly Progress Report No. 5, Apr. 1945, ibid.
[148] British Embassy in Chongqing to FO, 30 Apr. 1945, TNA, FO 371/46199. Amongst the redacted passages in an American report that mentions this affair is the name of the person who delivered the message to Reeves ('Japanese–Portuguese Relations and the "Macao Problem" (February–May 1945)', p. 10).
[149] FO to British Embassy in Chongqing, 19 May 1945, TNA, FO 371/46199.
[150] British Embassy in Chongqing to FO, 22 May 1945, TNA, ibid.
[151] Portuguese Embassy in London to FO, 1 Aug. 1945, ibid.
[152] M. Yu, *The Dragon's War: Allied Operations and the Fate of China, 1937–1945* (Annapolis, MD, 2006), p. 159.

perhaps it was that vagueness that made Reeves of interest to so many organisations.

Even if Reeves was seen as a potential liability, British intelligence's interest in Macau continued until the end of the war. In October and November 1944, enquiries were made in Lisbon, London and Macau about the possibility of 'having a reliable Portuguese agent' to provide funds in the enclave for 'financing special work'. Contacts in Lisbon were made by Mikhail Terestchenko, a Russian with a Nansen passport who had been minister of finance in Kerenski's government.[153] A businessman and a banker, Terestchenko had been spotted by the British in Mozambique. He had contacts in Eastern Europe and the Balkans and had been connected to British intelligence work in Lisbon.[154] Amongst the figures initially suggested were a Portuguese veterinary surgeon in Macau with friends in democratic circles, the manager of the BNU and even the governor.[155]

In late November, Terestchenko provided more specific data on eight possible recruits, including potential uses and ways of contacting them. Henrique Nolasco, the honorary Dutch consul in Macau, was the first. Other names put forward were recommended by the 'Lisbon Freemasons', an intriguing reference, given that Freemasonry was banned and persecuted under Salazar's regime. Even more surprisingly, amongst the suggested names was the former bishop of Macau, José da Costa Nunes, who, it was stated, would probably be able to indicate possible recruits in Macau.[156] This, allied to the fact that Reeves was a Freemason himself, points to other transnational networks connected to wartime Macau.[157]

Further enquiries were made in December and January 1945 about the Norwegian Reider Johannessen, one of the names proposed by Terestchenko. Johannessen had escaped to Macau via Hong Kong after being arrested by the Japanese in Shanghai. He then went to India in 1942, where he was appointed representative of the Norwegian Merchant Shipping Board.[158] MI5 had informed he was on friendly terms with the opium merchant Nemazee, who was favourably regarded by the Japanese and suspicious to the British. It is inconclusive if further enquiries led to Johannessen or of any of the others listed being recruited.[159] However, these fragmentary plans convey quite clearly the global connections shaping British understanding of neutrality and collaboration in Macau.

[153] TNA, HS 1/176. [154] TNA, HS 9/1451/8. [155] TNA, HS 1/176.

[156] 'Summary of the Conference Held in Lisbon between Mr T and F/A in November, 1944', 23 Nov. 1944, TNA, HS 1/176.

[157] Reeves, *The Lone Flag*, p. 118. [158] TNA, HS 1/176. [159] TNA, HS 9/799/1.

It is quite possible that enquiries about people and ways to send money into Macau were connected to the SOE's 'Operation Remorse', studied by Robert Bickers. Currency trading was the main activity in this scheme for purchasing 'quinine, influence, safety and food for prisoners, to smooth the British path into Hong Kong'.[160] Currency trading was indeed one of the key activities that made neutral Macau appealing to different actors. Remorse's commercial network through occupied and unoccupied China had a number of international connections, including to Lisbon, which adds credibility to a possible Macau link. This variety of international contacts attests to the important supporting role played by neutral Macau in a global Second World War.

Preparing a British Return to Hong Kong

Even though Hong Kong's colonial transplantation to Macau was a temporary endeavour that ended shortly after the Japanese surrender, its long-term impact was immense. A neutral Macau where a British consul operated relatively unhindered was an important factor in easing a British return to Hong Kong. The British consulate supported and was supported by numerous Hong Kong refugees, many of whom regarded a return to pre-war colonial rule as desirable, even though their actions in Macau stood for a much more open and fairer society, free of the racial prejudices many of them had experienced.

Macau was a place where the British reoccupation of Hong Kong was prepared, even though the preparations were not sanctioned by London and their actual implementation is unclear. Amongst the Braga Papers and a bound volume at the HKPRO one finds several pages of detailed plans for the post-war rehabilitation of Hong Kong made by refugees in Macau.[161] Covering issues such as housing, repatriation, food supplies or transportation, the plans attest to efforts to combine the expertise of those in Macau for the future prosperity of a British-ruled Hong Kong.

A letter containing a list of personnel mentioned that those participating included people receiving British consulate support and some who did not. Some names had been referred to Nationalist agents in Macau for their views, indicating a certain overlap of Chinese and British resistance networks in Macau. A list of those involved included several Portuguese

160 R. Bickers, 'The Business of a Secret War: Operation "Remorse" and SOE Salesmanship in Wartime China', *Intelligence and National Security*, 16/4 (2001), pp. 11–36, at pp. 12, 25–6.

161 For example, Minutes of meetings in Macau and other papers, NLA, MS 4300, Box 52, 8.1/10 and Box 53, 8.1/20; HKPRO, Book 940.53 SOM 1945, *Some Records of the Plans Made During the War Against Japan by British Residents in Macao.*

and Chinese, amongst others.[162] An accompanying letter from Jack Braga explained that it was the author's idea to gather some friends to 'draw up a study'. Reeves was approached and 'gave his blessing to the suggestion'.[163] Therefore, committees sprang up from local initiative and were unconnected to planning being done in London. These planning activities were a way for many Hong Kong people stranded in Macau to contribute to the war effort and to affirm their capacity to play active roles in the future of Hong Kong, a home where many had been marginalised by racist colonial hierarchies. Braga wrote:

> [I]f given a chance, the local fellows believe that they can contribute substantially in many ways to assist in the important phases of the rehabilitation of Hongkong, together with a contribution, if such should be needed, to the war effort, in case Hongkong should be utilized as a military base and use can be found for local people of ability, integrity and goodwill, whose loyalty is unquestioned. In other words, we feel we can show that we can, if given the opportunity, and assigned to those posts where our ability and qualifications can enable us to render good service, be of some help to the British Government.[164]

In sum, much like the refugee commissions covered in Chapter 3, the plans for a post-war Hong Kong devised in Macau sprang from civil society efforts. Non-state actors sought to play an active role in shaping a post-war future that, by 1945, was already possible to see in the horizon. These plans did not exist in isolation but were patronised by the British consul, even if they were not connected to metropolitan policymakers.

Indeed, in May 1945, the FO was informed of the existence of two committees comprising Portuguese, Indian, Eurasian and Chinese refugees in Macau drawing up plans for the future reoccupation and rehabilitation of Hong Kong. The information, provided by the BAAG representative in Macau and transmitted by Ride to the military attaché in Chongqing and from him to the CO, noted that both committees were 'fully chartered and authorized by the governing bodies in London' and there was a 'wild rumour' about how the two committees would function on a return to Hong Kong.[165] The FO expressed surprise and concern, as

[162] The list is too extensive to reproduce here. The first names listed were Reeves as 'Chairman', L. d'Almada e Castro, T. N. Chau, A. el Arculli and C. G. Anderson as 'Consultants', E. J. Figueiredo, C. Y. Kwan, W. C. Hung and R. Nazarin as 'Executives' and J. M. Braga, Dr S. N. Chau, J. S. Landolt, R. L. Noronha and M. U. Razack as 'Co-ordinators' (HKPRO, Book 940.53 SOM 1945).

[163] Braga to 'George', 14 July 1945, ibid. Although the letter is unsigned, a reference to 'my father, the late Mr. J.P. Braga, O.B.E.', and a copy of the letter amongst the Braga Papers confirm the authorship.

[164] Ibid.

[165] Ride to Military Attaché, British Embassy in Chongqing, 25 Apr. 1945, TNA, FO 371/46251.

if the idea of functioning committees of non-white British was both unimaginable and undesirable. It made clear that committees were certainly not London's doing, admitted the possibility of Reeves 'being duped by an enemy agent' and even entertained the possibility of having him replaced.[166] Suspicion of Reeves was linked to the discovery made in 1943 that Reeves was, without superior order, 'engaged in various unorthodox activities': there was information that he had disobeyed previous instructions to limit his activities to relief and consular duties and had been communicating with the OSS in China.[167] To investigate further, the possibility of getting Leo d'Almada e Castro, listed as one of the members of the 'Hong Kong Rehabilitation Committee', out of Macau was discussed.[168]

In Macau, where he arrived in April 1942 after having been arrested by the Japanese, d'Almada had been the liaison officer between the British consulate and the Macau government.[169] He agreed to come to London but insisted on bringing along his wife, Clothilde, much to the nervousness of the extraction organisers, who believed that the route from Macau via Yanping and Kunming was too difficult for a woman.[170] In the meantime, it was decided in London that he was no longer required, and the embassy in Chongqing was sent instructions for Reeves not to let d'Almada leave.[171] In a clear example of how wartime miscommunications could have unintended consequences, d'Almada had already left when the message arrived.[172] Given that fact, the CO accepted to employ him in the Hong Kong Planning Unit, after confirmation that he was in fact a British subject – yet another reminder that even the most loyal of imperial subjects had their Britishness questioned.[173] Enquiries about the confusion were to be dealt delicately because of his 'status as a leading Eurasian barrister' and a member of the Hong Kong Legislative Council.[174] It was, thus, by a series of misunderstandings, that a Portuguese Hongkonger ended up playing an important formal role in the British retaking of Hong Kong.

[166] F 2868/1147/10 minutes, ibid. [167] FO to CO, 23 May 1945, ibid.
[168] British Embassy in Chongqing to FO, 22 May 1945, ibid.
[169] Sá, *The Boys from Macau*, p. 164.
[170] British Military Attaché in Chongqing to CO, 23 May 1945, TNA, FO 371/46251.
[171] FO to Embassy in Chongqing, 19 June 1945, ibid.
[172] Seymour to FO, 28 June 1945, ibid.
[173] Alice Ruston, CO to L. H. Foulds, FO, 7 July 1945; FO to British Embassy in Chongqing, 12 July 1945, ibid.
[174] BAAG Kunming to British Consul General in Kunming, 8 July 1945, HKU, MF 2530701, Roll 15.

Smuggled by BAAG agents, d'Almada and his wife got to Kunming (via Yanping, Baise, Yulin and Nanning) and from there to India before they were flown to London in August.[175] When in London, d'Almada visited the Portuguese embassy, where he praised Teixeira and Lobo, stating that their skills in conducting difficult negotiations with the Japanese had spared the civilian population 'the horrors of an occupation'.[176] He also wrote to the FO commending Reeves and the governor of Macau for their assistance to refugees at a time of 'difficulties unparalleled in the history of any colonial administration'.[177] These remarks further evidence that, despite the challenges posed by Japanese military power, Anglo–Portuguese cooperation had been maintained in Macau, and this inter-imperial collaboration served a British reoccupation of Hong Kong well.

Several of the Hong Kong refugees who had played important roles in Macau during the war went on to have stellar post-war careers. D'Almada was appointed president of the General Military Court in Hong Kong and he was made Commander of the Order of the British Empire in 1953.[178]

Macau itself played a key part in the actual re-establishment of British authority over Hong Kong at the end of the war. The enclave's importance was twofold: it was an intermediary post for communications between British authorities in Chongqing and London and the pre-war colonial secretary before the occupation, Franklin Gimson, then interned at Stanley; and it was also a crucial purveyor of emergency supplies in the immediate aftermath of the war.

A few days elapsed after the Japanese surrender was acknowledged by military authorities in Hong Kong and British rule was re-established, in defiance of the known intentions of Chiang Kai-shek's government to place Hong Kong under Chinese authority. To ensure that the British government policy 'to restore British sovereignty and administration immediately' was carried out, it was considered a 'matter of great importance' to transmit a message to Franklin Gimson stating that, if released when the Japanese

175 BAAG Yanping to Kunming, ibid.; BAAG War Diary, July 1945, HKU, MF 2530701, Roll 2; British Embassy in Chongqing to Foreign Office, 10 and 26 July 1945, TNA, FO 371/46251; Sá, *The Boys from Macau*, p. 166.

176 Domingos de Sousa Holstein Beck, Portuguese Ambassador in London to Salazar, 20 Aug. 1945, TNA, HW 12/330.

177 D'Almada e Castro to David Scott, FO, 22 Aug. 1945, TNA, FO 371/46253.

178 A. M. P. J. Silva, *The Portuguese Community in Hong Kong: A Pictorial History* (Macau, 2011), p. 21; Sá, *The Boys from Macau*, p. 53. His wife, Clothilde Barretto, was one of the first female justices of the peace in Hong Kong.

capitulated in Hong Kong, he was to assume governing authority in the absence of a governor and before a British naval force arrived.[179] The transmission of such a vital message involved different British, Chinese and Portuguese intermediaries.

According to Brian Edgar, Selwyn Selwyn-Clarke, the director of medical services in Hong Kong, played an important role in convincing Gimson to form a British administration in the days following the end of the war. Gimson did not rush into it, supposedly to thwart any possibility of public violence if the Japanese military presence suddenly collapsed without either a British or a Chinese immediate replacement in Hong Kong, with the possibility of execution of British POWs and internees.[180]

Unaware of the London plans, Selwyn-Clarke asked Arthur May, an electrician who assisted him and who had claimed Irish nationality to avoid internment, to go to Macau.[181] The goal was to contact Reeves to get instructions from the secretary of state for the colonies via Lisbon so that Gimson could assume civil administration before an Allied commander arrived.[182] His trip coincided with Y. C. Liang's in the opposite direction. Although seemingly uncoordinated, Liang took a similar message to Gimson, travelling to Hong Kong with Roger Lobo, Eddie Gosano, Fung Bei and radio operator Lee Wai disguised as fishermen.[183] Gimson received it on 23 August, the same day that May first tried to leave Hong Kong.[184]

In Macau, where May eventually arrived on 27 August because of a typhoon, Jack Braga introduced him to the governor and to Pedro Lobo, who arranged for May's return to Hong Kong.[185] The message carried by May reached the secretary of state as intended, who approved of his plans. The secretary of state replied that Rear Admiral Harcourt was to establish a military administration by proclamation on arrival in Hong Kong, after which Gimson was to comply with his instructions.[186] Although actions on the ground were not always smoothly aligned, Macau was a common denominator in both May and Liang's

[179] FO to British Embassy in Chongqing, 11 and 13 Aug. 1945, TNA, FO 371/46251.
[180] B. Edgar, 'Myths, Messages and Manoeuvres: Franklin Gimson in August 1945', *Journal of the Royal Asiatic Society Hong Kong Branch*, 58 (2018), pp. 7–29.
[181] R. Taylor, *The Arthur May Story: Hong Kong 1941–1945* (2015), p. 91.
[182] S. Selwyn-Clarke, *Footprints: The Memoirs of Sir Selwyn Selwyn-Clarke* (Hong Kong, 1975), p. 99.
[183] S. J. Chan, *East River Column*, p. 92; Edgar, 'Myths, Messages and Manoeuvres', p. 17.
[184] S. J. Chan, *East River Column*, p. 93; Ride, *BAAG*, p. 299; Edgar, 'Myths, Messages and Manoeuvres', p. 17.
[185] Edgar, 'Myths, Messages and Manoeuvres', p. 16; Taylor, *Arthur May Story*, p. 94.
[186] FO to Chongqing, 28 Aug. 1945, TNA, FO 371/46256.

démarches. The enclave connected London and Hong Kong at a crucial time when the British were rushing to reach the occupied colony before Chinese forces. Macau's neutrality and geographical proximity to Hong Kong offered ideal conditions to facilitate the recolonisation of Hong Kong, against the Nationalists' will.

Immediately after the war had ended, Macau also provided Hong Kong with much-needed supplies. This had been a key concern of Selwyn-Clarke and Gimson.[187] The Macau Red Cross was contacted to ensure the urgent provision of food, medicine and fuel.[188] Jack Braga was credited with guaranteeing the first cargo of rice to Hong Kong after the conflict.[189] In a 1949 publication, Leo d'Almada connected the Portuguese contribution to the post-war rehabilitation of Hong Kong to the pioneering part that the community had played in the early years of the British colony.[190] Yet, despite the important role played by Portuguese Hongkongers, the British return to Hong Kong was the result of diverse layers of collaboration involving various actors; not only Portuguese, but also Chinese (e.g. Y. C. Liang) and British (e.g. Selwyn-Clarke).

Conclusion

Of the multiple layers of collaboration that marked wartime Macau, none was stronger than the Anglo–Portuguese connection, anchored in a centuries-old alliance that governing elites understood as essential to Portuguese colonial rule. From 1942 to 1945, Macau also was a lifeline for British colonialism in South China. The enclave played an important supportive role to many in and from Hong Kong during the Japanese occupation. It allowed for escapees to reach unoccupied China, for great numbers of refugees to receive assistance, for intelligence to be gathered and for resistance activities to be coordinated. Without a neutral Macau, the British reoccupation of Hong Kong would have been more difficult.

Just as it had played a crucial role in the first Sino–British contacts in the eighteenth and early nineteenth centuries, Macau was key to the British presence in South China during the Second World War through the functioning of its local consulate. Consul John Reeves managed a true colony within a colony. He coordinated humanitarian assistance, organised employment and leisure opportunities, monitored the Hong Kong

[187] Edgar, 'Myths, Messages and Manoeuvres', pp. 14, 22–3.
[188] Zindel to ICRC, 29 Sept. 1945, ICRC, B G 017 07–063.
[189] Koo, *The Portuguese in Hongkong*, p. 141.
[190] L. d'Almada e Castro, *Some Notes on the Portuguese in Hongkong* (Macau, 1949), p. 15.

refugees and set up an ad hoc intelligence network that both intersected with other Allied groups and was so independent that it exasperated authorities in London. Many of those who came to Macau supported the Allies in different ways. A particularly significant institution was the Macau Delegation of the Portuguese Red Cross Society. It assisted Allied POWs and civilian internees and their dependants in Hong Kong and Shanghai at a time when the British were unable to reach them on the ground or to organise their repatriation.

Although neutral Macau was a site where British power was exercised, it was also a stage for cooperative relations beyond that of the Portuguese and British authorities. Amongst those drawing relief from the British consulate, assisting escapees from Hong Kong and gathering intelligence for Reeves were, for example, many Chinese and Indians. Some of those involved in these efforts were closely linked to the Chinese Nationalists and to American forces and agents in China. Macau was, therefore, a centre of inter-Allied collaboration, spearheaded by the actions of individuals such as Jack Braga who had connections in different camps.

Anglo–Portuguese imperial collaboration is crucial to understanding neutrality in Macau as a key enabler of the post-war continuity of two colonial remnants in China: Macau and Hong Kong. However, the maintenance of colonial rule in Macau was not uncontested. As Chapter 6 will show, the (ab)uses of neutrality were confronted by different Chinese actors in their bumpy quest for justice in the early post-war years.

6 Seeking Justice and Recognition

Dealing with Neutrality and Collaboration after the War

In August 1946, a newsletter published by the Chinese Ministry of Information in London, *China Newsweek*, ran an article by a professor of economics at the National Central University in Nanjing advocating Macau's 'return to the motherland in order to clear away the last vestige of the unequal treaties'. The piece decried the 'unsettled problem in China's foreign relations', the 'clandestine dealings' still rampant in the enclave and how the territory had been serving 'as a perfect refuge for fugitives, gangsters and criminals'.[1] Almost a year had passed since the end of the war, but issues stemming from the ambiguities of Portuguese neutrality in China – and the layers of collaboration it enabled – remained unresolved. A minister plenipotentiary had yet to reach the Nationalist capital, the end of Portuguese extraterritoriality had not been negotiated and the extradition of suspects of war crimes and collaborations in Macau was far from settled. The maintenance of colonial rule over Macau was inextricable from these issues, a state of affairs due, in large measure, to wartime neutrality.

The importance of Nationalist China in post-war international politics and the complex dissolution of the Japanese wartime empire have been reassessed by historians since the 2010s. Placing the 'deimperialisation' of Japan at the centre but drawing attention to a constellation of actors at the imperial margins, Barak Kushner's three co-edited volumes have underscored the entanglements of this process – which unfolded beyond 1945 – with the post-war and early Cold War period in East Asia.[2] Two key works have shed significant light on the relationship between post-war trials and attempts to shore up the Nationalists' legitimacy at home and

[1] C. Chu, 'Macao's Return to China', *China Newsweek* (1 Aug. 1946), p. 4. Also in TNA, FO 371/53617.

[2] B. Kushner and S. Muminov (eds.), *The Dismantling of Japan's Empire in East Asia: Deimperialization, Postwar Legitimation and Imperial Afterlife* (London, 2017); B. Kushner and S. Muminov (eds.), *Overcoming Empire in Post-Imperial East Asia: Repatriation, Redress and Rebuilding* (London, 2019); B. Kushner and A. Levidis (eds.), *In the Ruins of the Japanese Empire: Imperial Violence, State Destruction, and the Reordering of Modern Japan* (Hong Kong, 2020).

internationally: Kushner's monograph on Chinese trials of Japanese accused of B and C class war crimes, and Yun Xia's book on the Nationalist policies regarding collaboration and trials of people accused of collaboration (much more numerous than the number of Japanese arrested in China for war crimes).[3]

Chinese authorities used these trials to affirm their regained sovereignty, but the trials also showcased the limitations – both external and internal – they faced in doing so. For the Nationalists, dealing with the legacies of the Japanese occupation happened concurrently with attempts to face the massive challenges of post-war reconstruction, as well as the problems of a recrudescent civil war with the Communists, which eroded support for Chiang Kai-shek's government both domestically and internationally. Still, regarding efforts of post-war recovery, the Nationalists engaged in international debates and with transnational institutions. Tehyun Ma's work on social policy planning, Rana Mitter's research on the United Nations (UN) Relief and Rehabilitation Administration in China and Jiayi Tao's study of the role of the CMC in restoring coastal lighthouses provide new insights into Nationalist state-building across the 1945 divide that dispute earlier assessments of administrative incompetence.[4] Nevertheless, the devastation caused by the war and the lingering postcolonial difficulties also shaped and often constrained those efforts.

Studies of China's diplomacy in the 1940s have largely centred on relations with major powers. With the exception of a few works probing engagements with the Netherlands, Italy and India, how China's new position as a war victor and postcolonial nation shaped its relationship with small powers and remnants of colonialism in its territory remains underexplored.[5] Building on recent scholarship that has reassessed the importance of Nationalist China in post-war international politics and the

[3] B. Kushner, *Men to Devils, Devils to Men: Japanese War Crimes and Chinese Justice* (Cambridge, MA, 2015); Y. Xia, *Down with Traitors: Justice and Nationalism in Wartime China* (Seattle, WA, 2017).

[4] T. Ma, '"The Common Aim of the Allied Powers": Social Policy and International Legitimacy in Wartime China, 1940–47', *Journal of Global History*, 9/2 (2014), pp. 254–75; R. Mitter, 'Imperialism, Transnationalism, and the Reconstruction of Post-war China: UNRRA in China, 1944–7', *Past & Present*, 218 (2013), pp. 51–69; R. Mitter, 'State-Building after Disaster: Jiang Tingfu and the Reconstruction of Post–World War II China, 1943–1949', *Comparative Studies in Society and History*, 61 (2019), pp. 176–206; J. Tao, '"Winning the Peace": The Chinese Maritime Customs Service, Foreign Technocrats, and Planning the Rehabilitation of Post-war China, 1942–1945', *Modern Asian Studies*, 56/6 (2022), pp. 1930–50.

[5] V. K. L. Chang, *Forgotten Diplomacy: The Modern Remaking of Dutch–Chinese Relations, 1927–1950* (Leiden, 2019); G. Samarani, 'The Evolution of Fascist Italian Diplomacy During the Sino–Japanese War, 1937–1943', in D. P. Barrett and L. N. Shyu (eds.), *China in the Anti-Japanese War, 1937–1945: Politics, Culture, and Society* (New York, 2001), pp. 65–87; T. Yang, 'Chiang Kai-shek and Jawaharlal Nehru', in H. van de Ven,

fates of imperialism in East Asia, this chapter explores the opportunities and difficulties that arose in China's diplomacy with Portugal in the late 1940s.

The ambiguities of wartime neutrality in Macau provided considerable room for political and diplomatic manoeuvring in the immediate post-war period as both the Chinese Nationalists and the Portuguese Estado Novo regime sought to assert sovereignty in a new, uncertain world order. The (ab)uses of neutrality during the war were central to post-war Sino–Portuguese relations. This chapter explores a series of issues left by the conflict: the re-establishment of regular diplomatic contacts, the handling of Japanese property, the extradition of suspects of war crimes and collaboration, the abolition of extraterritoriality, and critiques of neutrality in calls to return Macau to Chinese rule. These interconnected issues raised complicated sets of questions about the meaning of justice and who got to wield it that had increased significance for both China and Portugal in a period of great change.

The Allied victory in the Second World War saw China recognised as an important post-war power. This new international status is perhaps best illustrated by Nationalist China's role in the UN. Not only was China a founding member, it was also one of the few to hold a permanent seat on the UN Security Council. In contrast, Portugal was permitted to join the UN only in 1955 and remained a 'rogue state' in the subsequent decades due to its rulers' position on decolonisation.[6] In their relations with Portugal, the Nationalist authorities sought to affirm China's post-war position as a fully sovereign nation. Portuguese attempts to counter this by acting the sovereign in Macau provide new insight into the limits of decolonisation in South China in the late 1940s. Whilst some attempts were made to overcome disagreements and forge smoother Sino–Portuguese relations, often through elite personal connections, most wartime issues – with the exception of extraterritoriality – were left unsolved as the Chinese Civil War unfolded.

Resuming Official Contacts

The sudden end to the war, with Japan's surrender announced on 15 August 1945 and formally signed on 2 September, caught Portuguese representatives in Shanghai and Macau in a whirlwind of changes that they, like many other foreigners, were often unable to comprehend. After years

D. Lary and S. R. MacKinnon (eds.), *Negotiating China's Destiny in World War II* (Stanford, CA, 2015), pp. 127–40.

6 B. C. Reis, 'Portugal and the UN: A Rogue State Resisting the Norm of Decolonization (1956–1974)', *Portuguese Studies*, 29/2 (2013), pp. 251–76.

without a senior diplomat in the Nationalists' capital, Portugal took steps to resume official contacts in China. Initially, the significance of the Allies' success seemed to have escaped the Portuguese minister in Shanghai, João de Lebre e Lima. He declined an invitation from the French consul to celebrate the Allied victory, arguing that, since Portugal was neutral and kept a diplomatic representation in Japan, 'to celebrate the victory of one power could be interpreted as rejoicing in the defeat of another'.[7]

The Ministry of Foreign Affairs in Lisbon emphasised that Lima was authorised to participate in celebrations of victory, in which the government was 'directly interested', but the unease was evident.[8] A few weeks later, Lima informed Lisbon of his wish to leave for the United States at the earliest opportunity due to his wife's ill health.[9] To replace him, the ministry sent José Rodrigues Simões Affra as chargé d'affaires to Chongqing. There, he was told that the Chinese government considered Lima's presence in China undesirable and hoped for his replacement. This was because Lima 'had always refused to reside' in Chongqing, 'alleging difficulties of relocation that all other colleagues had managed to overcome'.[10]

Complaints about Lima had been made several times. A few months before, on a visit to the Ministry of Foreign Affairs in Lisbon, the first secretary of the Chinese legation had enquired about the delay in sending a chargé d'affaires to Chongqing who, months after being nominated, had not yet made the trip, alleging health reasons. The first secretary noted, disapprovingly, that during the war the Portuguese minister to China had stayed in Shanghai with no contact with the Chinese government. He had remained in occupied territory, generating 'a confused and "regrettable" diplomatic situation' that ought to be clarified with the end of hostilities.[11]

Proximity to the base of the Nationalist government was not a guarantee of better understanding. Affra spent six months in Chongqing from October 1945 and wrote a detailed report about the experience. Revealing a poor adaptation to life in the wartime capital and an incredible dearth of empathy for what the city had gone through, Affra concentrated on the failings of the Nationalists and what he saw – in

[7] Lima to Salazar, 14 Sept. 1945, AHD, 2P, A48, M212.
[8] Salazar to Portuguese Legation in Shanghai, 15 Sept. 1945, ibid.
[9] Lima to MNE, 6 Oct. 1945, ibid. Later correspondence to Lisbon reveals that the United States took almost one month to give Lima a visa on his diplomatic passport.
[10] Affra to MNE, 17 Oct. 1945, ibid.
[11] Note of conversation between the First Secretary of the Chinese Legation and Franco Nogueira, MNE, 13 Ago. 1945, ANTT, AOS, NE-2A2, cx. 422. Also in AHD, 2P, A48, M212 (the word 'regrettable' is not translated in the original; the rest of the document suggests that the conversation was held in French).

typical colonial parlance – as the ordeal of the 'foreigners born in civilized countries'.[12] He lived in a hotel owned by Vice Premier H. H. Kung (Kong Xiangxi), Chialing House (Jialing binguan), where many foreign diplomats resided. Although other accounts describe it as a space of relative luxury amidst the privations of the wartime capital,[13] Affra decried its supposedly appalling conditions, for which he blamed the Chinese government. The lack of privilege he was experiencing was doubly disconcerting: China was no longer treating all foreigners as superior, and Portugal's diplomatic presence in China was insignificant, having been the only country to have sent just one representative to Chongqing (Affra was even called the 'one man legation').[14] He moved to Shanghai in 1946 and then to Nanjing, but his description of the latter was also extremely critical.[15] Only in 1947 did Portugal send a minister plenipotentiary to China again, although his opinion of the Nationalists, as will be mentioned later, was probably worse than Affra's.[16]

In contrast, the Portuguese authorities in Macau were relatively quick to adapt to victory and to seek closer relations with the Nationalists, despite the difficulties springing from the volatile conditions in South China. In early September 1945, the situation around Macau reflected the confusion experienced in many other places when the war in Asia reached an abrupt end. The governor, Gabriel Maurício Teixeira, reported to Lisbon that some areas were occupied by Chongqing forces, others still by Japanese, and others were dominated by Communist guerrillas, none of whom advanced on Macau, where the Chinese community filled the streets commemorating peace.

Although the governor, afraid of Japanese reprisals, did not initially permit open celebrations of victory, when this danger was dispelled, he even joined in with the festivities.[17] In a public speech, Teixeira said 'long

[12] AHD, Relatório Anual, J. R. S. Affra, 'Chunking', June 1946, p. 29. On the devastating bombing of Chongqing, see E. Tow, 'The Great Bombing of Chongqing and the Anti-Japanese War, 1937–1945', in M. Peattie, E. Drea and H. van de Ven (eds.), *The Battle for China: Essays on the Military History of the Sino-Japanese War of 1937–1945* (Stanford, CA, 2011), pp. 256–82.

[13] For example, L. Stowe, *They Shall Not Sleep* (New York, 1944), pp. 34–5; G. Peck, *Two Kinds of Time* (Boston, MA, 1950), p. 131.

[14] Affra, 'Chunking', pp. 33, 38–9.

[15] AHD, Relatório Anual, J. R. S. Affra, 'O Pôsto de Nanquim' ('The Nanjing Post'), June 1948.

[16] 'New Portuguese Minister Arrives in Nanking', *China Newsweek* (13 Mar. 1947), p. 9.

[17] On the initial prohibition, see 'Economic Currents in Macao', p. 29. On the celebrations, see Teixeira to MC, 5 Sept. 1945, ANTT, AOS, NE-10A2, cx. 768; 'A grandiosa homenagem da população chinesa a Sua Exa. o Governador da Colónia Comandante

live' (*viva*) China and Chiang Kai-shek.[18] Representatives of the Chinese community in Macau, including the presidents of the Commercial Association, the Kiang Wu Hospital, the Tung Sin Tong Charitable Society and the Chinese Educational Association – key relief organisations during the war years – thanked Portuguese authorities for the 'benefits received' under Portuguese neutrality.[19] Two visions of sovereignty with rather opposing views towards colonialism coexisted in such celebrations: one marked China's victory in a war against imperialism, the other emphasised the shielding effects of a neutrality derived from colonial rule. This contradictory overlap was fragile and easily contested. Indeed, public celebrations of peace did not last for long.

A few days later, a Portuguese soldier disobeyed an order not to cross the border at the Barrier Gate, was caught by a group of Chinese collaborators and was subsequently held for ransom.[20] The governor appealed to Chinese authorities, whose regular armed forces were increasing in the vicinity, suggesting both impotence to deal with the matter and a desire to foster a constructive relationship with the Nationalists. However, the Nationalists' position was also far from stable, especially in a complex frontier area where the plurality of actors who had engaged in wartime resistance or collaboration (or both) was not always easy to disentangle. According to Teixeira, the Chinese government's forces were clashing with communist guerrillas whilst some islands near Macau remained under the control of 'pirates' and pro-Japanese Chinese.[21] The governor recommended that Chongqing appoint a trusted delegate to Macau because he had no way of knowing with whom to discuss matters given that many people came to him saying they were Nationalist officials.[22] Such confusion would mark the post-war years to a significant extent, though this was not due to domestic fractures within China alone but also amongst the Portuguese.

Nationalist military figures engaged in liberating Guangdong province from the Japanese saw a good opportunity to include Macau in their operations and prepared to oust the Portuguese by force. Liu Shaowu, who commanded a division under General Zhang Fakui, blockaded Macau between November and December, controlling water and land transport and preventing food and energy supplies from entering the

Gabriel Teixeira' ('The Grandiose Tribute of the Chinese Population to His Excellency the Governor, Commander Gabriel Teixeira'), *Renascimento* (7 Sept. 1945), p. 1.

18 'Palavras de S. Exa. o Governador' ('Words by His Excellency the Governor'), *Renascimento* (5 Sept. 1945), p. 1.

19 Teixeira to MC, 5 Sept. 1945, ANTT, AOS, NE-10A2, cx. 768.

20 Teixeira to MC, 11 Sept. 1945, ibid. 21 Teixeira to MC, 12 Sept. 1945, ibid.

22 Teixeira to MC, 27 Sept. 1945, ibid.

enclave.[23] Liu believed that he was strengthening the government's negotiating hand, but Minister of Foreign Affairs Wang Shijie considered that the time was not yet right to recover Macau. Chiang's government asked Zhang Fakui to order Liu to end the blockade.[24] The blockade was duly lifted, but only when Portugal accepted to undertake measures to extradite suspects of war crimes, hand over Japanese property and allow the nomination of a MOFA special commissioner to Macau.[25]

The retreat of Liu Shaowu ended KMT attempts to retake the enclave by force, but the unfinished business of Macau's decolonisation remained a matter of public discussion, not only for Chinese, but also for foreign audiences, as the 1946 *China Newsweek* article attests. The fact that this was read by members of the FO, stored in a folder on 'Chinese attitude to Macao', attests to how carefully British officials were monitoring the maintenance of Portuguese rule in the enclave, no doubt to gauge what possible moves the Chinese government might take towards Hong Kong.[26]

The Portuguese authorities did not regard Chinese nationalist aspirations towards Macau as legitimate, just as they would be unable to engage constructively with other forms of anti-imperialist nationalism elsewhere in the following decades. Nevertheless, some Portuguese policymakers did see these comparatively. In an illustrative example, Charles Stirling, a counsellor at the British embassy in Lisbon, noted how the director general of the Ministry of Foreign Affairs had told him in conversation that 'the attitude of the Chinese towards Macau was much the same as that of the Indian nationalists towards Goa'.[27]

Portuguese diplomats in China were unimpressed by the Nationalists' new international position and saw Portugal's inflexibility as evidence of the country's exceptionalism. In 1946, the consul in Guangzhou, Amaro Sacramento Monteiro, speculated that that was due 'to the susceptibility originating from the fact that a small power maintains a colony in Chinese territory when the great ones make concessions and court their good will' together with a heighted nationalism fuelled by 'the Americans' attitude who convinced them they also won the war'.[28]

Monteiro further expressed disregard for China's contribution to the war – which is now recognised as significant to the Allied victory[29] – in

[23] Zhang Fakui was serving as commander-in-chief of the Second Front Army in 1945, and he had accepted the Japanese surrender in Guangzhou.
[24] Wu, 'Shenzhang zhengyi', p. 134; Wu, 'Zhongguo kangzhan xia de Aomen juese', p. 48.
[25] Fernandes, *Confluência de Interesses*, pp. 44–6.
[26] TNA, FO 371/53617.
[27] C. N. Stirling to Foreign Secretary Ernest Bevin, 29 Ago. 1946, ibid.
[28] Monteiro to Salazar, 9 Jan. 1946, AHD, 2P, A48, M212.
[29] For example, Mitter, *China's War with Japan*.

another dispatch where he referred to the Chinese people as 'drunk with a victory for which they contributed little'.[30] In a fourteen-page-long dispatch to Lisbon, Affra, the chargé d'affaires then based in Shanghai, also expressed his very negative view of the Nationalists, stating that the KMT was 'discredited' and its administration was 'inefficient and supremely dishonest'.[31] He was particularly revolted when Lieutenant General Takashi Sakai, former commander of the Imperial Japanese Army in South China, who had interacted with Portuguese representatives in Guangzhou, was publicly executed in Nanjing.[32] In bluntly racist language, Affra referred to this event as defining of 'this sordid and barbaric people, in which a pseudo-millenarian civilisation had not managed to infuse a single attribute of moral decency'.[33] Anger at, and dismissal of, Nationalist China's post-war actions can be read as unsurprising given the obstinacy of the Estado Novo elites' colonialist world view. At least for some, an independent Asian nation serving justice against a former imperial occupier appears to have been difficult to process.

Contempt for China's post-war position as a major power in the international stage was also expressed a few years later by the Portuguese minister to China, João de Barros Ferreira da Fonseca, who did not hide a certain sympathy for defeated Japan, a country that was regarded quite favourably by some – but by no means all – Portuguese officials.[34] He believed that the new Chinese status had made Sino–Portuguese relations difficult because of the 'natural arrogance' of a country emerging victorious 'over the progressive Japanese empire', although he did admit that the anomalous wartime circumstances when Portugal 'lost contact with the central government' were also to blame.[35] In an unintended ironic statement – for Portugal itself was ruled by an authoritarian regime – Fonseca described the KMT as 'a form of national dictatorship, supported on a single party ... that everyone knows has as little of "democratic" as of "national" or "serious"'.[36] Another dispatch followed a similar logic, stating that some said that Chiang Kai-shek's government 'is little different from a modality of fascism, which the war had destined

30 Monteiro to Salazar, 23 Sept. 1946, AHD, 2P, A48, M212.
31 Affra to MNE, 22 July 1946, AHD, 2P, A47, M151.
32 On Sakai's trial, see Kushner, *Men to Devils, Devils to Men*, pp. 147–53.
33 Affra to MNE, 15 Sept. 1946, AHD, 2P, A47, M151.
34 Amongst those critical of wartime Japan was the diplomat Luís Esteves Fernandes, who served as minister in Tokyo during the conflict (Fernandes, *De Pequim a Washington*, pp. 95–122).
35 Fonseca to José Caeiro da Mata, Minister of Foreign Affairs, 29 Jan. 1949, AHD, 2P, A48, M211.
36 Fonseca to Caeiro da Mata, 22 Mar. 1947, AHD, 2P, A47, M151.

to be removed', a regime 'where individual freedoms and non-official expressions of thought are severely suppressed'.[37] Once again, this observation could also be applicable to the Estado Novo dictatorship.

Whilst one should be cautious to read these discriminatory remarks as the sole perspective on the Nationalists circulating in Portuguese diplomatic circles, they do expose the anxieties of a small European colonial power unable to come to terms with China's post-war status and an increasingly anti-colonial post-war order.[38] They also suggest a certain disjuncture between diplomats in mainland China and authorities in Macau, whose de facto dependency on Chinese goodwill no doubt informed their more accommodating position.

The Remains of the Empire: Japanese and Their Property in Portugal and Macau

China promptly embraced its role as a victorious nation, but this postcolonial reality found colonial powers such as Portugal disinclined to accept China's sovereignty in the legal adjudication of problems left by the war. Of central concern to the Chinese representatives was the management of alleged war criminals and their property. Writing to MOFA, the Chinese minister in Lisbon, Zhang Qian, noted that the news of Japan's surrender was received with joy by the people of Portugal. The Portuguese government had informed him that it would recover Timor and that the question of Macau, which had been through difficult times, could be later discussed. Zhang understood that Portugal was still harbouring colonial designs.[39]

The Chinese legation in Lisbon sent a note to the Portuguese Ministry of Foreign Affairs requesting that Portugal apply to 'all public and private Japanese assets in Portugal and Portuguese territory as well as to the assets owned or controlled from all territories occupied by Japan and Japanese satellites' the same provisions it had applied to German assets.[40] It would soon become apparent that it was easier for the Nationalists to be treated as a fully sovereign power abroad than in Macau, where their efforts to deal with wartime issues clashed with Portugal's moves to affirm its rule and protect the reputation of its administration. Unlike Portugal, Macau was two things the Nationalists

37 Fonseca to Caeiro da Mata, 23 May 1947, ibid.

38 These negative views contrast with more positive accounts written by diplomats who had witnessed Japanese wartime atrocities, such as the reports penned by the Portuguese consul in Guangzhou at the start of the war (*A Guerra vista de Cantão*).

39 Zhang to MOFA, 16 Aug. 1945, AH, Waijiaobu, 020000023906A.

40 Zhang to MOFA, 15 Aug. 1945, ibid.

wanted to change in the post-war period: a Chinese territory controlled by a foreign power, and a territory that had been subjected to a significant level of Japanese control. Whilst both Taiwan and Hong Kong had been ruled as colonies by Japan during the previous years, the Nationalist government had assumed control of the former and Hong Kong returned to the hands of Great Britain, China's wartime ally. Macau's neutrality placed it in a somewhat different position.

In Portugal, disposal of Japanese property was coordinated between China, Britain and the United States, an instance of relatively smooth international cooperation between the wartime allies. According to a report written in April 1947 by the American, British and Chinese members of a quadripartite committee for Japanese affairs (a representative of the USSR was absent because Portugal had no diplomatic relations with Moscow) for the chiefs of diplomatic missions of those countries, 'plans for taking in[to] custody the official Japanese property in Portugal were made in August 1945'.[41]

The following month, guards from the US Army were posted in the Japanese minister's residence, the chancery, and the military attaché and the naval attaché's offices. The last contained 'only office furniture and items without particular value or confidential character, other items having been either destroyed or consolidated in the Legation'. Analysis of the documents in the Japanese legation revealed 'nothing of any interest whatsoever'. After being questioned on this, the Japanese minister reported that 'everything of a confidential nature had been destroyed, on instructions, "immediately after the Potsdam declaration"'.[42] This matches communications intercepted in 1945 revealing that the Japanese legation in Lisbon destroyed telegrams and account books after the German surrender.[43]

If Japanese assets in Portugal were negligible, in Macau they were considerable and a joint action was harder to coordinate. Power-sharing with the other key Allied power represented in the territory, the United Kingdom, was not a priority for the Chinese government, then reeling from Britain's speedy reoccupation of Hong Kong in plain disregard of their wartime alliance. In September 1945, the Chinese legation in Lisbon wrote to the Portuguese Ministry of Foreign Affairs about

41 'Report of the Quadripartite Committee for Japanese Affairs to the Chiefs of the Diplomatic Missions of the United States, the United Kingdom and China at Lisbon, Portugal', 29 Apr. 1947, p. 1, AS-IMH, Waijiaobu, 078.3/0004, Jieshou Riben zhu geguo shi ling guan caichan (Received Property from Japanese Embassies and Consulates Abroad).

42 'Report of the Quadripartite Committee', pp. 1–2, ibid.

43 Japanese Minister in Lisbon to Foreign Minister Tokyo, 13 Aug. 1945, TNA, HW 12/329.

Japanese assets of 'considerable amount and quantity' accumulated in Macau. It proposed that a 'thorough investigation and inspection of these assets be conducted jointly by the representatives of the Chinese and Portuguese Government[s]'.[44]

The MOFA special commissioner appointed to Macau in 1945, Tang Liu, proceeded to transfer some of those assets to China, which motivated the British to try and guarantee that enemy property was dealt with in Macau as in any neutral territory. In September, the British ambassador in Chongqing, Horace Seymour, wrote to the vice minister for foreign affairs, Gan Naiguang, to ascertain if the British consul in Macau could be associated with the investigation into Japanese assets in Macau.[45] Repeated correspondence on this over the following year shows that the Nationalists regarded Japanese assets in Macau quite differently from those in Lisbon because the former was considered a Chinese territory. British proposals for holding Japanese funds in a joint account or leaving Japanese property under Portugal's control proved unattractive to the Chinese government.[46]

Taking over Japanese property was regarded by the Chinese government as a reasonable request in light of the massive destruction caused by Japan in eight years of war, but the processes of dealing with Japanese assets were not always smooth. In London, the Chinese ambassador, Wellington Koo, sent a memorandum to the FO in 1945 on China's desiderata relating to Japanese reparations. It proposed that the 'full title of property rights, interests and assets of whatever nature belonging to the Japanese Empire and Japanese nationals in the territory of the Chinese Republic ... be considered as having passed to the Chinese Government'.[47]

The British were cautious in their reply, underplaying the devastation China had experienced. The head of the Far Eastern Department of the FO, J. C. Sterndale Bennett, wrote to the Treasury that, whilst China had 'suffered much from looting, pillage and destruction by the Japanese armed forces', it had 'suffered nothing like the bomb damage which we in Britain have suffered', and destruction in the British colonies had to be considered. For the

44 Chinese Legation in Lisbon to MNE, 7 Sept. 1945, AHD, 2P, A48, M211. Also in ANTT, AOS, NE-2A2, cx. 422.

45 Seymour to Gan, 20 Sept. 1945, AS-IMH, Waijiaobu, 078.4/0003, Chuli Aomen diwei caichan (Dealing with Enemy and Puppet Property in Macau).

46 Seymour to Wang Shijie, Chinese Minister of Foreign Affairs, 24 Jan. 1946; Seymour to MOFA, 29 Oct. 1946, ibid.

47 Memorandum, 'China's Desiderata relating to Japanese Reparations', sent by Wellington Koo to Bevin, 20 Sept. 1945, TNA, FO 371/46214.

British, it was important to clarify whether assets were Japanese or seized from British owners.[48] The existence of places where both Chinese and British had competing claims on Japanese property complicated matters. Macau had long been claimed as part of China, but it had also been a territory within the British sphere of influence during the war, and these ambiguities complicated the assertion of Chinese sovereignty there in the post-war period. In May 1946, the British embassy in Chongqing enquired about the veracity of a report received from the consul in Macau that a cash sum in Chinese national dollars, property of the local branch of the Yokohama Specie Bank, had been sent by the MOFA special commissioner in the enclave to the Bank of China in Guangzhou. If confirmed, the British requested the funds be returned as they had been assured that 'no unilateral decision would be taken regarding the disposal of Japanese assets in Macao'.[49] The MOFA confirmed that the notes would be 'deposited in a special account and not touched pending discussions between the governments concerned regarding their disposition'.[50] It is likely that the records of the Japanese consulate in Macau were also taken to China in this period.[51]

Apart from material remains, another trace of Japan's presence in Macau merited international attention: several Japanese residing in the enclave. Their case shows how a neutral territory was part of the extensive repatriation drive at the end of the Japanese empire that involved the movement of some six million people, a process itself marked by complex ambiguities.[52] By the end of the war, more than fifty Japanese residing in Macau were eligible for repatriation. Lists compiled in January 1946 listed forty men, eight women and five children wanting to leave. Some expressed the desire to be repatriated at a later date, either to accompany family members (two women whose husbands were detained in Macau and Guangzhou) or to be able to liquidate their frozen businesses.[53]

[48] FO to Treasury, 27 Sept. 1945, ibid.

[49] British Embassy in Chongqing to MOFA, 22 May 1946, TNA, FO 371/53617.

[50] MOFA to British Embassy in Nanjing, 4 June 1946, ibid.

[51] They are currently held at the No. 2 Historical Archives of China in Nanjing, which contains a significant part of China's government records from the Republican period.

[52] For example, L. Watt, *When Empire Comes Home: Repatriation and Reintegration in Postwar Japan* (Cambridge, MA, 2009), p. 1; J. Sheng, 'Homeward Bound: The Postwar Repatriation of Japanese Civilians in Shanghai, 1945–1948', *Asia-Pacific Journal*, 23/2 (2020), apjjf.org/2020/23/Sheng.html.

[53] In addition to these, there were at least fifteen Japanese with residency in Macau who were not registered at the consulate, most of whom were traders (AM, MO/AH/AC/SA/01/19213, Repatriação dos súbditos japoneses residentes em Macau (Repatriation of Japanese subjects resident in Macau)).

Three Japanese subjects wanted to be repatriated to Formosa, which suggests that they were in fact Taiwanese with Japanese citizenship.

Other Japanese were not registered at the consulate, and the Americans believed some ten to fifteen might be hiding in Macau. Some were deemed of potential intelligence interest to the British authorities in Hong Kong, who wanted to take them to be interrogated there. This was the case of the vice consul, Asahina Taiki, who was believed to be a Kempeitai captain.[54] The Chinese General Headquarters of the National Military Council in Guangzhou was also interested in Japanese men in Macau, notably Fukasako Tomio, ex-manager of the Nan Xing Tobacco Company in Macau, which was described as 'the property of the ex-Puppet-Governor of Korea'.[55] There were some attempts at joint action in the South China region. For example, General Zhang Fakui asked for the cooperation of the governor of Hong Kong to have the wanted men arrested and sent to Guangzhou for trial. Competing national interests and jurisdictions, as well as complex identity matters, marred extradition procedures, however. Some Japanese ended up staying in Macau for good, a few seemingly switching sides to assist the United States or Nationalist China.[56]

Elusive *Hanjian*

Disagreements over Japanese property and extradition of alleged war criminals and collaborators were not only driven by Chinese grievances connected to what had happened during the war, but were also very much linked to the idea that the ability to serve justice was a marker of a sovereign state. In the uncharted terrain of a postcolonial and postwar new order, Portuguese officials made the most of the control they retained over Macau, meeting Chinese attempts to seek justice for wartime misdeeds with their own sets of conditions. To the Portuguese authorities, handing alleged Chinese traitors (*hanjian*) to the Nationalists was even more problematic than extraditing Japanese subjects, who were considerably less numerous. Furthermore, amongst those suspected of collaboration were figures connected to crucial sectors of

[54] Lt. Col. A. S. Roger, Defence Security Officer, Hong Kong, to Secretariat Civil Affairs, Hong Kong, 29 Jan. 1946, HKPRO, HKRS, 163–1–72.

[55] Zhang Fakui to Mark Young, Governor of Hong Kong, 3 June 1946, ibid.

[56] See the case of Ogata Shunsako mentioned in Jorge and Coelho, *Roque Choi*, p. 79, and in G. Horne, *Race War! White Supremacy and the Japanese Attack on the British Empire* (New York, 2004), p. 291. An entry in a list of Japanese and alleged traitors in the Braga Papers on Allied intelligence states that Ogata 'registered as a Portuguese, for the purpose of maintaining his properties in this colony' (first entry in handwritten list under the header 'Economic', NLA, MS 4300, Box 169, 8.1/29).

Macau's economy and, if proven guilty, their closeness to the Portuguese administration would complicate the latter's record of 'strict neutrality'.

In November 1945, an editorial in the *Jianguo ribao* urged 'the early repossession of Macao by the Chinese', and the *Dagongbao* reported that Zhongshan authorities were blockading the territory because of the 'misbehaviour of the Macao authorities for harbouring traitors, conniving smugglers, gamblers, and opium-smokers'. According to the *Dagongbao*, a 'large number of traitors' who had been 'naturalized as Portuguese only by paying several tens of Macao currency dollars as fees' planned to escape to Lisbon on a repatriation ship.[57] The SS *Colonial* left Macau in September 1945 and arrived in the Portuguese capital in March 1946. The Chinese legation in Lisbon asked the Portuguese Ministry of Foreign Affairs if there were any 'enemy persons and traitors' and their property on board. The Portuguese secret police guaranteed that no Chinese or Japanese subjects had arrived in Lisbon on the repatriation ship.[58] Even if that was the case, the ship's passengers had something to say on wartime collaboration, including criticisms of the governor's conduct. Americans in Lisbon got a 'reliable source' to interview some of them. The information was compiled by the US naval attaché in Lisbon in a report that painted a grim picture of Macau as a site of quasi-occupation and collaboration:

> The Japanese Army completely controlled Macau. The Portuguese officials, the Chinese resident there and even the Japanese Consul were entirely subservient to them. Receiving orders only from Canton headquarters and acting independently of other Japanese armies in China, the war lords had their General Staff headquarters in Macau, and used it as a pleasure resort where officers spent their leave. Macau was run by brute force during this period, and famine, starvation, disregard of law and order, murder, etc. were rampant. Hundreds of Chinese died on the streets every day, and for a time it is said that their flesh was sold in restaurants as 'smuggled pork from the Japanese zone'. Many Chinese got rich in the service of the Japanese, carrying on murder, gambling and the opium trade.[59]

The situation was more nuanced than this report suggests; nevertheless, it constitutes a telling example of some of the strongest critiques of Portuguese unneutral conduct articulated in the post-war period. Both

[57] Extracts from Guangzhou press on 27 Nov. 1945 sent by British Consul General in Guangzhou to Commander-in-Chief in Hong Kong, 29 Nov. 1945, TNA, FO 371/53617.

[58] Chinese Legation in Lisbon to MNE, 23 Mar. 1946; MNE to State Surveillance and Defence Police (PVDE) Director, 24 Apr. 1946; PVDE to MNE, 30 Apr. 1946, AHD, 2P, A48, M212.

[59] Copy of report by US Naval Attaché in Lisbon, 26 Apr. 1946, TNA, FO 371/53617. About 100 Portuguese army personnel stationed in Macau and 259 passengers were repatriated on the ship.

Chinese and Americans saw the war as a turning point for democracy and anti-colonialism, values the Estado Novo leaders did not share and fought against. Thus, Portuguese officials, acting the sovereign in an international environment hostile to right-wing authoritarianism, sought ways to obstruct reasonable Chinese requests to investigate wartime issues after the conflict. The attitude of Portuguese authorities and the apparent passivity of Allied powers other than China in the face of it generated disappointment amongst many who had supported the Allies in Macau, who lamented that 'those who collaborated flagrantly with the Japanese, piling up fortunes' were 'still able to do business freely and openly' in the post-war period.[60]

Those who stayed in Macau were of as much concern to the Chinese officials as any potential escapees, but Portuguese authorities imposed some conditions to assist with extradition. A memorandum from the Portuguese legation in Chongqing in December 1945 stated: 'The Portuguese Government had commit[t]ed itself to refuse asylum to war criminals and to surrender those who eventually took refuge in Portuguese territory at the request of an allied nation, presented to it through regular diplomatic channels.' But to 'avoid any arbitrary action', it would surrender only 'those individuals whose names were included on lists of war criminals approved by a responsible government and containing the indication of the tribunal by which their trials would be conducted', excluding 'members of the Japanese armed forces and common law criminals' who 'would be surrendered without those formalities'. The memorandum further stated that, until then, the Portuguese government had not received from the Chinese 'any request of such kind' despite 'arbitrary action of some Chinese army officers' who sought to interfere with the Portuguese administration.[61]

From October 1945, the Portuguese authorities in Macau had been visited by different figures that claimed to be representing the Nationalist government. Delegates of the Chinese War Crimes Commission came to see the governor, asking for names of Japanese collaborators, and some were given.[62] The situation soon became confusing, with representatives of that commission, of the Guangdong provincial authorities and of what the governor considered as members of the Blue Shirts competing to take over *hanjian* and seize their assets. The Portuguese authorities stalled demands,

[60] OSS, China Theatre, X-2 Branch Report 'Political Situation in Macau', p. 1, 16 Apr. 1946, NARA, RG226, UD 173, Box 9. See also Matthews to Indiv., 21 Jan. 1946, NARA, RG226, UD 140, Box 53.

[61] Memorandum from the Portuguese Legation in Chongqing, 13 Dec. 1945, AH, Waijiaobu, 020000003315A.

[62] Teixeira to MC, 2 Oct. 1945, ANTT, AOS, NE-10A2, cx. 768.

partly in an attempt to understand where power lay, partly – it seems – out of fear of the possibility of a Chinese takeover of Macau. The Chinese minister to Portugal had requested that property belonging to the RNG in Macau should be handed over to the Chinese authorities. The Portuguese agreed, as long as there were no doubts that it had belonged to them and that the request was presented in Lisbon through diplomatic channels.[63] In theory, this would illustrate Portuguese sovereignty over Macau and, in practice, it would lengthen procedures.

The overlapping layers of wartime collaboration proved to be liabilities in the post-war period. Governor Teixeira expressed concern over the possibility of Chinese authorities asking for 'some of the Macau Chinese [who] cooperated with us', distancing himself from them by noting that they were not 'people of good character' (*não sejam boas rezes*).[64] Chinese authorities compiled lists with hundreds of pages of the alleged *hanjian* from Macau that contained information on a variety of people, mainly Chinese but also some Japanese (possibly Taiwanese). Their suspicious activities were mostly of an economic nature.[65]

One high-profile case was that of Gao Kening, accused of being an 'economic traitor'. Gao's case is paradigmatic of the ambiguities around alleged collaboration, with parallels to some cases of elites in mainland China.[66] As addressed in Chapter 4, he was the co-owner of the company with the exclusive gambling rights in Macau, as well as a key figure in the legal opium trade, the pawnshop business (important local financial institutions that were especially relevant during the war) and transportation.[67] He was a major philanthropist who had contributed greatly to a number of relief initiatives in wartime Macau, both Chinese and Portuguese, which earned him several decorations from the Portuguese authorities.[68]

Between 1946 and 1947, China attempted to have Gao extradited, but the Portuguese authorities constantly refused, arguing that accusations against him were inconsistent, that his good conduct was well known, that he had purchased food provisions for the people and that he had not aided the enemy. Emphasising Gao's charity work as being of greater significance than his wartime businesses

63 Salazar to Portuguese Legation in Shanghai, 27 July 1946, AHD, 2P, A48, M211.
64 Teixeira to MC, 4 Oct. 1945, ANTT, AOS, NE-10A2, cx. 768.
65 AS-IMH, Waijiaobu, 078.4/0007, Aomen de dichan, jianshang, Hanjian diaocha mingce (Survey of Macau Enemy Property, Profiteers and Traitors).
66 For example, Brook, *Collaboration*.
67 Gao's partner in the gambling business, Fu Deyin, was also accused of being a traitor; he was tried in Guangzhou and was acquitted.
68 Y. Huang, 'Ru shang bense: Gao Kening de cishan shiye' ('Confucian Merchant: Gao Kening's Charitable Activities'), *Wenhua zazhi* (*Review of Culture*), 93 (2014), pp. 38–44.

affirmed him as someone who served the Chinese at a time of need, whilst distancing the Portuguese state that had decorated him from negative associations with collaboration. Whatever Gao – and the Portuguese administration – had done during the conflict under economic and military pressure, was justified by the greater good of social relief. Arguments justifying dealing with Japanese agents to ensure the survival of Chinese civilians did not always work when those on trial were RNG high officials.[69] Gao was a private citizen living in an unoccupied neutral territory, however, and he had a strong base of foreign and local elite backing. Major personalities in associational circles in Macau supported him, such as the representative of the Chinese community, Lu Rongxi, the vice chairman of the Kiang Wu Hospital, Ho Yin, the chairman of the Tung Sin Tong, Huang Weilin, and the chairman of the Commercial Association, Liu Baiying.[70] Gao remained in Macau and his patriotic wartime record, notably his charitable work and financial support to the resistance, was brought forward by his colonial and local elite supporters. The Guangdong High Court decided not to prosecute in December 1948.[71]

Dealing with alleged collaborators saw both sides seeking to affirm their sovereignty and, relating to it, the right to manage judicial procedures over people caught in the middle of the ambiguities of Portugal's presence in China. The following two cases of non-elite men accused of treason – Huang Gongjie and Lourenço Oswaldo de Senna – illustrate this in greater detail.

Arguably, no *hanjian* in Macau seems to have been more sought after than Huang Gongjie. A Portuguese missionary stated that Huang and his wife 'were the greatest criminals in Macao'.[72] Huang, who was in his late thirties or early forties during the war, worked for the Japanese special services in the territory. He headed a group of armed men deemed responsible for assassinating many Chinese and also linked to the murder of the president of the Macau branch of the Portuguese Red Cross. The attempts by the Chinese government to have Huang handed over for trial in China proved unfruitful and his death is revealing of the unsolved problems left by an ambivalent neutrality. Chinese sources

69 D. Hwang, 'Wartime Collaboration in Question: An Examination of the Postwar Trials of the Chinese Collaborators', *Inter-Asia Cultural Studies*, 6/1 (2005), pp. 75–97.

70 Y. Huang, *Tong Shan Tang yu Aomen Huaren shehui* (*The Tung Sin Tong and Macau's Chinese Society*) (Beijing, 2012), pp. 301–2.

71 Huang, 'Ru shang bense', p. 43.

72 M. Teixeira, 'The Bonnie and Clyde of Macao', in D. Pittis and S. J. Henders (eds.), *Macao: Mysterious Decay and Romance* (Hong Kong, 1997), pp. 3–13, at p. 8.

show that the Chinese government requested that the Portuguese authorities arrest and extradite Huang.[73] The Portuguese were also interested in keeping him as he threatened to provide sensitive information on Portuguese dealings with Japan during the war if he was handed over to the Nationalist authorities. If the country was shown to have been excessively close to Japanese interests, this would tarnish Portugal's reputation, strengthening the Chinese arguments against colonial rule.

The East River Column issued a manifesto in December 1945 concerning 'the war criminal' Huang Gongjie. It stated they had captured Huang and his subordinates and that, 'after long and careful trials', the prisoners were to be 'sentenced to death according to the law of punishment for War Criminals'. However, because Huang and his subordinates had been active in Macau, causing much suffering not only to Chinese but also to Portuguese, the Column had accepted the request to hand them over to the Macau authorities 'for public trial'.[74]

Portuguese accounts stated that, after escaping from Macau at the end of the war, Huang was caught on an island west of Hong Kong by the chief of a special brigade of the Macau police, Sebastião Voltaire Pinto de Morais, in an operation that involved Macau policemen (both Portuguese and Chinese), British intelligence agents and the co-opting of a Communist guerrilla general with whom Huang had planned to link up.[75] As the manifesto suggests, the guerrillas regarded his wartime crimes as deserving of exemplary punishment. According to the governor, he paid 200,000 patacas – Nationalist documents mention other sums – in exchange for the prisoner.[76] After being caught, Huang was brought back to Macau from Hong Kong where, according to some Portuguese accounts, Morais managed to bypass the British, whose intelligence services were also interested in capturing Huang.[77]

Once arrested, Huang wrote to the governor of Macau to plea for mercy. He stressed his affection for the city and the role he had

[73] AS-IMH, Waijiaobu, 074/0001, Huang Gongjie.
[74] 'Handed to Macao – Alleged War Criminal Arrested by Guerrillas', *SCMP* (10 Dec. 1945), AHD, 2P, A48, M212.
[75] Teixeira, 'The Bonnie and Clyde of Macao', p. 11.
[76] Teixeira to MC, 10 Dec. 1945, ANTT, AOS, NE-10A2, cx. 768; AS-IMH, Waijiaobu, 074/0001.
[77] For example, Teixeira, 'The Bonnie and Clyde of Macao', pp. 11–13; J. C. Rêgo (Filho), *Os Feitos do Capitão Ribeiro da Cunha durante o Período da Guerra do Pacífico em Macau* (*The Feats of Captain Ribeiro da Cunha during the Pacific War Period in Macau*) (n.p., 1996), pp. 83–4.

played to 'save' it, using his favour with the Japanese to guarantee that the territory did not suffer major aggression. He also recalled that he had once been a Chinese patriot who had worked for the resistance as an undercover agent, before divisions in his group forced him to seek alternative work in Macau.[78] This rather self-serving confession seems to be corroborated with earlier Portuguese intelligence that stated Huang had for a while worked for Zhou Yongneng, who had led the KMT branch in Macau, before he left the territory for unoccupied China in 1942. After Zhou departed to Chongqing, and facing destitution, Huang began to work for the Japanese. He and his gang operated in and around Macau, controlling rice supplies to the enclave, blackmailing and allegedly torturing and killing local traders and going after those deemed enemies of Japan (there was a hit list).[79]

In his letter to the governor, Huang defended his actions, explaining that he had not been the only one to, in his words, 'pursue the path of friendship with [the] Japs' and, therefore, it was terribly unfair that he was now labelled such a great criminal when 'the real sinners in society are allowed to remain'. Addressing Portuguese neutrality with a mixture of praise and threat, he suggested the real danger to Portuguese rule in Macau was coming from the Nationalists who were already blockading Macau on the pretext of 'cleaning up ... bandits and taking over ... enemy property'.[80] By exploiting Portuguese colonial anxieties, Huang's words reference an often overlooked feature of post-war China: the consolidation of the Nationalists as an anti-imperialist force. Their new international status made the authorities from a small colonial power such as Portugal somewhat uncomfortable.

The Nationalists sought to assert China's new role in the international community, as well as their domestic authority, through organising war crimes and collaboration trials.[81] The insistence for people like Huang to be handed over for trial spoke to these national and transnational dimensions of post-war justice. Under Chiang Kai-shek's instructions, the MOFA delegate in Macau, Tang Liu, wrote to the governor in late December 1945 asking for Huang to be extradited to Guangzhou to be

[78] Wong Kong Kit (Huang Gongjie) to Governor of Macau, 19 Dec. 1945, AHU, Espólio Gabriel Maurício Teixeira.

[79] See several intelligence-related documents amongst the governor papers in AHU, Espólio Gabriel Maurício Teixeira.

[80] Wong to Governor of Macau, 19 Dec. 1945 AHU, Espólio Gabriel Maurício Teixeira.

[81] Kushner, *Men to Devils, Devils to Men*; Y. Xia, 'Traitors in Limbo: Chinese Trials of Russian Spies, 1937–1948', *Nationalities Papers*, 49/6 (2021), pp. 1096–1112, at pp. 1096–7.

tried. After failed attempts to get the Portuguese to hand Huang over, they finally agreed to do it.[82]

However, in early January 1946, as Huang was being moved from one detention centre to another under very suspicious circumstances, he was shot dead after allegedly trying to escape. The local newspapers reported that he had attempted to flee and was pursued by the police who shot him several times. He was then sent to a hospital, where he died. The Chinese authorities sought to investigate Huang's suspicious death. Tang presented a series of demands to the governor of Macau to ensure this would not happen again. Dai Li, the head of Juntong, had investigated the case and concluded in February that the Macau government had collaborated with the Japanese and, worried that Huang Gongjie might reveal secrets to the Chinese, had spent money to get him back to Macau to be killed. The explanation that he had tried to flee was false. Later accounts of the case take for granted that the Portuguese deliberately shot Huang.[83]

The strange death of Huang in Portuguese custody contrasts with the efforts of the Nationalists to give him a proper trial. Justice was a key arena for affirming sovereignty and, tellingly, the twists and turns of its exercise in Huang's case reflect the problems of dealing with the legacies of an ambivalent neutrality in a contested jurisdiction.

Huang Gongjie may have been the most notorious, but he was certainly not the only alleged *hanjian* at the centre of difficult negotiations between the Nationalist government and the Portuguese authorities. Unresolved debates about the nature of Portuguese sovereignty in Macau, as well as about the classification of *hanjian* as war criminals, also marred a process that was marked not only by Portuguese reluctance to hand over suspects to the Chinese authorities, but also by internal conflicts with those in charge of dealing with extradition issues on the Chinese side. Wu Su-feng observed that bribery and obstruction accompanied the attempts of extraditing alleged *hanjian* hiding in Macau, with competing Nationalist officials involved in the process, colonial authorities resisting attempts to extradite some suspects and widespread irregularities, including powerful individuals paying for police protection and avoiding extradition. Impecunious suspects who were arrested in Macau and sent to the mainland were usually acquitted by the Guangdong High Court because they were found not guilty or because there was a lack of evidence.[84] Highlighting practices of

[82] AS-IMH, Waijiaobu, 074/0001.
[83] Ibid.; Rêgo, *Os Feitos*, p. 84; Pinto, 'Guerra em Paz', p. 87
[84] Wu, 'Shenzhang zhengyi', p. 157.

corruption, Wu links the limitations of the post-war pursuit of justice to the lack of decolonisation in 1940s Macau. As it ruled the enclave as a colony, Portugal was able to act like a sovereign and hamper Nationalist agents' efforts to exercise justice as thoroughly as the Nationalists had intended.

If Huang Gongjie's case exposed the thin line between those acting for resistance and collaboration and the failure to pursue regular legal channels, the case of Lourenço Oswaldo de Senna is suggestive of the flexible definition of *hanjian* and the intricacies of legal procedures at a time when extraterritoriality was being abolished. This case is also revealing of the ambiguities of nationality and how different states could – not always successfully – claim authority over 'in-between people' in the post-war order when citizenship became more narrowly defined than before.

Senna, a Portuguese citizen born in Shanghai of a Portuguese father and a Chinese mother, was detained in Chongqing from 1944 to 1949.[85] A Eurasian, he assumed a Chinese identity on certain occasions – under the name Luo Mingzhi – and wrote to the Portuguese consulate in English only (sometimes signing as Lou de Senna). When the Sino–Japanese hostilities began in 1937, he left for Macau where he served in the police force. In October 1943, he resigned and went to mainland China in search of a better salary. He adopted a Chinese name and lived first in Guilin and then in Kunming, where he worked for the American Red Cross, and he is likely to have provided information to the OSS.[86]

In December 1944, Senna was arrested for espionage while he was with his Chinese wife and son, and was brought to Chongqing. Chinese authorities accused him of having raided a clandestine radio station in the house of a Chinese man in Macau who was arrested, to have had repeated contacts with Japanese in the enclave, including with the consulate, to have handed a few 'Chinese patriots' to the Japanese and to have spied for the Japanese special service in Macau whilst in China. Senna claimed he was tortured and forced to sign a confession in Chinese he could not read and that during the trial he was not given an interpreter and had to use Mandarin, a language he did not master (though he was fluent in spoken Shanghainese and Cantonese).[87]

[85] 'Portuguese to Face Trial on Espionage Count', *China Daily Tribune* (8 Oct. 1946) and other files in AHD, 2P, A59, M263 and in AHD, Arquivo do Consulado de Portugal em Xangai, M37, Correspondência Classificada de 1946 (Classified Correspondence from 1946).

[86] There are references to 'Lawrence Senna' as a source for some of the information in the report 'Japanese Installations in Macao / Hong Kong / Kwangchowan and Occupied China'.

[87] Affra to MNE, 2 Mar. 1946 and Senna to António Alves Lico, acting consul general for Portugal in Shanghai, 9 Oct. 1946, AHD, 2P, A59, M2623.

For Portuguese diplomats, who ensured Senna's legal costs were covered, as a Portuguese citizen in China, he was still protected under extraterritoriality (which, in Portugal's case, was not abolished until 1947), and, in any case, he could not be tried in Chinese courts for his acts in a Portuguese colony whilst on police duty.[88] The Macau authorities confirmed Senna's defence, including that he had even been given a reference by the British consul in Macau before leaving for mainland China.[89] Senna's ordeal was to last throughout the Civil War, the outcome of which would ultimately save him.

Although in August 1946, Senna was reportedly freed,[90] in October, he was sentenced to 'imprisonment for an indefinite period of time' and to have his property confiscated by the Sichuan Higher Court for having collaborated with the enemy 'in gathering for it military, political an[d] economical information' about Allied forces in China.[91] He decided to appeal to the highest court in Nanjing, insisting that the verdict was 'a most terrible miscarriage of justice' and that he was 'innocent of any crime or intention against the Chinese Government or any government'.[92] Senna had been charged 'not as a spy, but as a traitor', and he wondered how he could have been one if he was not Chinese.[93] Although unusual, his case was not unique, as Chinese authorities tried to bring to justice other foreigners accused of being *hanjian*, notably French and Russians as well as people whose Chinese citizenship was, in legal terms, uncertain at best at the time, such as Taiwanese.[94]

Senna's appeal noted that he had helped the Allies, using his connection with the Macau police to 'furnish the British consulate with information obtained by him from the Japanese' and, after the latter became suspicious, he had decided to leave for Free China. He stated that in Macau, only the British consul knew where he was going, although in his memoirs the consul did not seem entirely convinced of Senna's innocence.[95]

[88] Affra to MNE, 3 June 1946, ibid.
[89] A. Telles de Vasconcellos, Macau Civil Administration Services to Affra, 23 July 1946, ibid.
[90] Salazar to Portuguese Legation in China, 13 Ago. 1946, ibid.
[91] Copy in English of the Sichuan Higher Court No. 1 Sub-court Criminal Case Decision, 15 Oct. 1946, ibid.
[92] Senna to Lico, 15 Oct. 1946, ibid.
[93] Senna to Lico, undated, copy attached to dispatch from Affra to MNE, 17 Dec. 1946, ibid.
[94] M. C. Bergère, 'The Purge in Shanghai, 1945–6: The Sarly Affair and the End of the French Concession', in W. H. Yeh (ed.), *Wartime Shanghai* (London, 1998), pp. 161–80; Xia, *Down with Traitors*, pp. 141–72; Xia 'Traitors in Limbo'.
[95] Copy of 'Petition incorporating additional grounds for appeal against decision of High Court at Chungking, submitted to the Highest Court at Nanking' sent with letter from

Portuguese diplomats in China and the Ministry of Foreign Affairs in Lisbon tried to clarify Senna's situation with Chinese authorities on several occasions, to no effect.[96] Chinese representatives used the case to affirm their regained sovereignty in the post-war period. In September 1948, the Chinese minister in Lisbon said the case would be retried, but with courts being independent there was a limit to what the government could do. The minister stressed that Senna had confessed to the acts of treason he was accused of, for which the sentence was usually the death penalty, and only because of his confession had it been commuted to life.[97]

In early November 1949, Senna was condemned again.[98] Statements backing his defence had been written in Macau by, amongst others, the governor and the former British consul, but these were deemed too vague in court.[99] A letter to the Chinese minister to Portugal, Wang Huazheng, pleaded that the Portuguese government expected from the Chinese government an 'attitude of generosity' similar to that shown by the British government when it had freed and deported Rogério de Menezes, a Portuguese citizen who had been sentenced to death for espionage.[100]

The comparison is intriguing, for Menezes was indeed guilty of spying for the Germans when working for the Portuguese legation in London.[101] The reply was similar to that of Wang's predecessor's the year before: he would relay the request to his government for consideration.[102] At the end of November, Senna was finally freed, as the warden of Chongqing prison received orders to release all prisoners as the Nationalists fled the city. His escape is revealing of the networks to which foreigners in China could resort in troubled times – and how these were still standing in the 1949 transition to communist rule.

Senna left Chongqing with the help of the Paris Foreign Missions Society, travelling by boat to Hankou, where he reported to the British consulate, which looked after Portuguese interests. In Hankou, he asked for help at the Colombian Catholic Mission and stayed with Portuguese

Tsai Kuo Han, attorney-at-law, to Lico, 1 Feb. 1947, AHD, 2P, A59, M263; Reeves, *The Lone Flag*, p. 103.

96 Affra to MNE, 26 Jan. 1948, AHD, 2P, A59, M263.

97 A. da Faria, MNE, note of conversation with the Chinese Minister to Portugal, 23 Sept. 1948, ibid.

98 Senna to Fonseca, 3 Nov. 1949 and Affra (in Macau) to MNE, 9 Nov. 1949, ibid.

99 See files in AHD, 2P, A59, M263.

100 V. Cunha, MNE to Wang, 14 Nov. 1949, ibid.

101 J. A. Barreiros, *O Homem das Cartas de Londres* (*The Man of the London Letters*) (Lisbon, 2003); Pimentel, *Espiões em Portugal*, pp. 281–7.

102 Caeiro da Mata to Affra, 14 Nov. 1949, AHD, 2P, A59, M263.

friends, but was taken by the police and was questioned over a few days. According to Senna's statement, the Communists treated him quite nicely, only asking him for information on British, American and missionary contacts. After being offered a book of Mao Zedong's writings, he was expelled to Hong Kong via Guangzhou. At the Hong Kong border, as he had no passport, Senna once again assumed a Chinese identity to enter the British colony and from there he went to Macau.[103]

This case highlights how the ambivalence of the Portuguese presence in China could intersect with issues of collaboration and the misunderstandings these generated in the post-war period when attempts were made to impose a nation-state-based sovereign order through decisions on who was a citizen, who was a 'traitor' and how – and by whom – justice should be administered. For the Portuguese authorities, Senna's case was a vivid example of the shortcomings of Chinese justice with its Kafkaesque delays and refusals to accept the arguments provided to justify the innocence of a foreign citizen.

From a Chinese perspective, suspicions about Senna were arguably also understandable. He was seen as Chinese and the Nationalist government did not treat collaboration lightly. Whilst in China, Senna had assumed a Chinese identity and lived with his Chinese family. The fact that he had worked for the police in Macau and then appeared in cities in unoccupied China with a strong presence of Allied intelligence without, it seems, assuming his Portuguese nationality, would have seemed odd. Furthermore, it was well known that Portuguese citizenship had been granted to people with spurious claims on it during the war, so brandishing it might have not been given too much credit.[104]

Like other allegations of Portuguese wartime misconduct, Senna's case was dropped at the end of the Civil War and was left lying largely hidden

[103] Report written by Senna sent by Affra, from Macau, to MNE, 7 Fev. 1950, ibid.

[104] Writing to Lisbon on the cold reception given by the new mayor of Shanghai, K. C. Wu (Wu Guozhen), to a courtesy visit by the Portuguese consul, José Francisco Teixeira, on his appointment, the Portuguese chargé d'affaires to China, who had met Wu several times in Chongqing, noted that Portugal's consulate in Shanghai enjoyed 'a very sad reputation'. The former consul, José Augusto Ribeiro de Melo, was rumoured to have practiced irregularities that brought scandal to the consulate, notably registering as Portuguese citizens people of various nationalities, particularly Chinese (Affra to Salazar, 6 June 1946, AHD, 2P, A48, M212). Melo arrived in Shanghai after serving as consul in Hamburg, where he granted visas to help European Jews leave for Portugal (M. M. Ramalho, *O Essencial Sobre os Salvadores Portugueses* (*The Essential about the Portuguese Saviours*) (Lisbon, 2021), p. 58). I have found evidence suggesting that he also assisted Jewish refugees who went to Shanghai by registering them as Portuguese (see files on Anni Samueldsdorff, Natalia Matilde Rosental and the businessman Leopold Silberstein (AHD, Arquivo do Consulado de Portugal em Xangai, M39, Correspondência de 1947 (1947 Correspondence) and AHD, Arquivo do Consulado de Portugal em Xangai, M26, Correspondência de 1942 (1942 Correspondence)).

in the archives.[105] It is yet another forgotten example of the problems between the Portuguese and the Nationalists in the changing post-war order, when it suddenly became paramount to draw clear lines between 'patriots' and 'traitors' and matters of jurisdiction over mobile people such as Senna became more contentious and inflexible.

Abolishing Extraterritoriality

As Senna's trials and tribulations indicate, a key element of tension in solving wartime issues and exercising Chinese sovereignty pertained to the remnants of extraterritoriality. Extraterritoriality was a legal regime that permitted citizens of countries with such rights in China to be placed outside its jurisdiction, answering to its resident consul and facing trial in consular courts. It had long been one of the most contentious issues in Republican China's foreign relations. Chinese governments, particularly after the end of the First World War, had strongly opposed extraterritoriality and its abolition began to be seriously negotiated when the Nationalists came to power in the late 1920s, although the start of the Second Sino–Japanese War halted the process.[106] In a first phase, discussions for its abolition were postponed, but the later globalisation of the conflict precipitated the end of the system when the United States and the United Kingdom both took steps to abolish extraterritorial rights on paper in 1943, reflecting the fact that they had already been abolished in practice. Contrary to what is often mentioned, negotiations for the end of extraterritoriality with other countries actually continued during the post-war period. The Portuguese government managed to stall the process for longer than most, only renouncing extraterritoriality in 1947, although the main reason for doing so was not resistance to give up rights in mainland China but its refusal to include Macau in the negotiations.

Chinese diplomats in Lisbon had tried several times to address extraterritoriality during the war, but the matter was constantly postponed by Portugal. In 1944, the first secretary in Lisbon was told that Portugal would make a decision when the act of abolishing extraterritoriality would

[105] The case is briefly mentioned in Fernandes, *Confluência de Interesses*, pp. 46–7.

[106] On the complexity of this legal regime, see P. K. Cassel, *Grounds of Judgment: Extraterritoriality and Imperial Power in Nineteenth-Century China and Japan* (Oxford, 2012); on its abolition, see W. R. Fishel, *The End of Extraterritoriality in China* (Berkeley, CA, 1974); on remnants after the war, see B. A. Elleman, 'The End of Extraterritoriality in China: The Case of the Soviet Union, 1917–1960', *Republican China*, 21/2 (1996), pp. 65–89, and Y. Zheng, 'A Specter of Extraterritoriality: The Legal Status of U.S. Troops in China, 1943–1947', *Journal of American–East Asian Relations*, 22/1 (2015), pp. 17–44.

not be seen as an action against one of the belligerents.[107] Such an agreement with Chiang's government could instigate retaliation from Japan, including a potential occupation of Macau that, with the war still ongoing, would benefit neither the Portuguese nor the Nationalists. Portuguese policymakers were closely following the developments of other countries' negotiations with China, asking their diplomats in differ ent European countries and in Brazil for information on their cases.

France, also a colonial power with interests in China, was an important reference. The Chinese government had unilaterally denounced all French privileges when it broke off relations with the Vichy regime, but this decision was not immediately accepted by the post-war French government. Eventually, France reached an agreement on the return to Chinese sovereignty of the leased territory of Guangzhouwan in 1945, before negotiating the end of extraterritoriality in late February 1946.[108] However, there was an important difference between the French and the Portuguese positions. In French concessions in China and in Guangzhouwan, occupation by Japan and handover to the RNG had paved the way to de facto decolonisation. In Macau, neutrality had spared the Portuguese the precedent of being removed from power.

Soon after the war ended, the Chinese legation in Lisbon insisted that the Portuguese government begin negotiations to abolish extraterritoriality. In September, Minister Zhang Qian went to the Ministry of Foreign Affairs to press Portugal to relinquish its rights in China.[109] The Sino–Portuguese treaty signed in Nanjing in December 1928 had scheduled the abolition of extraterritoriality for 1930, provided that the Chinese government signed agreements with the signatory powers of the 1921–2 Washington Treaties and made detailed agreements with Portugal for the matter.[110] With the end of the war, the Portuguese government was pressured to initiate negotiations. In 1945, on the ROC national day, 10 October, a note was delivered to the Chinese minister in Lisbon, declaring the Portuguese government's decision to renounce extraterritoriality and that it should come into effect after the signing of a Sino–Portuguese convention yet to be negotiated.[111] The note was relayed to Chongqing at the end of the month.[112]

[107] Notes on talk between Franco Nogueira, MNE and the First Secretary of the Chinese Legation, 16 June 1944, AHD, 2P, A48, M211.
[108] Portuguese Legation in Paris to MNE, 12 Sept. 1945; Portuguese Legation in Chongqing to MNE, 1 Mar. 1946, ibid.
[109] Zhang to MOFA, 19 Sept. 1945, AH, Waijiaobu, 020000006303A.
[110] Project of note, Sept. 1945, AHD, 2P, A48, M211.
[111] MNE to Portuguese Legation in Shanghai, 10 Oct. 1945, ibid.
[112] Zhang to MOFA, 28 Oct. 1945, AH, Waijiaobu, 020000023906A.

Before such an agreement was sealed, however, a number of contentious issues hampered the negotiations. In December 1945, the Chinese legation in Lisbon stated that the consular courts of all powers had ceased to operate in China, and Portugal was to be no exception.[113] Portugal refused, as it had not yet finished negotiating the relinquishment of its extraterritorial privileges.[114] The issue was particularly significant given the detention of some Portuguese citizens in China accused of different crimes, including collaboration, against which legal protection from facing trial in a Chinese court could be useful.

Then there was the ever-thorny question of Macau. If it was treated as a foreign concession, the door would be open for decolonisation. The Chinese government intended to reserve its position on Macau, but, predictably, this was deemed unacceptable by the Portuguese authorities, as the Portuguese chargé d'affaires relayed to the Chinese vice minister of foreign affairs in Nanjing.[115] The only reservation the Portuguese government would be open to consider was on the borders of Macau, not on Portuguese sovereignty over the enclave.[116]

Metropolitan and local approaches to Macau did differ at times. The governor saw in the extraterritoriality negotiations a good opportunity to fix the disputed borders of the territory to Portugal's advantage. He advised the minister of colonies that, although it might be difficult, Portugal should try to obtain Montanha (Da Hengqin) Island in exchange for clearly renouncing Lappa and Dom João (Xiao Hengqin) – none of which Portugal de facto controlled.[117] The fact that a 1946 official map excluded the islands from the country's jurisdiction suggests that the Portuguese government took a different position from the Macau authorities.[118] In November 1946, without Lisbon's knowledge, the latter banned the distribution of an edition of the *South China Morning Post* due to a news report on Sino–Portuguese negotiations for the abolition of extraterritoriality on the pretext that it suggested that Macau was equivalent to other foreign concessions in China.[119]

The Chinese government had prepared a draft for a Sino–Portuguese treaty with fourteen articles to be celebrated, possibly in Lisbon, and that

113 Chinese Legation in Lisbon to MNE, 18 Dec. 1945, AHD, 2P, A48, M211.
114 Affra to MNE, 15 Feb. 1946, ibid.
115 MNE to Portuguese Legation in Chongqing and Embassies in London and Washington, 16 Mar. 1946; Portuguese Legation in China (Nanjing) to MNE, 25 July 1946, ibid.
116 Salazar to Portuguese Legation in Shanghai, 2 Sept. 1946, ibid.
117 Ministry of Colonies to MNE, 21 Jan. 1946, ibid.
118 Fernandes, *Confluência de Interesses*, p. 68.
119 'Hongkong Paper Banned by Macao', *North China Daily News* (24 Nov. 1946); Acting Governor of Macau to MC, Dec. 1946, AHD, 2P, A48, M211.

included the transfer of the administration and control of Macau to the ROC.[120] Unsurprisingly, the Portuguese government did everything in its power to prevent the Macau issue from being linked to its renunciation of extraterritorial rights in China. It is important to note that the Estado Novo regime's intransigence regarding its colonial possessions was not a matter for open public debate. The majority of people in Portugal were kept in the dark about the foreign policy decisions made by the country's leaders. Indeed, unlike in China, there was no news in the Portuguese press when notes with China were eventually exchanged.[121]

After a lengthy impasse, an agreement was reached between Portugal and the ROC to postpone indefinitely the discussion of the 'Macau problem' and thus withdraw the major impediment to the negotiations for the abolition of Portuguese extraterritorial rights in China. It has been argued that with civil war looming, it became pressing for Chiang Kai-shek's regime to secure a diplomatic victory – even without Macau's handover – in order to appease sectors of the Chinese public who were becoming increasingly hostile to the KMT.[122] However, in 1947, the Nationalists' defeat was not yet a fait accompli and, in any case, the agreement with Portugal was far from a major breakthrough. There were also advantages to Portugal in reaching a settlement, as this agreement restored Sino–Portuguese relations to normalcy after years of ambivalent practice during the war, and left Macau with the guarantee of a continued status quo.

Notes 'for the relinquishment by Portugal of its rights relating to the consular jurisdiction in China and the adjustment of certain other matters' were finally exchanged between the Portuguese minister, João de Barros Ferreira da Fonseca, and Chinese Minister of Foreign Affairs Wang Shijie, in Nanjing on 1 April 1947.[123] The notes abrogated all the 'provisions of treaties or agreements in force [the wording 'in force' allowed for the exclusion of Macau, the jurisdiction of which had never been unequivocally clarified] between both countries which authorize the Government of Portugal or its representatives to exercise consular jurisdiction over nationals or companies of the Republic of Portugal in the

[120] AH (Xindian), Xingzheng yuan (Executive Yuan), 01400000186A, ZhongPu qianding pingdeng xinyue an (Signing of a New Equal Treaty between China and Portugal).

[121] Fernandes, *Confluência de Interesses*, p. 82. For Chinese news reports, see, for example, 'Pu quxiao zai Hua tequan' ('Portugal Abolishes Privileges in China'), *Shenbao* (2 Apr. 1947).

[122] Fernandes, *Confluência de Interesses*, pp. 72–3.

[123] AH, Waijiaobu, 020000023907A, Putaoya za juan (er) (Portugal–Miscellaneous (II)); also in AH, Guomin zhengfu, 001000005349A, Lingshi caipan quan chefei (wu) (Abolition of Consular Jurisdiction (V)) and AH, Xingzheng yuan, 01400000186A.

territory of the Republic of China'.[124] Excluding a financial agreement between China and Macau and an arrangement between the Macau authorities and CMC concerning smuggling between Macau and South China signed in 1948,[125] the notes relinquishing consular jurisdiction were the last diplomatic agreement between Portugal and the ROC to be signed until the official breaking of diplomatic ties between the two countries in 1975.[126]

Calls to Retake Macau (but Not Right Now)

The absence of Macau in the 1947 notes did not settle the problems left by its ambiguous wartime neutrality. After Portuguese extraterritoriality was officially abolished, calls for the retrocession of the territory intensified in the Chinese press. A critical discourse on the ambiguities of wartime experience was key to those calls, in line with critical views on the 'immorality' of neutrality in post-1945 Europe.[127] The non-democratic nature of the Portuguese regime and the existence of 'immoral activities' in Macau (gambling, opium and prostitution) were also pointed out.

Critics claimed that the enclave 'had been the centre of Japanese espionage and refuge for "collaborationists" during the war', that neutrality had not been maintained and that Portugal had 'helped the enemy'.[128] A letter to the editor of the *China Weekly Review* went as far as to portray the governor during the war as 'a warm-hearted collaborator with the "Imperial Army"'.[129] The shortcomings of the Portuguese administration during the war, in particular its relative disregard for the Chinese population when compared with the welfare of Portuguese officials sent from Europe and Portuguese refugees, and closeness to Japanese and collaborator business activities was still fresh in people's minds.

A post-war report made a blunt assessment of the public mood: '[T]here is no doubt at all but that the Chinese population of Macao would be only too happy to see Macao taken over by China.'[130] Reflecting this, a resolution

[124] Ministry of Foreign Affairs, *Treaties between the Republic of China and Foreign States (1927–1957)* (Taipei, 1958), pp. 412, 414.

[125] Ministry of Foreign Affairs, *Treaties*, pp. 415–21.

[126] On the closing of the ROC legation in Lisbon, see files in AS-IMH, Waijiaobu, 310.11/006, Wo guanbi zhu Pu gongshiguan (Our Closing of the Legation in Portugal). On Portugal's diplomatic switch from the ROC to the PRC, see Fernandes, *Confluência de Interesses*, pp. 345–461, and M. S. Fernandes, 'The Normalisation of Portuguese–Chinese Relations and Macao's Handover to Mainland China, 1974 –79', *China: An International Journal* 13/1 (2015), pp. 3–21.

[127] On the latter see, for example, Abbenhuis, *An Age of Neutrals*, pp. 6–10.

[128] Fonseca to Caeiro da Mata, 29 Jan. 1949, AHD, 2P, A48, M211.

[129] 'Return of Macao', *CWR* (17 May 1947), p. 305.

[130] 'Economic Currents in Macao', p. 30.

was passed by members of the People's Political Council (PPC) asking the government for Macau's return, as the issue had not been included in the agreement abolishing extraterritoriality.[131] The following month, twenty-one PPC members presented recommendations to the president of the Executive Yuan, Zhang Qun, advocating 'the immediate recovery of Macau' and arguing that 'during the war, Portugal violated her neutrality to the detriment of China's war efforts'.[132] In July, the Legislative Yuan decided that steps should be made for the 'recovery' (*shouhui*) of Macau 'at the earliest possibility' (*zui duan shi nei*). The government ordered the Executive Yuan to start negotiations with the relevant authorities.[133]

Macau was portrayed as a place where suspects of war crimes and collaboration avoided Chinese justice. An article in the KMT's official newspaper, *Zhongyang ribao* (*Central Daily News*), labelled Macau a 'criminals' playground' (*fanzuizhe de leyuan*).[134] In an attempt to placate this sort of attack, which damaged Portuguese prestige by questioning the legitimacy of its sovereignty claims, the consul in Hong Kong, Eduardo Brazão, approached the British authorities in search of some inter-imperial solidarity, playing on yet another of the ambiguities that had shaped the war years in Macau. The response was lukewarm. Taking a different stand on the matter, the consul in Guangzhou, José Calvet de Magalhães, argued that a joint action with Britain would not be advantageous to Portugal and the country should act independently.[135] Sino–British interactions had been experiencing a number of clashes linked to the Kowloon Walled City, including the burning of the British consulate in Guangzhou in January 1948. In contrast, relations with Portugal entered a more positive track.

Elite personal connections were crucial to the gradual improvement in relations between the Portuguese and the Nationalist authorities in the late 1940s. In August 1947, shortly after a branch of the Chinese Central News Agency was established in Macau,[136] Sun Fo (Sun Ke), Sun Yat-sen's son and president of the Legislative Yuan since 1932 (who would become premier in 1948), was invited by the governor to visit Macau where some of his family, including his mother, still lived. In the run-up to his visit, the MOFA delegate in Hong Kong told the Portuguese consul

[131] 'China Wants Return of Macao', *China Mail* (12 Apr. 1947), AHD, 2P, A48, M212.
[132] 'Return of Macao', *SCMP* (22 May 1947), ANTT, AOS, UL-10A3, cx. 769, Pt. 1.
[133] Chiang Kai-shek, Chinese Government to Executive Yuan, 8 July 1947, AH, Xingzheng yuan, 01400000186A.
[134] 'Fanzuizhe de leyuan, Aomen' ('Macau, Criminals' Playground'), *Zhongyang ribao* (*Central Daily News*) (10 July 1947).
[135] J. C. Magalhães, *Macau e a China no Após Guerra* (*Macau and China in the Post-war*) (Macau, 1992), p. 31.
[136] Fernandes, *Confluência de Interesses*, p. 96.

that he was worried that the Macau government would exaggerate the reception for Sun Fo, making his visit appear to be an official one, which could be interpreted as a tacit acknowledgement of Portuguese sovereignty over Macau.[137] Although labelling it a 'personal visit', authorities in Macau gave Sun a grand welcome and the consul concluded that Sun's passage through Macau as a 'guest of honour' was of 'great utility'.[138] Sun's words on Sino–Portuguese friendship at a banquet made the news even in Lisbon.[139]

At the end of the month, it was reported that Chiang Kai-shek had ordered Chinese newspapers in Guangdong to stop their calls for the handover of Macau.[140] The Portuguese could read visits such as Sun Fo's as *their* success and as an implicit recognition of their sovereignty in Macau even if they had nothing to do with sanctioning Portugal's colonial rule. The enthusiastic welcome Sun received from Macau's residents can, in fact, be seen as an expression of Chinese patriotism. Still, the pursuit of good relations with the Nationalists illustrated that the Portuguese in China knew where the ultimate decision-making power over Macau lay: not in Lisbon but in the Chinese capital.

This restoration of amiable ties with Nationalist figures can be understood in a context of changing priorities in the region, notably the co-option of foreign circles to secure a pro-Chiang, anti-communist redoubt in South China.[141] Personal connections, some forged during the war, were important for this. In September 1947, a new governor arrived in Macau, Albano Rodrigues de Oliveira. He had lived in China from 1937 to 1938, having been interim consul general at Guangzhou, where he had befriended the then governor, Wu Tiecheng. Oliveira went on an official visit to the city the same month he assumed the governorship.[142] He was received by General Zhang Fakui, Provincial Governor Luo Zhuoying, Mayor of Guangzhou Ouyang Ju, and Admiral Chan Chak (Chen Ce). Oliveira was also taken to important local sites such as the Sun Yat-sen

137 Brazão to MNE, 20 Ago. 1947, AHD, 2P, A48, M212.

138 Brazão to MNE, 25 Ago. 1947, ibid.

139 'É Necessário que Não Haja Razões que Possam Destruir a Amizade que Existe entre Portugal e a China' ('There Must Not Be Any Reasons to Destroy the Friendship That Exists between Portugal and China'), *O Século* (23 Ago. 1947), ibid.

140 'Ordem Sensacional de Chiang Kai Shek' ('Chiang Kai-shek's Sensational Order'), *Notícias de Macau* (27 Ago. 1947), p. 1; 'Return of Macao', *SCMP* (27 Aug. 1947), p. 1; on Chiang's intervention, see also Fonseca to MNE, 4 Sept. 1947, AHD, 2P, A47, M151; Fonseca to Caeiro da Mata, 29 Jan. 1949, AHD, 2P, A48, M211.

141 H. T. Lin and S. F. Wu, 'America's China Policy Revisited: Regionalism, Regional Leaders, and Regionalized Aid (1947–49)', *Chinese Historical Review*, 19/2 (2012), pp. 107–27.

142 'Visita a Cantão de S. Exa. o Governador de Macau' ('His Excellency the Governor of Macau's Visit to Canton'), *Notícias de Macau* (22 Sept. 1947), p. 1.

Memorial Hall and the Mausoleum of the Seventy-Two Martyrs, as well as to university campuses.[143] The itinerary projected confidence, showcasing China's achievements in areas such as education.

Elite connections continued to be nurtured in the following years, with Oliveira considering Wu Tiecheng 'an old friend'.[144] Wu was appointed minister of foreign affairs at the end of 1948. When he met the Portuguese minister in Nanjing at the first audience given to members of the diplomatic corps, Wu referred to the 'very good personal and official relations' he had had with the governor of Macau in the past.[145] Bilateral relations also improved markedly after the appointment of Premier T. V. Soong as governor of Guangdong in the same month.[146] Soong – Chiang Kai-shek's brother-in-law and minister of foreign affairs during the war – had told the consul in Guangzhou, Calvet de Magalhães, that he expected Portuguese cooperation so that asylum was not given in Macau to 'political discontents' of the region, a likely reference to the CCP and other opponents of Chiang.[147] Chinese relations with Portugal and Macau improved significantly due in part to the very cordial relations that developed between Soong and Calvet de Magalhães (see Figure 6.1). In a fifteen-page dispatch, the consul exposed his appreciation for Soong, who he perceived positively as the most Westernised politician in China who wanted to modernise China along Western models – a description that matches similar accounts of the period such as *Thunder out of China*, which the consul quoted.[148]

Highlighting the new state of relations, the Chinese Double Ten (10 October) national day was effusively celebrated in Macau in 1947. The main Portuguese-language newspaper went so far as to post on the front page portraits of Sun Yat-sen, Lei Peng Seak, president of the Macau Branch of the KMT, and of Guo Zefan, the MOFA delegate since 1946, accompanied by quotes on democracy – a concept controversial in Portugal's Estado Novo.[149] The Nationalists also won a symbolic victory when Portuguese authorities finally agreed to ban opium in Macau, a decision the Portuguese would likely not have taken of their own volition. The trade was banned in late 1945 and opium houses were closed in mid-

[143] 'A Viagem Triunfal de S. Exa. o Governador' ('His Excellency the Governor's Triumphal Trip'), *Notícias de Macau* (25 Sept. 1947), p. 1.
[144] Oliveira quoted in dispatch from MC to MNE, 30 Ago. 1948, AHD, 2P, A47, M151.
[145] Fonseca to MNE, 30 Dec. 1948, ibid.
[146] T. V. Soong remained governor of Guangdong province until 1949.
[147] Calvet de Magalhães to MNE, 20 Oct. 1947, AHD, 2P, A47, M151.
[148] T. H. White and A. Jacoby, *Thunder Out of China* (New York, 1946, repr. 1975), pp. 263–6; Calvet de Magalhães para Caeiro da Mata, 28 Nov. 1947, AHD, 2P, A47, M151.
[149] 'O Duplo Dez' (Double Ten), *Notícias de Macau* (12 Oct. 1947), p. 1.

Figure 6.1 T. V. Soong, his wife, Zhang Leyi, and the Portuguese consul in Guangzhou, José Calvet de Magalhães, January 1948. PT/MNE/ AHD/ C. E.18 P.2 UI/999 (2P, A47, M151). Courtesy of Instituto Diplomático

1947, after the implementation of rehabilitation plans for addicts.[150] This shows that the Nationalists were able to shape developments in post-war Macau even without retaking control of its administration.

The Nationalists were also successful in ending Portuguese claims over islands around the enclave. In January 1948, T. V. Soong asked Calvet de Magalhães – who had come to see him about rice supplies – to intervene with the Macau government to recall the Portuguese policemen posted at Maliaohe, on Montanha Island.[151] Two policemen had remained there since the war, when Governor Barbosa had tried to use the Japanese invasion as a pretext to extend Portuguese control over the islands through a police presence, as seen in Chapter 2. Chinese control over the island finally resumed in full. Despite an improvement in bilateral relations, the Nationalists did not give up on the goal of affirming their sovereignty over

[150] On the abolition of the government's Opium Regie, see *Boletim Oficial de Macau* (*Macau Official Bulletin*), no. 52, 31 Dec. 1946, p. 1007. Opium suppression measures were regarded as a way of placating Chinese claims to retake Macau, but their implementation in the enclave was seen as only partially effective ('Macao Hits the Doldrums', *CWR* (6 Sept. 1947), p. 12).

[151] MNE to Ministry of Colonies, 23 Jan. 1948, AHD, 2P, A47, M151.

Macau. Amongst the proposals presented at the National Assembly in April 1948 was one calling for the retrocession of the territory.[152]

As relations between the Nationalists and the Portuguese took a more positive turn, the uncomfortable ambiguities of neutrality were reinterpreted in a more favourable light. In April 1948, during commemorations in Macau marking the twentieth anniversary of Salazar's appointment as minister of finance, figures of the Chinese community praised Portugal's role in the war, dispelling accusations of collaboration. Guo Zefan highlighted the ceding of basing rights in the Azores as a valuable act of Portuguese cooperation with the Allies.[153] Then the chairman of the board of directors of the Commercial Association, Liu Baiying, mentioned how many 'cultivated individuals, merchants and capitalists' from all over China had sought refuge in Macau during the war and contributed to the development of the enclave's commerce and industry, an observation that can be prone to different readings given how some of these figures had been intermediaries between the Portuguese authorities and Japanese and RNG authorities.[154]

The importance of personal connections with certain notable figures of late-KMT rule on the mainland was stressed by Portuguese actors until a fairly late stage of the Civil War, but there was a limit to what these connections could achieve. In 1948, the Portuguese minister to China wrote several times to Lisbon recommending the upgrade of the Portuguese legation to embassy, stressing that only a few countries still kept legations instead of embassies and ministers plenipotentiary instead of ambassadors. Given Portuguese interests in China, he noted, this matter could affect the country's prestige.[155] Despite this suggestion, the legation's status was not elevated.

As the Nationalists lost ground to the CCP in the Civil War, Portugal, like most other countries, remained neutral. The experience of neutrality during China's War with Japan provided a peculiar 'blueprint' for Portuguese actions on the ground. Just as they had done during the war with RNG officials in Guangdong, authorities in Macau dispatched a few envoys to forge links with the Communists to ensure the status quo of colonial rule. One of these envoys was Pedro Lobo, who was sent as 'special emissary' to deal with the future authorities of neighbouring districts to guarantee the 'regular supply of goods' needed by the enclave.[156]

[152] Fonseca to MNE, 20 Apr. 1948, AHD, 2P, A47, M151.
[153] 'Programa' (Programme), p. 9, ANTT, AOS, UL-10A3, cx. 769, Pt. 2.
[154] Ibid., p. 13. [155] Fonseca to Caeiro da Mata, 19 July 1948, AHD, 2P, A48, M212.
[156] Pereira, *Accommodating Diversity*, p. 39.

Another envoy was Captain Francisco da Costa Gomes, who would become the second president of the Portuguese Republic after the end of the Estado Novo dictatorship. He later stated that before the end of the Civil War he went on a 'secret mission' to hand over two CCP members detained in Macau to prevent them from falling into Nationalists' hands. He claimed he 'had always had good relations with the Chinese Communists' knowing they 'did not intend to attack Macau'.[157]

In the 1940s, the KMT was arguably perceived as more anti-imperialist than the CCP by some Portuguese figures, and the Communists' accommodating stance – as their main adversary was, then, the Nationalists – eased communications with the Macau representatives. In fact, as Fernandes noted, Mao had made his position on Macau clear to a Soviet envoy in early 1949: although eradicating imperialist privileges and agents in China were priorities for the CCP, he advocated 'more flexible solutions or a peaceful transition policy that required more time'.[158] Meanwhile, the Portuguese minister to China, admittedly unsure of the CCP's ideological alignments with the USSR, decided to remain in Nanjing instead of accompanying the Nationalists to Taiwan, just as his predecessor had stayed in occupied Shanghai instead of going to Chongqing.[159]

In September 1949, a secret *pro memoria* from the British embassy in Lisbon asked the Portuguese government if they 'would be prepared in principle to support their [British government] policy of maintaining a foothold in China as long as possible'.[160] The Portuguese did manage to keep a foothold in China, even for longer than the British, but they did not follow their old ally when, the following month, the British embassy informed Portugal of its government's intention to recognise the recently established PRC – which Britain recognised in January 1950.[161] Despite

[157] A. Caeiro, *Peregrinação Vermelha: O Longo Caminho até Pequim* (*Red Pilgrimage: The Long Path to Beijing*) (Lisbon, 2016), pp. 16–17. Gomes was chief of staff of the Portuguese military garrison in Macau.

[158] Fernandes, *Confluência de Interesses*, p. 114. A similar account is given in C. K. Mark, *Hong Kong and the Cold War: Anglo–American Relations 1949–1957* (Oxford, 2004), pp. 26–7.

[159] Fonseca to MNE, 29 Jan. 1949, AHD, 2P, A48, M211.

[160] *Pro memoria* from the British Embassy in Lisbon, 1 Sept. 1949, ANTT, AOS, NE-2A2, cx. 422.

[161] Aide-mémoire from the British Embassy in Lisbon, 5 Oct. 1949, ibid. On Britain's recognition of the PRC, see D. C. Wolf, '"To Secure a Convenience": Britain Recognizes China – 1950', *Journal of Contemporary History*, 18/2 (1983), pp. 299–326; L. Xiang, 'The Recognition Controversy: Anglo–American Relations in China, 1949', *Journal of Contemporary History*, 27/2 (1992), pp. 319–43; C. K. Mark, *The Everyday Cold War: Britain and China, 1950–1972* (London, 2017), pp. 14–31.

some in the diplomatic corps favouring it, the Portuguese government preferred to wait, as did the French, although Portugal ended up waiting longer than France to establish official diplomatic relations with Beijing.[162] This did not happen until 1979, making Portugal the last European country to establish relations with the PRC. But, as throughout Macau's history, official diplomatic channels were not the only ones available; unofficial relations between the Portuguese administration and Communist authorities continued for decades via Macau.[163] These too were marked by pragmatic arrangements springing from the ambiguities of neutrality, this time neutrality in the Civil War.

Conclusion

This chapter has argued that post-war Sino–Portuguese relations were impacted by the ambiguities of wartime neutrality in Macau. Those ambiguities provided leeway for political manoeuvring in the aftermath of the war when China sought to assert its sovereignty in a new world order. Portugal's Estado Novo, itself uncertain of its international status in an increasingly postcolonial world, also tried to act the sovereign by defending its record of neutrality – and, by association, its colonial rule in Macau.

Disagreements on issues left by the war were inextricably connected to China and Portugal's radically different views on colonialism in the late 1940s. Nationalist China emerged from the Second World War as a victorious, anti-imperialist world power that, after a century of foreign impositions, had regained control over most foreign-ruled territories in the country. Interactions with Portugal reveal not only the Nationalists' determination to assume their heightened post-war status but also the difficulties in doing so in the face of Portuguese efforts to retain colonial rule over Macau. Because of wartime neutrality, the enclave had avoided the transfer of power that the war had brought about elsewhere. Tackling perceived unneutral actions that occurred in the mainland and in Macau during the war, the Nationalists sought to deal with enemy property and alleged criminals and collaborators as a sovereign state – like they attempted in mainland China, as scholars such as Barak Kushner have shown.[164]

However, Nationalist efforts were marred by internal division and external prejudice. Sino–Portuguese relations reveal limitations in China's

[162] Pereira, *Accommodating Diversity*, p. 49. France recognised the PRC in 1964.
[163] For example, Fernandes, *Confluência de Interesses*; Pereira, *Accommodating Diversity*.
[164] Kushner, *Men to Devils, Devils to Men*.

exercise of its new position, from difficulties in getting people extradited to the option of not retaking Macau immediately after the war, despite its return to Chinese rule being advocated by some as a way of dealing with its complicated wartime record. Portugal's flexible neutrality had multiple beneficiaries, including those on the winners' side, so it could easily be portrayed as having been advantageous for China (e.g. refugee relief) rather than a cause for condemnation (e.g. collaboration with Japan) – that is, it could be deployed to support Portuguese sovereignty claims rather than to confirm their illegitimacy.

The hazy identities of several of those who had operated in and around the shadowlands of Macau during the war were a pointed example of the difficulty of labelling people when exercising post-war justice, as in the case of a collaborationist gang leader who began as an agent for the resistance or that of a Portuguese Eurasian policeman who found himself on trial as a Chinese traitor. As Timothy Brook and others have demonstrated, the wartime record of individuals and institutions was far more complicated than a clear-cut binary of resistance and collaboration.[165] This was particularly evident in in-between neutral spaces such as Macau.

Although post-war Sino–Portuguese relations were haunted by the ghosts of wartime collaboration, their record was mixed. The Nationalists succeeded in negotiating with Portugal the abolition of extraterritoriality and in getting the infamous opium trade in Macau prohibited. These were Chinese anti-imperialist success stories that pre-dated 1949. From 1947, more cordial bilateral relations began to take shape through personal connections, further stalling any radical moves to force the Portuguese to leave the enclave. The Civil War ultimately derailed a Nationalist-led decolonisation of Macau.

[165] See, for example, Brook, *Collaboration*; Martin, 'Collaboration within Collaboration'; Mitter, *China's War with Japan*.

Epilogue

Enduring Legacies of a Globally Connected Periphery

The Second World War has inspired a spectacular industry of film and television productions in China that has grown exponentially since the turn of the twenty-first century. Macau can be glimpsed in a few of these, its neutral setting offering opportunities aplenty for fictional entertainment. The Macau Tourism Office supported one of them, the 2006 fiction film *Haoqing suiyue / Love in Macau.*[1] Shot on location, the film chronicles a love story between a refugee from North China (played by Aisin-Gioro Qixing, a descendant of the former Manchu royal family) and a Cantonese reporter working underground for the resistance. One would not guess how cosmopolitan wartime Macau actually was from this film – even the representation of the local colonial authorities is largely limited to a scene at the police station in which a Chinese actor plays a Portuguese policeman, Officer Martins (Ma Dingshi), a character who speaks only in Chinese (either Cantonese or Mandarin, depending on the film's audio version).[2] The portrayal of neutrality in this film is telling: the Portuguese are shown as acting unneutrally to both sides, at times seeming to assist the Japanese and *hanjian* but ultimately helping their opponents. Chinese resistance takes centre stage and an explicit link is made between the war and current Chinese politics. The narrative ends not in the 1940s, but in the 2000s, celebrating both victory over Japanese imperialism in China and the end of Portuguese rule, with the narrator proudly stating that, sixty years after the events depicted, the PRC flag now flies over Macau's government house. The connection is interesting for what it leaves out, namely how neutrality played a crucial role in delaying the decolonisation of Macau.

[1] Macau Government Tourism Office, '"Love in Macau" Premiere's [*sic*] in Beijing', Macao Tourism Industry Net (2006). https://bit.ly/3HGhBHZ.

[2] *Haoqing suiyue / Love in Macau* (2006), directed by Chen Yifeng. DVD distributed by My Way Film Company and Kam & Ronson, Kowloon, Hong Kong.

This book has explored the intricacies and ambiguities of neutrality in Macau and how its practice was marked by different forms of collaboration. Global connections were ever-present in the territory's wartime experience, an experience that transcended partial narratives of unaided Chinese resistance or of colonial benevolence and exceptionalism. During the eight years of warfare in East Asia and the trying post-war years that followed, Macau was both profoundly connected to the war and a site of refuge in a neutral peace, which was often more imagined than real. During these years, the territory experienced different levels of pressure from the belligerents and multiple and evolving connections that ended up keeping it unoccupied through somewhat unneutral ways.

To an extent, Macau's wartime experience was not completely new. Cooperation for mutual interests and relative autonomy had centuries-old precedents that had been continuously reinvented, with practices at the margins of legality featuring prominently long before the 1930s. However, the Second World War posed a series of challenges on a scale unprecedented before or since, challenges connected in different ways to the arrival of hundreds of thousands of refugees of various nationalities. Amongst those who arrived and made their fortunes in wartime Macau were some of the architects of its post-war economy who, in turn, were unassuming pioneers of contemporary Chinese global capitalist development.

Chapter 1 placed Macau in the history of China's war with Japan, revealing how its neutrality turned it into a space of refuge, mobilisation and mediation for and between different Chinese forces. The chapter unpacked the entangled realities of local contacts and understandings in Macau and of Chinese diplomacy with Portugal on the international stage. Macau and Portuguese neutrality became elements in the Chinese government's active diplomacy to harness support for resistance, as well as in the pragmatic use that Wang Jingwei and his followers made of the enclave to co-opt potential supporters.

Chapter 2 detailed the growing level of pressure that Macau was subjected to from 1937 by expanding the web of international and imperial contacts that framed its experience before the occupation of Hong Kong. The Macau Portuguese administration was committed to keeping colonial control. The Portuguese were players and were played in a web of competing, even contradictory imperial interests from the wooing and coercion of Japanese forces to hands-off Anglo–Portuguese solidarity. They sought to engage in new realities in South China, where neutrality was increasingly challenged by direct and indirect involvement in warfare around Macau's borders. As with Chinese actors operating in the enclave, new collaborative relations at the international level began to be forged in the late 1930s and were developed in subsequent years.

Chapter 3 delved into how Macau's neutrality made it a haven for hundreds of thousands of refugees fleeing Shanghai and Guangdong province. Through the analysis of the interactive state–society response to the refugee crisis in Macau, the chapter explored different forms of collaboration for relief. Refugees brought social, cultural and financial capital from treaty-port metropolises such as Shanghai and Guangzhou and transformed Macau from a sleepy backwater into a globally connected educational, artistic and economic urban centre, important for China on a scale unseen for centuries.

Wartime refuge was, however, vulnerable to shifting political, economic and military conditions beyond Macau's borders. Chapter 4 exposed how layers of collaboration were at the centre of what were arguably the most dramatic years of Macau's twentieth century. After the occupation of Hong Kong, pressure from the Japanese forces and the RNG authorities – which did not always act in tandem – reached a peak. The Portuguese administration and its associates in Macau resorted to multiple contacts to keep Macau nominally neutral and to remain in power. In doing so, the local authorities ended up engaging in unneutral actions that underscored the limits to Portuguese colonial control. The Chinese central government and its agents kept monitoring how Portuguese neutrality was being maintained and how Chinese citizens were affected by the fluctuating practices of Portuguese neutrality, not only in Macau, but also in Lisbon and Timor.

Other effects generated by the Japanese occupation of Hong Kong are detailed in Chapter 5, which considers the hitherto understudied process of colonial transplantation from the British colony to the neighbouring enclave. A neutral Macau served British citizens and interests well, allowing for escapes to Free China to be organised, assistance to be dispensed, intelligence to be collected and the reoccupation of Hong Kong to be prepared. Cooperation with the British is another dimension that brought several Portuguese and Chinese together. The legacies of these layers of collaboration proved difficult to manage in the immediate post-war period, however.

As Chapter 6 showed, questionable practices of neutrality and ambiguous collaborative ties resurfaced in the post-war years and affected Sino–Portuguese bilateral relations and local developments in Macau. China's efforts to deal with what had taken place during the war were made difficult by the scepticism of those who belittled its contribution to the war and its new international status. Those efforts were also weakened by internal division. Meanwhile, whilst past relations of collaboration were decried by some, other ties were forged anew.

Macau's wartime position as a twilight zone at the confluence of different empires had contradictory effects. Initially, it was a relevant channel for the Nationalists to acquire necessary materials for the interior, an intelligence collection station and a mobilisation centre targeting the local Chinese population and overseas Chinese. However, the Portuguese authorities in the enclave progressively conceded to more and more Japanese demands, thus affecting Chinese resistance efforts in Macau. Furthermore, they remained close to the British due to an imperial solidarity at odds with China's anti-imperialist position during the war. In later stages of the conflict, contacts between the Macau government and communist guerrillas forged a relatively positive view of the CCP amongst Portuguese officials that eased their future relationship with the PRC authorities, despite the absence of diplomatic recognition. In the immediate post-war period, pressures from certain Nationalist sectors to retake Macau and disagreements between figures on the ground fuelled a negative image of Chiang's rule, which likely further eroded chances of a stable relationship despite a relative rapprochement during T. V. Soong's governorship of Guangdong from 1947 to 1949. Also, for many in Macau, wartime solidarity with communist agents engaged in healthcare and anti-Japanese resistance in and around Macau was a positive legacy that harnessed popular support in the late 1940s, although the Nationalists too were involved in this in the context of the Second United Front. The Nationalists' concern for Chinese people in Macau during the war no doubt also ensured that pockets of KMT support remained relatively active in the enclave until they were forced to shut down in the late 1960s.

Ambiguous circumstances springing from Portugal's neutrality made Macau a site of interactions for actors with various, often conflicting interests, who found enough freedom for their actions in this grey zone. This book has argued that neutrality led to unneutral actions, with different layers of collaboration marking the enclave's wartime and post-war experience, involving Chinese, Portuguese, Japanese, British and other actors. This study re-evaluates Macau's importance in the history of China's Second World War, in particular its links and similarities with more studied colonial territories such as Shanghai. It is centred on a neglected aspect of the historiography of Chinese diplomacy in the period, which has privileged relations with major powers, and adds to the scholarship on neutrality, which has been dominated by Eurocentric accounts. By looking into China's interactions with a small European country, this book presents a countercurrent case study in which the Chinese – the central government or collaborationist RNG authorities and local elites – were more often than not in a position of strength vis-à-vis a European imperial power and its representatives. In so doing, the study problematises narratives of the European presence in East Asia. Although this work does not shy away from addressing practices of blunt racism and discrimination that tend to be underplayed in some accounts of Portuguese colonialism in Asia, it also highlights the importance of Chinese agency and places Macau as a key location to understand China's global Second World War. From its opening salvo in East Asia, the war involved a variety of international actors in official and unofficial contacts and actions that connected Europe and Asia. Because of its neutrality, Macau was an important meeting place.

It is precisely the importance of these webs of connections linking different people and locales near and far that is emphasised here. Macau's relative isolation as a 'lone island' not only hampered some of these networks, but it also created new ones or enhanced declining ones, such as those linking it to Southeast Asia. The importance of connections is also explored through the figures of middlemen. A link between the war and the post-war period is discernible in the emergence of powerful economic magnates who became key intermediaries for the Portuguese administration for decades to come. Men such as Stanley Ho and Ho Yin became leading figures in Macau's economic and political affairs after the war, especially after the founding of the PRC in 1949. They and others in Macau helped maintain commercial and other connections between Mao's China and the world even at a time when the Portuguese government did not recognise the PRC. These intermediaries and Macau itself played a role in the origins of Chinese economic development from the late 1970s Reform and Opening period in very similar ways as those of Hong Kong and its neighbouring Bao'an county (now the Shenzhen Special Economic Zone) – they simply have not received the same level of scholarly attention.[3] These experiments of shadowy exchanges in the liminal frontiers of legality, challenging embargoes and ideological prescriptions had had a crucial predecessor in the experience of a connected neutral Macau during the Second World War. Part of the story of how Guangdong came to be 'one step ahead in China' is thus to be found in

[3] Fernandes, 'How to Relate to a Colonial Power on Its Shore'; T. Simpson, 'Macao, Capital of the 21st Century?', *Environment and Planning D: Society and Space*, 26 (2008), pp. 1053–79; P. E. Hamilton, *Made in Hong Kong: Transpacific Networks and a New History of Globalization* (New York, 2021); T. Zhou, 'Leveraging Liminality: The Border Town of Bao'an (Shenzhen) and the Origins of China's Reform and Opening', *Journal of Asian Studies*, 80/2 (2021), pp. 337–61.

peripheral Macau.[4] Macau's present-day prosperity as the world-leading centre of casino capitalism owes much to its postcolonial policies, but its character as an unassuming place of opportunity for all sorts of unlikely actors remains as it was under Portuguese rule; one only has to think of the role it currently plays in enabling some North Korean connections to the world.[5]

Macau's wartime experience is also essential in understanding why total decolonisation was not achieved in South China in the immediate post-war period. Neutrality facilitated the maintenance of Portuguese colonialism in China in stark contrast to what occurred with the British in Shanghai's International Settlement or the French in their concessions, including the leased territory of Guangzhouwan. British colonialism did return to Hong Kong and, for that, as this book shows, some credit is also owed to neutrality in wartime Macau. The ambiguities and contradictions of neutrality ultimately made the Chinese Nationalists' post-war attempts to solve issues such as extradition of alleged war criminals and direct actions for Macau's retrocession more difficult and, in the context of a restarted Civil War, these came to be insurmountable obstacles to a complete decolonisation of South China in the 1940s.

The disruption the Second World War caused had a lasting effect on relations between the ROC and Portugal. Although officially relations were maintained until 1975, the post-war emergence of Chiang's China as an internationally recognised anti-imperialist power keen on retaking Macau was not particularly appealing for Portugal, despite the shared anti-communism of both regimes. Smooth relations were prevented from developing during the war in part because the Portuguese chose not to send their minister in China to the wartime capital of Chongqing. Even though the ROC kept its diplomats in Lisbon, dialogue was difficult. The only interest the Estado Novo elites had in China was ensuring that Macau remained under colonial rule and, for that, the Nationalists were of no importance after 1949. Still, many KMT supporters found a haven in the enclave as they had done during the war.

The war period had striking parallels with some post-1949 developments, in terms both of bilateral Sino–Portuguese relations and of local practices in Macau. Diplomatic relations between Salazar and Chiang's governments were maintained, but the two countries were far from close. Although the ROC kept its legation in Lisbon open, staffed and functioning, Portugal never sent a diplomat to Taipei – a striking contrast to

[4] E. F. Vogel, *One Step Ahead in China: Guangdong under Reform* (Cambridge, MA, 1989).
[5] For example, 'The Lazarus Heist: How North Korea Almost Pulled Off a Billion-Dollar Hack', *BBC News* (21 June 2021). www.bbc.co.uk/news/stories-57520169.

Franco's Spain, with which Chiang's China had not even had relations before the war but with which friendly links were forged afterwards.[6] In Macau, everyday life was dependent on a peaceful relationship with the communist authorities across the border. It was not that far removed from the war period, when the Macau experience was marked by pressures, concessions and interactions to guarantee food supplies or, in the case of the Portuguese authorities, to ensure that their nominal colonial control was kept intact – even though time and again their powerlessness became evident.

New waves of refugees arrived, some relocating from Shanghai and Guangdong province as many others had done during the war with Japan.[7] Others arrived later from Indonesia and Vietnam.[8] Responses in Macau were, in many ways, fairly similar to what happened during the war: accommodation, shadow diplomacy and a dependence on increasingly powerful local intermediaries involved in smuggling, several of whom had emerged precisely during the Second World War. The centrality of these figures outlived Portuguese colonial rule: the first chief executive of the Macau Special Administrative Region of the PRC was Ho Yin's son, Edmund Ho (He Houhua).

The war period in Macau may also be regarded as a peak in Macau's popular image as a 'sin city' for, arguably, its contradictions were never more evident than during the conflict. It was a safe haven and a killing ground. It was a bustling 'dancing world' with a new-found cosmopolitanism borrowed from Shanghai and Hong Kong, and a hell of piled-up cadavers and poor so famished they ate fellow human beings.[9] It was a land of spies, traitors and patriotic heroes, many as ambiguous as the enclave itself. It is this allure that has inspired popular culture, especially in recent years. It was not just Chinese audiovisual fiction that found in the territory fertile ground for wartime narratives: novels in Portuguese and English, and even a podcast series, have turned to the ambiguities of neutrality and collaboration in Macau.[10]

[6] Despite this, Spain broke off relations with the ROC in 1973 to establish relations with the PRC, two years before Portugal did the same.

[7] A. G. Dias, *Refugiados de Xangai, Macau (1937–1964)* (*Shanghai Refugees, Macau (1937–1964)*) (Macau, 2015).

[8] 'Indonesian–Chinese Refugees' Plight', *SCMP* (16 May 1963), p. 6; 'For Refugees from Vietnam, a Catch-22 in Macao', *NYT* (17 Aug. 1981), p. A2; Maxwell, 'Macao: The Shadow Land', p. 89; S. Miller and R. Allego, 'A Safe Haven', *Ariana*, 4 (2019), pp. 96–105. issuu.com/arianalife/docs/ariana04/s/10126112.

[9] I am borrowing the term 'dancing world' from A. D. Field, *Shanghai's Dancing World: Cabaret Culture and Urban Politics, 1919–1954* (Hong Kong, 2010).

[10] For audiovisual fiction see, for example, the thirty-episode TV series set in wartime Macau, *Jing hai fengyun* (international title: *Nature Situation*), produced by China

The idea of inaction associated with Macau's neutrality in W. H. Auden's poem that opened this book is as much a fantasy as some of these recent fictional reimaginings. In a world conflict of unprecedented scale and transformative consequences, neutrality was not completely attainable and led to multiple forms of collaboration. These collaborations may have been built on centuries-old precedents of accommodation and global connections, but the opportunities and compromises forged during the Second World War transcended them. The experience of wartime neutrality profoundly shaped the post-war period and, eventually, the postcolonial future of Macau and neighbouring areas in South China.

Central Television in 2009 and aired in 2011. Novels include Carvalho, *A Mãe*, based on a true story of a family of Russian refugees; C. Petit, *Deep Night* (New York, 2008); J. Lees, *The Fan Tan Players* (Dingwall, 2009), inspired by the life story of the author's mother, a Russian woman who lived in wartime Macau; B. Castro, *Shanghai Dancing* (New York, 2003), based on the Australian author's Portuguese family in wartime Shanghai; I. Valadão, *O Rio das Pérolas* (*The Pearl River*) (Lisbon, 2017); J. R. Santos, *A Amante do Governador* (*The Governor's Lover*) (Lisbon, 2018), F. Sobral, *A Grande Dama do Chá* (*The Great Tea Lady*) (Lisbon, 2021), and French, *Strangers on the Praia*, based on his 2019 podcast series for Radio Television Hong Kong on the experience of a Jewish refugee from Shanghai en route to Guangzhouwan.

Appendix 1: Net Entries and Departures to and from Macau by Land and by Water

Table A.1 *Net entries and departures to and from Macau by land and by water*

Year	Chinese	Foreigners	Total
1940	+30,757	+132	+30,889
1941	+85,855	−356	+85,499
1942	−36,977	+1,137	−35,840
1943	+65,478	+813	+66,291
1944	+80,620	+1,527	+82,147
1945	−18,240	−1,770	−20,010
			TOTAL: +208,976

Source: Repartição Central dos Serviços de Administração Civil – Secção de Estatística, *Anuário Estatístico de Macau. Ano de 1949* (*Macau Statistical Yearbook. Year of 1949*) (Macau, 1950), pp. 32–3. Calculations by the author.

Appendix 2: Selected List of Relief Providers That Assisted Refugees Who Went to Macau

In Shanghai and Hong Kong

- Club Lusitano, Shanghai
- 廣東旅滬同鄉會 Guangdong Native Place Association in Shanghai
- Club Lusitano, Hong Kong
- Relief Commission (Comissão de Socorros)
- Portuguese Consulates in Shanghai and Hong Kong

In Macau

- 慈善救濟委員會 Charity and Relief Commission (Comissão de Assistência e Beneficência)
- 鏡湖醫院 Kiang Wu Hospital
- 同善堂 Tung Sin Tong Charitable Society
- 難民救濟委員會 Refugee Relief Commission (Comissão de Assistência aos Refugiados)
- 澳門四界救災會 Macau Four Circles Disaster Relief Association
- 澳門各界救災會 Macau All Circles Relief Organisation
- 澳門中國婦女慰勞會 Macau Chinese Women's Support Association
- 澳僑協助難民回鄉會 Macau Overseas Chinese Association for Assisting Refugees to Return Home
- Executive Commission for Refugees (Comissão Executiva de Refugiados)
- Catholic Diocese of Macau
- British Consulate

Glossary of Chinese Names

An Puling (Father Serafim Brum Amaral) 安普靈

Bi Lüjian (Butt Lui-kim) 畢侶儉

Cai Zengji (Jun Ke Choy) 蔡增基

Chen Bijun 陳璧君

Chen Ce (Chan Chak) 陳策

Chen Chunpu 陳春圃

Chen Guangfu (K. P. Chen) 陳光甫

Chen Jie 陳介

Chen Shaoling 陳少陵

Chen Shaomu (Chan Chiu-mok) 陳少木

Chen Yaozu 陳耀祖

Chu Minyi 褚民誼

Cui Leqi (Roque Choi) 崔樂其

Cui Nuozhi (Joel José Choi Anok) 崔諾枝

Dai Ensai 戴恩賽

Dai Li 戴笠

Diao Zuoqian (Philip K. C. Tyau) 刁作謙

Gan Naiguang 甘乃光

Gao Kening (Kou Ho Neng) 高可寧

Gao Jianfu 高劍父

Geng Tingzhen 耿廷楨

Gu Weijun (V. K. Wellington Koo) 顧維鈞

Guan Shanyue 關山月

Guo Jingqiu (Helena Kuo) 郭鏡秋

Guo Taiqi 郭泰祺

Guo Zefan 郭則范

Feng Zhuwan 馮祝萬

Fu Deyin (Fu Tak Iam) 傅德蔭

He Dong (Robert Ho Tung) 何東

He Hongshen (Stanley Ho) 何鴻燊

He Weihan (Ho Wai-hon) 何維漢

He Xian (Ho Yin) 何賢

Huang Gongjie (Wong Kong Kit) 黃公傑

Huang Huilan (Oei Hui-lan / Madame Wellington Koo) 黃蕙蘭

Huang Weilin 黃渭霖

Jiang Jieshi (Chiang Kai-shek) 蔣介石

Kang Youwei 康有為

Ke Lin (O Lon) 柯麟

Ke Zhengping (O Cheng Ping) 柯正平

Kong Xiangxi (H. H. Kung) 孔祥熙

Li Jinlun (Frank W. Chinglun Lee) 李錦綸

Li Shizhong (Chet Chong Li) 李世中

Li Tian'ai (Florence Tim Oi Li) 李添嬡

Liang Houyuan (Leong Hau-Un) 梁後源

Liang Runchang (Y. C. Liang) 梁潤昌

Liang Yanming 梁彥明

Liao Deshan 廖德山

Liao Fengji 廖奉基

Liao Fengling (Fung Ling Liu) 廖奉靈

Liao Jintao 廖錦濤

Lin Zhuofu 林桌夫

Ling Shifen (Andrew S. F. Lin) 凌士芬

Liu Baiying (Lao Pak Ieng) 劉柏盈

Liu Shaowu 劉紹武

Liu Yulin (Lew Yuk Lin) 劉玉麟

Lu Lianruo (Lou Lim Ieoc) 盧廉若

Lu Muzhen 盧慕貞

Lu Rongxi (Lo Wing Sik) 盧榮錫

Luo Chun 羅春

Luo Mingzhi (Lourenço Oswaldo de Senna) 羅明志

Luo Zhuoying 羅卓英

Ma Zhanshan 馬占山

Ou Chu 歐初

Ouyang Ju 歐陽駒

Qu Renze (Watt Yue-chat) 屈仁則

Sa Kongliao 薩空了

Shi Liang 史良

Song Ziwen (T. V. Soong) 宋子文

Sun Ke (Sun Fo) 孫科

Sun Zhongshan (Sun Yat-sen) 孫中山

Tang Liu (Tong Lau) 唐榴

Tang Shaoyi 唐紹儀

Wang Chonghui 王寵惠

Wang Jingwei 汪精衛

Wang Jinling (Warren Wong Achuck) 王金鈴

Wang Shijie 王世杰

Wang Tingzhang (J. Ouang Ting-chang) 王廷璋

Wang Zhengting 王正廷

Wu Guozhen (K. C. Wu) 吳國楨

Wu Tiecheng 吳鐵城

Xu Shiying 許世英

Xu Weimin (Hue Wai-man) 許偉民

Ye Ting 葉挺

Yu Hanmou 余漢謀

Zhang Fakui 張發奎

Zhang Huichang (Chang Wai Cheung) 張惠長

Zhang Qian (Henry Kunghui Chang) 張謙

Zhang Qun 張群

Zhang Xinzhi (Cheung Sun-chao) 張新之

Zhang Youyun 張幼雲

Zhao Ping (Chue Peng) 趙平

Zheng Guanying 鄭觀應

Zhou Bingsan 周秉三

Zhou Fohai 周佛海

Zhou Yongneng 周雍能

Zhu Jiahua 朱家驊

Bibliography

Archives

Academia Historica / Guoshiguan (Xindian Branch), New Taipei City, Taiwan

Xingzheng yuan (Executive Yuan)

01400000186A, ZhongPu qianding pingdeng xinyue an (Signing of a New Equal Treaty Between China and Portugal).

Academia Historica / Guoshiguan, Taipei, Taiwan

Waijiaobu (Ministry of Foreign Affairs)

020000003314A, Aomen yindu hanjian zhanfan deng an (Records of Extradition of Traitors, War Criminals and Others from Macau).

020000003315A, Aomen wenti (Macau Question).

020000003319A, Di tu jianshi Aomen (Surveillance of Enemy Plans in Macau).

020000039817A, Zhongliguo zhi taidu (Attitudes of Neutral Countries).

020000006303A, Putaoya zhu Hua gongshi Lima Feileila rennei (Portuguese Ministers in China: Period in Office of Lima and Ferreira da Fonseca).

020000023906A, Putaoya za juan (Portugal–Miscellaneous).

020000023907A, Putaoya za juan (er) (Portugal–Miscellaneous (II)).

Guomin zhengfu (National Government)

001000004794A, Gang'Ao huashang juankuan jiuzai (yi) (Relief Contributions from Hong Kong and Macau Chinese Businessmen (I)).

001000004795A, Gang'Ao huashang juankuan jiuzai (san) (Relief Contributions from Hong Kong and Macau Chinese Businessmen (III)).

001000005349A, Guomin zhengfu lingshi caipan quan chefei (wu) (Abolition of Consular Jurisdiction by the National Government (V)).

Academia Sinica, Institute of Modern History Archives, Taiwan

Waijiaobu (Ministry of Foreign Affairs)

063.1/001, Zai Hua waiqiao ji haiwai huaqiao zhanshi sunshi peichang (Reparations for War Losses of Foreigners in China and Chinese Overseas).

074/0001, Huang Gongjie.

078.3/0004, Jieshou Riben zhu geguo shi ling guan caichan (Received Property from Japanese Embassies and Consulates Abroad).

078.4/0003, Chuli Aomen diwei caichan (Dealing with Enemy and Puppet Property in Macau).

078.4/0007, Aomen de dichan, jianshang, hanjian diaocha mingce (Survey of Macau Enemy Property, Profiteers and Traitors).

310.11/006, Wo guanbi zhu Pu gongshiguan (Our Closing of the Legation in Portugal).

312.8/0001, Putaoya Aomen shijian (Portugal, Macau Incidents).

Archives Research Centre of the Presbyterian Church of Aotearoa New Zealand, Dunedin, Aotearoa New Zealand

AA11/6, Union Normal & Middle School Canton (1937–1948), Missions Committee-Subject Files.

Proceedings of the General Assembly of the Presbyterian Church of New Zealand (Dunedin, 1940).

Arquivo de Macau / Aomen dang'an guan (Archives of Macau), Macau, SAR, China

Administração Civil (Civil Administration)

MO/AH/AC/SA/01/13673, Conflito Sino–Japonês (Sino–Japanese Conflict).

MO/AH/AC/SA/01/13827, Conflito Sino–Japonês (Sino–Japanese Conflict).

MO/AH/AC/SA/01/16831, Acêrca do Conflito Sino–Nipónico (On the Sino–Japanese Conflict).

MO/AH/AC/SA/01/17164, Condecoração concedida por Sua Majestade o Imperador do Japão ao Capitão Carlos de Sousa Gorgulho (Decoration Awarded by His Majesty the Emperor of Japan to Captain Carlos de Sousa Gorgulho).

MO/AH/AC/SA/01/17228, Acêrca do bombardeamento da Missão Portuguesa de Shiu Hing pela aviação Japonesa (On the Bombing of the Portuguese Mission of Zhaoqing by Japanese Aviation).

MO/AH/AC/SA/01/18103, Repatriação para Shanghai de vários indivíduos (Repatriation of Several Individuals to Shanghai).
MO/AH/AC/SA/01/18210, Auto de Corpo delicto indirecto instaurado pelo crime de ofensas corporais em que é presumido delinquente o subdito japonês Hirochi Sakurai (Report of the Indirect Evidence of the Crime of Corporal Offense in Which the Presumed Delinquent Is the Japanese Subject Hirochi Sakurai).
MO/AH/AC/SA/01/18566, Delegação em Macau, da Sociedade Portuguesa da Cruz Vermelha (Macau Delegation of the Portuguese Red Cross Society).
MO/AH/AC/SA/01/19213, Acêrca da repatriação dos súbditos japoneses residentes nesta Colónia (On the Repatriation of Japanese Subjects Resident in This Colony).
MO/AH/AC/SA/01/25240, Documentos enviados e recebidos de vários consulados portugueses e estrangeiros (Documents Sent to and Received from Various Portuguese and Foreign Consulates).
MO/AH/AC/SA/01/25736, Correspondência recebida de Rádio Clube de Macau, da Cruz Vermelha Portuguesa, e de Pui Ching Middle School (Correspondence Received from the Macau Radio Club, the Portuguese Red Cross, and the Pui Ching Middle School).
MO/AH/AC/SA/01/25738, Comissão de Assistência e Beneficência (Charity and Relief Commission).
MO/AH/AC/SA/01/25726, Governos Estrangeiros (Foreign Governments).
MO/AH/AC/AC1/35/13, Assistência aos refugiados chineses da Ilha de Coloane (Assistance to the Chinese Refugees on Coloane Island).

Educação (Education)
AH/EDU/3174.
AH/EDU/3180.
AH/EDU/3187.
AH/EDU/3194.

Leal Senado (Loyal Senate)
AH/LS/184.

Arquivo Histórico da Cruz Vermelha Portuguesa (Historical Archives of the Portuguese Red Cross Society), Lisbon, Portugal

CV/3513–3514.
CV/4742–4805.
Delegação de Macau, 1ª Pasta (1915–74).

Arquivo Histórico-Diplomático do Ministério dos Negócios Estrangeiros (Historical Archives of the Ministry of Foreign Affairs), Lisbon, Portugal

2P, A47, M151.
2P, A48, M175.
2P, A48, M176.
2P, A48, M211.
2P, A48, M212.
2P, A48, M217.
2P, A48, M221.
2P, A49, M115.
2P, A59, M263.
3P, A9, M125.
3P, A9, M128–129.
3P, A9, M132–133.
3P, A9, M134.
3P, A9, M135.
Arquivo do Consulado de Portugal em Cantão, No. 199–203.
Arquivo do Consulado de Portugal em Xangai, M26, Correspondência de 1942 (1942 Correspondence).
Arquivo do Consulado de Portugal em Xangai, M37, Correspondência Classificada de 1946 (Classified Correspondence from 1946).
Arquivo do Consulado de Portugal em Xangai, M39, Correspondência de 1947 (1947 Correspondence).

Relatórios anuais (Annual Reports)
João Rodrigues Simões Affra, 'Chunking', June 1946.
João Rodrigues Simões Affra, 'O Pôsto de Nanking' ('The Nanjing Post'), June 1948.

Arquivo Histórico da Caixa Geral de Depósitos (Caixa Geral de Depósitos Historical Archives), Lisbon, Portugal

Banco Nacional Ultramarino (National Overseas Bank)
AG-012–22–117 – Relatório de Exercício de 1938 a 1945 da Filial de Macau (Macau Branch Activity Report from 1938 until 1945).
AG-011–7–185.

Arquivo Histórico Ultramarino (Overseas Historical Archives), Lisbon, Portugal

Ministério das Colónias (Ministry of Colonies)
157, 1A, MU, GM, MÇ, 1938.
236, 1E, MU, GM, MÇ, 1942.

Espólio Gabriel Maurício Teixeira (Gabriel Maurício Teixeira Papers)
Documentos relativos a Macau (Macau-Related Documents).

Arquivo Nacional Torre to Tombo (National Archives), Lisbon, Portugal

Arquivo Oliveira Salazar (Oliveira Salazar Archives)
AOS, NE-2A2, cx. 422.
AOS, NE-10A2, cx. 768.
AOS, NE-2F1, Pt. 41.
AOS, NE-7B, Pt. 40.
AOS, PC-2D, cx. 587.
AOS, UL-5A, cx. 750.
AOS, UL-10A1, cx. 767.
AOS, UL-10A3, cx. 769.

Centre des Archives diplomatiques de La Courneuve (Diplomatic Archives at La Courneuve), Paris, France

Direction d'Asie et d'Océanie (Asia and Oceania Division), Goa – Macau – Timor, 1944–1967
125QO/6, Macao, Dossier general (Macau, General Folder).
125QO/7, Timor, Dossier general (Timor, General Folder).

Série Asie 1918–1940, sous-série Chine (Series Asia 1918–1940, Sub-series China)
32CPCOM/761, Maintien du traité des neuf puissances (Continuation of the Nine-Power Treaty).
32CPCOM/784, Portugal–Chine (Portugal–China).
32CPCOM/795, Concession française de Canton (French Concession in Guangzhou).

Vichy Guerre, 1939–1945, Asie (Vichy War, 1939–1945, Asia)
3GMII/93, Corps diplomatique étranger en Chine (Foreign Diplomatic Corps in China).
3GMII/94, Corps diplomatique chinois (Chinese Diplomatic Corps).
3GMII/122, Question de la reconnaissance du gouvernement de Nankin par les autres pays (Question of the Recognition of the Nanjing Government by Other Countries).

Franklin D. Roosevelt Presidential Library, New York, USA

Collection FDR-FDRPSF, Diplomatic Correspondence, 1933–1945, China, 1938: catalog.archives.gov/id/16618367.

Hong Kong Public Records Office, Hong Kong, SAR, China

Book 940.53 SOM 1945, Some Records of the Plans Made during the War against Japan by British Residents in Macao.
HKRS 30–1–1, Documents Presented to the P. R. O. by Mr Y. C. Liang, C. B. E., concerning Wartime Activities in Hong Kong & Macao in Which He Was Involved.
HKRS, 163–1–72, Repatriation of Japanese Civilians in Macao, 1946.
HKRS 170–1–333, Case Histories of Persons Authorised to Return from Macao to Hongkong, etc.
HKRS 170–1–334, Case Histories of Persons Authorized to Return from Macao to Hong Kong, 1945.
HKRS 170–1–359, Immigration: Applications Sent from B. C. Macao from Persons Desirous of Returning to Hongkong.

Imperial War Museum, London, UK

23=(512.318) 15 (Gossano [*sic*], Eddie), *Hong Kong Farewell.*
97/40/1, Private Papers of Mrs Fletcher.

Sound Archive
Catalogue no. 19926, Interview with Bernard Felix Xavier (1999).

International Committee of the Red Cross Archives, Geneva, Switzerland

B G 017 07–063, Prisonniers à Hong Kong (Prisoners in Hong Kong).
B G 017 07–068, Prisonniers à Hong Kong (Prisoners in Hong Kong).
B G 017 07–077, Prisonniers à Macao (Prisoners in Macau).
D AO CHINE1 01–086, Portuguese Red Cross Society, Macao.

National Archives and Records Administration, College Park, Maryland, USA

Record Group 38: Records of the Office of the Chief of Naval Operations
A1 27, Records of Inactive Naval Stations, Box 59.

Record Group 165: Records of the War Department General and Special Staffs

NM84 421, American–British Conversations Correspondence relating to Organizational Planning and Combat Operations, 1940–48, Box 37: 014. Japan Sec. 29 to Sec. 33.

Record Group 226: Records of the Office of Strategic Studies

UD 140, Washington and Pacific Coast Field Station Files, Boxes 53 and 54.

UD 173, Official Subject Records, Box 9.

National Archives of Australia, Canberra, Australia

Series no. A1539, 1942/W/2712, National Security (Exchange Control) Regulations – Trading with the Enemy Act 1939–1940 – Remittances to Portuguese Macao.

National Library of Australia, Canberra, Australia

Papers of J. M. Braga

MS 4300, Box 9, 3.2/2, Historical Work, Charles Boxer, Correspondence and Related Papers, 1936–1941.

MS 4300, Box 14, 4.1/15, Business and Community Affairs, Pre–World War II, 1920–1942.

MS 4300, Box 16, 4.2/2, Business and Community Affairs, Companhia das Aguas de Macau, 1929–1948.

MS 4300, Box 26, 4.7/1, Business and Community Affairs, Sir Robert Ho Tung, 1938–1957.

MS 4300, Box 52, 8.1/10, World War II, Reports, Minutes, Notes and Related Papers, Primarily re Conditions in Macau during the War and Plans for the Post-war Rehabilitation of Hong Kong, 1943–1945.

MS 4300, Box 52, 8.1/11, World War II, Correspondence, Notes, Ration Cards, Printed Material and Related Papers, 1942–1948.

MS 4300, Box 52, 8.1/14, World War II, Correspondence, Minutes, Reports, Postcards, Telegrams, Newsletters, Printed Material and Related Papers, Primarily re Life in Wartime Macau and Hong Kong, 1938–1945.

MS 4300, Box 52, 8.1/15, World War II, Invitations, Programs, Orders of Service and Other Ephemera, Primarily re Cultural Activities in Wartime Macau, 1942–1945.

MS 4300, Box 53, 8.1/18, World War II, Correspondence, Telegrams, News Summaries and Related Papers, Particularly re Braga's Work for Various Press Agencies Reporting on Life in Post-war Macau and Hong Kong, 1945–1946.

MS 4300, Box 53, 8.1/20, World War II, Correspondence, Reports, Minutes, Notes and Related Papers, Primarily re Plans for the Post-war Rehabilitation of Hong Kong, 1944–1945.
MS 4300, Box 84, 14.2/14, Newspaper Cuttings, Macau, 1927–1971.
MS 4300, Box 169, 8.1/27, Items on the Operations of the Allied Secret Service in Macao during WWII.
MS 4300, Box 169, 8.1/29, Items on the Operations of the Allied Secret Service in Macao during WWII.
MS 4300, Photographs, Box 14.

The British Library, London, UK

India Office Records and Private Papers

BL, IOR/L/PJ/8/334, Maintenance of Portuguese and Others Evacuated from Macao.

The National Archives, Kew, UK

Cabinet Office

CAB 121/508, Proposed Participation of Portugal in the War against Japan.

Colonial Office

CO 129/579/11/2, Sino–Japanese War: Seizure of Unauthorized Wireless Transmitting Apparatus.
CO 825/30/12, War with Japan: Hong Kong and Malayan Residents in Macao.

Foreign Office

FO 369/3267, Relief to Distressed British Subjects in Macao.
FO 371/20988, China.
FO 371/23427, Export of Arms to China.
FO 371/23501, China.
FO 371/24688, Hong Kong: Immigration: Defence: Evacuation.
FO 371/24700, China.
FO 371/24704, China.
FO 371/31630, Situation in Macao.
FO 371/31679, Work of the British Embassy at Chungking and Events in Free China.
FO 371/35731, Macao Electric Company.
FO 371/35732, Macao Electric Company.
FO 371/35733, Macao Electric Company.
FO 371/35734, Macao Electric Company.
FO 371/35735, Macao Electric Company.
FO 371/35736, Macao Electric Company.

FO 371/41564, Refugee Relief Department in Chungking.
FO 371/41619, Conditions in Macao.
FO 371/41620, Conditions in Macao.
FO 371/41662, Kwangsi–Kwangtung Leaders.
FO 371/46196, Clandestine Organisations in China and Indo-China.
FO 371/46199, Situation in the Portuguese Colony of Macao.
FO 371/46214, Situation in China, etc.
FO 371/46224, Overseas Chinese: Position in Malaya and Other Territories.
FO 371/46251, Administration and Future of Hong Kong after Japanese Surrender, etc.
FO 371/46253, Administration and Future of Hong Kong after Japanese Surrender, etc.
FO 371/46256, Administration and Future of Hong Kong after Japanese Surrender, etc.
FO 371/53617, Chinese Attitude to Macao: Future of Macao.
FO 676/410, Wang Ching Wei.

Special Operations Executive
HS 1/176, Miscellaneous; Portuguese Colony of Macao; VODKA Operation.
HS 9/799/1, Reider A Johannessen.
HS 9/1451/8, Michel Terestchenko.

Government Code and Cypher School
Diplomatic Section and Predecessors – Decrypts of Intercepted Diplomatic Communications:
HW 12/275.
HW 12/293.
HW 12/315.
HW 12/316.
HW 12/319.
HW 12/325.
HW 12/327.
HW 12/329.
HW 12/330.
Security of Allied Cyphers Sections – Security Files on Allied World War II Communications:
HW 40/84 – Enemy Exploitation of Communications related to Macao.

The University of Hong Kong Libraries Special Collections, Hong Kong, SAR, China

Personal Papers of Sir Lindsay Tasman Ride
MF 2530701, Rolls 2, 15, 18, 19.

Published Primary Sources

Auden, W. H., and C. Isherwood, *Journey to a War* (London, 1939, repr. 1973).

Blair, M., *Gudao, Lone Islet: The War Years in Shanghai* (Victoria, 2007).

Boletim Oficial da Colónia de Macau (*Official Bulletin of the Colony of Macau*) (1937–46).

Brandão, C. C., *Funo: Guerra em Timor* (*Funo: War in Timor*) (Oporto, 1953).

Cai, P. (ed.), *Koushu lishi: KangRi zhanzheng shiqi de Aomen* (*Oral History: Macau during the War of Resistance*) (Macau, 2005).

Callinan, B. J., *Independent Company: The 2/2 and 2/4 Australian Independent Companies in Portuguese Timor, 1941–1943* (London, 1953).

Campbell, A., *The Double Reds of Timor* (Swanbourne, 1995).

Cardoso, A. M., *Timor na 2ª Guerra Mundial: O Diário do Tenente Pires* (*Timor in the Second World War: Lieutenant Pires' Diary*) (Lisbon, 2007).

Chinese Ministry of Information, *China Handbook 1937–1945: A Comprehensive Survey of Major Developments in China in Eight Years of War* (New York, 1947).

The Chinese Year Book 1936–37 (Shanghai, 1937).

The Chinese Year Book 1940–1941 (Chongqing, 1941).

Choy, J. K., *My China Years 1911–1945: Practical Politics in China after the 1911 Revolution* (San Francisco, CA, 1974).

Collins, G. *Chinese Red* (London, 1932).

The Conference of Brussels November 3–24, 1937 (Washington, DC, 1938).

Cruz Vermelha Portuguesa (Portuguese Red Cross), *Boletim Oficial 1943* (*Official Bulletin 1943*), 1st semester (1943).

D'Almada e Castro, L., *Some Notes on the Portuguese in Hongkong* (Macau, 1949).

'Declarações do Sr. Governador de Macau à Imprensa' ('The Words of the Governor of Macau to the Press'), *Boletim Geral das Colónias* (*General Bulletin of the Colonies*), 22/254–55 (1946), pp. 7–11.

Epstein, I., *My China Eye: Memoirs of a Jew and a Journalist* (San Francisco, CA, 2005).

Fernandes, L. E., *De Pequim a Washington: Memórias de um Diplomata Português* (*From Beijing to Washington: Memoirs of a Portuguese Diplomat*) (Lisbon, 2007).

Field, E., *Twilight in Hong Kong* (London, 1960).

Fleming, Ian, *Thrilling Cities* (London, 2013).

Guangdong Provincial Archives, *Guangdong Aomen dang'an shiliao xuanbian* (*Selected Historical Materials about Macau from Guangdong*) (Beijing, 1999).

A Guerra vista de Cantão: Os relatórios de Vasco Martins Morgado, Cônsul-Geral de Portugal em Cantão, sobre a Guerra Sino-Japonesa (*The War Seen from Canton: The Reports of Vasco Martins Morgado, Portugal's Consul-General in Canton, about the Sino–Japanese War*), ed. A. V. Saldanha (Macau, 1998).

Guo, H., and Z. Luo (eds.), *Liang Yanming lieshi jinianji* (*Martyr Liang Yanming Memorial Collection*) (Beijing, 1946).

Harrop, P., *Hong Kong Incident* (London, 1943).

Koo, H. L., *An Autobiography As Told to Mary Van Rensselaer Thayer* (New York, 1943).

Kuo, H., *I've Come a Long Way* (New York, 1943).

Kuomintang Central Committee, *Zhongguo Guomindang zai haiwai* (*The KMT Overseas*) (Taipei, 1961).

Kuomintang Hong Kong–Macau General Branch, *Gang'Ao kangzhan xunguo lieshi jiniance* (*Album of Martyrs from Hong Kong and Macau during the War of Resistance*) (Hong Kong, 1946).

Li, F. T. O., and T. Harrison, *Much Beloved Daughter* (London, 1985).

Lima, F., and E. C. Torres, *Macau entre Dois Mundos* (*Macau between Two Worlds*) (Lisbon, 2004).

Lin, F., and Jiang, C. (eds.), *Pingmin shengyin: Aomen yu kangRi zhanzheng koushu lishi* (*Civilian Voices: Oral History of Macau in the War of Resistance*) (Guangzhou, 2015).

Lo, P. F., *It Is Dark Underground* (New York, 1946).

Macau Government Tourism Office, '"Love in Macau" premiere's [*sic*] in Beijing', Macao Tourism Industry Net (2006). https://bit.ly/3HGhBHZ.

Magalhães, J. C., *Macau e a China no Após Guerra* (*Macau and China in the Post-war*) (Macau, 1992).

McGivering, J., *Macao Remembers* (Oxford, 1999).

Ministry of Foreign Affairs, *Treaties between the Republic of China and Foreign States (1927–1957)* (Taipei, 1958).

Peck, G., *Two Kinds of Time* (Boston, MA, 1950).

Reeves, J. P., *The Lone Flag: Memoir of the British Consul in Macao during World War II*, ed. C. Day and R. Garrett (Hong Kong, 2014).

Repartição Central dos Serviços de Administração Civil: Secção de Estatística, *Anuário Estatístico de Macau: Ano de 1949* (*Macau Statistical Yearbook: Year of 1949*) (Macau, 1950).

Selwyn-Clarke, S., *Footprints: The Memoirs of Sir Selwyn Selwyn-Clarke* (Hong Kong, 1975).

Silva, A. A., *Eu estive em Macau durante a Guerra* (*I Was in Macau during the War*) (Macau, 1991).

Silva, A. P., 'Life and Learning in Wartime Macau', *UMA News Bulletin* 32/1 (2009), pp. 8–11. www.uma-casademacau.com/files/9212/9669/0353/UMA_News_Bulletin__All_Summer_2009.pdf.

Stowe, L., *They Shall Not Sleep* (New York, 1944).

Teixeira, M., '"A Alfandega Roubada" e "O Barco Roubado"' ('The Stolen Customs Station' and 'The Stolen Boat'), *Boletim Eclesiástico da Diocese de Macau* (*Macau Diocese Ecclesiastic Bulletin*), 885 (1978), pp. 522–6.

Teixeira, M., 'The Bonnie and Clyde of Macao', in D. Pittis and S. J. Henders (eds.), *Macao: Mysterious Decay and Romance* (Hong Kong, 1997), pp. 3–13.

Teixeira, M., 'Macau durante a Guerra: Doce Visão de Paz! ('Macau during the War: Sweet Vision of Peace!'), *Boletim Eclesiástico da Diocese de Macau* (*Macau Diocese Ecclesiastic Bulletin*), 885 (1978), pp. 497–518.

White, T. H., and A. Jacoby, *Thunder Out of China* (New York, 1946, repr. 1975).

Wright-Nooth, G., and M. Adkin, *Prisoner of the Turnip Heads: Horror, Hunger and Humour in Hong Kong, 1941–1945* (London, 1994).

Wu, Y. F., 'Women in the War', *Chinese Recorder and Educational Review*, 71/6 (1940), pp. 369–73.

Yu, P., 'Wartime Experiences in Hong Kong and China (Part 2)', in C. Matthews and O. Cheung (eds.), *Dispersal and Renewal: Hong Kong University during the War Years* (Hong Kong, 1998), pp. 313–34.

Zhang, K. (ed.), *Eyewitnesses to the Massacre: American Missionaries Bear Witness to Japanese Atrocities in Nanjing* (New York, 2001).
Zhou, Y., *Zhou Yongneng xiansheng fangwen jilu* (*The Reminiscences of Mr Chou Yung-neng*) (Taipei, 1984).

Books and Articles

Abbenhuis, M., *An Age of Neutrals: Great Power Politics, 1815–1915* (Cambridge, 2014).
af Malmborg, M., *Neutrality and State-Building in Sweden* (Hampshire, 2001).
Adelman, J., 'What Is Global History Now?', *Aeon*, 2 Mar. 2017. aeon.co/essays/is-global-history-still-possible-or-has-it-had-its-moment.
Alden, D., *Charles R. Boxer: An Uncommon Life* (Lisbon, 2001).
Allsop, A., 'A Borrowed Place: Jewish Refugees in Hong Kong, 1938–1949' (PhD thesis, King's College London, 2022).
Alves, J. M. S., *Macau: O Primeiro Século de um Porto Internacional* (*Macau: The First Century of an International Port*) (Lisbon, 2007).
Amaro, A. M., 'Sons and Daughters of the Soil', *Review of Culture*, 20 (1994), pp. 16–67.
The Art of Kao Chien-Fu (Hong Kong, 1978).
Bailey, S. K., 'Briefing Failure in Ready Room 4: The Question of Culpability for U.S. Navy Air Strikes on Macau, 16 January 1945', *Journal of the Royal Asiatic Society Hong Kong Branch*, 58 (2018), pp. 30–54.
Baker, M., 'City Limits on China's Central Plains: Zhengzhou, Kaifeng, and the Making of Spatial Inequality, 1900–1960' (PhD thesis, Yale University, 2017).
Barreiros, J. A., *O Homem das Cartas de Londres* (*The Man of the London Letters*) (Lisbon, 2003).
Barreto, I. L. F. (ed.), *Macau during the Sino–Japanese War / Kangzhan shiqi de Aomen / Macau Durante a Guerra Sino-Japonesa* (Macau, 2002).
Barreto, L. F., *Macau: Poder e Saber – Séculos XVI e XVII* (*Macau: Power and Knowledge – 16th and 17th Centuries*) (Lisbon, 2006).
Barrett, D. P., 'The Wang Jingwei Regime, 1940–1945: Continuities and Disjunctures with Nationalist China', in D. P. Barrett and L. N. Shyu (eds.), *Chinese Collaboration with Japan, 1932–1945: The Limits of Accommodation* (Stanford, CA, 2001), pp. 102–15.
Barrett, D. P., and L. N. Shyu (eds.), *Chinese Collaboration with Japan, 1932–1945: The Limits of Accommodation* (Stanford, CA, 2001).
Bastid-Bruguière, M., 'Les Relations entre l'Indochine de Decoux et le Gouvernement de Wang Jingwei Pendant la Deuxième Guerre Mondiale' ('Relations between Decoux's Indochina and the Wang Jingwei Government during the Second World War'), in L. Cesari and D. Varaschin (eds.), *Les Relations Franco–Chinoises au Vingtième Siècle et leurs Antécédents* (*Sino–French Relations in the Twentieth Century and Their Antecedents*) (Arras, 2003), pp. 217–47.
Benton, G., *New Fourth Army: Communist Resistance along the Yangtze and the Huai, 1938–1941* (Berkeley, CA, 1999).

Bergère, M. C., 'The Purge in Shanghai, 1945–6: The Sarly Affair and the End of the French Concession', in W. H. Yeh (ed.), *Wartime Shanghai* (London, 1998), pp. 161–80.

Bergère, M. C., *Shanghai: China's Gateway to Modernity* (Stanford, CA, 2009).

Bethencourt, F., 'Political Configurations and Local Powers', in F. Bethencourt and D. R. Curto (eds.), *Portuguese Oceanic Expansion, 1400–1800* (Cambridge, 2007), pp. 197–254.

Bethencourt, F., and D. R. Curto, 'Introduction', in F. Bethencourt and D. R. Curto (eds.), *Portuguese Oceanic Expansion, 1400–1800* (Cambridge, 2007), pp. 1–18.

Bickers, R., *Britain in China: Community, Culture and Colonialism, 1900–1949* (Manchester, 1999).

Bickers, R., 'The Business of a Secret War: Operation "Remorse" and SOE Salesmanship in Wartime China', *Intelligence and National Security*, 16/4 (2001), pp. 11–36.

Bickers R., 'The Chinese Maritime Customs at War, 1941–45', *Journal of Imperial and Commonwealth History*, 36/2 (2008), pp. 295–311.

Bickers, R., *Empire Made Me: An Englishman Adrift in Shanghai* (London, 2004).

Bickers, R., *Out of China: How the Chinese Ended the Era of Western Domination* (London, 2017).

Boecking, F., *No Great Wall: Trade, Tariffs, and Nationalism in Republican China, 1927–1945* (Cambridge, MA, 2017).

Botas, J. F. O., *Macau 1937–1945: Os Anos da Guerra* (*Macau 1937–1945: The War Years*) (Macau, 2012).

Boxer, C. R., *Fidalgos in the Far East 1550–1770* (Oxford, 1948, repr. 1968).

Boxer, C. R., *The Portuguese Seaborne Empire, 1415–1825* (London, 1969, repr. 1977).

Boyle, J. H., *China and Japan at War, 1937–1945: The Politics of Collaboration* (Stanford, CA, 1972).

Braga, I. M. P., *Macau Durante a II Guerra Mundial: Sociedade, Educação Física e Desporto* (*Macau during World War II: Society, Physical Education and Sport*) (Macau, 2003).

Braga, J. M., *Hong Kong and Macao* (Hong Kong, 1960).

Braga, S., 'Nossa Gente (Our People): The Portuguese Refugee Community in Wartime Macau', in G. C. Gunn (ed.), *Wartime Macau: Under the Japanese Shadow* (Hong Kong, 2016), pp. 116–40.

Braga, S., 'Rescued from Certain Death', *Casa Down Under Newsletter*, 23/4 (2011), pp. 1–4. casademacau.org.au/wp-content/uploads/newsletters/11_4CasaOct2011.pdf.

Brook, T., *Collaboration: Japanese Agents and Local Elites in Wartime China* (Cambridge, MA, 2005).

Brook, T., 'Collaborationist Nationalism in Occupied Wartime China', in T. Brook and A. Schmid (eds.), *Nation Work: Asian Elites and National Identities* (Ann Arbor, MI, 2000), pp. 159–90.

Brooks, C., *American Exodus: Second-Generation Chinese Americans in China, 1901–1949* (Oakland, CA, 2019).

Bunker, G. E., *The Peace Conspiracy: Wang Ching-wei and the China War, 1937–1941* (Cambridge, MA, 1972).

Cabral, J. P., 'A Composição Social de Macau' ('Macau's Social Composition'), in F. Bethencourt and K. Chaudhuri (eds.), *História da Expansão Portuguesa, Vol. V: O Último Império e Recentramento (1930–1998)* (*History of the Portuguese Expansion, Vol. V: The Last Empire and Recentring (1930–1998)*) (Lisbon, 1999), pp. 275–301.

Cabral, J. P., 'The "Ethnic" Composition of Macao', *Review of Culture*, 20 (1994), pp. 229–38.

Caeiro, A., *Peregrinação Vermelha: O Longo Caminho até Pequim* (*Red Pilgrimage: The Long Path to Beijing*) (Lisbon, 2016).

Calthorpe, D., 'About *The Lone Flag* and John Pownall Reeves', in J. P. Reeves, *The Lone Flag*, ed. C. Day and R. Garrett (Hong Kong, 2014), pp. 167–80.

Camacho, J. M. S., *Chinese Mexicans: Transpacific Migration and the Search for a Homeland, 1910–1960* (Chapel Hill, NC, 2012).

Cannon, M. D., 'Experience, Memory and the Construction of the Past: Remembering Macau 1941–1945' (MA thesis, University of British Columbia, 2001).

Carroll, J. M., 'Chinese Collaboration in the Making of British Hong Kong', in T. W. Ngo (ed.), *Hong Kong's History: State and Society under Colonial Rule* (London, 1999), pp. 13–29.

Carroll, J. M., *The Hong Kong–China Nexus* (Cambridge, 2022).

Carvalho, R. L., *A Mãe* (*The Mother*) (Pedreiras, 2001).

Cassel, P. K., *Grounds of Judgment: Extraterritoriality and Imperial Power in Nineteenth-Century China and Japan* (Oxford, 2012).

Castro, B., *Shanghai Dancing* (New York, 2003).

Ch'i, H. S., 'The Military Dimension, 1942–1945', in J. C. Hsiung and S. I. Levine (eds.), *China's Bitter Victory: The War with Japan 1937–1945* (Armonk, NY, 1992), pp. 157–84.

Chan, C. S., *The Macanese Diaspora in British Hong Kong: A Century of Transimperial Drifting* (Amsterdam, 2021).

Chan, C. S., 'Macau Martyr of Portuguese Traitor? The Macanese Communities of Macau, Hong Kong and Shanghai and the Portuguese Nation', *Historical Research*, 93/262 (2020), pp. 754–68.

Chan, G. Y. M., *The Chinese Communists' East River Column, Guangdong, 1937–1945* (Leeds, 1998).

Chan, G. Y. M., 'Hong Kong and Communist Guerrilla Resistance in South China, 1937–1945', *Twentieth-Century China*, 29/1 (2003), pp. 39–63.

Chan, M. K., *The Luso–Macau Connections in Sun Yatsen's Modern Chinese Revolution* (Macau, 2011).

Chan, S. J., *East River Column: Hong Kong Guerrillas in the Second World War and After* (Hong Kong, 2009).

Chan Lau, K. C., *China, Britain and Hong Kong, 1895–1945* (Hong Kong, 1990).

Chang, V. K. L., *Forgotten Diplomacy: The Modern Remaking of Dutch–Chinese Relations, 1927–1950* (Leiden, 2019).

Chen, J. C., *Guilty of Indigence: The Urban Poor in China, 1900–1953* (Princeton, NJ, 2012).
'Chen Shaoling', in *Baidu baike*. baike.baidu.com/item/陈少陵.
Chen, W., 'Guan Shanyue', Grove Art Online (2002). doi.org/10.1093/gao/9781884446054.article.T097478.
Chen, Z., 'The Rise of Macao Chinese Cultural Nationalism during the Anti-Japanese War' (MA thesis, University of Macau, 2013).
Cheng, C. M. B., *Macau: A Cultural Janus* (Hong Kong, 1999).
Cheung, R., 'Wartime Feminists in the City of Ram: Women's Movement in the City of Guangzhou during the Second World War', *UCLA Center for the Study of Women* (2009). eprints.cdlib.org/uc/item/77k5j421.
Ching, M. B., 'Itinerant Singers: Triangulating the Canton–Hong Kong–Macau Soundscape', in E. Tagliacozzo, H. F. Siu and P. C. Perdue (eds.), *Asia Inside Out: Itinerant People* (Cambridge, MA, 2019), pp. 244–70.
Chiu, L. M. W., 'The South China Daily News and Wang Jingwei's Peace Movement, 1939–41', *Journal of the Royal Asiatic Society Hong Kong Branch*, 50 (2010), pp. 343–70.
Christensen, E. J., *In War and Famine: Missionaries in China's Honan Province in the 1940s* (Montreal, 2005).
Chu, C. Y. Y., *The Maryknoll Sisters in Hong Kong, 1921–1969: In Love with the Chinese* (New York, 2004).
Clarence-Smith, G., *The Third Portuguese Empire 1825–1975: A Study in Economic Imperialism* (Manchester, 1985).
Clayton, C., 'The Hapless Imperialist? Portuguese Rule in 1960s Macau', in B. Goodman and D. S. G. Goodman (eds.), *Twentieth-Century Colonialism and China: Localities, the Everyday and the World* (Abingdon, 2012), pp. 212–23.
Clayton, C., *Sovereignty at the Edge: Macau & the Question of Chineseness* (Harvard, MA, 2009).
Cleary, P., *The Men Who Came Out of the Ground* (Sydney, 2010).
Coates, A., *Macao and the British 1637–1842: Prelude to Hong Kong* (Oxford, 1988).
Coble, P. M., *China's War Reporters: The Legacy of Resistance against Japan* (Cambridge, MA, 2015).
Coble, P. M., 'Chinese Capitalists and the Japanese: Collaboration and Resistance in the Shanghai Area, 1937–45', in *Wartime Shanghai*, ed. W. H. Yeh (London, 1998), pp. 57–77.
Coble, P. M., *Chinese Capitalists in Japan's New Order: The Occupied Lower Yangzi, 1937–1945* (Berkeley, CA, 2003).
Coble, P. M., 'The National Salvation Movement and Social Networks in Republican Shanghai', in N. Dillon and J. C. Oi (eds.), *At the Crossroads of Empires: Middlemen, Social Networks, and State-Building in Republican Shanghai* (Stanford, CA, 2008), pp. 110–30.
Cole, R., *Propaganda, Censorship and Irish Neutrality in the Second World War* (Oxford, 2006).
Conceição, D. *Cheong-Sam: A Cabaia (Cheongsam)* (Macau, n.d.).

Cónim, C. N. P. S., and M. F. B. Teixeira, *Macau e a sua População, 1500–2000: Aspectos Demográficos, Sociais e Económicos* (*Macau and Its Population, 1500–2000: Demographic, Social, and Economic Aspects*) (Macau, 1998).

Cornet, C., 'The Bumpy End of the French Concession and French Influence in Shanghai, 1937–1946', in C. Henriot and W. H. Yeh (eds.), *In the Shadow of the Rising Sun: Shanghai under Japanese Occupation* (Cambridge, 2004), pp. 257–76.

Craft, S. G., 'Opponents of Appeasement: Western-Educated Chinese Diplomats and Intellectuals and Sino-Japanese Relations, 1932–37', *Modern Asian Studies*, 35/1 (2001), pp. 195–216.

Croizier, R., *Art and Revolution in Modern China: The Lingnan (Cantonese) School of Painting, 1906–1951* (Berkeley, CA, 1988).

Culp, R., *Articulating Citizenship: Civic Education and Student Politics in Southeastern China, 1912–1940* (Cambridge, MA, 2007).

Cunha, L., *A Publicidade em Macau (1822–1965)* (*Advertising in Macau (1822–1965)*) (Macau, 2000).

Cunha, L., 'Timor: A Guerra Esquecida' ('Timor: The Forgotten War'), *Macau*, 45 (1996), pp. 32–46.

d'Água, F. B., *Le Timor Oriental face à la Seconde Guerra Mondiale (1941–1945)* (*East Timor in the Second World War (1941–1945)*) (Lisbon, 2007).

Day, C., 'Not Just Refugee Relief: John Reeves' Work As British Consul in Macao in WWII', *Journal of the Royal Asiatic Society Hong Kong Branch*, 60 (2020), pp. 115–37.

Deng, K. S, *Aomen lishi (1840–1949 nian)* (*History of Macau (1840–1949)*) (Macau, 1995).

Deng, K. S., and X. M. Lu (eds.), *Yue Gang Ao jindai guanxi shi* (*Modern History of Guangdong–Hong Kong–Macau Relations*) (Guangzhou, 1996).

Deng, K. S., J. M. Lu, and R. F. Yang, *Aomen shihua* (*A Brief History of Macau*) (Beijing, 2011).

Dias, A. G., *Diáspora Macaense: Macau, Hong Kong, Xangai (1850–1952)* (*Macanese Diaspora: Macau, Hong Kong, Shanghai (1850–1952)*) (Lisbon, 2014).

Dias, A. G., 'The Origins of the Macao Community in Shanghai: Hong Kong's Emigration (1850–1909)', *Bulletin of Portuguese–Japanese Studies*, 17 (2008), pp. 197–224.

Dias, A. G., *Portugal, Macau e a Internacionalização da Questão do Ópio (1909–1925)* (*Portugal, Macau and the Internationalization of the Opium Question (1909–1925)*) (Macau, 2004).

Dias, A. G., 'Os Refugiados de Hong Kong (1942)' ('The Hong Kong Refugees (1942)'), *Revista de Cultura* (*Review of Culture*), 34 (2010), pp. 117–28.

Dias, A. G., *Refugiados de Xangai, Macau (1937–1964)* (*Shanghai Refugees, Macau (1937–1964)*) (Macau, 2015).

Dillon, N., 'Middlemen in the Chinese Welfare State: The Role of Philanthropists in Refugee Relief in Wartime Shanghai', *Studies in Comparative International Development*, 46 (2011), pp. 22–45.

Dillon, N., 'The Politics of Philanthropy: Social Networks and Refugee Relief in Shanghai, 1932–1949', in N. Dillon and J. C. Oi (eds.), *At the Crossroads of*

Empires: Middlemen, Social Networks, and State-Building in Republican Shanghai (Stanford, CA, 2008), pp. 179–205.

Drayton R., and D. Motadel, 'Discussion: The Futures of Global History', *Journal of Global History*, 13 (2018), pp. 1–21.

Edgar, B., 'Myths, Messages and Manoeuvres: Franklin Gimson in August 1945', *Journal of the Royal Asiatic Society Hong Kong Branch*, 58 (2018), pp. 7–29.

Elleman, B. A., 'The End of Extraterritoriality in China: The Case of the Soviet Union, 1917–1960', *Republican China*, 21/2 (1996), pp. 65–89.

Elphick, P., *Far Eastern File: The Intelligence War in the Far East, 1930–1945* (London, 1997).

Evans, B., *Ireland during the Second World War: Farewell to Plato's Cave* (Manchester, 2014).

Faure, D., *Emperor and Ancestor: State and Lineage in South China* (Stanford, CA, 2007).

Fedorowich, K., 'Doomed from the Outset? Internment and Civilian Exchange in the Far East: The British Failure over Hong Kong, 1941–45', *Journal of Imperial and Commonwealth History*, 25/1 (1997), pp. 113–40.

Fei C., *Aomen sibai nian* (*Macau 400 Years*) (Shanghai, 1988).

Fei C., *Macao 400 Years* (Shanghai, 1996).

Feng, C., and Q. Xia, 'Bentu zhi wai: Aomen kangRi zhanzheng yanjiu shuping' (Outside the Territory: Studies on the War of Resistance against Japan in Macau), *Minguo dang'an* (*Republican Archives*), 3 (2013), pp. 125–33.

Ferlanti, F., 'The New Life Movement in Jiangxi Province, 1934–1938', *Modern Asian Studies*, 44/5 (2010), pp. 961–1000.

Fernandes, H. S., *Mong-Há* (Macau, 1998).

Fernandes, H. S., *Nam Van: Contos de Macau* (*Nanwan: Macau Short Stories*) (Macau, 1997).

Fernandes, M. S., *Confluência de Interesses: Macau nas Relações Luso–Chinesas Contemporâneas 1945–2005* (*Confluence of Interests: Macau in Contemporary Portuguese–Chinese Relations 1945–2005*) (Lisbon, 2008).

Fernandes, M. S., 'How to Relate to a Colonial Power on Its Shore: Macau in the Chinese Foreign Policy, 1949–1965', *Bulletin of Portuguese–Japanese Studies*, 17 (2008), pp. 225–50.

Fernandes, M. S., 'The Normalisation of Portuguese–Chinese Relations and Macao's Handover to Mainland China, 1974–79', *China: An International Journal*, 13/1 (2015), pp. 3–21.

Fernandes, M. S., *Sinopse de Macau nas Relações Luso–Chinesas – 1945–1995: Cronologia e Documentos* (*Synopsis of Portuguese–Chinese Relations – 1945–1995: Chronology and Documents*) (Lisbon, 2000).

Ferreira, J. M., 'Timor', in F. Rosas and J. M. B. Brito (eds.), *Dicionário de História do Estado Novo* (*Estado Novo History Dictionary*), vol. 2 (Lisbon, 1996), pp. 974–6.

Field, A. D., *Shanghai's Dancing World: Cabaret Culture and Urban Politics, 1919–1954* (Hong Kong, 2010).

Fishel, W. R., *The End of Extraterritoriality in China* (Berkeley, CA, 1974).

Fodor, D. J., *The Neutrals* (Alexandria, VA, 1983).

Fok, F. C., *O Dr. Sun Yat-sen e a sua Profissão Médica em Macau* (*Dr Sun Yat-sen and His Medical Profession in Macau*) (Macau, 2014).
Fok, F. C., *Estudos sobre a Instalação dos Portugueses em Macau* (*Studies on the Portuguese Settlement in Macau*) (Lisbon, 1996).
Fragomen Jr, A. T., 'The Refugee: A Problem of Definition', *Case Western Reserve Journal of International Law*, 3/1 (1970), pp. 45–69.
French, P., *Strangers on the Praia: A Tale of Refugees and Resistance in Wartime Macao* (Hong Kong, 2020).
Fu, P., *Passivity, Resistance, and Collaboration: Intellectual Choices in Occupied Shanghai, 1937–1945* (Stanford, CA, 1993).
Gang'Ao dabaike quanshu (*Encyclopedia of Hong Kong & Macao*) (Guangzhou, 1993).
Garrett, R. J., *The Defences of Macao: Forts, Ships and Weapons over 450 Years* (Hong Kong, 2010).
Garver, J. W., 'China's Wartime Diplomacy', in J. C. Hsiung and S. I. Levine (eds.), *China's Bitter Victory: The War with Japan 1937–1945* (Armonk, NY, 1992), pp. 3–32.
Gin, O. K., 'Cash and Blood: The Chinese Community and the Japanese Occupation of Borneo, 1941–45', in C. de Matos and M. E. Caprio (eds.), *Japan As the Occupier and the Occupied* (London, 2015), pp. 152–71.
Glang, N. F., 'Back-Channel Diplomacy and the Sino–German Relationship, 1939–1945' (PhD thesis, University of Sheffield, 2014).
Godinho, J., 'A History of Games of Chance in Macau: Part 2 – The Foundation of the Macau Gaming Industry', *Gaming Law Review and Economics*, 17/2 (2013), pp. 107–16.
Goodman, B., and D. S. G. Goodman, 'Introduction: Colonialism in China', in B. Goodman and D. S. G. Goodman (eds.), *Twentieth-Century Colonialism and China: Localities, the Everyday and the World* (Abingdon, 2012), pp. 1–22.
Goto, K., *Tensions of Empire: Japan and Southeast Asia in the Colonial and Postcolonial World* (Athens, OH, 2003).
Gunn, G. C., 'The British Army Aid Group (BAAG) and the Anti-Japanese Resistance Movement in Macau', in G. C. Gunn (ed.), *Wartime Macau: Under the Japanese Shadow* (Hong Kong, 2016), pp. 141–65.
Gunn, G. C., 'Hunger amidst Plenty: Rice Supply and Livelihood in Wartime Macau', in G. C. Gunn (ed.), *Wartime Macau: Under the Japanese Shadow* (Hong Kong, 2016), pp. 72–93.
Gunn, G. C., 'Introduction', in G. C. Gunn (ed.), *Wartime Macau: Under the Japanese Shadow* (Hong Kong, 2016), pp. 1–24.
Gunn, G. C. (ed.), *Wartime Macau: Under the Japanese Shadow* (Hong Kong, 2016).
Gunn, G. C., 'Wartime Macau in the Wider Diplomatic Sphere', in G. C. Gunn (ed.), *Wartime Macau: Under the Japanese Shadow* (Hong Kong, 2016), pp. 25–54.
Gunn, G. C., *Wartime Portuguese Timor: The Azores Connection* (Clayton, 1988).
Guo, L., 'Shilun Aomen zai Guangdong kangzhan zhong de diwei he zuoyong' ('On Macau's Position and Function in the War of Resistance in Guangdong'),

Zhanjiang shifan xueyuan xuebao (*Journal of Zhanjiang Teachers College*), 20/4 (1999), pp. 99–104.
Hamilton, P. E., *Made in Hong Kong: Transpacific Networks and a New History of Globalization* (New York, 2021).
Hao, Y., and J. Wang (eds.), *Macao and Sino–US Relations* (Lanham, MD, 2011).
Hayashi, H., 'Massacre of Chinese in Singapore and Its Coverage in Postwar Japan', in A. Yoji and Y. Mako (eds.), *New Perspectives on the Japanese Occupation in Malaya and Singapore, 1941–1945* (Singapore, 2008), pp. 234–49.
Hei, R., and H. Chen, '1927–1949 nian Guomindang Aomen zhibu de dangwu kaocha' ('The Party Affairs of the KMT Macau Branch in 1927–1949'), *Aomen yanjiu* (*Journal of Macau Studies*), 54/10 (2009), pp. 131–5.
Henriot, C., 'Rice, Power and People: The Politics of Food Supply in Wartime Shanghai (1937–1945)', *Twentieth-Century China*, 26/1 (2000), pp. 41–84.
Henriot, C., 'Shanghai and the Experience of War: The Fate of Refugees', *European Journal of East Asian Studies*, 5/2 (2006), pp. 215–45.
Henriot, C., Shi L., and C. Aubrun, *The Population of Shanghai (1865–1953)* (Leiden, 2019).
Henriot, C., and W. H. Yeh, 'Introduction', in C. Henriot and W. H. Yeh (eds.), *In the Shadow of the Rising Sun: Shanghai under Japanese Occupation* (Cambridge, 2004), pp. 1–14.
Hofer, W., *Neutrality As the Principle of Swiss Foreign Policy* (Zurich, 1957).
Horne, G., *Race War! White Supremacy and the Japanese Attack on the British Empire* (New York, 2004).
Huang, M., and H. Yang, 'Nationalist China's Negotiating Position during the Stalemate, 1938–1945', in D. P. Barrett and L. N. Shyu (eds.), *Chinese Collaboration with Japan, 1932–1945: The Limits of Accommodation* (Stanford, CA, 2001), pp. 56–76.
Huang, Q. H., *ZhongPu guanxi shi (1513–1999)* (*History of Sino–Portuguese Relations, 1513–1999*), vol. 3 (Hefei, 2006).
Huang, W., and L. Chen (eds.), *Haojiang fengyun er'nü: Aomen sijie jiuzaihui kangRi jiuguo shiji* (*Children of Haojiang: Macau's Four Circles Disaster Relief Association Activities of Resistance Against the Japanese and for National Salvation*) (Macau, 1990).
Huang, Y., 'Ru shang bense: Gao Kening de cishan shiye' ('Confucian Merchant: Gao Kening's Charitable Activities'), *Wenhua zazhi* (*Review of Culture*), 93 (2014), pp. 38–44.
Huang, Y., *Tong Shan Tang yu Aomen huaren shehui* (*The Tung Sin Tong and Macau's Chinese Society*) (Beijing, 2012).
Hung, C. T., *War and Popular Culture: Resistance in Modern China* (Berkeley, CA, 1994).
Hwang, D., 'Wartime Collaboration in Question: An Examination of the Postwar Trials of the Chinese Collaborators', *Inter-Asia Cultural Studies*, 6/1 (2005), pp. 75–97.
Israel, J., *Lianda: A Chinese University in War and Revolution* (Stanford, CA, 1998).

Jackson I., *Shaping Modern Shanghai: Colonialism in China's Global City* (Cambridge, 2018).

Janeiro, H. P., *Salazar e Pétain: Relações Luso-Francesas durante a Segunda Guerra Mundial (1940–44)* (*Salazar and Pétain: Portuguese–French Relations during the Second World War (1940–44)*) (Lisbon, 1998).

Jin, G. P., and Z. Wu, 'Teria havido acordos secretos entre Portugal e o Japão surante a Segunda Guerra Mundial?' (Were There Secret Agreements between Portugal and Japan during the Second World War?), *Administração* 14/51 (2001), pp. 239–75.

Jordan, D. A., *China's Trial by Fire: The Shanghai War of 1932* (Ann Arbor, MI, 2001).

Jorge, C., and R. B. Coelho, *Roque Choi: Um Homem Dois Sistemas* (*Roque Choi: A Man Two Systems*) (Macau, 2015).

Karsh, E., *Neutrality and Small States* (London, 1988).

King, F. H. H., *The History of the Hongkong and Shanghai Banking Corporation, Volume III – The Hong Kong Bank between the Wars and the Bank Interned, 1919–1945: Return from Grandeur* (Cambridge, 1988).

Kong, V., 'Exclusivity and Cosmopolitanism: Multi-ethnic Civil Society in Interwar Hong Kong', *Historical Journal*, 63/5 (2020), pp. 1281–1302.

Koo, B. H. M., *The Portuguese in Hongkong and China: Their Beginning, Settlement and Progress to 1949*, vol. 2 (Macau, 2013).

Kuo, H. Y., *Networks beyond Empires: Chinese Business and Nationalism in the Hong Kong–Singapore Corridor, 1914–1941* (Leiden, 2014).

Kushner, B., *Men to Devils, Devils to Men: Japanese War Crimes and Chinese Justice* (Cambridge, MA, 2015).

Kushner, B., *The Thought War: Japanese Imperial Propaganda* (Honolulu, HI, 2006).

Kushner, B., and A. Levidis (eds.), *In the Ruins of the Japanese Empire: Imperial Violence, State Destruction, and the Reordering of Modern Japan* (Hong Kong, 2020).

Kushner, B., and S. Muminov (eds.), *The Dismantling of Japan's Empire in East Asia: Deimperialization, Postwar Legitimation and Imperial Afterlife* (London, 2017).

Kushner B., and S. Muminov (eds.), *Overcoming Empire in Post-Imperial East Asia: Repatriation, Redress and Rebuilding* (London, 2019).

Lam, N. L., '"The Song of Selling Olives": Acoustic Experience and Cantonese Identity in Canton, Hong Kong, and Macau across the Great Divide of 1949', *China Perspectives*, 3 (2019), pp. 9–16.

Lary, D., *The Chinese People at War: Human Suffering and Social Transformation, 1937–1945* (Cambridge, 2010).

Lary, D., 'A Ravaged Place: The Devastation of the Xuzhou Region, 1938', in D. Lary and S. MacKinnon (eds.), *Scars of War: The Impact of Warfare on Modern China* (Vancouver, 2001), pp. 98–116.

Lees, J. *The Fan Tan Players* (Dingwall, 2009).

Leitz, C., *Nazi Germany and Neutral Europe during the Second World War* (Manchester, 2000).

Levi, W., 'Portuguese Timor and the War', *Far Eastern Survey*, 15/14 (1946), pp. 221–3.

Li, Y. H., 'Lunxian qian guomin zhengfu zai Xianggang de wenjiao huodong' ('Culture and Education Activities by the National Government in Hong Kong before the Occupation'), in *Gang'Ao yu jindai Zhongguo xueshu yanjiuhui lunwen ji* (*A Summary of the Symposium on Hong Kong, Macao and Modern China*) (Taipei, 2000), pp. 440–76.

Li, Y. H., 'Wu Tiecheng yu zhanshi Guomindang zai Gang'Ao de dangwu huodong' ('Wu Tiecheng and Kuomintang Party Activities in Hong Kong and Macau during the War'), in H. Y. Chen (ed.), *Wu Tiecheng yu jindai Zhongguo* (*Wu Tiecheng and Modern Chinese History*) (Taipei, 2012), pp. 64–88.

Li, Z., 'Approaches of Chinese Newspapers in Macau and Their Roles in Four Fields under the Influence of Nationalism during the Sino–Japanese War (1937–1945)' (MA thesis, University of Macau, 2013).

Liao, H., '*Shang* and *Shan*: Charitable Networks of the "Four Great Department Stores" and Their Associated Chinese–Australian Families 1900–1949 (PhD thesis, Swinburne University of Technology, 2018).

Lin, F., and X. Wang (eds.), *Gudao yingxiang: Aomen yu kangRi zhanzheng tuzhi* (*Lone Island Images: Pictorial History of Macau and the War of Resistance against Japan*) (Guangzhou, 2015).

Lin, H. T., and S. F. Wu, 'America's China Policy Revisited: Regionalism, Regional Leaders, and Regionalized Aid (1947–49)', *Chinese Historical Review*, 19/2 (2012), pp. 107–27.

Lin, M. H., 'Overseas Chinese Merchants and Multiple Nationality: A Means for Reducing Commercial Risk (1895–1935)', *Modern Asian Studies*, 35/4 (2001), pp. 985–1009.

Lincoln, T., 'Fleeing from Firestorms: Government, Cities, Native Place Associations and Refugees in the Anti-Japanese War of Resistance', *Urban History*, 38/3 (2011), pp. 437–56.

Lincoln, T., *Urbanizing China in War and Peace: The Case of Wuxi County* (Honolulu, HI, 2015).

Liu, G. (ed.), *Zhongguo Guomindang bai nian renwu quanshu* (*Book of 100 Years of KMT Figures*) (Beijing, 2005).

Liu, J., 'Defiant Retreat: The Relocation of Middle Schools to China's Interior, 1937–1945', *Frontiers of History in China*, 8/4 (2013), pp. 558–84.

Liu, L., 'Imagining the Refugee: The Emergence of a State Welfare System in the War of Resistance', in J. A Cook, J. Goldstein, M. D. Johnson and S. Schmalzer (eds.), *Visualizing Modern China: Image, History, and Memory, 1750–Present* (Lanham, MD, 2014), pp. 165–83.

Liu, X., and H. Huang, 'Aomen Zhongwen baozhi zai kangzhan moqi de xinwen bianji kuangjia yanjiu' ('The Frame of Macau Chinese Newspaper at the End of the Anti-Japanese War'), *Guoji xinwen jie* (*International Press*), 1 (2013), pp. 134–42.

Lochery, N., *Lisbon: War in the Shadows of the City of Light, 1939–1945* (New York, 2011).

Lopes, H. F. S., 'The Impact of Refugees in Neutral Hong Kong and Macau', *Historical Journal*, 66/1 (2023), pp. 210–36.

Lopes, H. F. S., 'Inter-imperial Humanitarianism: The Macau Delegation of the Portuguese Red Cross during the Second World War', *Journal of Imperial and Commonwealth History*, 46/6 (2018), pp. 1125–47.

Lopes, H. F. S., 'The Red Cross in Wartime Macau and Its Global Connections', in N. Wylie, M. Oppenheimer and J. Crossland (eds.), *The Red Cross Movement: Myths, Practices and Turning Points* (Manchester, 2020), pp. 264–81.

Lopes, H. F. S., 'Wartime Education at the Crossroads of Empires: The Relocation of Schools to Macao during the Second World War, 1937–1945', *Twentieth-Century China*, 46/2 (2021), pp. 130–52.

Lopez, K., *Chinese Cubans: A Transnational History* (Chapel Hill, NC, 2013).

Lottaz, P., 'Neutral States and Wartime Japan: The Diplomacy of Sweden, Spain and Switzerland toward the Empire' (PhD thesis, National Graduate Institute for Policy Studies, 2018).

Lottaz, P., and I. Ottosson, *Sweden, Japan, and the Long Second World War 1931–1945* (London, 2021).

Lou, S., 'Acerca das Características do Corporativismo de Macau' ('On the Characteristics of Macau's Corporatism'), *Administração*, 65 (2004), pp. 783–823.

Lu, Y., 'Together with the Homeland: Civic Activism for National Salvation in British Hong Kong', *Modern China*, 40/6 (2014), pp. 639–74.

Luk, B. H. K., 'War, Schools, China, Hong Kong: 1937–1949', in James Flath and Norman Smith (eds.), *Beyond Suffering: Recounting War in Modern China* (Vancouver, 2011), pp. 36–58.

Ma, T., '"The Common Aim of the Allied Powers": Social Policy and International Legitimacy in Wartime China, 1940–47', *Journal of Global History*, 9/2 (2014), pp. 254–75.

MacKinnon, S., 'Refugee Flight at the Outset of the Anti-Japanese War', in D. Lary and S. MacKinnon (eds.), *Scars of War: The Impact of Warfare on Modern China* (Vancouver, 2001), pp. 118–34.

MacKinnon, S., *Wuhan, 1938: War, Refugees and the Making of Modern China* (Berkeley, CA, 2008).

Macri, F. D., *Clash of Empires in South China: The Allied Nations' Proxy War with Japan, 1935–1941* (Lawrence, KS, 2012).

Madeira, L. A., 'Introdução' ('Introduction'), in L. A. Madeira (ed.), *Correspondência de um Diplomata no III Reich* (*Correspondence of a Diplomat in the Third Reich*) (Coimbra, 2005), pp. 15–33.

Man-Cheong, I., 'Macao: An Early Modern Cosmopolis', in C. X. G. Wei (ed.), *Macao: The Formation of a Global City* (Abingdon, 2014), pp. 143–55.

Mark, C. K., *The Everyday Cold War: Britain and China, 1950–1972* (London, 2017).

Mark, C. K., *Hong Kong and the Cold War: Anglo–American Relations 1949–1957* (Oxford, 2004).

Martin, B. G., 'Collaboration within Collaboration: Zhou Fohai's Relations with the Chongqing Government, 1942–1945', *Twentieth-Century China*, 34/2 (2008), pp. 55–88.

Martin, B. G., '"The Pact with the Devil": The Relationship between the Green Gang and the Shanghai French Concession Authorities, 1925–1935', in

F. Wakeman Jr and W. H. Yeh (eds.), *Shanghai Sojourners* (Berkeley, CA, 1992), pp. 266–304.

Martin, B. G., 'Du Yuesheng, the French Concession, and Social Networks in Shanghai', in N. Dillon and J. C. Oi (eds.), *At the Crossroads of Empires: Middlemen, Social Networks, and State-Building in Republican Shanghai* (Stanford, CA, 2008), pp. 65–84.

Matos, P. F., *As Côres do Império: Representações Raciais no Império Português* (*The Colours of the Empire: Racialized Representations in the Portuguese Colonial Empire*) (Lisbon, 2012).

Maxwell, K., 'Macao: The Shadow Land', *World Policy Journal*, 16/4 (1999–2000), pp. 73–95.

Meneses, F. R., *Salazar: A Political Biography* (New York, 2009).

Milhazes, J., *Rússia e Europa: Uma Parte do Todo* (*Russia and Europe: Part of the Whole*) (Lisbon, 2016).

Miller, S., and R. Allego, 'A Safe Haven', *Ariana*, 4 (2019), pp. 96–105. issuu.com/arianalife/docs/ariana04/s/10126112.

Mitter, R., *China's War with Japan, 1937–1945: The Struggle for Survival* (London, 2013).

Mitter, R., 'Classifying Citizens in Nationalist China during World War II, 1937–1941', *Modern Asian Studies*, 45/2 (2011), pp. 243–75.

Mitter, R., 'Imperialism, Transnationalism, and the Reconstruction of Post-war China: UNRRA in China, 1944–7', *Past & Present*, 218 (2013), pp. 51–69.

Mitter, R., *The Manchurian Myth: Nationalism, Resistance, and Collaboration in Modern China* (Berkeley, CA, 2000).

Mitter, R., 'State-Building after Disaster: Jiang Tingfu and the Reconstruction of Post–World War II China, 1943–1949', *Comparative Studies in Society and History*, 61 (2019), pp. 176–206.

Mo, S. X., 'Kangzhan qijian PuRi heliu kuitan' ('A Probe into Portugal–Japan Collusion during the War of Resistance against Japan'), *Aomen ligong xuebao / Revista do Instituto Politécnico de Macau* (*Macau Polytechnic Institute Journal*), 16/2 (2013), pp. 42–52.

Mo, Y., *Touring China: A History of Travel Culture, 1912–1949* (Ithaca, NY, 2021).

Moore, A. W., 'Kunming Dreaming: Hope, Change, and War in the Autobiographies of Youth in China's Southwest', in T. Lincoln and T. Xu (eds.), *The Habitable City in China: Urban History in the Twentieth Century* (New York, 2017), pp. 43–70.

Moreli, A., 'The War of Seduction: The Anglo–American Struggle to Engage with the Portuguese Ruling Elite (1943–1948)', *International History Review* 40/3 (2018), pp. 654–82.

Morier-Genoud, E., and M. Cahen, 'Introduction: Portugal, Empire, and Migrations – Was There Ever an Autonomous Social Imperial Space?', in E. Morier-Genoud and M. Cahen (eds.), *Imperial Migrations: Colonial Communities and Diaspora in the Portuguese World* (Basingstoke, 2012), pp. 1–27.

Motta, C. T., *O Caso de Timor na II Guerra Mundial: Documentos Britânicos* (*The Case of Timor in World War II: British Documents*) (Lisbon, 1997).

Muscolino, M. S., *The Ecology of War in China: Henan Province, the Yellow River, and Beyond, 1938–1950* (Cambridge, 2015).
Muscolino, M. S., 'Violence against People and the Land: The Environment and Refugee Migration from China's Henan Province, 1938–1945', *Environmental History*, 17 (2011), pp. 291–311.
Musgrove, C. D., 'Cheering the Traitor: The Post-war Trial of Chen Bijun, April 1946', *Twentieth-Century China*, 30/2 (2005), pp. 3–27.
Nash, D., 'Gao Jianfu', Grove Art Online (2003). doi.org/10.1093/gao/9781884446054.article.T030631.
Netto, A. F., *Breve Notícia Histórica da Missão de Shiu-Hing na Província de Cantão* (*Brief Historical Account of the Shiu-Hing Mission in Canton Province*) (Macau, 1924).
Newitt, M., *A History of Portuguese Overseas Expansion, 1400–1668* (London, 2005).
Nield, R., *China's Foreign Places: The Foreign Presence in China in the Treaty Port Era, 1840–1943* (Hong Kong, 2015).
Ninhos, C. *Portugal e os Nazis: Histórias e Segredos de uma Aliança* (*Portugal and the Nazis Histories and Secrets of an Alliance*) (Lisbon, 2017).
O'Halpin, E., *Spying on Ireland: British Intelligence and Irish Neutrality during the Second World War* (Oxford, 2008).
O'Keefe, A., 'Stars in the Nation's Skies: The Ascent and Trajectory of the Chinese Aviation Celebrity in the Prewar Decade', in P. Pickowicz (ed.), *Liangyou: Kaleidoscopic Modernity, and the Shanghai Global Metropolis, 1926–1945* (Leiden, 2013), pp. 135–59.
Ogley, R., *The Theory and Practice of Neutrality in the Twentieth Century* (London, 1970).
Osterhammel, J., 'Semi-colonialism and Informal Empire in Twentieth-Century China: Towards a Framework of Analysis', in W. J. Mommsen (ed.), *Imperialism and After: Continuities and Discontinuities* (London, 1986), pp. 290–314.
Ou, T. C., 'Education in Wartime China', in P. K. T. Sih (ed.), *Nationalist China during the Sino-Japanese War, 1937–1945* (Hicksville, NY, 1977), pp. 99–103.
Pan, Y., 'Feminism and Nationalism in China's War of Resistance against Japan', *International History Review*, 19/1 (1997), pp. 115–30.
Parobo, P. D., 'Tristão Bragança Cunha and Nationalism in Colonial Goa: Mediating Difference and Essentialising Nationhood', *Economic & Political Weekly*, 1/31 (2015), pp. 61–8.
Patrikeeff, F., *Russian Politics in Exile: The Northeast Asian Balance for Power, 1924–1931* (Oxford, 2012).
Peattie, M., E. Drea, and H. van de Ven (eds.), *The Battle for China: Essays on the Military History of the Sino-Japanese War of 1937–1945* (Stanford, CA, 2011).
Pereira, B. F., *A Diplomacia de Salazar (1932–1949)* (*Salazar's Diplomacy (1932–1949)*) (Lisbon, 2012).
Pereira, F. G., *Accommodating Diversity: The People's Republic of China and the 'Question of Macau' [1949–1999]* (Lisbon, 2013).
Petit, C., *Deep Night* (New York, 2008).
Pimentel, I. F., *Espiões em Portugal durante a II Guerra Mundial* (*Spies in Portugal during World War II*) (Lisbon, 2013).

Pimentel, I. F., *Judeus em Portugal durante a II Guerra Mundial: Em Fuga de Hitler e do Holocausto* (*Jews in Portugal during World War II: Fleeing Hitler and the Holocaust*) (Lisbon, 2006).

Pimentel, I. F., 'Refugiados' (Refugees), in F. Rosas and J. M. B. Brito (eds.), *Dicionário de História do Estado Novo* (*Estado Novo History Dictionary*), vol. 2 (Lisbon, 1996), pp. 823–5.

Pimentel, I. F., and Ninhos, C., *Salazar, Portugal e o Holocausto* (*Salazar, Portugal and the Holocaust*) (Lisbon, 2013).

Pinto, R., 'A Grande Evasão' ('The Great Escape'), *Macau*, 43 (1995), pp. 90–7.

Pinto R., 'Guerra em Paz' ('War in Peace'), *Macau*, 43 (1995), pp. 54–89.

Pires, B. V., 'Origins and Early History of Macau', in R. D. Cremer (ed.), *Macau: City of Commerce and Culture* (Hong Kong, 1987), pp. 7–21.

Pons, P., *Macao*, trans. S. Adams (London, 2002).

Ptak, R., *China, the Portuguese, and the Nanyang: Oceans and Routes, Regions and Trade (c. 1000–1600)* (Aldershot, 2004).

Puga, R. M., *The British Presence in Macau, 1635–1793* (Hong Kong, 2013).

Ramalho, M. M., *O Essencial Sobre os Salvadores Portugueses* (*The Essential about the Portuguese Saviours*) (Lisbon, 2021).

Reis, B. C., 'Portugal and the UN: A Rogue State Resisting the Norm of Decolonization (1956–1974)', *Portuguese Studies*, 29/2 (2013), pp. 251–76.

Reginbogin, H. R., *Faces of Neutrality: A Comparative Analysis of the Neutrality of Switzerland and Other Neutral Nations during WWII* (Bern, 2006).

Rêgo (Filho), J. C., *Os Feitos do Capitão Ribeiro da Cunha durante o Período da Guerra do Pacífico em Macau* (*The Feats of Captain Ribeiro da Cunha during the Pacific War Period in Macau*) (n.p., 1996).

Rhoads, E. J. M., *China's Republican Revolution: The Case of Kwangtung, 1895–1913* (Cambridge, MA, 1975).

Ride, E., *BAAG Hong Kong Resistance 1942–1945* (Hong Kong, 1981).

Rihal, D., 'The French Concession in Hankou 1938–43: The Life and Death of a Solitary Enclave in an Occupied City', in R. Bickers and I. Jackson (eds.), *Treaty Ports in Modern China* (Milton Park, 2016), pp. 220–42.

Ristaino, M. R., *The Jacquinot Safety Zone: Wartime Refugees in Shanghai* (Stanford, CA, 2008).

Robinson, R., 'Non-European Foundations of European Imperialism: Sketch for a Theory of Collaboration', in R. Owen and B. Sutcliffe (eds.), *Studies in the Theory of Imperialism* (London, 1972), pp. 117–42.

Rodao, F., *Franco y el Emperio Japonés: Imágenes y Propaganda en Tiempos de Guerra* (*Franco and the Japanese Empire: Images and Propaganda in Wartime*) (Barcelona, 2002).

Rodao, F., 'Franco's Spain and the Japanese Empire, 1937–45', *Bulletin of Portuguese–Japanese Studies*, 10–11 (2005), pp. 243–62.

Rodao, F., 'Japan and the Axis, 1937–8: Recognition of the Franco Regime and Manchukuo', *Journal of Contemporary History*, 44/3 (2009), pp. 431–47.

Rodao, F., 'Japanese Relations with Neutrals, 1944–1945: The Shift to Pragmatism', in W. P. Brecher and M. W. Myers (eds.), *Defamiliarizing Japan's Asia-Pacific War* (Honolulu, HI, 2019), pp. 104–36.

Rosas, F., *Portugal entre a Paz e a Guerra 1939–1945* (*Portugal between Peace and War 1939–1945*) (Lisbon, 1995).

Rosas, F., 'Portuguese Neutrality in the Second World War', in N. Wylie (ed.), *European Neutrals and Non-belligerents during the Second World War* (Cambridge, 2001), pp. 268–83.

Sá, L. A., *The Boys from Macau: Portugueses em Hong Kong* (*The Boys from Macau: Portuguese in Hong Kong*) (Macau, 1999).

Sá, L. A., *A História na Bagagem: Crónicas dos Velhos Hotéis de Macau* (*History in the Luggage: Chronicles of Macau's Old Hotels*) (Macau, 1989).

Saldanha, A. V., *Negociações e Acordos Luso-Chineses sobre os Limites de Macau no século XIX* (*Sino–Portuguese Negotiations and Agreements on Macau's Borders in the Nineteenth Century*) (Lisbon, 2010).

Saldanha, A. V., *O Tratado Impossível: Um Exercício de Diplomacia Luso–Chinesa num Contexto Internacional em Mudança, 1842–1887* (*The Impossible Treaty: An Exercise in Portuguese–Chinese Diplomacy in a Changing International Context, 1842–1887*) (Lisbon, 2007).

Samarani, G., 'The Evolution of Fascist Italian Diplomacy during the Sino–Japanese War, 1937–1943', in D. P. Barrett and L. N. Shyu (eds.), *China in the Anti-Japanese War, 1937–1945: Politics, Culture, and Society* (New York, 2001), pp. 65–87.

Sand, J., 'Subaltern Imperialists: The New Historiography of the Japanese Empire, *Past & Present*, 225/1 (2014), pp. 273–88.

Santa, J. D., *Australianos e Japoneses em Timor na II Guerra Mundial, 1941–1945* (*Australians and Japanese in Timor in World War II, 1941–1945*) (Lisbon, 1997).

Santos, B. S., 'Between Prospero and Caliban: Colonialism, Postcolonialism, and Inter-identity', *Luso–Brazilian Review*, 39/2 (2002), pp. 9–43.

Santos, J. R., *A Amante do Governador* (*The Governor's Lover*) (Lisbon, 2018).

Schneider, H. M., 'Mobilising Women: The Women's Advisory Council, Resistance and Reconstruction during China's War with Japan', *European Journal of East Asian Studies*, 11/2 (2012), pp. 213–36.

Schoppa, R. K., *In a Sea of Bitterness: Refugees during the Sino–Japanese War* (Cambridge, MA, 2011).

Serfass, D., 'Collaboration and State Making in China: Defining the Occupation State, 1937–1945', *Twentieth-Century China*, 47/1 (2022), pp. 71–80.

Shacknove, A. E., 'Who Is a Refugee?', *Ethics* 95/2 (1985), pp. 274–84.

Shaplen, R., *A Corner of the World* (London, 1950).

Sheng, J., 'Homeward Bound: The Postwar Repatriation of Japanese Civilians in Shanghai, 1945–1948', *Asia-Pacific Journal*, 23/2 (2020). apjjf.org/2020/23/Sheng .html.

Silva, A. M. P. J., *The Portuguese Community in Hong Kong: A Pictorial History* (Macau, 2011).

Silva, A. M. P. J., *The Portuguese Community in Shanghai: A Pictorial History* (Macau, 2012).

Simpson, T., 'Macao, Capital of the 21st Century?', *Environment and Planning D: Society and Space*, 26 (2008), pp. 1053–79.

Sit, V. F. S., *Macau through 500 Years: Emergence and Development of an Untypical Chinese City* (Singapore, 2013).

Siu, H. F., *Agents and Victims in South China: Accomplices in Rural Revolution* (New Haven, CT, 1989).
Siu, H. F., *Tracing China: A Forty-Year Ethnographic Journey* (Hong Kong, 2016).
Smith, R., 'Keeping the Flag Flying: John Reeves and the British Consulate in Macao, 1941–45', in R. Pastor-Castro and M. Thomas (eds.), *Embassies in Crisis: Studies of Diplomatic Missions in Testing Situations* (London, 2020), pp. 55–70.
Snow, P., *The Fall of Hong Kong: Britain, China and the Japanese Occupation* (New Haven, CT, 2003).
So, W. C., 'Race, Culture, and the Anglo–American Powers: The Views of Chinese Collaborators', *Modern China*, 37/1 (2011), pp. 69–103.
Sobral, F., *A Grande Dama do Chá* (*The Great Tea Lady*) (Lisbon, 2021).
Souza, G. B., *The Survival of Empire: Portuguese Trade and Society in China and the South China Sea, 1630–1754* (Cambridge, 1986).
Stone, G., *The Oldest Ally: Britain and the Portuguese Connection, 1936–1941* (Suffolk, 1994).
Stranahan, P., 'Radicalization of Refugees: Communist Party Activity in Wartime Shanghai's Displaced Persons Camps', *Modern China*, 26/2 (2000), pp. 166–93.
Studwell, J., *Asian Godfathers: Money and Power in Hong Kong and South-East Asia* (London, 2007).
Sullivan, M., *Art and Artists of Twentieth-Century China* (Berkeley, CA, 1996).
Sun, C. H. R., 'The Holocaust and Hong Kong: An Overlooked History', *Holocaust Studies* (2022), pp. 1–21. doi.org/10.1080/17504902.2022.2057118.
Sun, C. H. R., 'More Than a Transit Port, but Less Than a Refuge: Hong Kong and Jewish Refugee Transmigration, 1938–1941' (MA thesis, University of British Columbia, 2019).
Tan, Z. Q., *Aomen zhuquan wenti shimo: 1553~1993* (*Disputes concerning Macau's Sovereignty between China and Portugal (1553–1993)*) (Taipei, 1994).
Tang, K. J., 'Os desportos modernos de Macau no Período Republicano: Formação e desenvolvimento' ('Macau Modern Sports during the Republican Period: Formation and Development'), *Administração*, 68 (2005), pp. 757–806.
Tang, X., 'Street Theater and Subject Formation in Wartime China: Toward a New Form of Public Art', *Cross-Currents: East Asian History and Culture Review*, 18 (2016), pp. 21–50.
'Tang Liu', in *Baidu baike*. baike.baidu.com/item/唐榴
Tao, J., '"Winning the Peace": The Chinese Maritime Customs Service, Foreign Technocrats, and Planning the Rehabilitation of Post-War China, 1942–1945', *Modern Asian Studies*, 56/5 (2022), pp. 1930–50.
Tarling, N., 'Britain, Portugal and East Timor in 1941', *Journal of Southeast Asian Studies*, 27/1 (1996), pp. 132–8.
Taylor, J. E., *Iconographies of Occupation: Visual Cultures in Wang Jingwei's China, 1939–1945* (Honolulu, HI, 2020).
Taylor, R., *The Arthur May Story: Hong Kong 1941–1945* (n.p., 2015).
Teixeira, M., *Bela Vista Hotel* (Macau, 1978).
Teixeira, M., *A Educação em Macau* (*Education in Macau*) (Macau, 1982).

Teixeira, M., 'The Origin of the Macanese', *Review of Culture*, 20 (1994), pp. 157–67.

Telo, A. J., *A Neutralidade Portuguesa e o Ouro Nazi* (*Portuguese Neutrality and Nazi Gold*) (Lisbon, 2000).

Telo, A. J., *Portugal na Segunda Guerra* (*Portugal in the Second World War*) (Lisbon, 1987).

Telo, A. J., *Portugal na Segunda Guerra: 1941–1945* (*Portugal in the Second World War: 1941–1945*), 2 vols. (Lisbon, 1991).

Thai, P., *China's War on Smuggling: Law, Economic Life, and the Making of the Modern State, 1842–1965* (New York, 2018).

Thorne, C., *Allies of a Kind: The United States, Britain, and the War against Japan, 1941–1945* (London, 1978).

Tillman, M. M., *Raising China's Revolutionaries: Modernizing Childhood for Cosmopolitan Nationalists and Liberated Comrades, 1920s–1950s* (New York, 2018).

Tinti, P., and T. Reitano, *Migrant Refugee Smuggler Saviour* (London, 2018).

Tow, E., 'The Great Bombing of Chongqing and the Anti-Japanese War, 1937–1945', in M. Peattie, E. Drea and H. van de Ven (eds.), *The Battle for China: Essays on the Military History of the Sino-Japanese War of 1937–1945* (Stanford, CA, 2011), pp. 256–82.

Tsang, S., *A Modern History of Hong Kong* (London, 2004).

Valadão, I. *O Rio das Pérolas* (*The Pearl River*) (Lisbon, 2017).

Van de Ven, H., 'Wartime Everydayness: Beyond the Battlefield in China's Second World War', *Journal of Modern Chinese History*, 13/1 (2019), pp. 1–23.

Van Dyke, P. A., *Merchants of Canton and Macao: Politics and Strategies in Eighteenth-Century Chinese Trade* (Hong Kong, 2012).

Viana, V., and K. Y. Kim, 'Rice Scarcity in World War II Macao: The Local Experience Revisited', *Urban History*, 46/3 (2019), pp. 518–41.

Vogel, E. F., *One Step ahead in China: Guangdong under Reform* (Cambridge, MA, 1989).

Wakeman Jr, F., 'A Revisionist View of the Nanjing Decade: Confucian Fascism', *China Quarterly*, 150 (1997), pp. 395–432.

Wakeman, Jr, F., *The Shanghai Badlands: Wartime Terrorism and Urban Crime, 1937–1941* (Cambridge, 1996).

Wakeman Jr, F., *Spymaster: Dai Li and the Chinese Secret Service* (Berkeley, CA, 2003).

Wang, D., *China's Unequal Treaties: Narrating National History* (Lanham, MD, 2005).

Ward, R., 'The Asia-Pacific War and the Failed Second Anglo-Japanese Civilian Exchange, 1942–45', *Asia-Pacific Journal*, 13/12/4 (2015). apjjf.org/2015/13/11/Rowena-Ward/4301.html.

Wasserstein, B., 'Ambiguities of Occupation: Foreign Resisters and Collaborators in Wartime Shanghai', in W. H. Yeh (ed.), *Wartime Shanghai* (London, 1998), pp. 24–41.

Watt, L., *When Empire Comes Home: Repatriation and Reintegration in Postwar Japan* (Cambridge, MA, 2009).

Whewell, E., *Law across Imperial Borders: British Consuls and Colonial Connections on China's Western Frontiers, 1880–1943* (Manchester, 2020).

Wolf, D. C., '"To Secure a Convenience": Britain Recognizes China – 1950', *Journal of Contemporary History*, 18/2 (1983), pp. 299–326.

Wong, W. Y. C., 'Shifting Memories: An Oral Study of the Canton Young Women's Christian Association in the 1940s', *Social Sciences and Missions*, 33 (2020), pp. 157–89.

Wordie, J., 'The Hong Kong Portuguese Community and Its Connections with Hong Kong University 1914–1941', in K. C. Chan Lau and P. Cunich (eds.), *An Impossible Dream: Hong Kong University from Foundation to Re-establishment, 1910–1950* (Hong Kong, 2002), pp. 163–73.

Worster, W. T., 'The Evolving Definition of the Refugee in Contemporary International Law', *Berkeley Journal of International Law*, 30/1 (2012), pp. 94–160.

Wu, S. F., 'Shenzhang zhengyi? Zhanhou yindu taoni Aomen hanjian (1945–1948)' ('Justice Served? Postwar Extradition of Traitors from Macao by the Nationalist Government (1945–1948)'), *Guoshiguan xueshu jikan* (*Bulletin of Academia Historica*), 1 (2001), pp. 128–60.

Wu, S. F., 'Zhongguo kangzhan xia de Aomen juese' ('Macau's Role in China's War of Resistance'), in *Jiang Jieshi yu kangzhan shiqi de Zhongguo* (*Chiang Kai-shek and China during the War of Resistance*) (Yilan, 2013), pp. 43–8. ccfd.org.tw /ccef001/filesys/files/dl/CKS-manual.pdf.

Wu, Z., *Segredos da Sobrevivência: História Política de Macau* (*Secrets of Survival: Political History of Macau*) (Macau, 1999).

Wylie, N., *Britain, Switzerland, and the Second World War* (Oxford, 2003).

Wylie, N. (ed.), *European Neutrals and Non-belligerents during the Second World War* (Cambridge, 2001).

Xavier, R. E., 'The Macanese at War: Survival and Identity among Portuguese Eurasians during World War II', in G. C. Gunn (ed.), *Wartime Macau: Under the Japanese Shadow* (Hong Kong, 2016), pp. 94–115.

Xia, Y., *Down with Traitors: Justice and Nationalism in Wartime China* (Seattle, WA, 2017).

Xia, Y., 'Traitors in Limbo: Chinese Trials of Russian Spies, 1937–1948', *Nationalities Papers*, 49/6 (2021), 1096–1112.

Xiang, L., 'The Recognition Controversy: Anglo–American Relations in China, 1949', *Journal of Contemporary History*, 27/2 (1992), pp. 319–43.

Xie, C., 'China's Casablanca: Refugees, Outlaws, and Smugglers in France's Guangzhouwan Enclave', in J. S. Esherick and M. T. Combs (eds.), *1943: China at the Crossroads* (Ithaca, NY, 2015), pp. 391–425.

Xu, L. 'Little Teachers: Children's Drama, Travelling, and Ruptured Childhoods in 1930s and 1940s China', *Twentieth-Century China*, 42/2 (2016), pp. 180–200.

Yan, X., 'The Language Situation in Macao', *Current Issues in Language Planning*, 18/1 (2017), pp. 241–61.

Yang, T., 'Chiang Kai-shek and Jawaharlal Nehru', in H. van de Ven, D. Lary, and S. R. MacKinnon (eds.), *Negotiating China's Destiny in World War II* (Stanford, CA, 2015), pp. 127–40.

Yap, F., 'Portuguese Communities in East and Southeast Asia during the Japanese Occupation', in L. Jarnagin, *The Making of the Luso–Asian World: Intricacies of Engagement* (Singapore, 2011), pp. 205–28.

Yeh, W. H., 'Prologue: Shanghai Besieged, 1937–45', in Y. H. Yeh (ed.), *Wartime Shanghai* (London, 1998), pp. 1–15.

Yeh, W. H., 'Urban Warfare and Underground Resistance: Heroism in the Chinese Secret Service during the War of Resistance', in Y. H. Yeh (ed.), *Wartime Shanghai* (London, 1998), pp. 111–32.

Yeh, W. H. (ed.), *Wartime Shanghai* (London, 1998).

Yick, J. K. S., '"Pre-collaboration": The Political Activity and Influence of Chen Bijun in Wartime China', *Southeast Review of Asian Studies*, 36 (2014), pp. 58–74.

Yick, J. K. S., '"Self-Serving Collaboration": The Political Legacy of "Madame Wang" in Guangdong Province, 1940–1945', *American Journal of Chinese Studies*, 21/217 (2014), pp. 217–34.

Yu, M., *The Dragon's War: Allied Operations and the Fate of China, 1937–1945* (Annapolis, MD, 2006).

Zanasi, M., 'Globalizing *Hanjian*: The Suzhou Trials and the Post–War II Discourse on Collaboration', *American Historical Review*, 113/3 (2008), pp. 731–51.

Zanasi, M., 'New Perspectives on Chinese Collaboration', *Asia-Pacific Journal*, 6/7 (2008). apjjf.org/-Margherita-Zanasi/2828/article.html.

Zhang, L., 'Aomen tongbao zhiyuan zuguo kangzhan chutan' ('The Support of Compatriots in Macau to the Homeland's War of Resistance'), *KangRi zhanzheng yanjiu* (*Journal of Studies of China's Resistance War against Japan*), 1 (2003), pp. 101–14.

Zhang, X., 'Kangzhan qianqi Aomen de jingji shehui' ('Macau's Economy and Society during the Early Phase of the War of Resistance'), *Minguo dang'an* (*Republican Archives*), 3 (2005), pp. 82–9.

Zheng, Y., 'A Specter of Extraterritoriality: The Legal Status of U.S. Troops in China, 1943–1947, *Journal of American–East Asian Relations*, 22/1 (2015), pp. 17–44.

Zheng, Z., *1940 niandai de Aomen jiaoyu* (*Macau Education in the 1940s*) (Beijing, 2016).

Zheng, Z., '1941–1945 nianjian Aomen jiaoyujie dui jiaoshi he xuesheng de jiuji gongzuo' ('Macau Education Circles' Relief Work for Teachers and Students in the 1941–1945 Period'), *Minguo dang'an* (*Republican Archives*), 3 (2013), pp. 134–41.

Zhongguo zhu wai ge gong/dashiguan liren guanzhang xian mingbiao (*Chronological List of Chinese Embassies/Legations Abroad*) (Taipei, 1989).

Zhonghua Minguo shi waijiao zhi (chu gao) (*Diplomatic History of the Republic of China*) (Taipei, 2002).

Zhou, T., 'Leveraging Liminality: The Border Town of Bao'an (Shenzhen) and the Origins of China's Reform and Opening', *Journal of Asian Studies*, 80/2 (2021), pp. 337–61.

Zou, J. H., 'Qianxi kangzhan zhong de Aomen sijie jiuzaihui' ('On Macau's Four Circles Relief Association'), *Xiandai qiye jiaoyu* (*Modern Enterprise Education*), 16 (2012), p. 146.

Zurndorfer, H., 'Wartime Refugee Relief in Chinese Cities and Women's Political Activism, 1937–1940', in B. K. L. So and M. Zelin (eds.), *New Narratives of Urban Space in Republican Chinese Cities: Emerging Social, Legal and Governance Orders* (Leiden, 2013), pp. 65–91.

Index

For EU product safety concerns, contact us at Calle de José Abascal, 56–1°,
28003 Madrid, Spain or eugpsr@cambridge.org.

www.ingramcontent.com/pod-product-compliance
Ingram Content Group UK Ltd.
Pitfield, Milton Keynes, MK11 3LW, UK
UKHW020142020925
462469UK00009BA/224
9781009311762